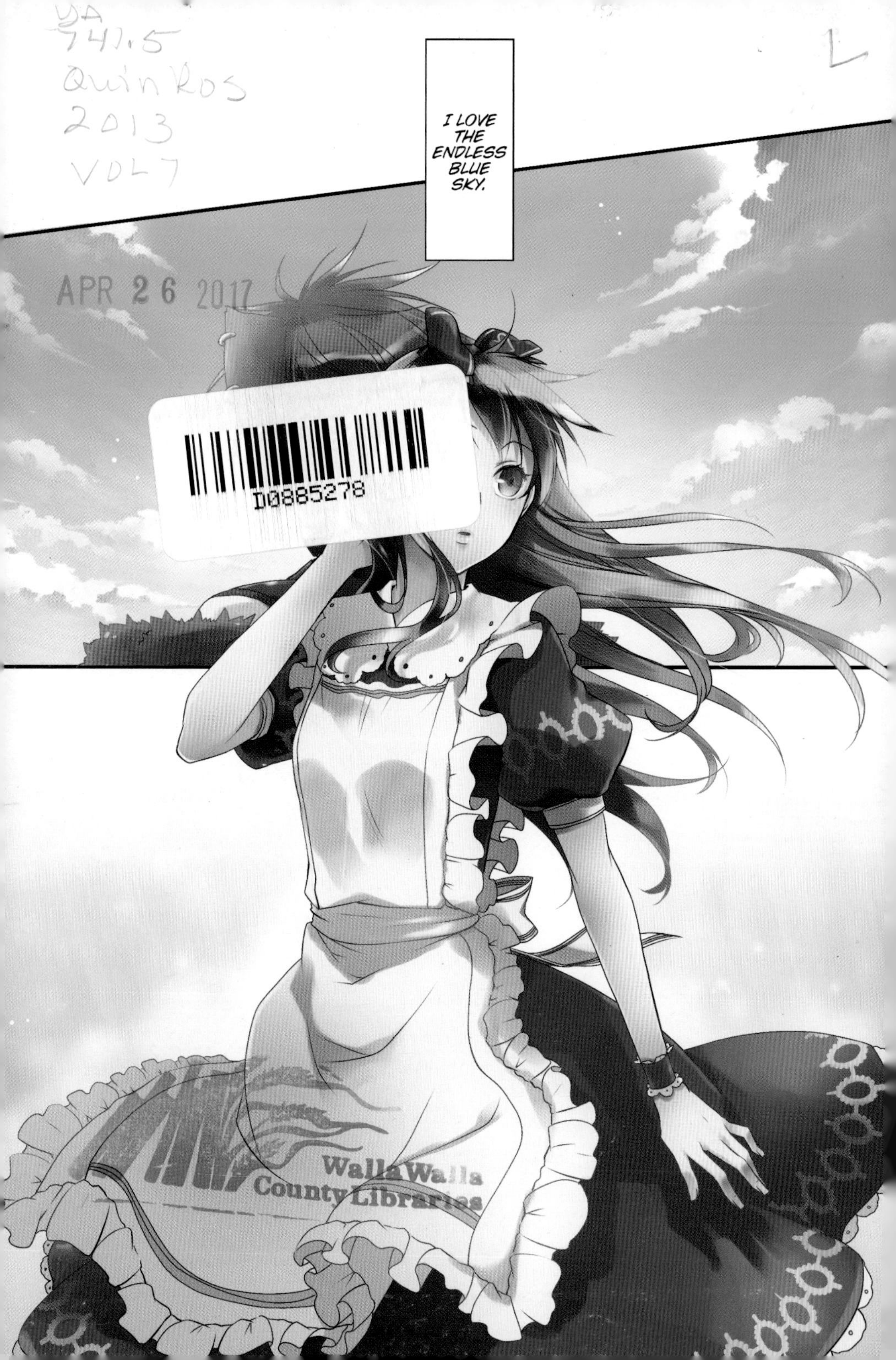
I LOVE THE ENDLESS BLUE SKY.

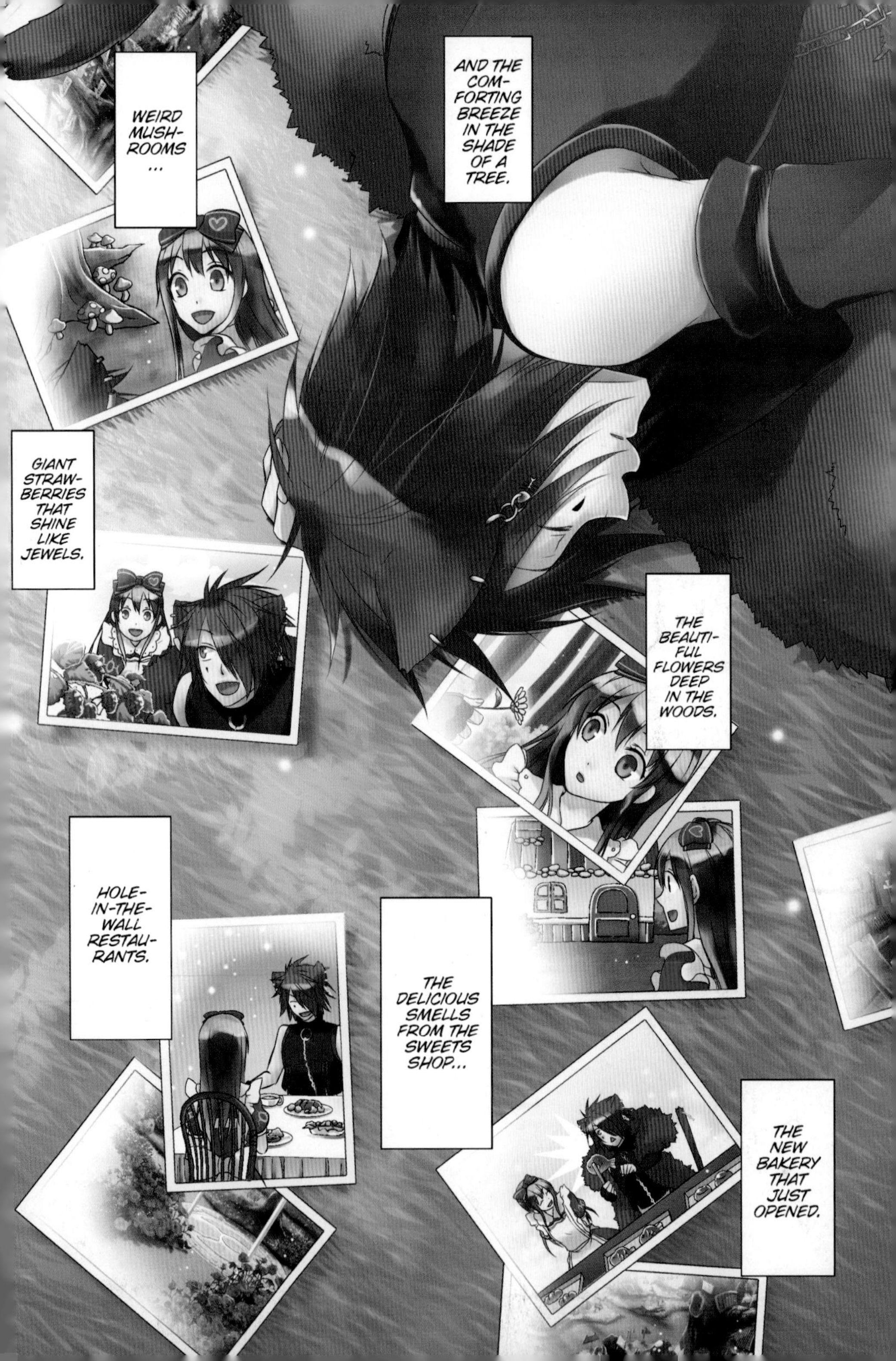

AND THE COM-FORTING BREEZE IN THE SHADE OF A TREE.
WEIRD MUSH-ROOMS ...
GIANT STRAW-BERRIES THAT SHINE LIKE JEWELS.
THE BEAUTI-FUL FLOWERS DEEP IN THE WOODS.
THE NEW BAKERY THAT JUST OPENED.
THE DELICIOUS SMELLS FROM THE SWEETS SHOP...
HOLE-IN-THE-WALL RESTAU-RANTS.

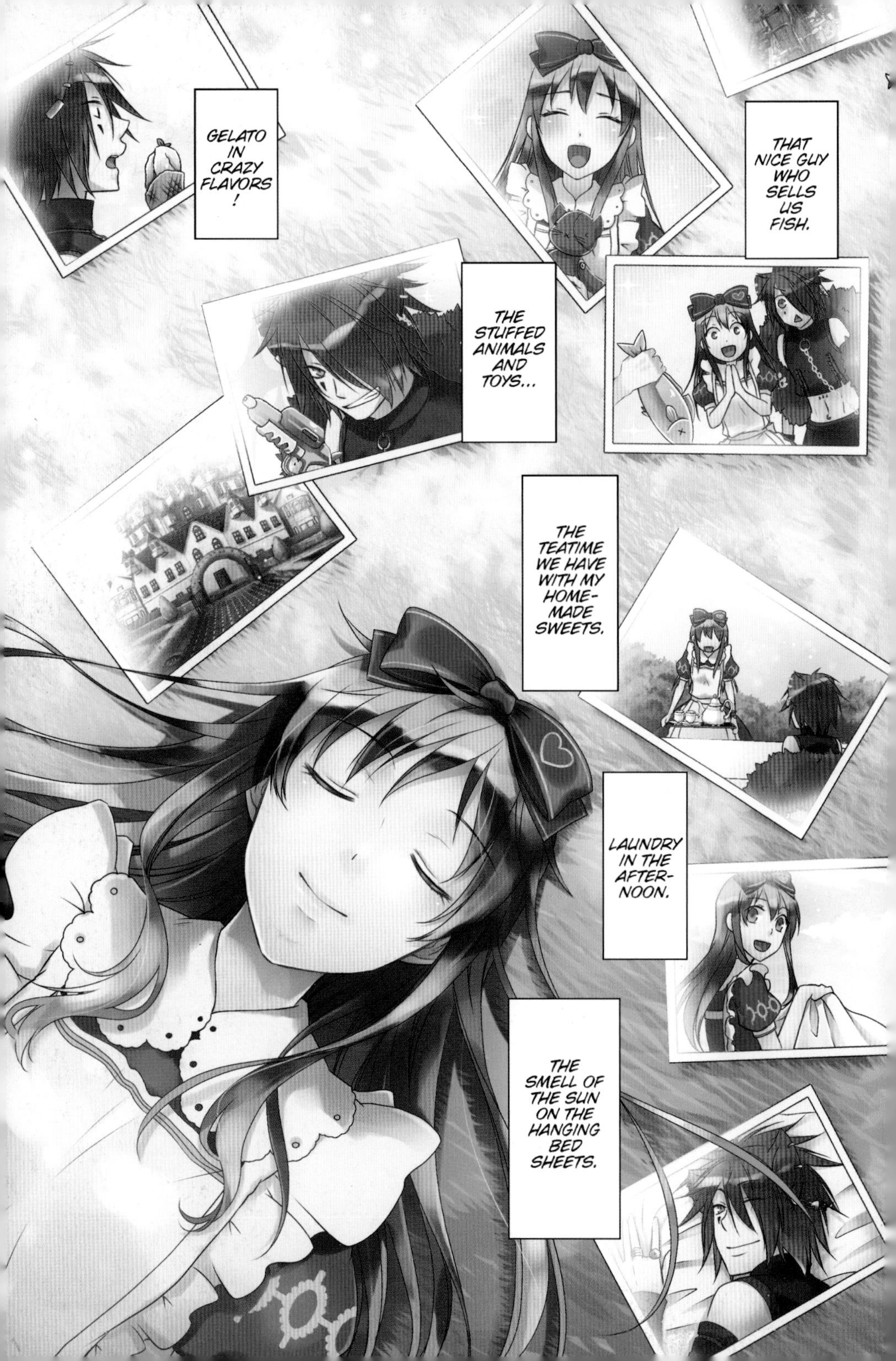
THAT NICE GUY WHO SELLS US FISH.
GELATO IN CRAZY FLAVORS!
THE STUFFED ANIMALS AND TOYS...
THE TEATIME WE HAVE WITH MY HOME-MADE SWEETS.
LAUNDRY IN THE AFTER-NOON.
THE SMELL OF THE SUN ON THE HANGING BED SHEETS.

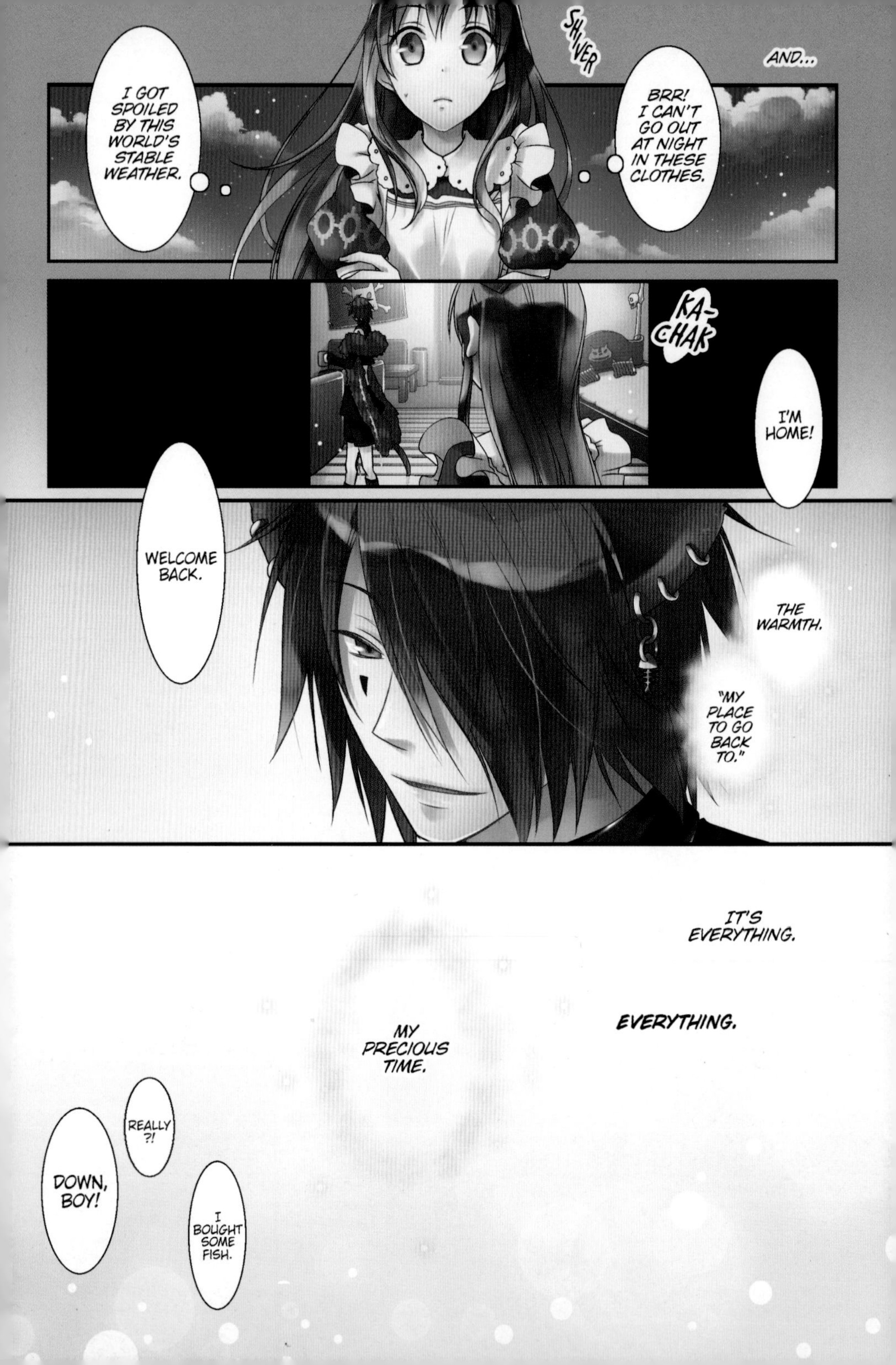
AND...
SHIVER
BRR! I CAN'T GO OUT AT NIGHT IN THESE CLOTHES.
I GOT SPOILED BY THIS WORLD'S STABLE WEATHER.
KA-CHAK
I'M HOME!
WELCOME BACK.
THE WARMTH.
"MY PLACE TO GO BACK TO."
IT'S EVERYTHING.
EVERYTHING.
MY PRECIOUS TIME.
I BOUGHT SOME FISH.
REALLY?!
DOWN, BOY!

Alice in the Country of Clover
~Cheshire Cat Waltz~

Mamenosuke Fujimaru

藤丸 豆ノ介

Alice IN THE COUNTRY OF Clover
CHESHIRE CAT WALTZ
VOLUME 7

story by QuinRose

art by Mamenosuke Fujimaru

STAFF CREDITS

translation **Angela Liu**

adaptation **Lianne Sentar**

lettering **Roland Amago**

layout **Bambi Eloriaga-Amago**

cover design **Nicky Lim**

proofreader **Shanti Whitesides**

editor **Adam Arnold**

publisher **Jason DeAngelis**
Seven Seas Entertainment

ALICE IN THE COUNTRY OF CLOVER: CHESHIRE CAT WALTZ VOL. 7
Copyright © Mamenosuke Fujimaru / QuinRose 2011
First published in Japan in 2011 by ICHIJINSHA Inc., Tokyo.
English translation rights arranged with ICHIJINSHA Inc., Tokyo, Japan.

ISBN: 978-1-937867-74-4

Printed in Canada

First Printing: November 2013

10 9 8 7 6 5 4 3 2 1

FOLLOW US ONLINE: www.gomanga.com

READING DIRECTIONS

This book reads from *right to left*, Japanese style.
If this is your first time reading manga, you start
reading from the top right panel on each page and
take it from there. If you get lost, just follow the
numbered diagram here. It may seem backwards
at first, but you'll get the hang of it! Have fun!!

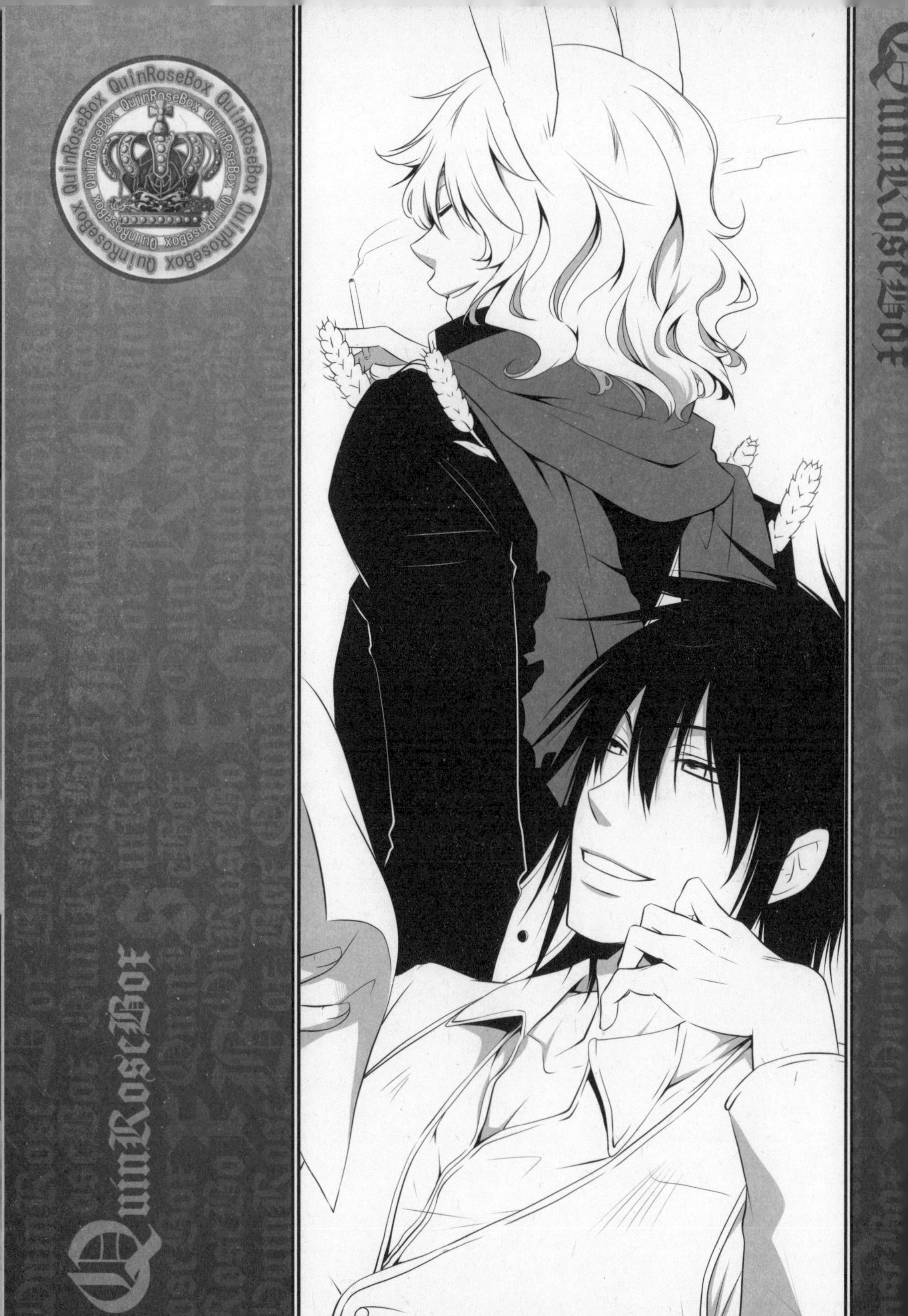
QuinRoseBox

Alice in the Country of Clover
クローバーの国の
アリス
~Wonderful Wonder World~

- STORY -

In *Alice in the Country of Clover*, the game starts with Alice having not fallen in love, but still deciding to stay in Wonderland.

She's acquainted with all the characters from the previous game, *Alice in the Country of Hearts.*

Since love would now start from a place of friendship rather than passion with a new stranger, she can experience a different type of romance from that in the previous game. Her dynamic with the characters is different through this friendship—characters can't always be forceful with her, and in many ways it's more comfortable to grow intimate. The relationships *between* the Ones With Duties have also become more of a factor.

In this game, the story focuses on the mafia. Alice attends the suited meetings (forcefully) and gets involved in various gunfights (forcefully), among other things.

Land fluctuations, sea creatures in the forest, and whispering doors—it's a game more fantastic and more eerie than the first.

Will our everywoman Alice be able to have a romantic relationship in a world devoid of common sense?

Alice in the Country of Clover
Character Information

Elliot March
VA: Tsuguo Mogami

Blood's right-hand man has a criminal past... and a temperamental present. But he's not as bad as he used to be, so that's something. Joining Blood has been good(?) for him.

Blood Dupre
VA: Katsuyuki Konishi

The head of the mafia Hatter Family, Blood is a cunning yet moody puppet-master. Alice now has the pleasure of having him for a landlord.

Alice Liddell
VA: Rie Kugimiya

A normal girl with a bit of a chip on her shoulder. Deciding to stay in the Wonderland she was carried to, she's adapted to her strange new lifestyle.

Vivaldi
VA: Yuuko Kaida

The beautiful Queen of Hearts has an unrivaled temper—which is really saying something in Wonderland. Although a picture-perfect Mad Queen, she cares for Alice as if Alice were her little sister...or a very interesting plaything.

Tweedle Dum
VA: Jun Fukuyama

The second "Bloody Twin" is equally cute and equally scary. In *Clover*, Dum can also turn into an adult.

Tweedle Dee
VA: Jun Fukuyama

One of the "Bloody Twin" gatekeepers of the Hatter territory, Dee can be cute when he's not being terrifying. In *Clover*, he sometimes turns into an adult.

Boris Airay
VA: Noriaki Sugiyama

This riddle-loving cat has a signature smirk— and in *Clover*, a new toy. One of his favorite pastimes is giving the Sleepy Mouse a hard time.

Ace
VA: Daisuke Hirakawa

The unlucky knight of Hearts was a former subordinate of Vivaldi and is perpetually lost. Even though he's depressed to be separated from his friend and boss Julius, he stays positive and tries to overcome it with a smile. He seems like a classic nice guy... or is he?

Peter White
VA: Kouki Miyata

The Prime Minister of Heart Castle—who has rabbit ears growing out of his head—invited (kidnapped) Alice to Wonderland. He loves Alice and hates everything else. His cruel, irrational actions are disturbing, but he acts like a completely different person (rabbit?) when in the throes of his love for Alice.

Gray Ringmarc
VA: Kazuya Nakai

Nightmare's subordinate in *Clover*. He used to have strong social ambition and considered assassinating Nightmare... but since Nightmare was such a useless boss, Gray couldn't help but feel sorry for him and ended up a dedicated assistant. He's a sound thinker with a strong work ethic. He's also highly skilled with his blades, rivaling even Ace.

Nightmare Gottschalk
VA: Tomokazu Sugita

A sickly nightmare who hates the hospital and needles. He has the power to read people's thoughts and enter dreams. Even though he likes to shut himself away in dreams, Gray drags him out to sulk from time to time. He technically holds a high position and has many subordinates, but since he can't even take care of his own health, he leaves most things to Gray.

Pierce Villiers
VA: Souichirou Hoshi

New to *Clover*, Pierce is an insomniac mouse who drinks too much coffee. He loves Nightmare (who can help him sleep) and hates Boris (who terrifies him). He dislikes Blood and Vivaldi for discarding coffee in favor of tea. He likes Elliot and Peter well enough, since rabbits aren't natural predators of mice.

Alice IN THE COUNTRY OF Clover

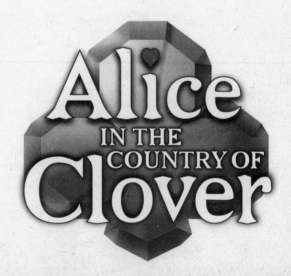

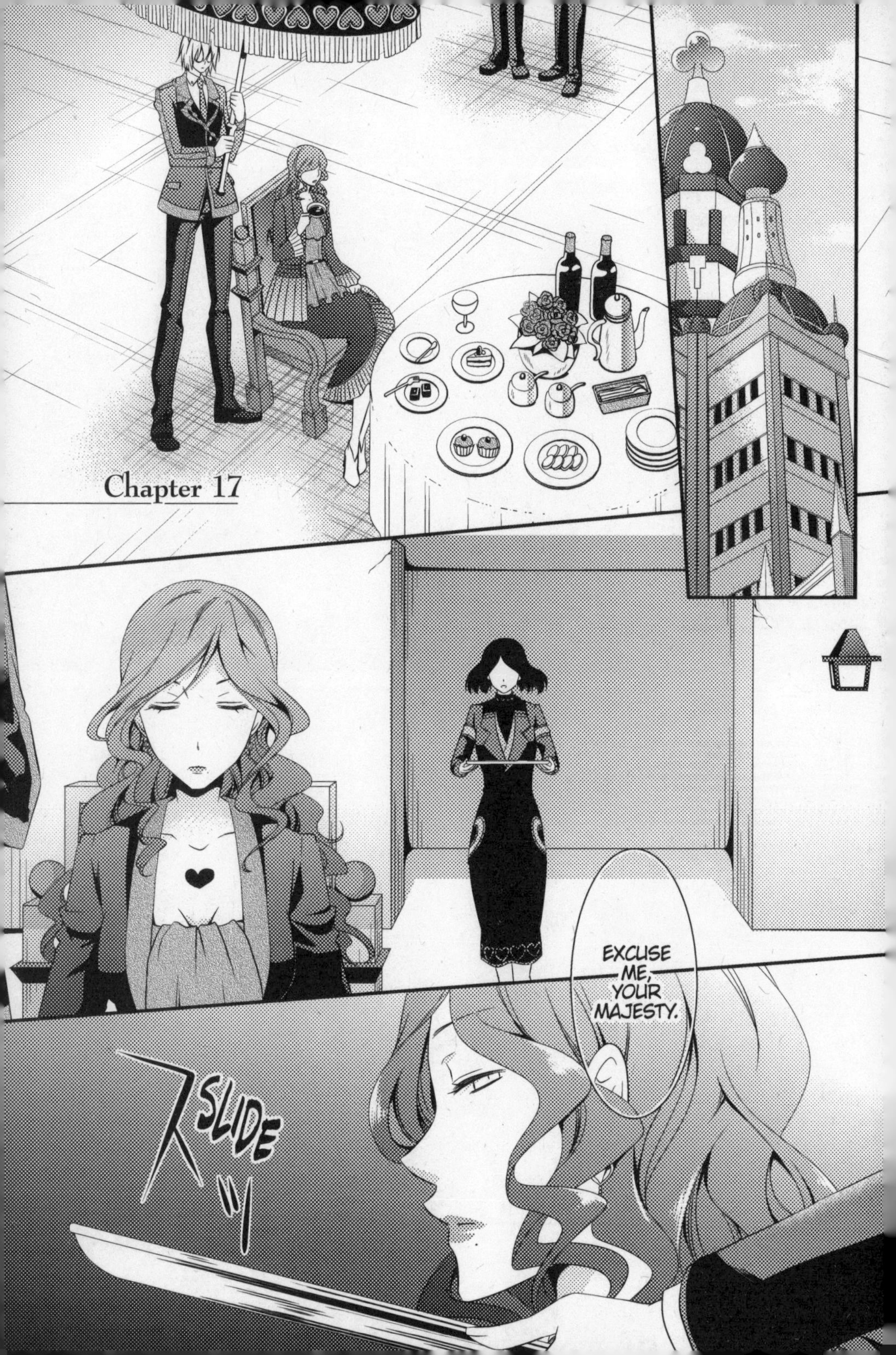
Chapter 17
EXCUSE ME, YOUR MAJESTY.
SLIDE

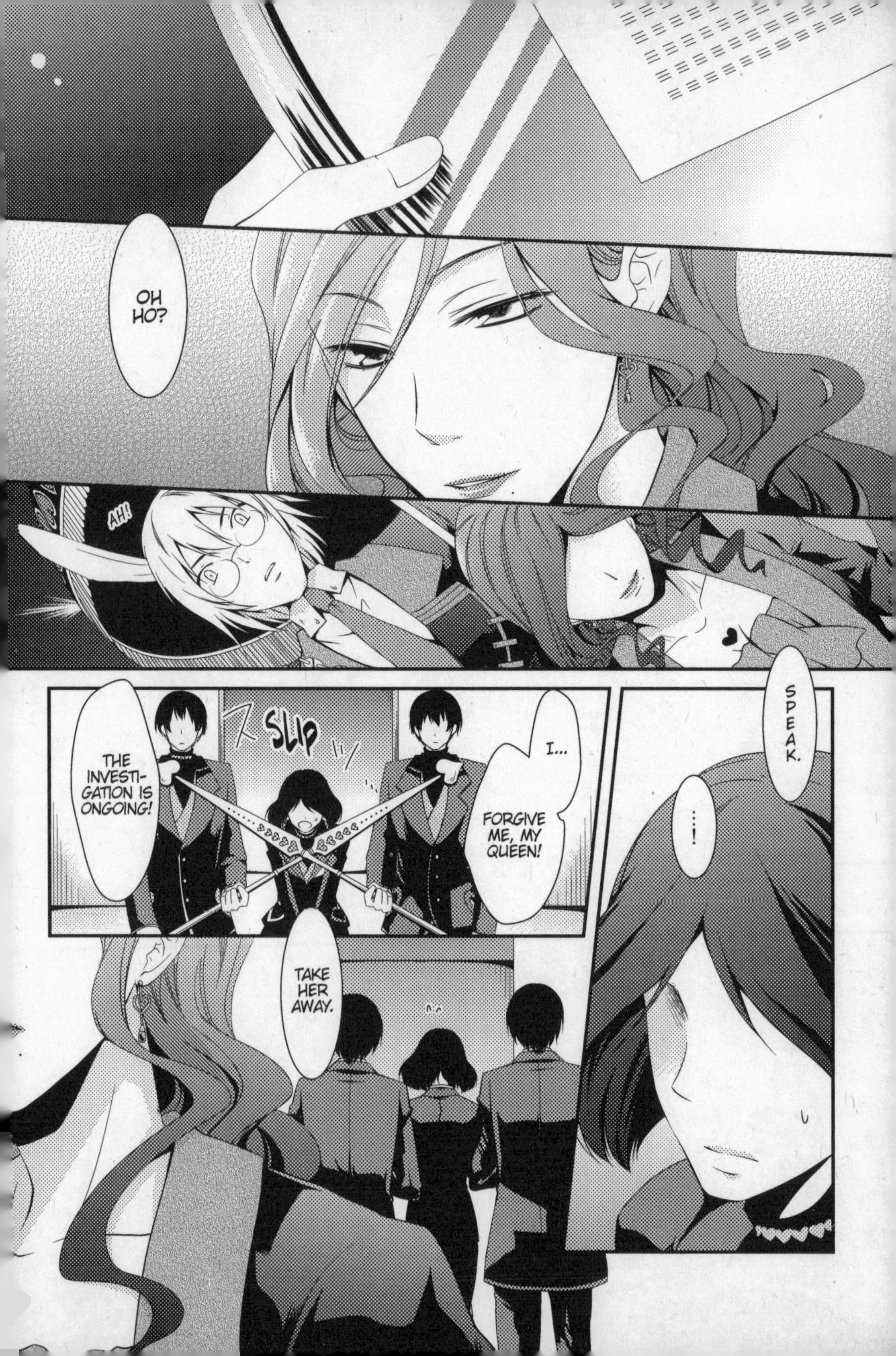
OH HO?
AH!
SPEAK.
...!
I...
FORGIVE ME, MY QUEEN!
SLIP
THE INVESTIGATION IS ONGOING!
TAKE HER AWAY.

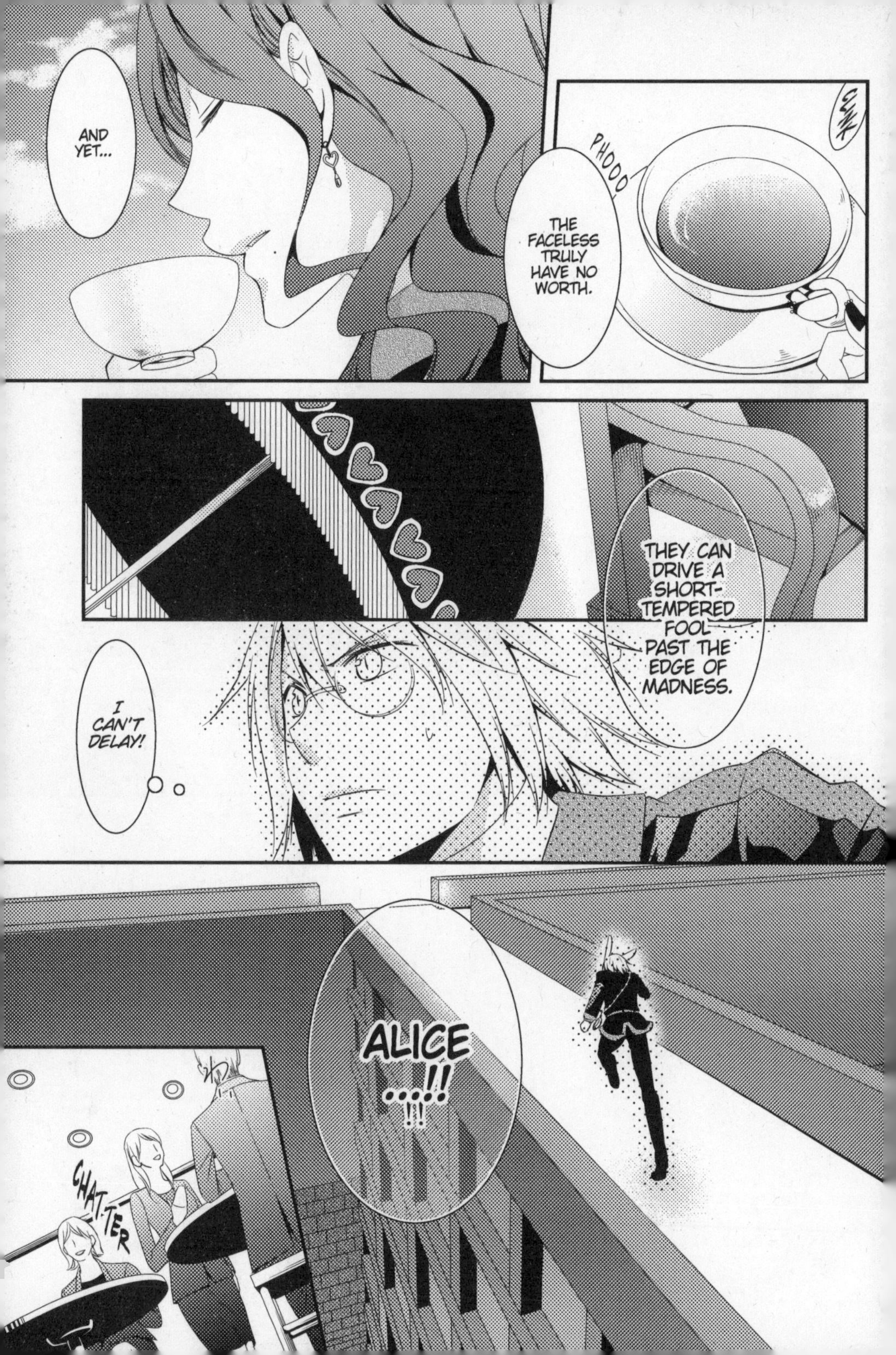
CLINK
PHOOO
THE FACELESS TRULY HAVE NO WORTH.
AND YET...
THEY CAN DRIVE A SHORT-TEMPERED FOOL PAST THE EDGE OF MADNESS.
I CAN'T DELAY!
ALICE ...!! !!
CHAT-TER

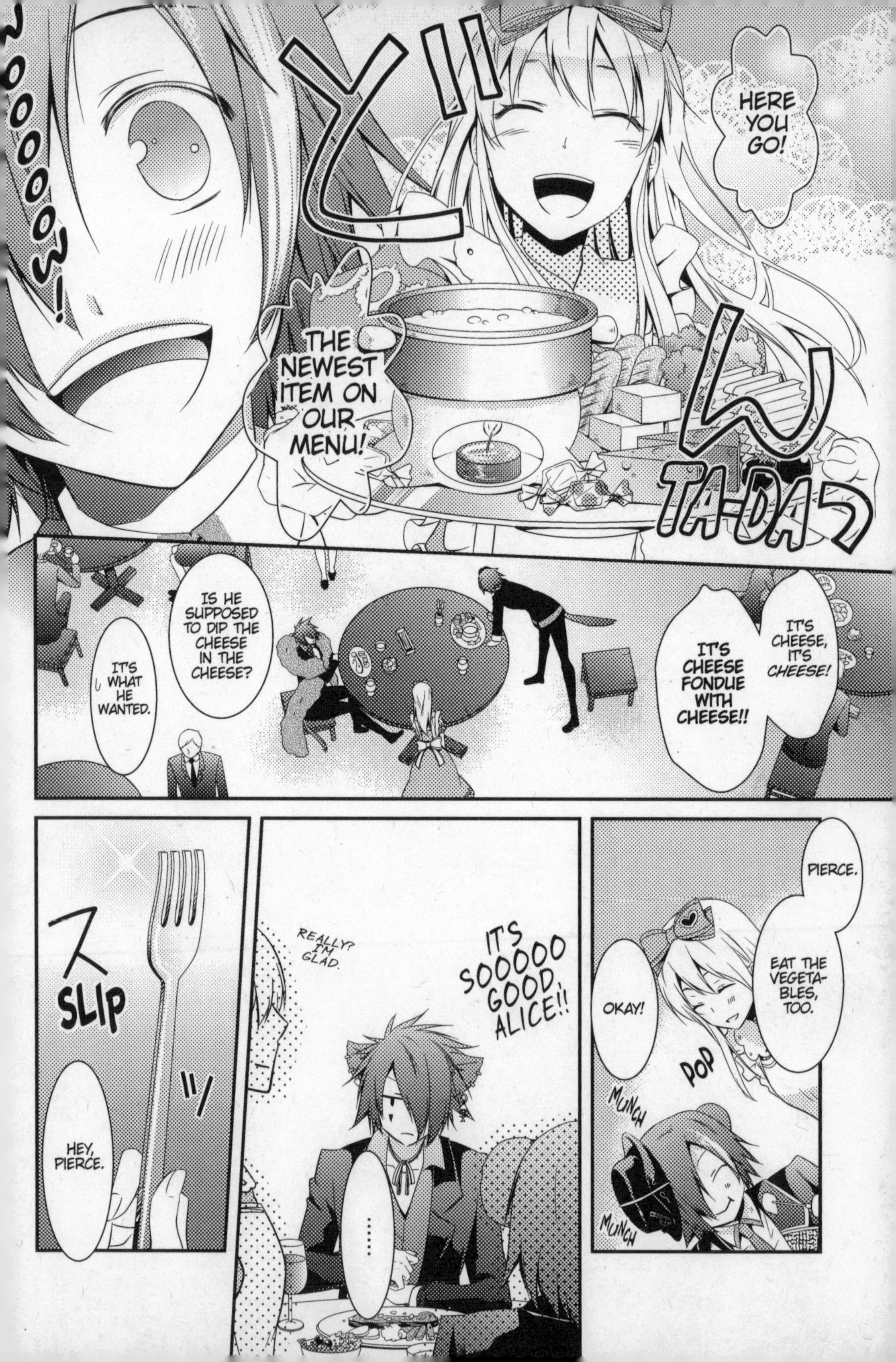
HERE YOU GO!
TA-DA
THE NEWEST ITEM ON OUR MENU!
WOOOOOOW!
IT'S CHEESE, IT'S CHEESE!
IT'S CHEESE FONDUE WITH CHEESE!!
IS HE SUPPOSED TO DIP THE CHEESE IN THE CHEESE?
IT'S WHAT HE WANTED.
PIERCE.
EAT THE VEGETA-BLES, TOO.
OKAY!
POP
MUNCH
MUNCH
IT'S SOOOOO GOOD ALICE!!
REALLY? I'M GLAD.
......
ス
SLIP
HEY, PIERCE.

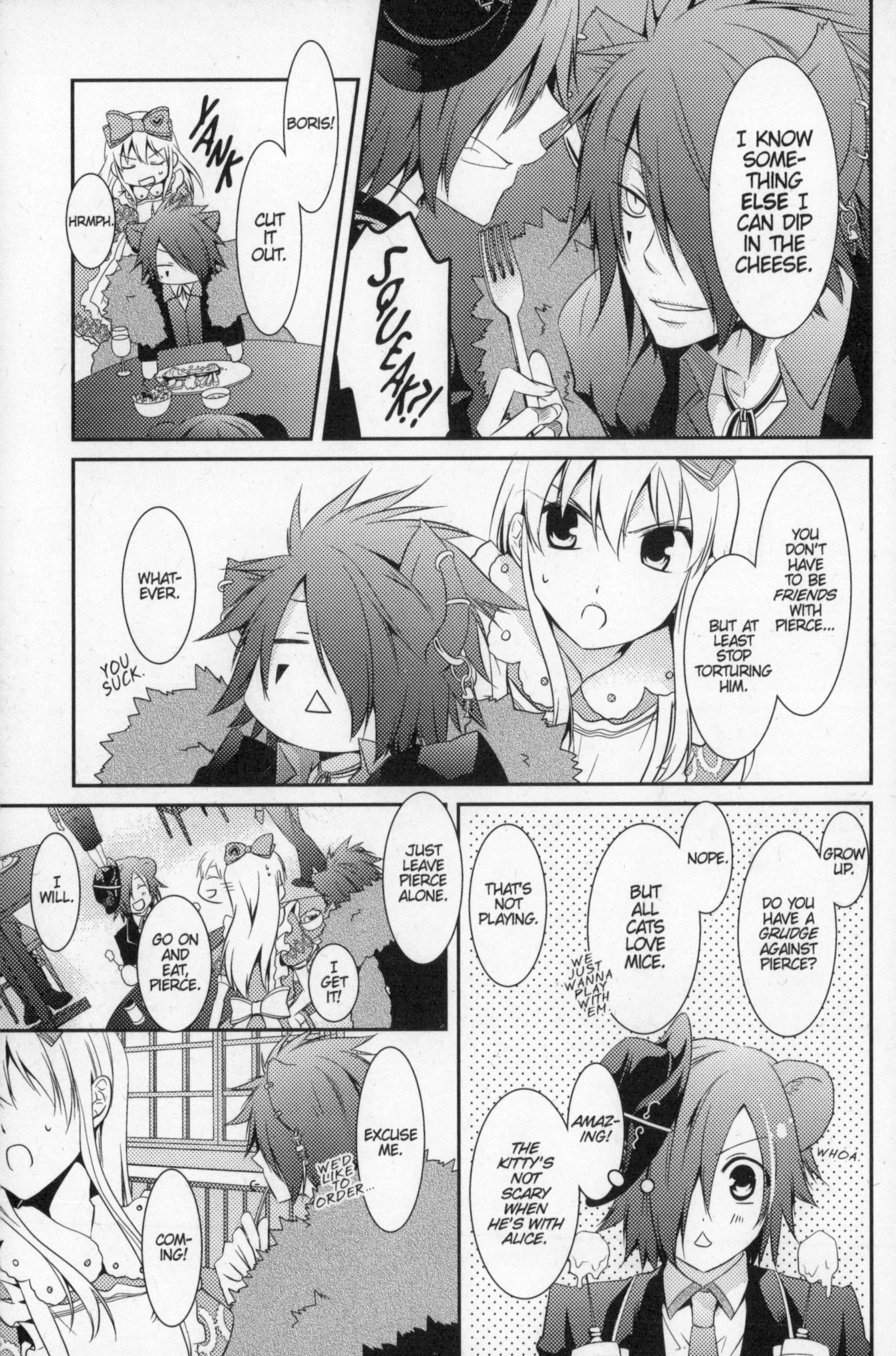
I KNOW SOME-THING ELSE I CAN DIP IN THE CHEESE.
SQUEAK?!
BORIS!
YANK
CUT IT OUT.
HRMPH.
YOU DON'T HAVE TO BE FRIENDS WITH PIERCE...
BUT AT LEAST STOP TORTURING HIM.
WHAT-EVER.
YOU SUCK.
GROW UP.
DO YOU HAVE A GRUDGE AGAINST PIERCE?
NOPE.
BUT ALL CATS LOVE MICE.
WE JUST WANNA PLAY WITH 'EM.
THAT'S NOT PLAYING.
AMAZ-ING!
THE KITTY'S NOT SCARY WHEN HE'S WITH ALICE.
WHOA.
JUST LEAVE PIERCE ALONE.
I GET IT!
GO ON AND EAT, PIERCE.
I WILL.
EXCUSE ME.
WE'D LIKE TO ORDER...
COM-ING!

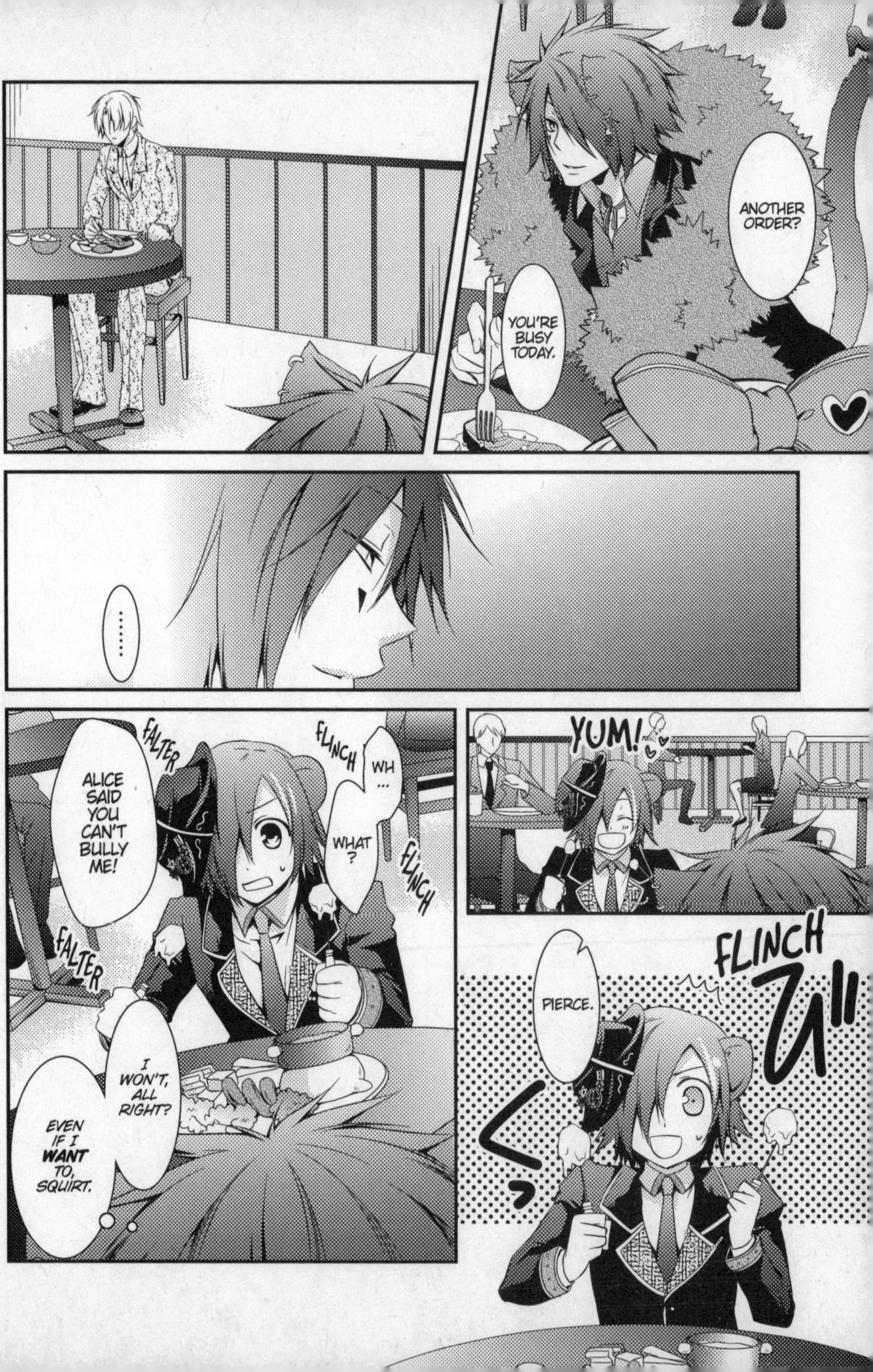
ANOTHER ORDER?
YOU'RE BUSY TODAY.
......
YUM!
PIERCE.
FLINCH
FLINCH
WH...
WHAT?
FLINCH
FALTER
ALICE SAID YOU CAN'T BULLY ME!
FALTER
I WON'T, ALL RIGHT?
EVEN IF I **WANT** TO, SQUIRT.

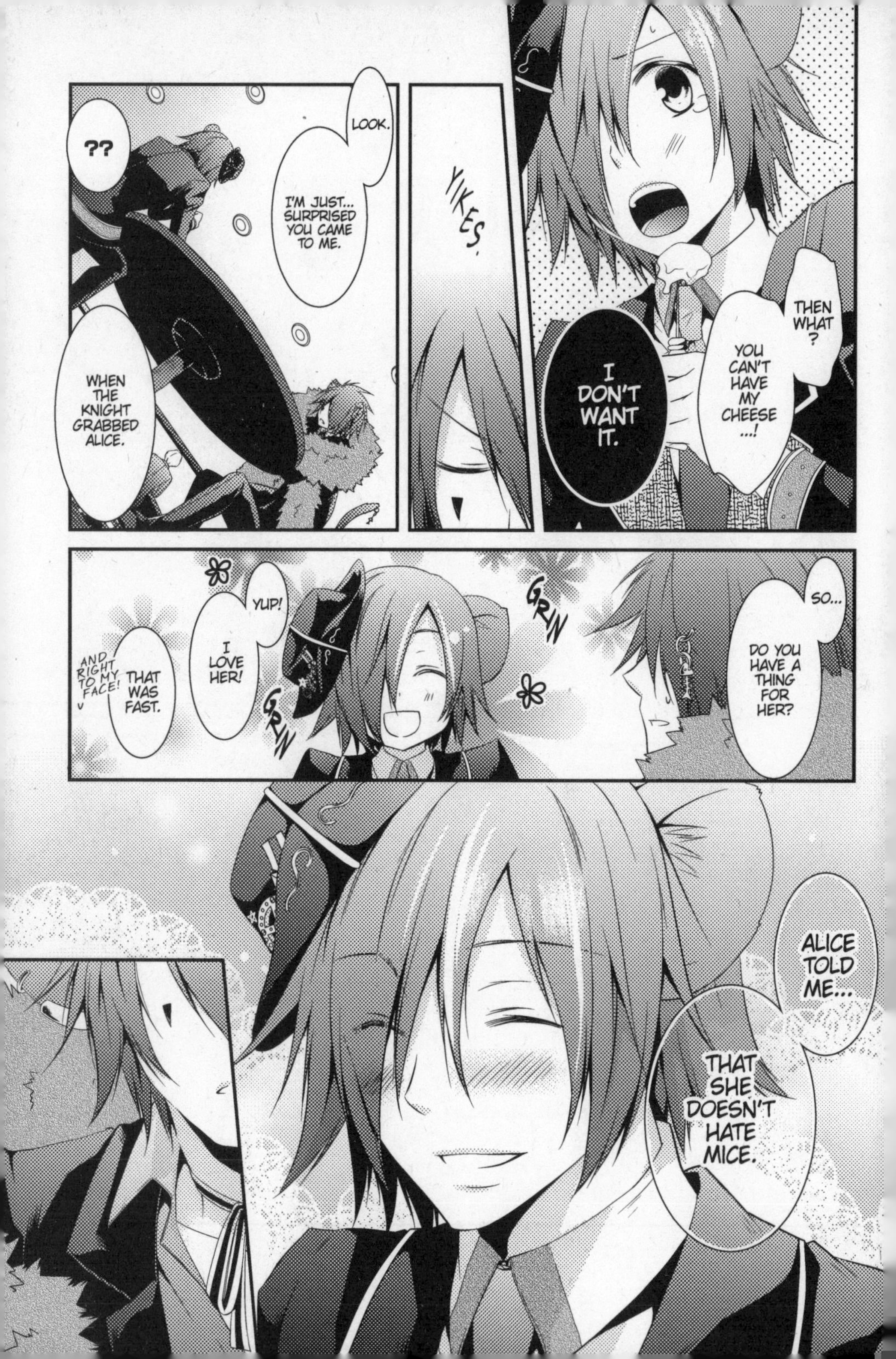
THEN WHAT?
YOU CAN'T HAVE MY CHEESE ...!
I DON'T WANT IT.
YIKES.
LOOK.
I'M JUST... SURPRISED YOU CAME TO ME.
??
WHEN THE KNIGHT GRABBED ALICE.
SO...
DO YOU HAVE A THING FOR HER?
GRIN
GRIN
YUP!
I LOVE HER!
THAT WAS FAST.
AND RIGHT TO MY FACE!
ALICE TOLD ME...
THAT SHE DOESN'T HATE MICE.

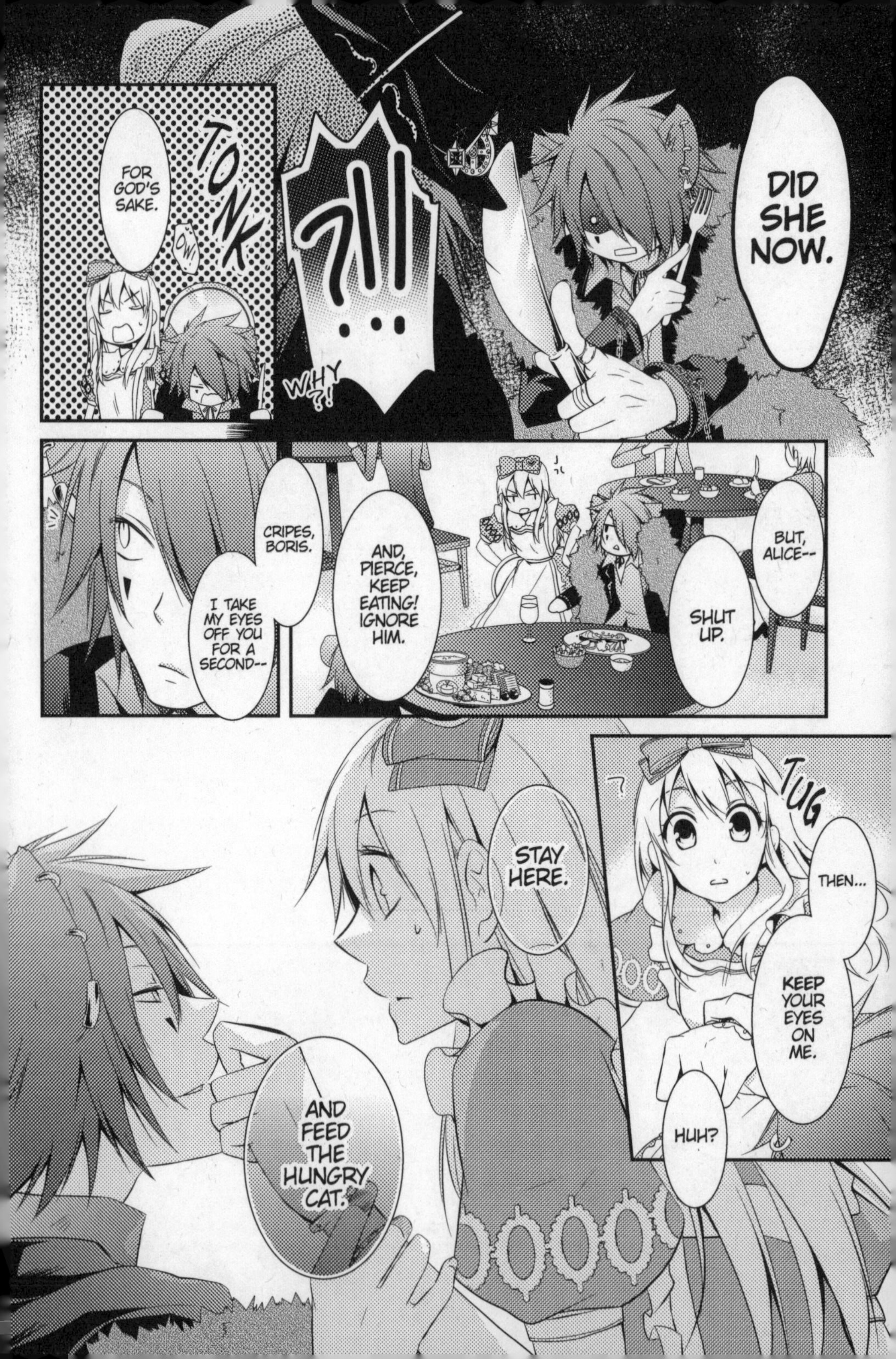
DID SHE NOW.
?!!
...
WHY?!!
TONK
OW!
FOR GOD'S SAKE.
BUT, ALICE--
SHUT UP.
AND, PIERCE, KEEP EATING! IGNORE HIM.
CRIPES, BORIS.
I TAKE MY EYES OFF YOU FOR A SECOND--
TUG
?
THEN...
KEEP YOUR EYES ON ME.
HUH?
STAY HERE.
AND FEED THE HUNGRY CAT.

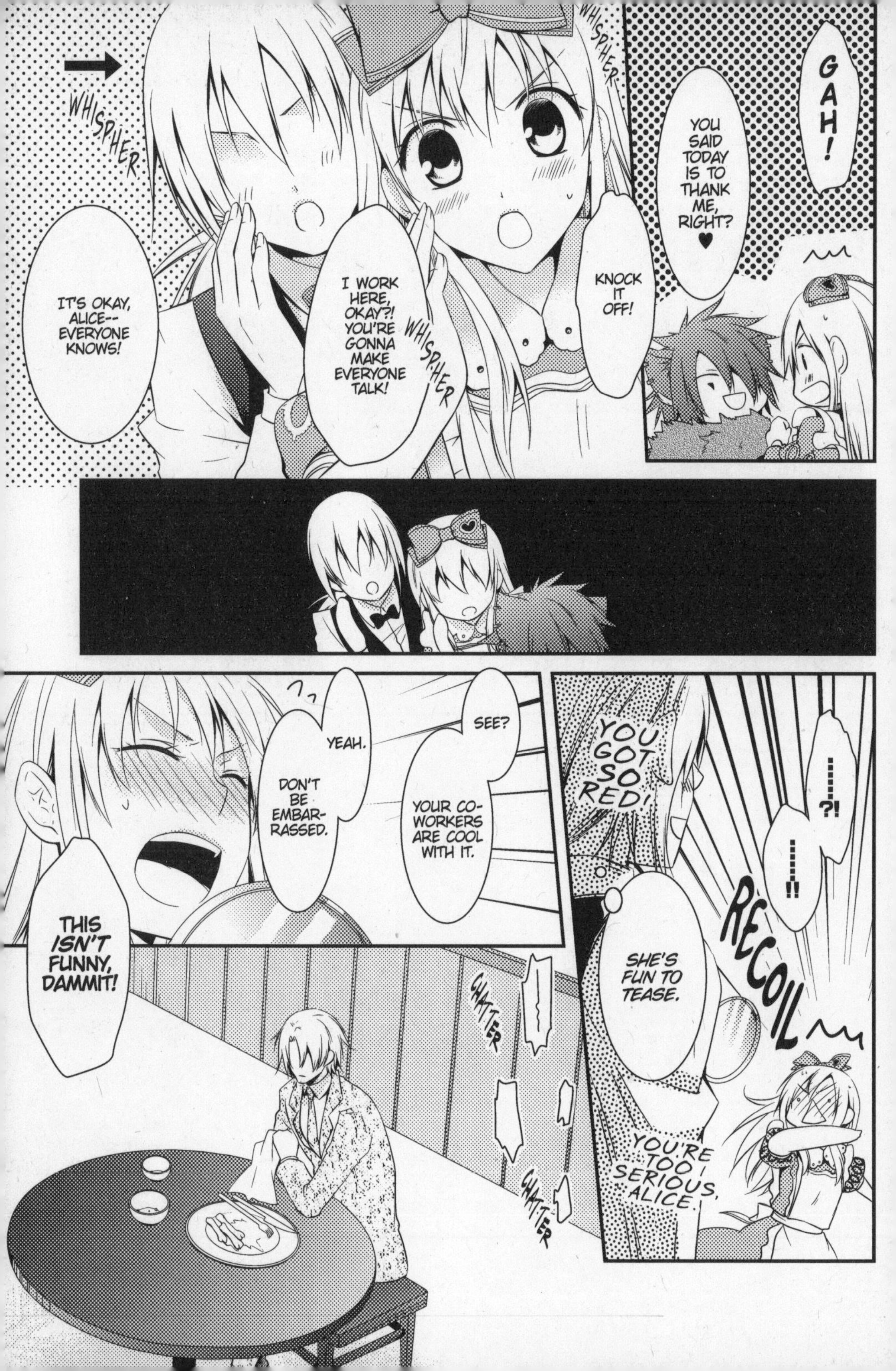

GAH!
YOU SAID TODAY IS TO THANK ME, RIGHT? ♥
KNOCK IT OFF!
WHISPHER
I WORK HERE, OKAY?! YOU'RE GONNA MAKE EVERYONE TALK!
WHISPHER
WHISPHER
IT'S OKAY, ALICE-- EVERYONE KNOWS!
...?!
...!!
YOU GOT SO RED!
RECOIL
SHE'S FUN TO TEASE.
YOU'RE TOO SERIOUS, ALICE.
SEE?
YOUR CO-WORKERS ARE COOL WITH IT.
YEAH.
DON'T BE EMBARRASSED.
THIS *ISN'T* FUNNY, DAMMIT!
CHATTER
CHATTER

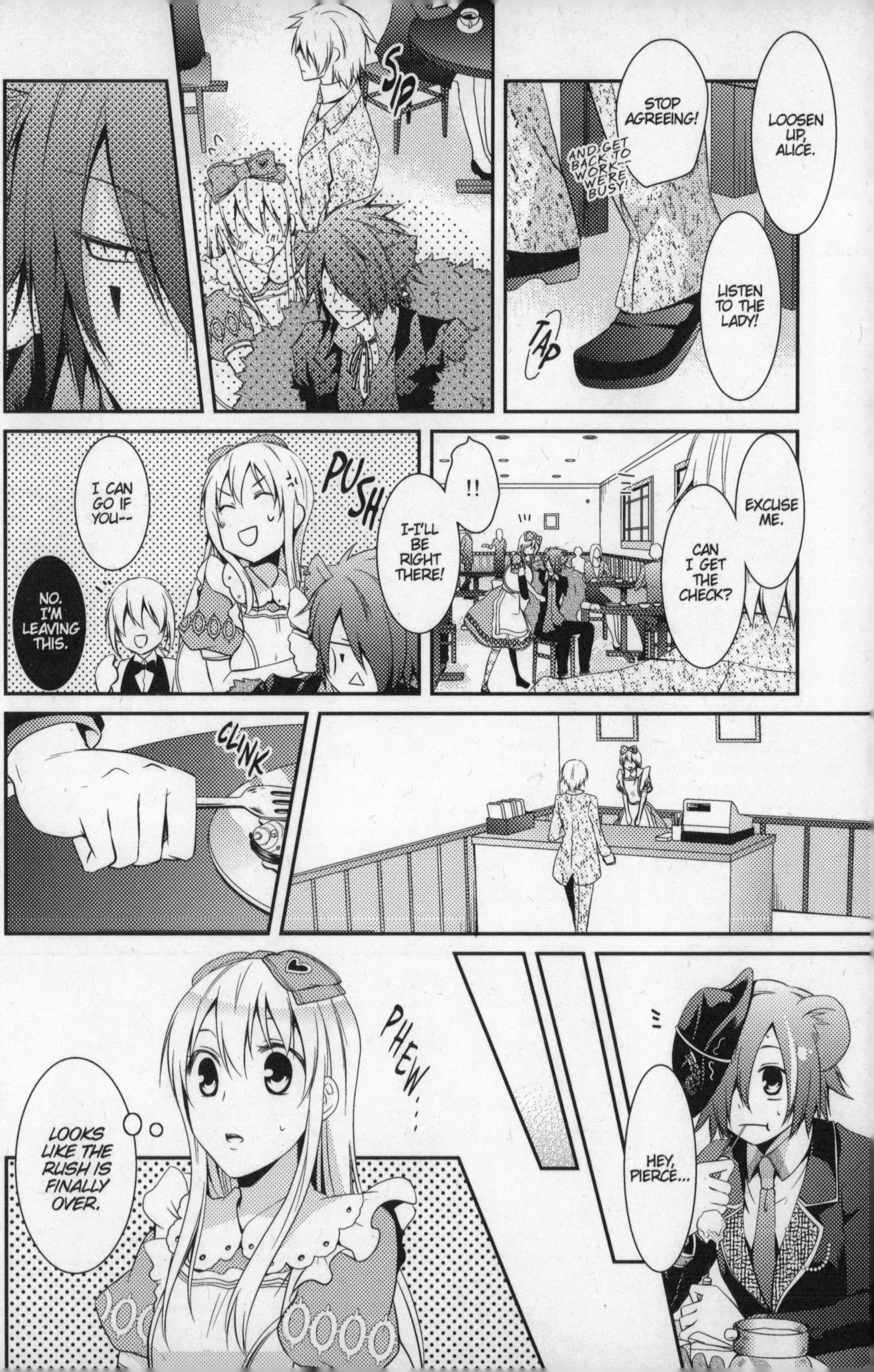
LOOSEN UP, ALICE.
STOP AGREEING!
AND GET BACK TO WORK--WE'RE BUSY!
LISTEN TO THE LADY!
TAP
SIP
EXCUSE ME.
CAN I GET THE CHECK?
!!
I-I'LL BE RIGHT THERE!
PUSH
I CAN GO IF YOU--
NO. I'M LEAVING THIS.
CLINK
HEY, PIERCE...
PHEW...
LOOKS LIKE THE RUSH IS FINALLY OVER.

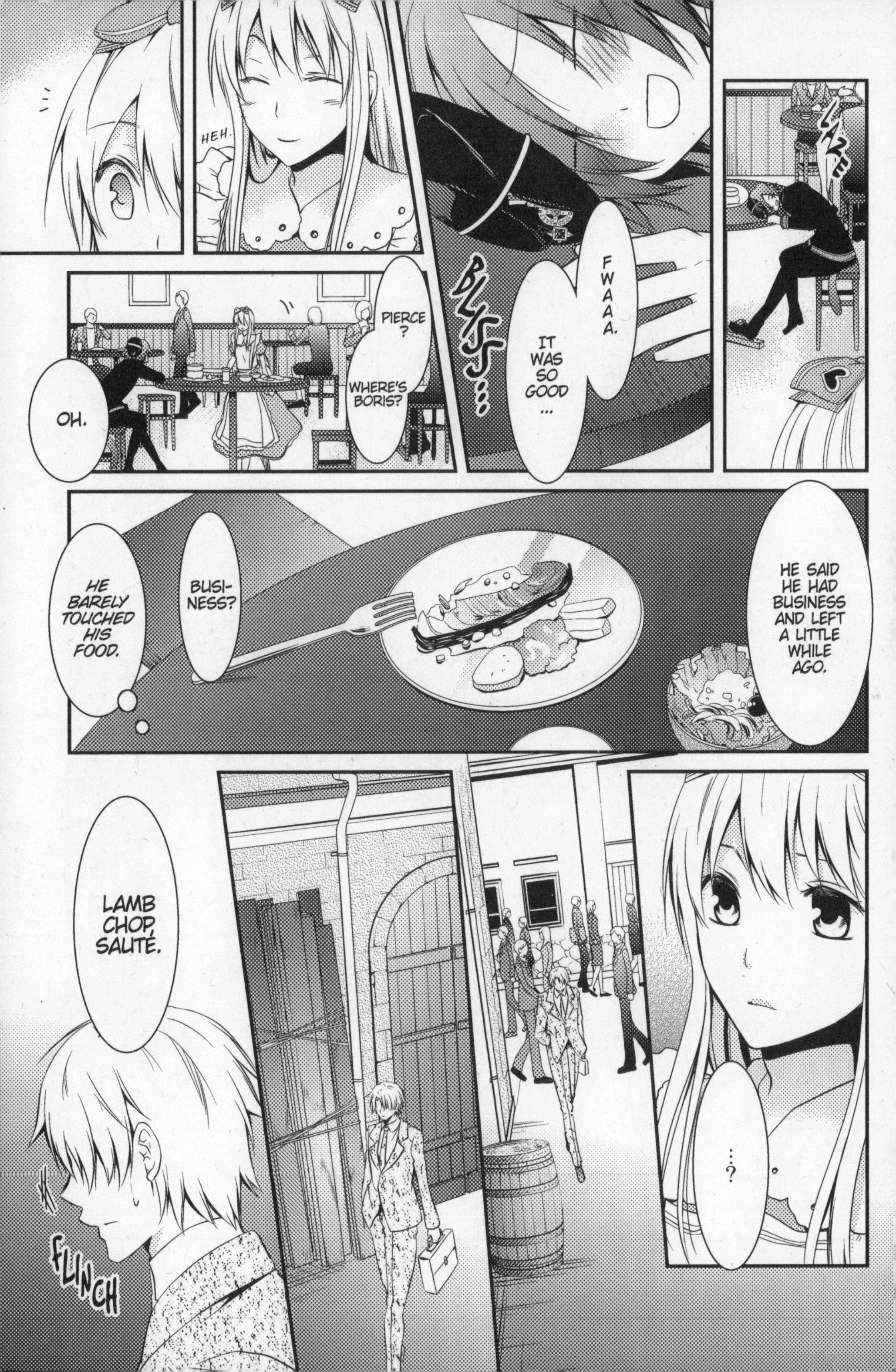

LAZE
FWAAA.
IT WAS SO GOOD...
BLISS...
HEH.
PIERCE?
WHERE'S BORIS?
OH.
HE SAID HE HAD BUSINESS AND LEFT A LITTLE WHILE AGO.
BUSINESS?
HE BARELY TOUCHED HIS FOOD.
...?
LAMB CHOP, SAUTÉ.
FLINCH

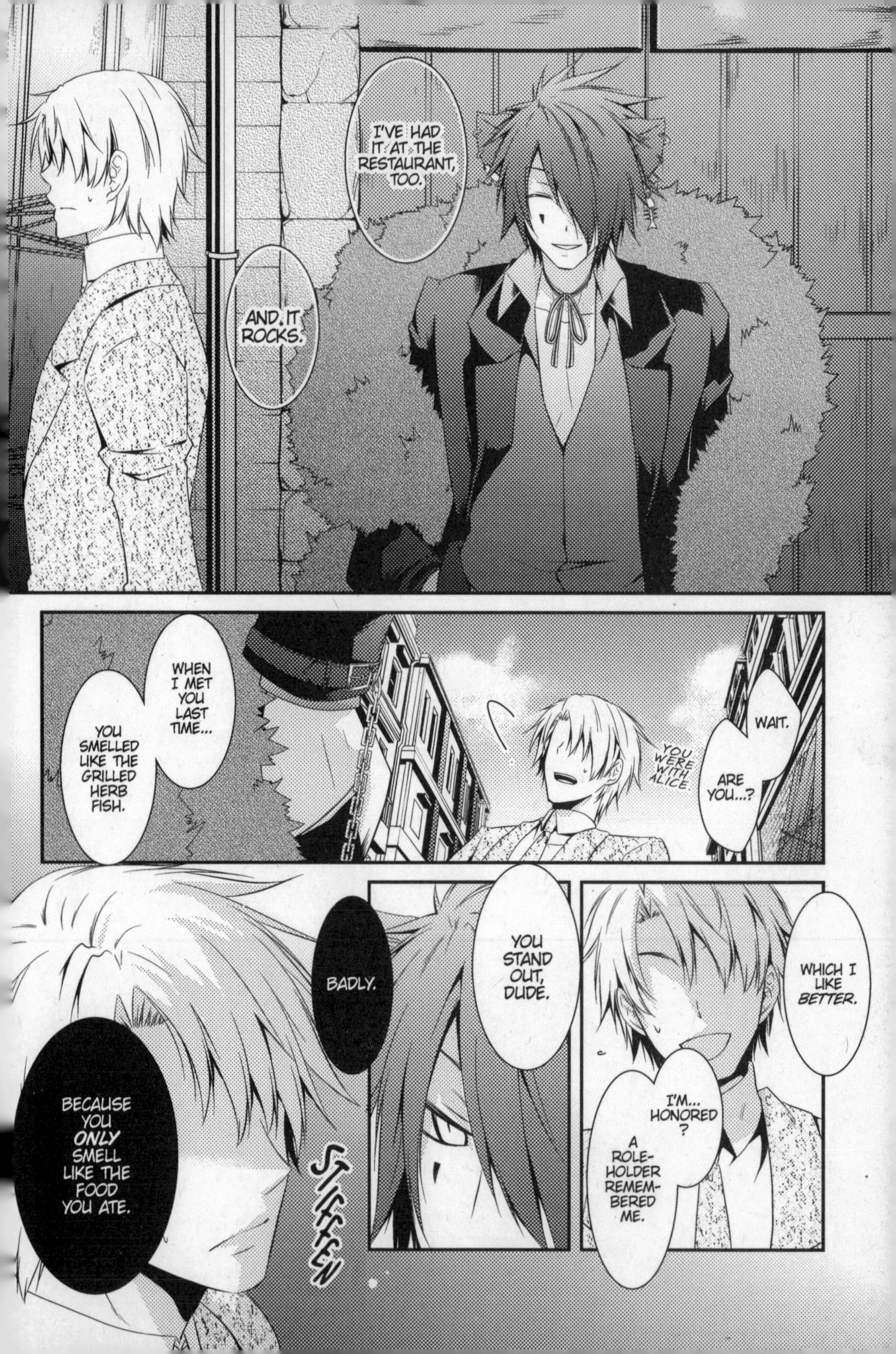
I'VE HAD IT AT THE RESTAURANT, TOO.
AND IT ROCKS.
WAIT.
ARE YOU...?
YOU WERE WITH ALICE.
WHEN I MET YOU LAST TIME...
YOU SMELLED LIKE THE GRILLED HERB FISH.
WHICH I LIKE *BETTER*.
I'M... HONORED?
A ROLE-HOLDER REMEMBERED ME.
YOU STAND OUT, DUDE.
BADLY.
BECAUSE YOU *ONLY* SMELL LIKE THE FOOD YOU ATE.
STIFFEN

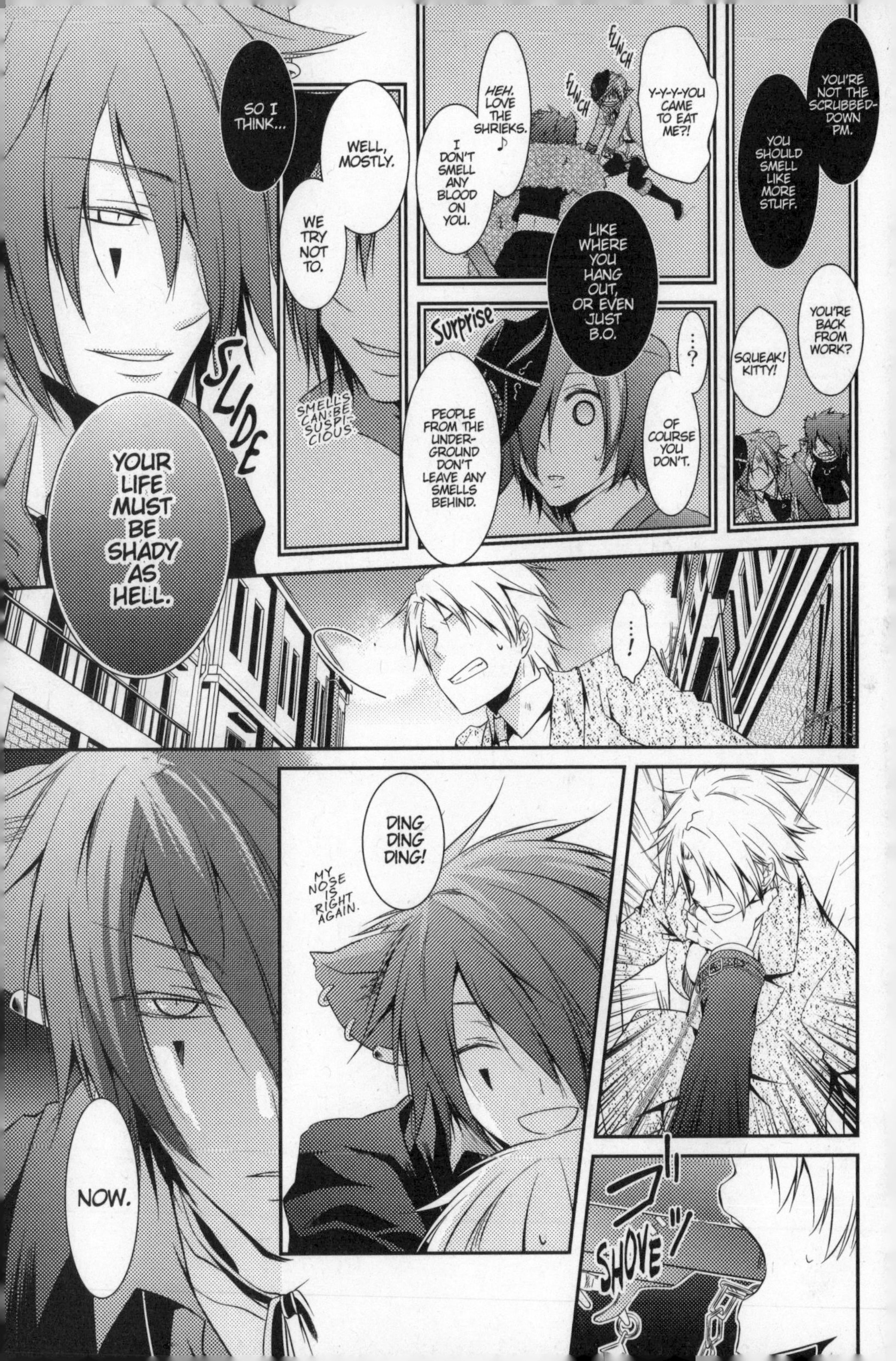

YOU'RE NOT THE SCRUBBED-DOWN PM.
YOU SHOULD SMELL LIKE MORE STUFF.
YOU'RE BACK FROM WORK?
SQUEAK! KITTY!
FLINCH
FLINCH
Y-Y-Y-YOU CAME TO EAT ME?!
HEH. LOVE THE SHRIEKS. ♪
I DON'T SMELL ANY BLOOD ON YOU.
...?
OF COURSE YOU DON'T.
LIKE WHERE YOU HANG OUT, OR EVEN JUST B.O.
Surprise
PEOPLE FROM THE UNDER-GROUND DON'T LEAVE ANY SMELLS BEHIND.
WELL, MOSTLY.
WE TRY NOT TO.
SMELLS CAN BE SUSPI-CIOUS.
SO I THINK...
SLIDE
YOUR LIFE MUST BE SHADY AS HELL.
...!
DING DING DING!
MY NOSE IS RIGHT AGAIN.
NOW.
SHOVE

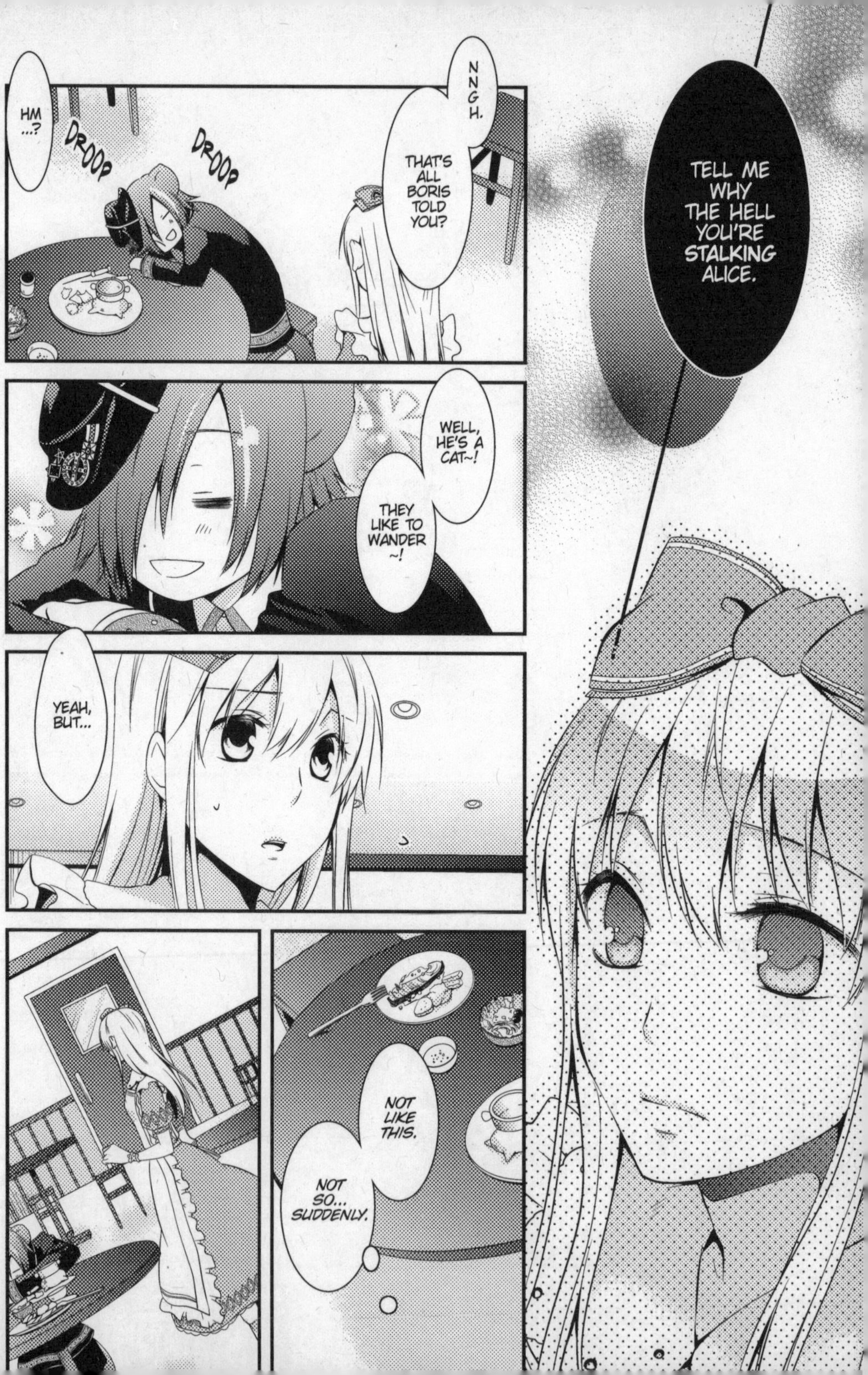
TELL ME WHY THE HELL YOU'RE STALKING ALICE.
NNGH.
THAT'S ALL BORIS TOLD YOU?
DROOP
DROOP
HM ...?
WELL, HE'S A CAT~!
THEY LIKE TO WANDER ~!
YEAH, BUT...
NOT LIKE THIS.
NOT SO... SUDDENLY.

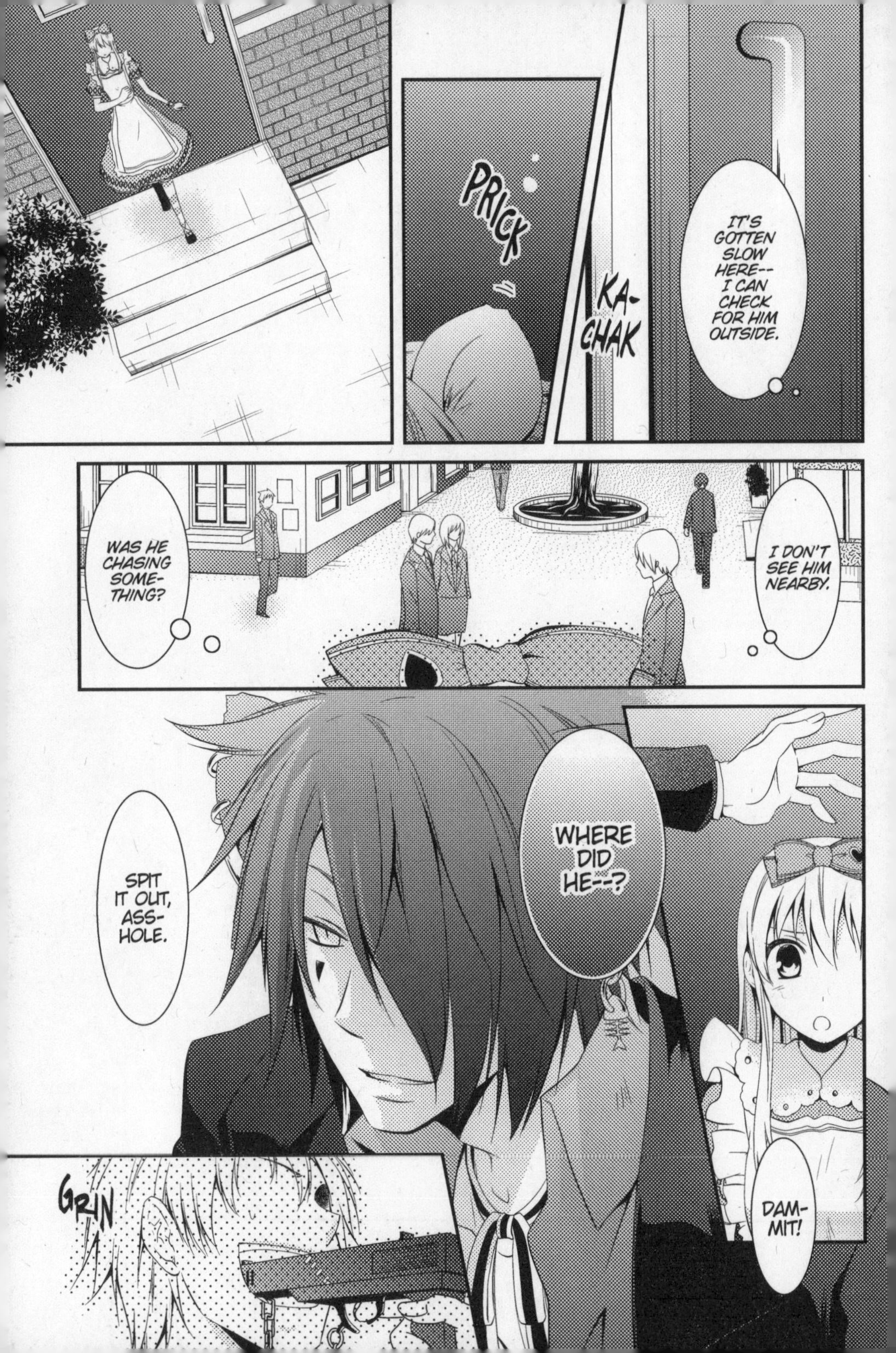

IT'S GOTTEN SLOW HERE-- I CAN CHECK FOR HIM OUTSIDE.
KA-CHAK
PRICK
I DON'T SEE HIM NEARBY.
WAS HE CHASING SOME-THING?
WHERE DID HE--?
SPIT IT OUT, ASS-HOLE.
DAM-MIT!
GRIN

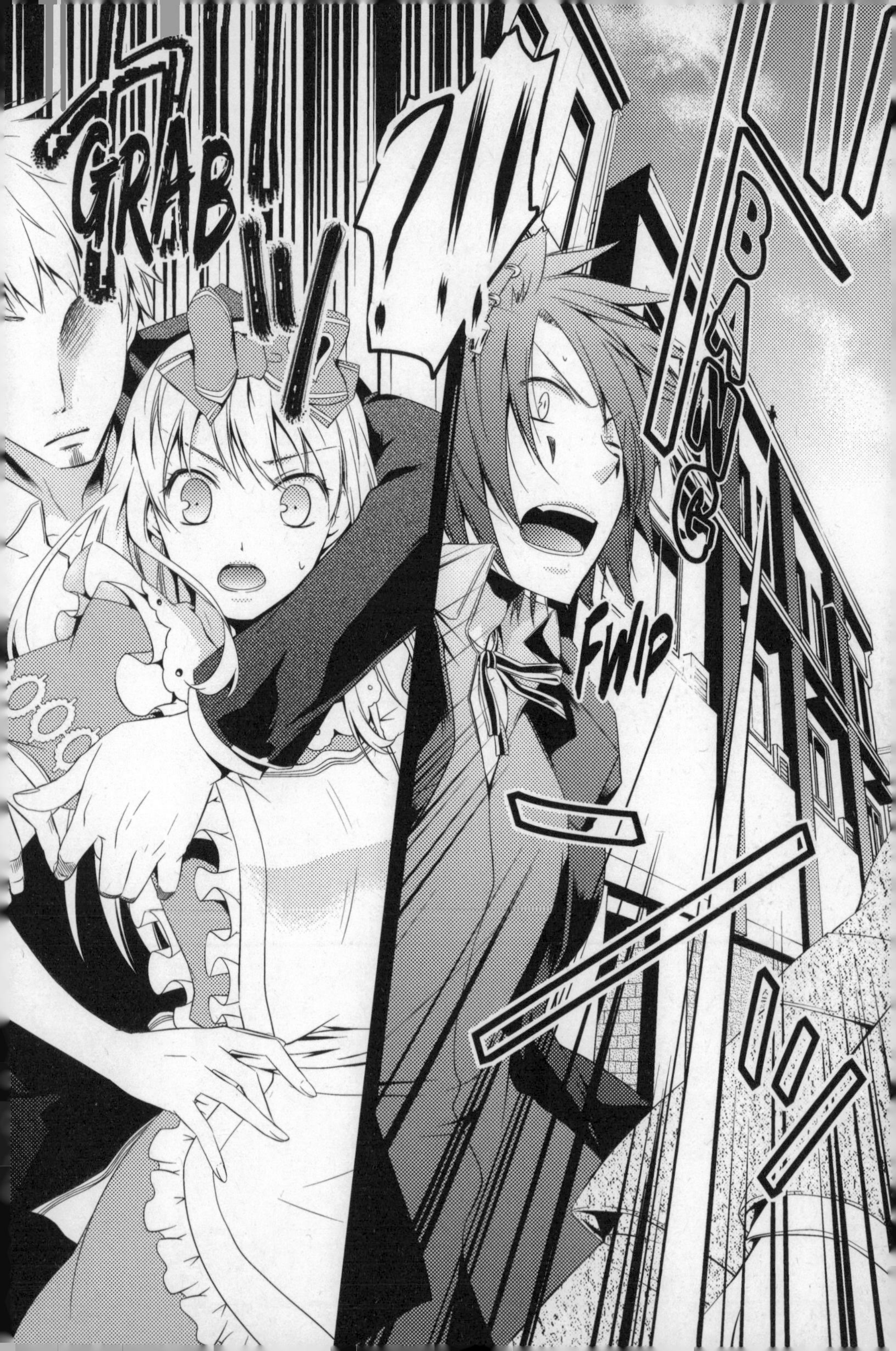
BANG
FWIP
GRAB

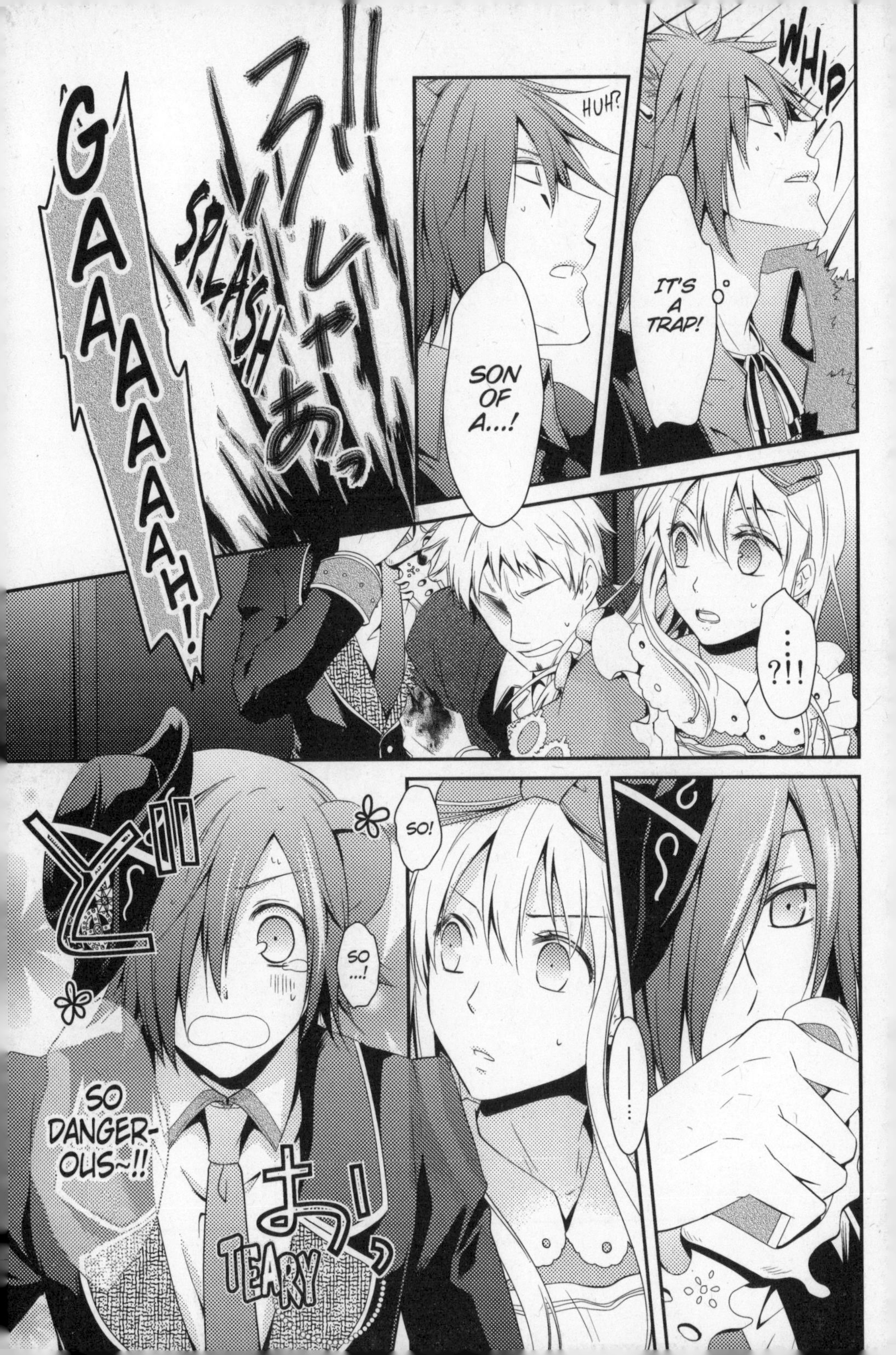
WHIP
IT'S A TRAP!
HUH?
SON OF A...!
GAAAAAAH!
SPLASH
...?!!
—...
SO!
SO ...!
SO DANGER-OUS~!!
TEARY

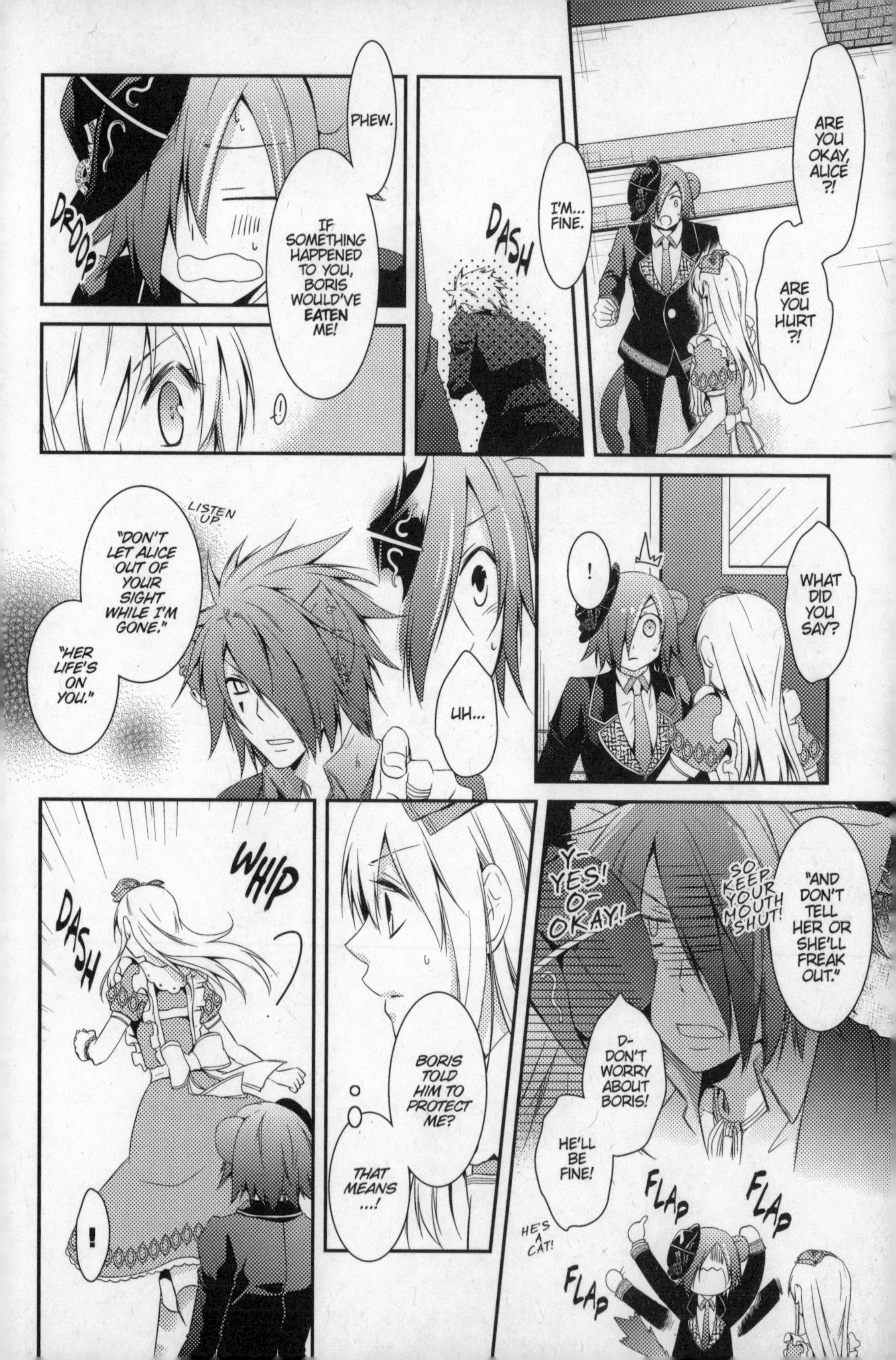
ARE YOU OKAY, ALICE?!
ARE YOU HURT?!
DASH
I'M... FINE.
PHEW.
IF SOMETHING HAPPENED TO YOU, BORIS WOULD'VE EATEN ME!
DROOP
!
!
WHAT DID YOU SAY?
UH...
LISTEN UP
"DON'T LET ALICE OUT OF YOUR SIGHT WHILE I'M GONE."
"HER LIFE'S ON YOU."
"AND DON'T TELL HER OR SHE'LL FREAK OUT."
SO KEEP YOUR MOUTH SHUT!
Y-YES! O-OKAY!
D-DON'T WORRY ABOUT BORIS!
HE'LL BE FINE!
FLAP
FLAP
HE'S A CAT!
FLAP
BORIS TOLD HIM TO PROTECT ME?
THAT MEANS...!
WHIP
DASH
!

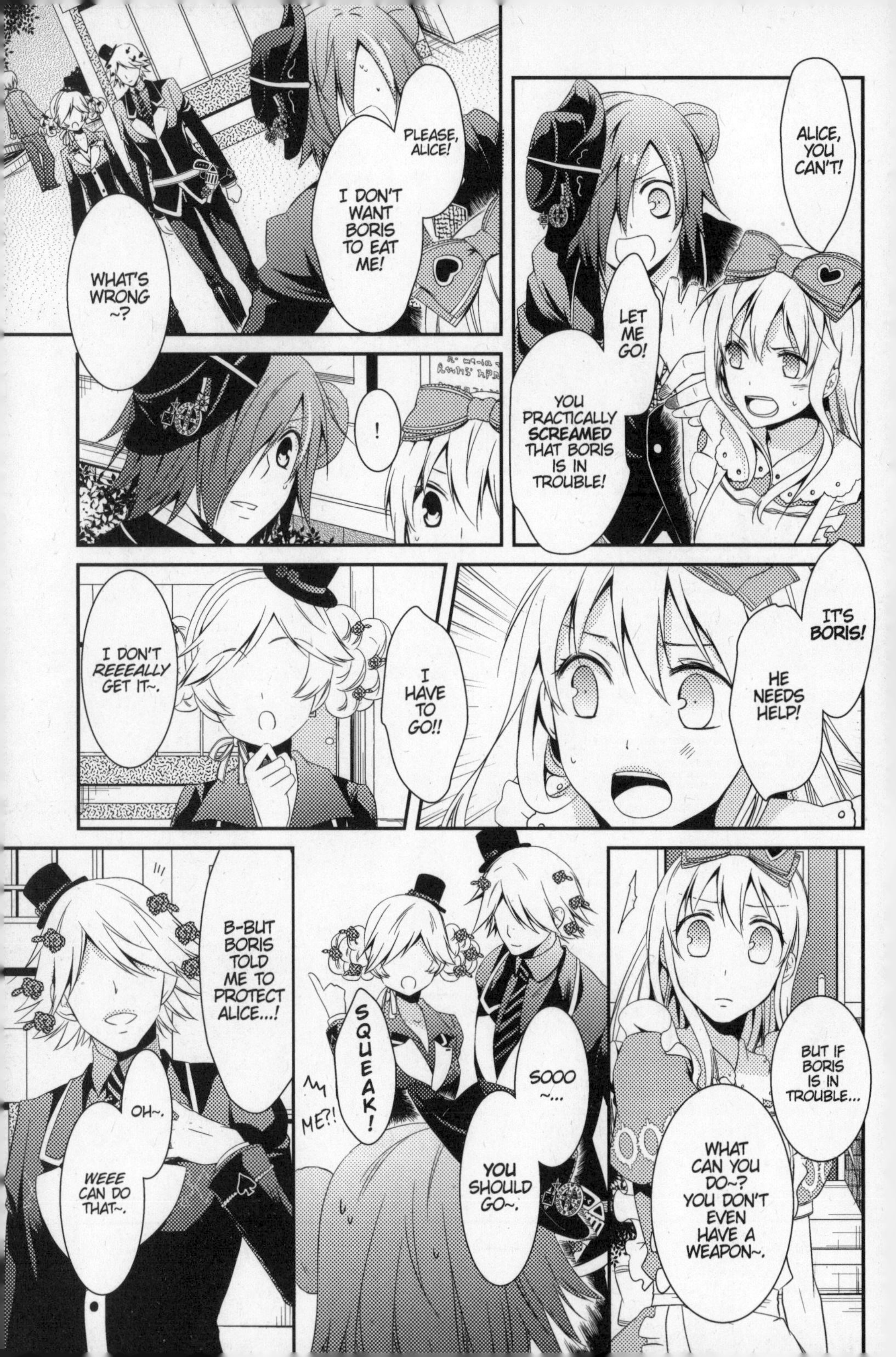
ALICE, YOU CAN'T!
LET ME GO!
YOU PRACTICALLY SCREAMED THAT BORIS IS IN TROUBLE!
PLEASE, ALICE!
I DON'T WANT BORIS TO EAT ME!
WHAT'S WRONG ~?
!
IT'S BORIS!
HE NEEDS HELP!
I HAVE TO GO!!
I DON'T REEEALLY GET IT~.
BUT IF BORIS IS IN TROUBLE...
WHAT CAN YOU DO~? YOU DON'T EVEN HAVE A WEAPON~.
SOOO ~...
YOU SHOULD GO~.
SQUEAK!
ME?!
B-BUT BORIS TOLD ME TO PROTECT ALICE...!
OH~.
WEEE CAN DO THAT~.

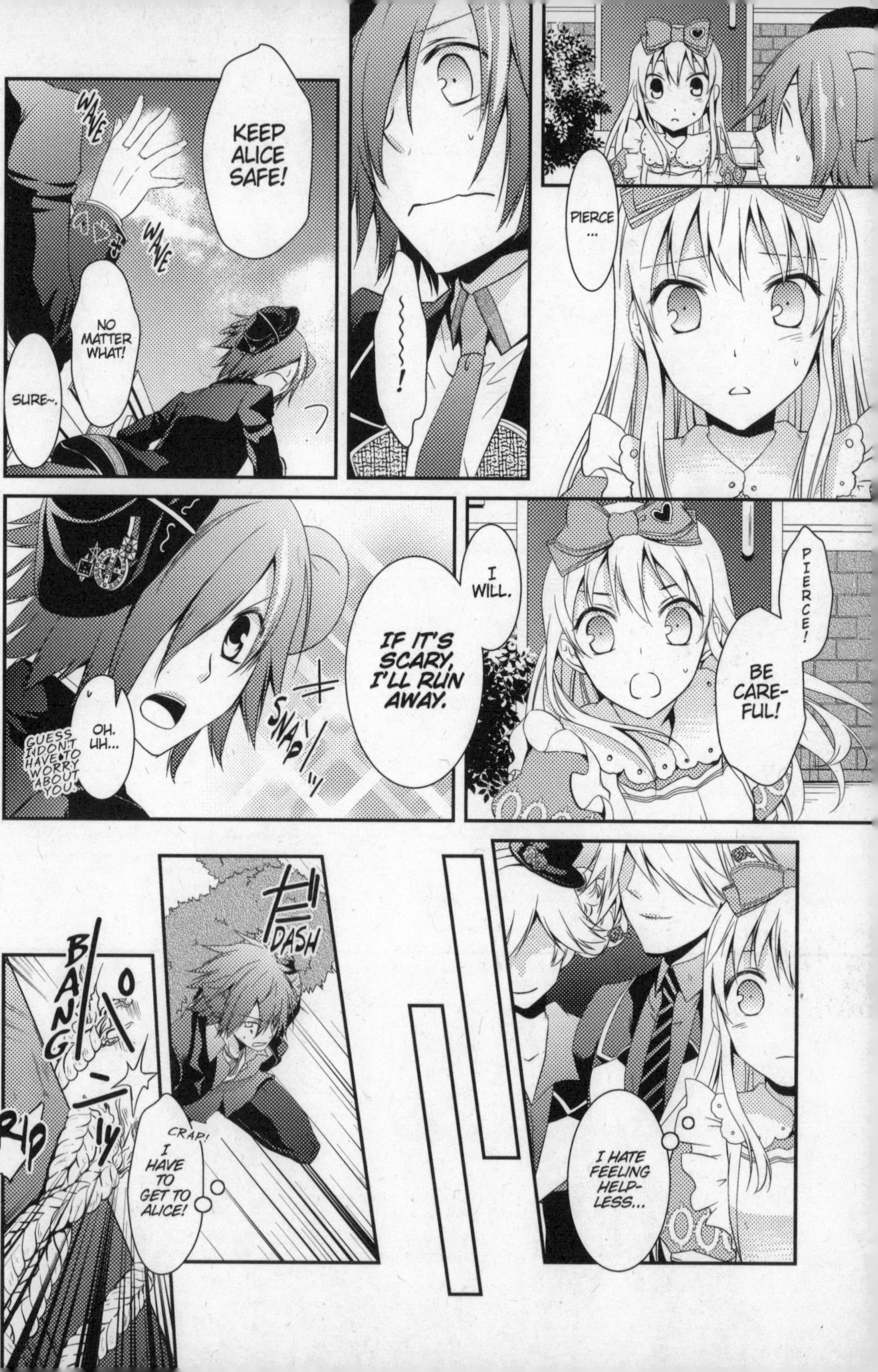
PIERCE ...
~~~~!
KEEP ALICE SAFE!
WAVE
WAVE
NO MATTER WHAT!
SURE~.
PIERCE!
BE CARE-FUL!
I WILL.
IF IT'S SCARY, I'LL RUN AWAY.
SNAP
OH. UH...
GUESS I DON'T HAVE TO WORRY ABOUT YOU.
I HATE FEELING HELP-LESS...
DASH
CRAP!
I HAVE TO GET TO ALICE!
BANG
RIP
~~~~

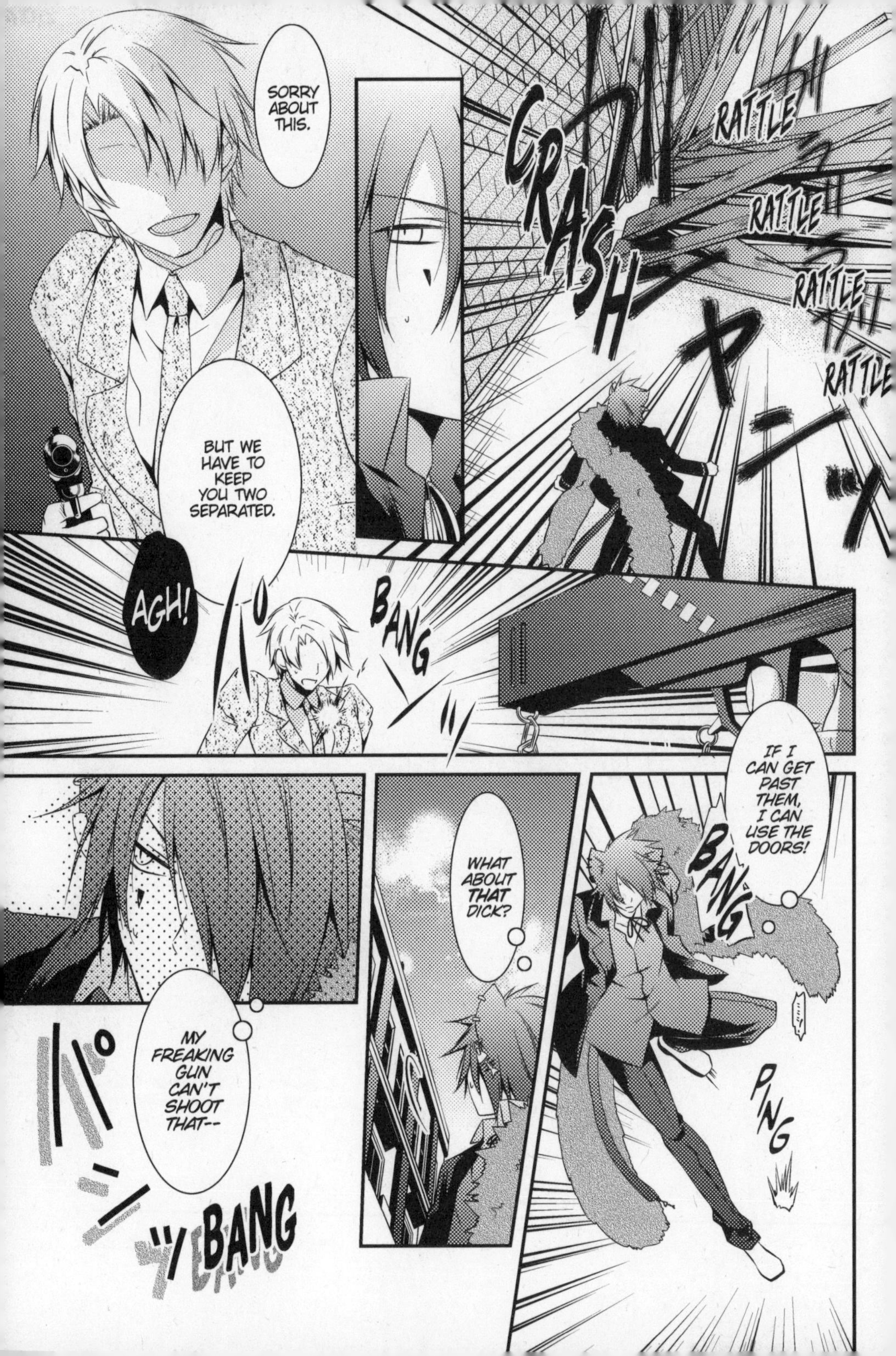

CRASH
RATTLE
RATTLE
RATTLE
RATTLE
SORRY ABOUT THIS.
BUT WE HAVE TO KEEP YOU TWO SEPARATED.
BANG
AGH!
IF I CAN GET PAST THEM, I CAN USE THE DOORS!
BANG
PING
WHAT ABOUT THAT DICK?
MY FREAKING GUN CAN'T SHOOT THAT--
BANG

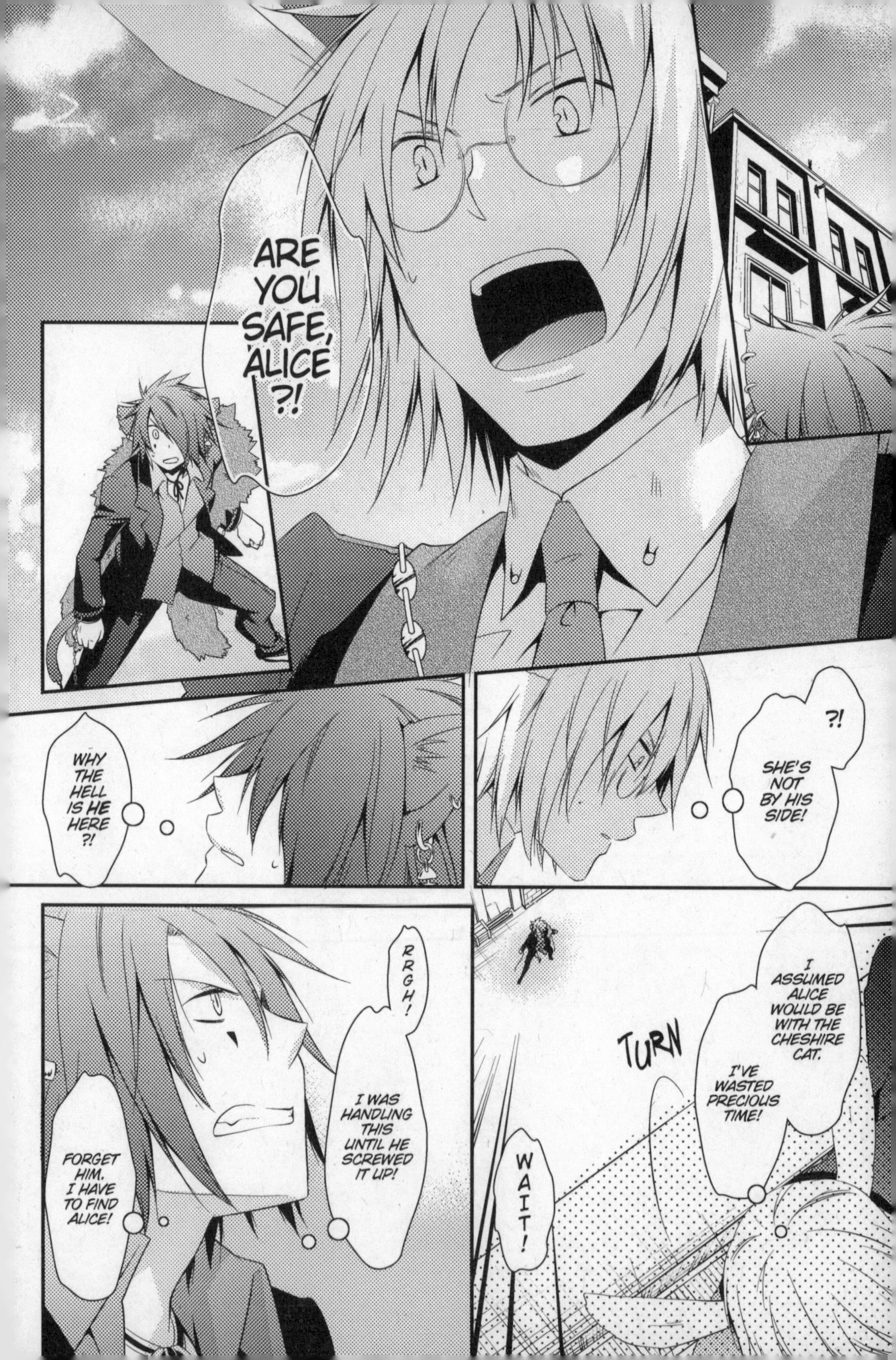
ARE YOU SAFE, ALICE ?!
?!
SHE'S NOT BY HIS SIDE!
WHY THE HELL IS HE HERE ?!
I ASSUMED ALICE WOULD BE WITH THE CHESHIRE CAT.
I'VE WASTED PRECIOUS TIME!
TURN
WAIT!
RRGH!
I WAS HANDLING THIS UNTIL HE SCREWED IT UP!
FORGET HIM. I HAVE TO FIND ALICE!

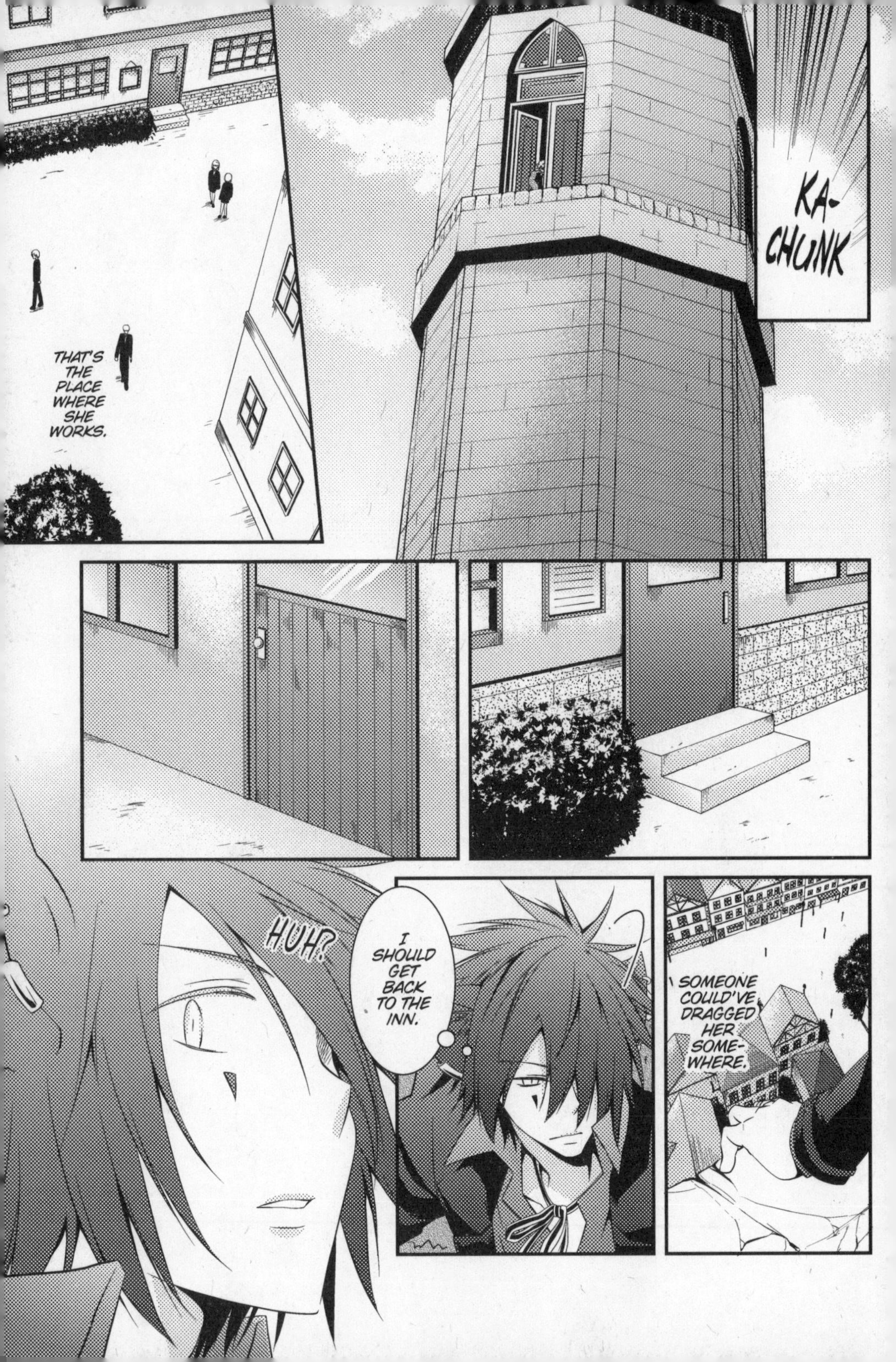
KA-CHUNK
THAT'S THE PLACE WHERE SHE WORKS.
SOMEONE COULD'VE DRAGGED HER SOME-WHERE.
I SHOULD GET BACK TO THE INN.
HUH?

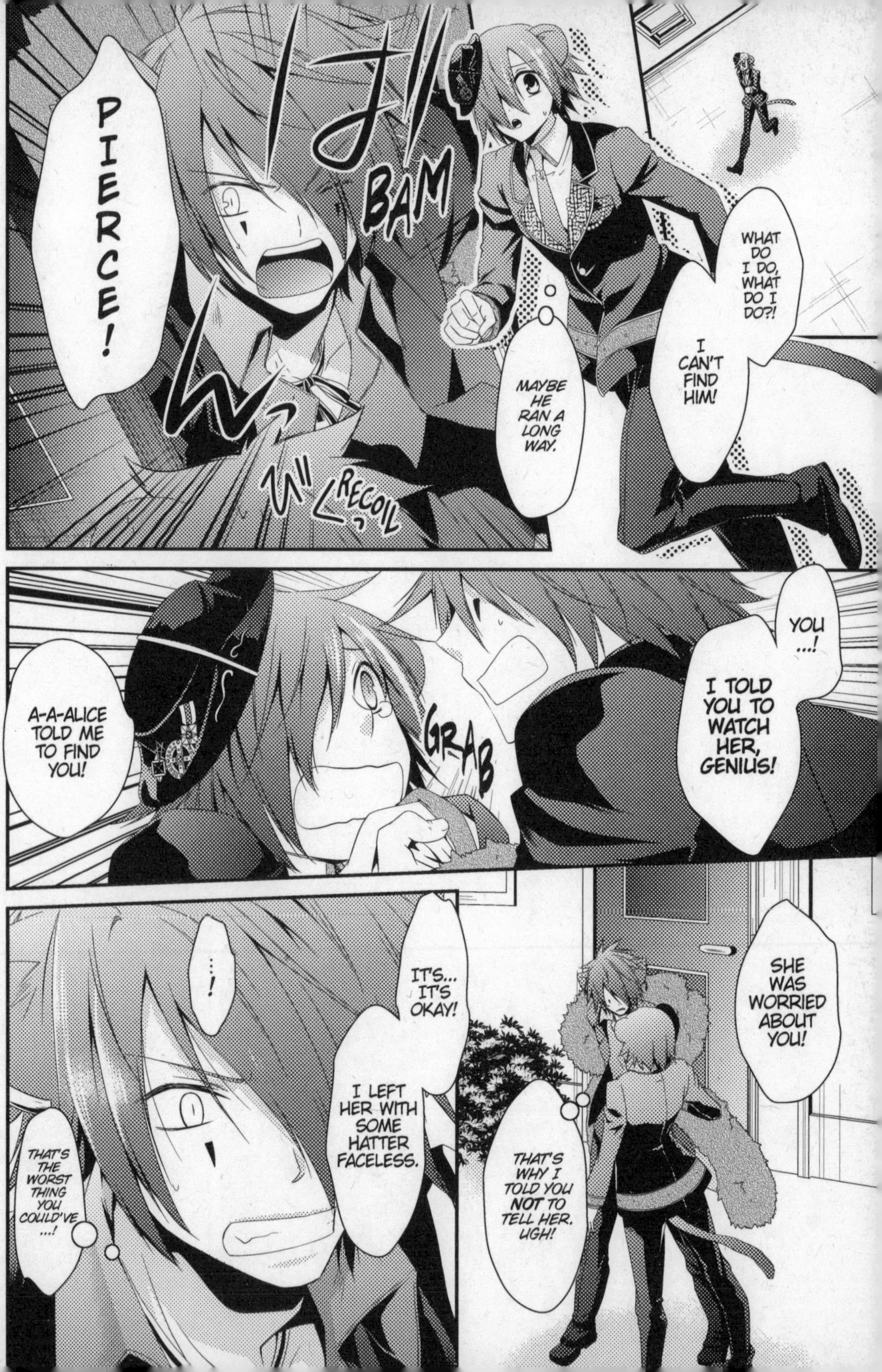
WHAT DO I DO, WHAT DO I DO?!
I CAN'T FIND HIM!
MAYBE HE RAN A LONG WAY.
BAM
PIERCE!
RECOIL
YOU ...!
I TOLD YOU TO WATCH HER, GENIUS!
GRAB
A-A-ALICE TOLD ME TO FIND YOU!
SHE WAS WORRIED ABOUT YOU!
THAT'S WHY I TOLD YOU **NOT** TO TELL HER. UGH!
IT'S... IT'S OKAY!
...!
I LEFT HER WITH SOME HATTER FACELESS.
THAT'S THE WORST THING YOU COULD'VE ...!

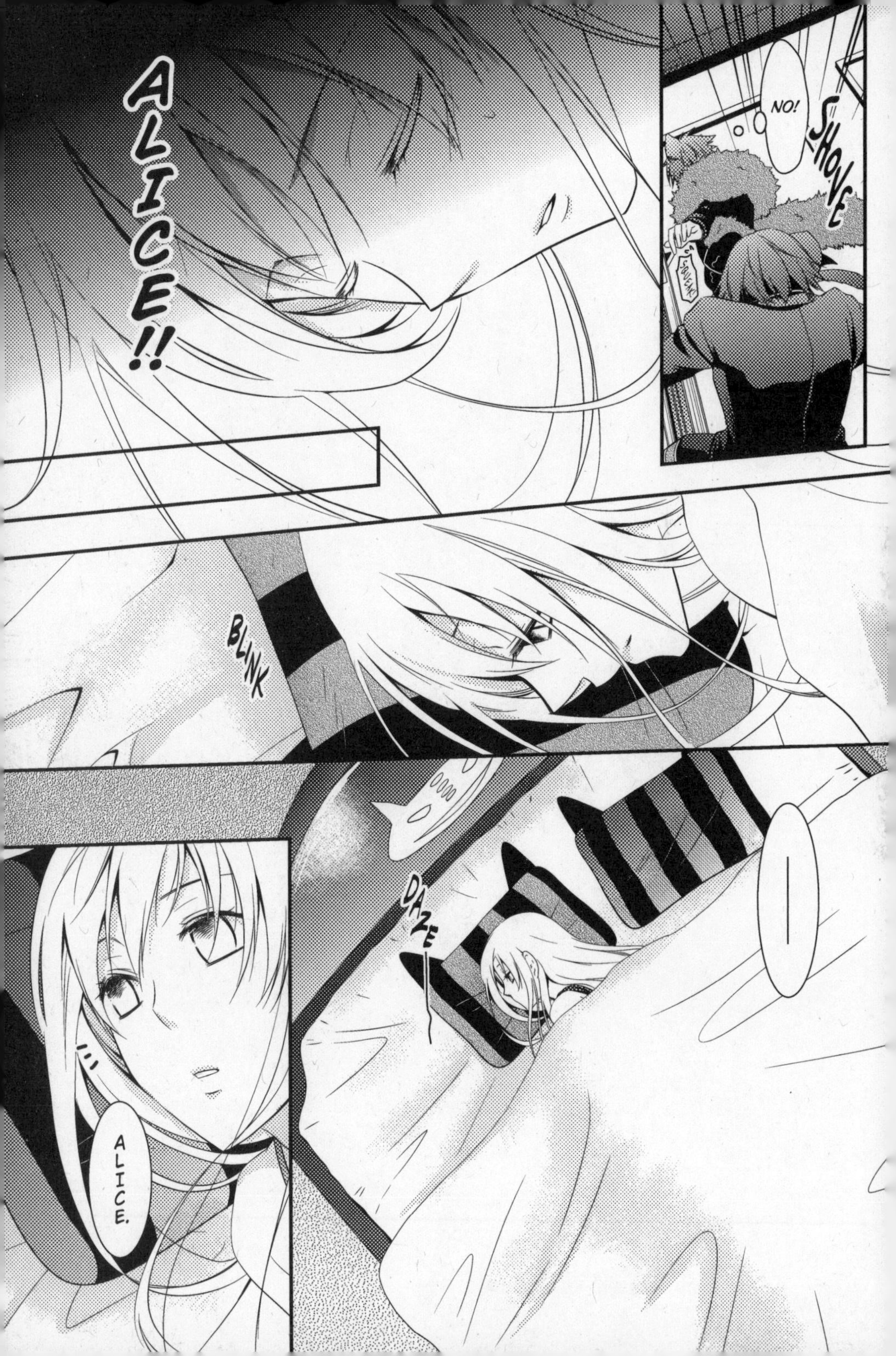
NO!
SHOVE
SQUEAK!
ALICE!!
BLINK
......
—
DAZE
!!
ALICE.

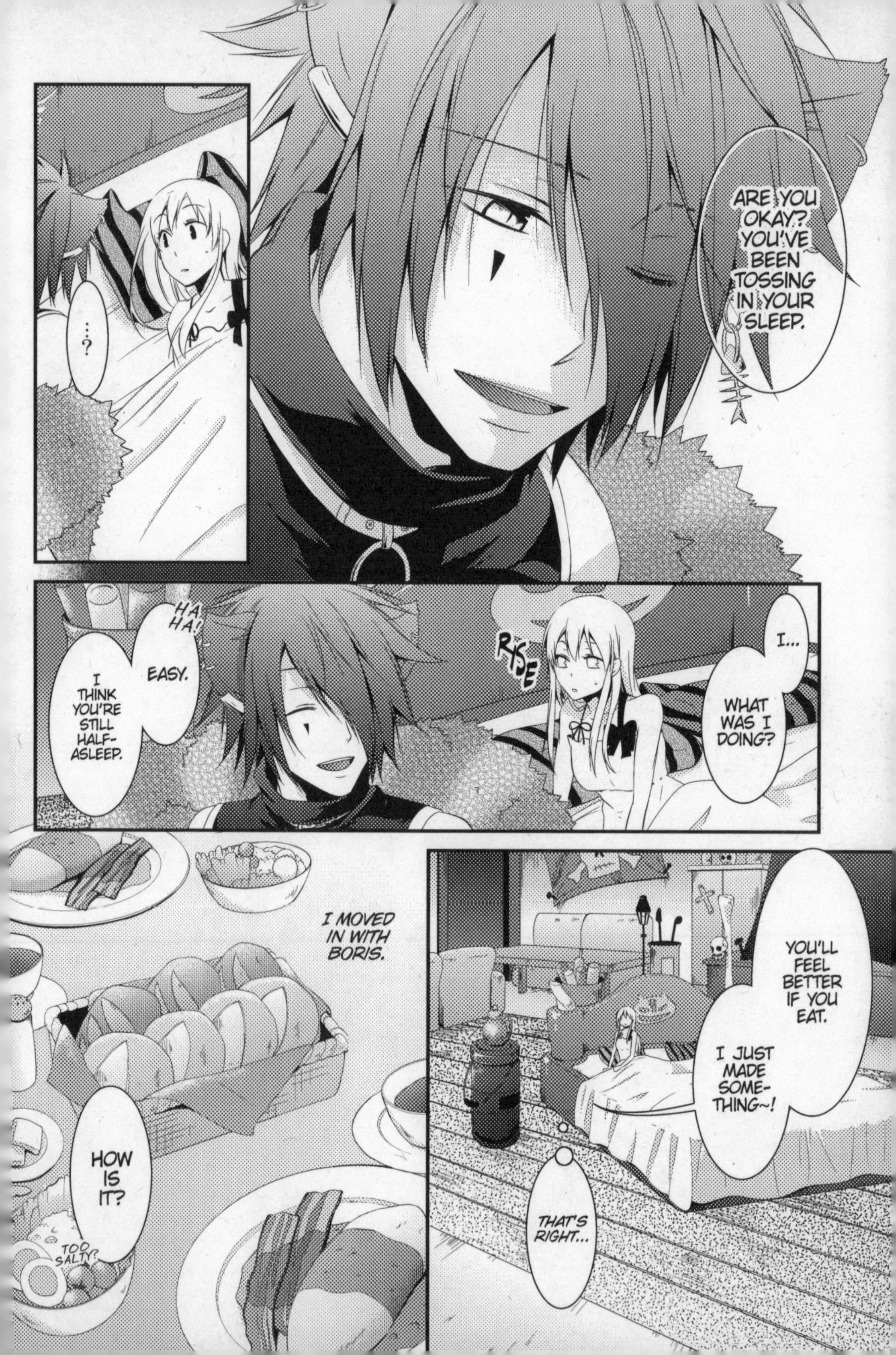
ARE YOU OKAY? YOU'VE BEEN TOSSING IN YOUR SLEEP.
...?
I...
WHAT WAS I DOING?
RISE
HA HA!
EASY.
I THINK YOU'RE STILL HALF-ASLEEP.
YOU'LL FEEL BETTER IF YOU EAT.
I JUST MADE SOME-THING~!
THAT'S RIGHT...
I MOVED IN WITH BORIS.
HOW IS IT?
TOO SALTY?

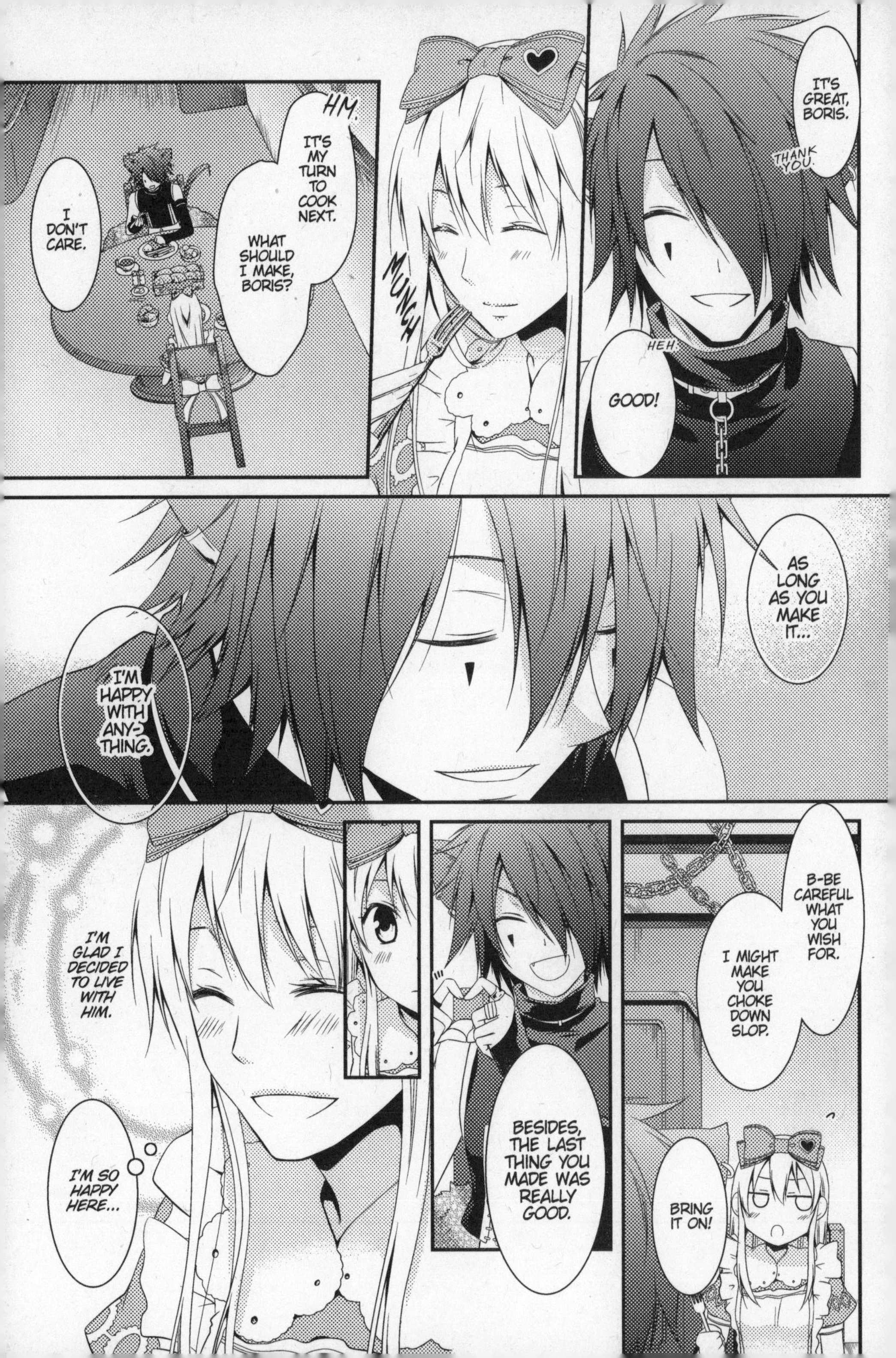
IT'S GREAT, BORIS.
THANK YOU.
HEH.
GOOD!
MUNCH
HM.
IT'S MY TURN TO COOK NEXT.
WHAT SHOULD I MAKE, BORIS?
I DON'T CARE.
AS LONG AS YOU MAKE IT...
I'M HAPPY WITH ANY-THING.
B-BE CAREFUL WHAT YOU WISH FOR.
I MIGHT MAKE YOU CHOKE DOWN SLOP.
BRING IT ON!
BESIDES, THE LAST THING YOU MADE WAS REALLY GOOD.
I'M GLAD I DECIDED TO LIVE WITH HIM.
I'M SO HAPPY HERE...

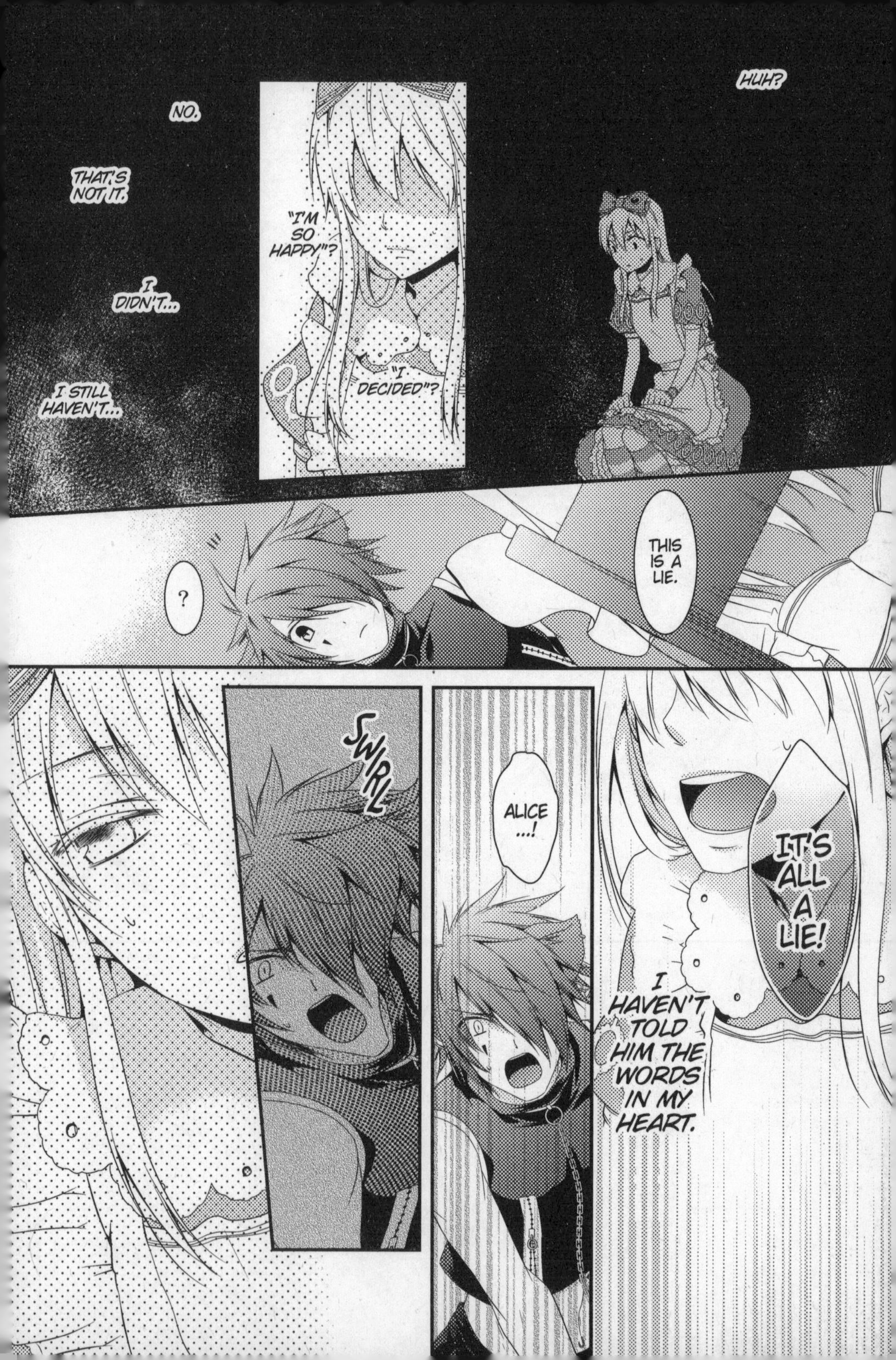
HUH?
"I'M SO HAPPY"?
"I DECIDED"?
NO.
THAT'S NOT IT.
I DIDN'T...
I STILL HAVEN'T...
THIS IS A LIE.
?
IT'S ALL A LIE!
I HAVEN'T TOLD HIM THE WORDS IN MY HEART.
ALICE ...!
SWIRL

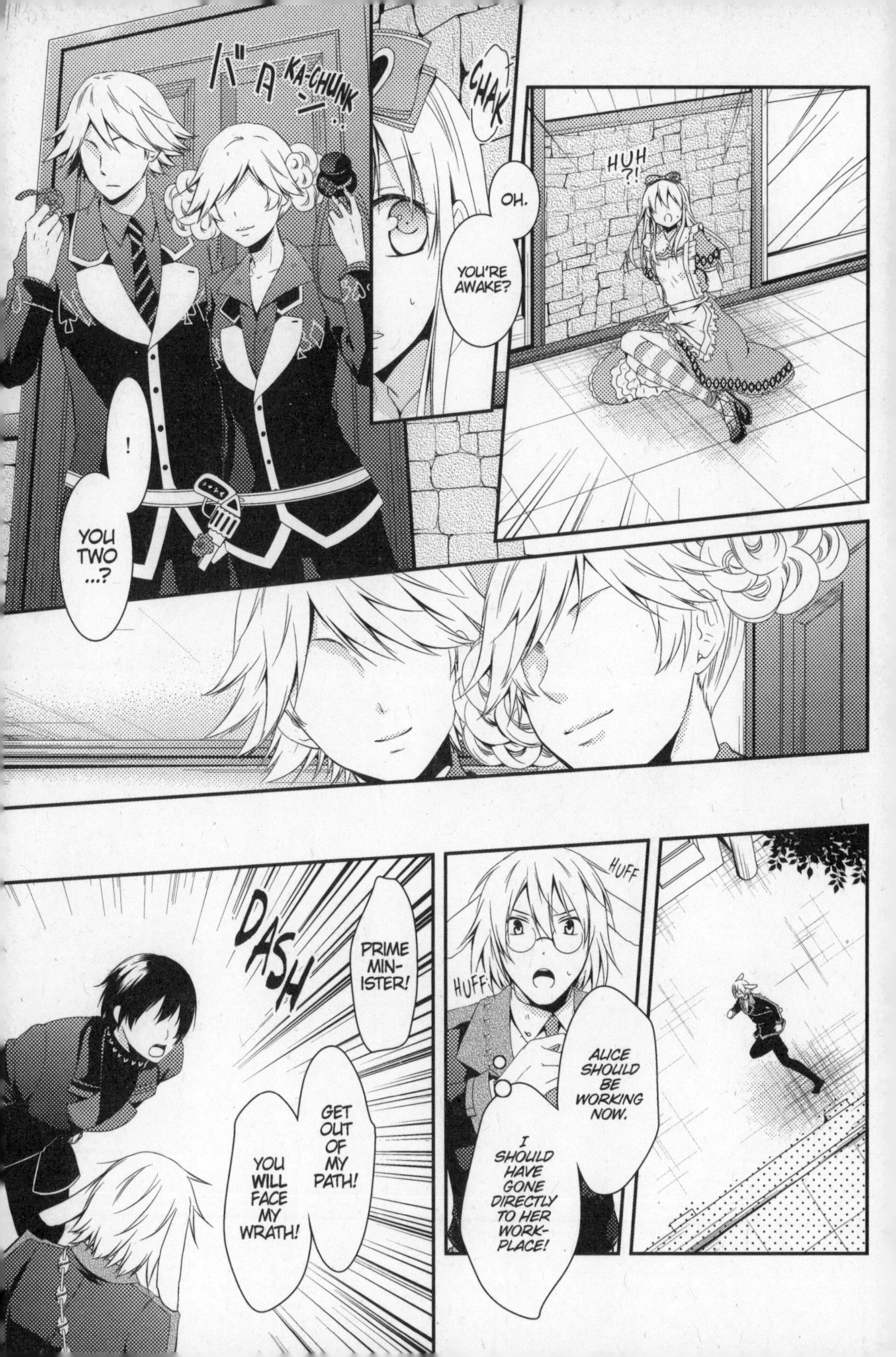
HUH ?!
CHAK
OH.
YOU'RE AWAKE?
KA-CHUNK
!
YOU TWO ...?
HUFF
HUFF
ALICE SHOULD BE WORKING NOW.
I SHOULD HAVE GONE DIRECTLY TO HER WORK-PLACE!
DASH
PRIME MIN-ISTER!
GET OUT OF MY PATH!
YOU WILL FACE MY WRATH!

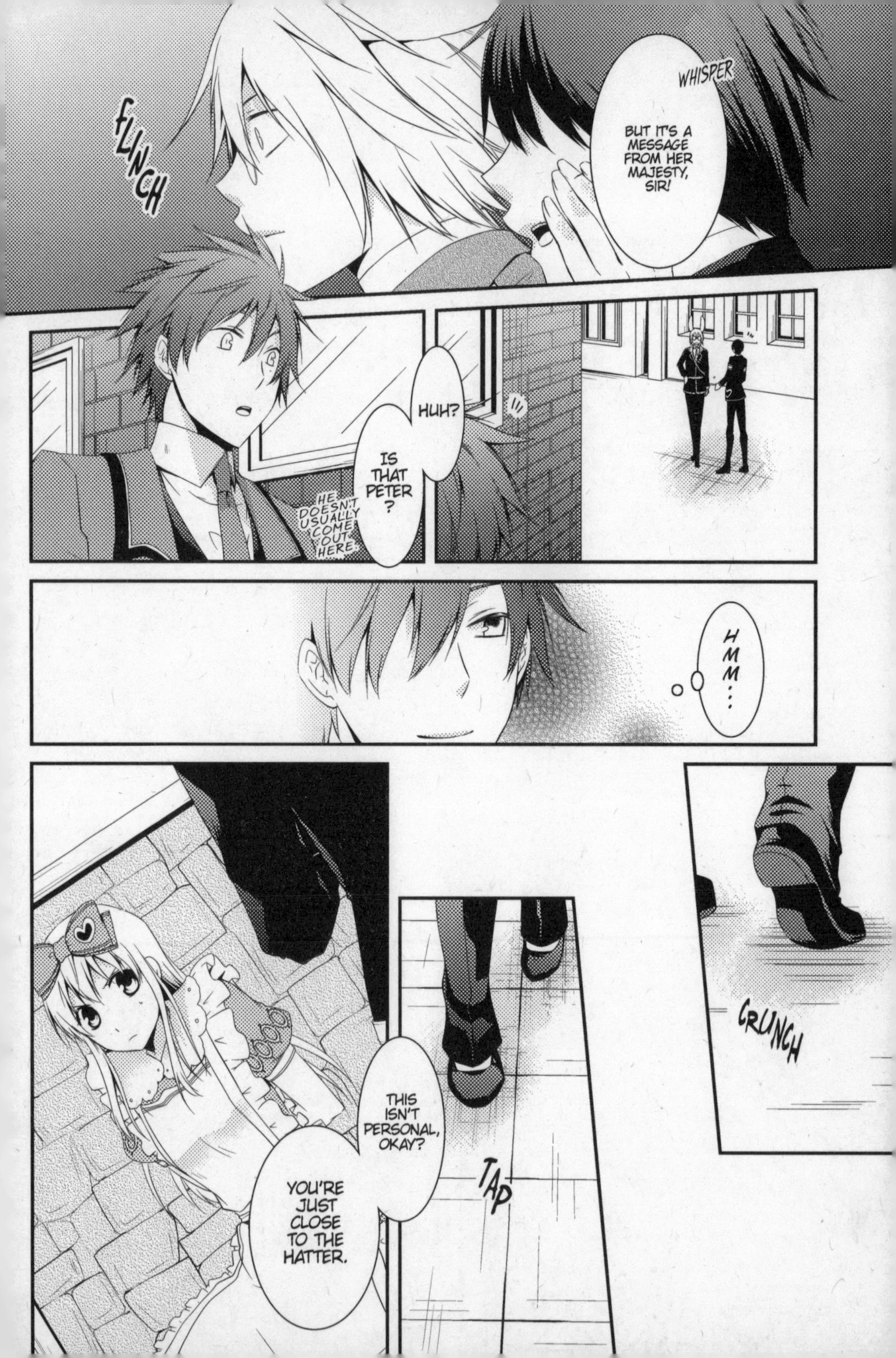
WHISPER
BUT IT'S A MESSAGE FROM HER MAJESTY, SIR!
FLINCH
HUH?
IS THAT PETER?
HE DOESN'T USUALLY COME OUT HERE.
HMM...
CRUNCH
TAP
THIS ISN'T PERSONAL, OKAY?
YOU'RE JUST CLOSE TO THE HATTER.

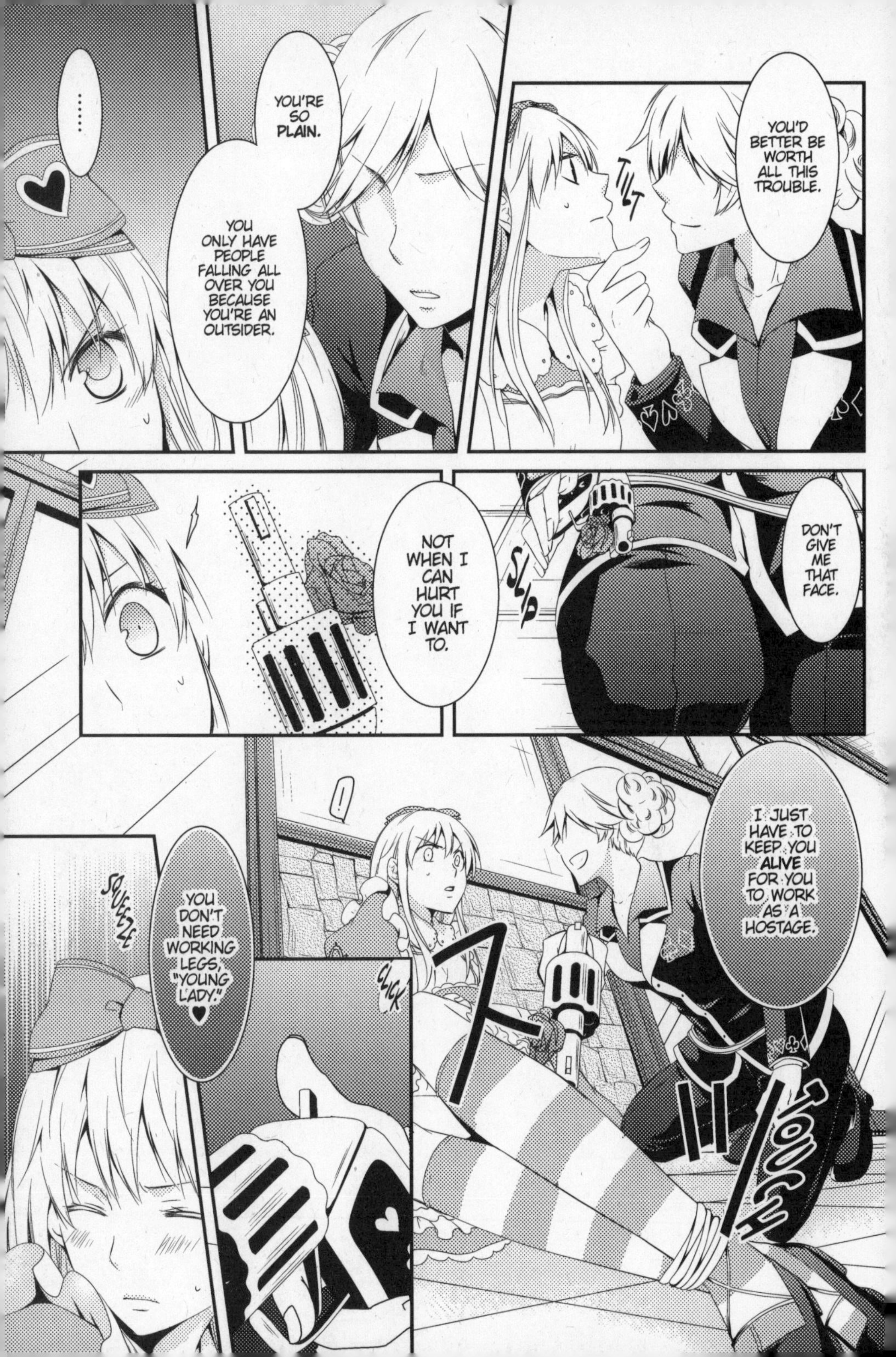
YOU'D BETTER BE WORTH ALL THIS TROUBLE.
TILT
YOU'RE SO PLAIN.
YOU ONLY HAVE PEOPLE FALLING ALL OVER YOU BECAUSE YOU'RE AN OUTSIDER.
......
DON'T GIVE ME THAT FACE.
SLIP
NOT WHEN I CAN HURT YOU IF I WANT TO.
I JUST HAVE TO KEEP YOU ALIVE FOR YOU TO WORK AS A HOSTAGE.
TOUCH
!
YOU DON'T NEED WORKING LEGS, "YOUNG LADY." ♥
SQUEEZE
CLICK

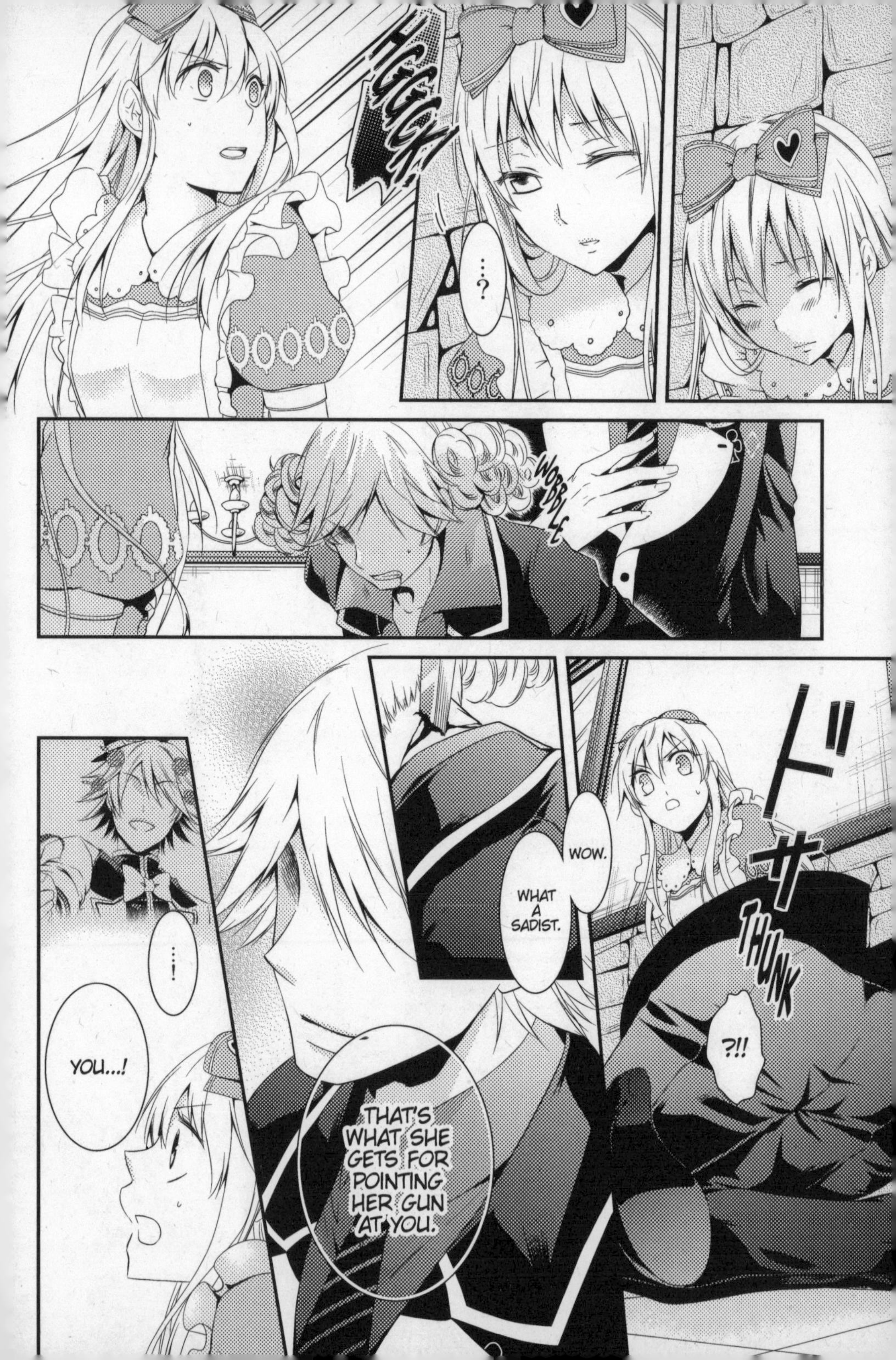

...?
HGGCK!
WOBBLE
ドサ
THUNK
?!!
WOW.
WHAT A SADIST.
THAT'S WHAT SHE GETS FOR POINTING HER GUN AT YOU.
...!
YOU...!

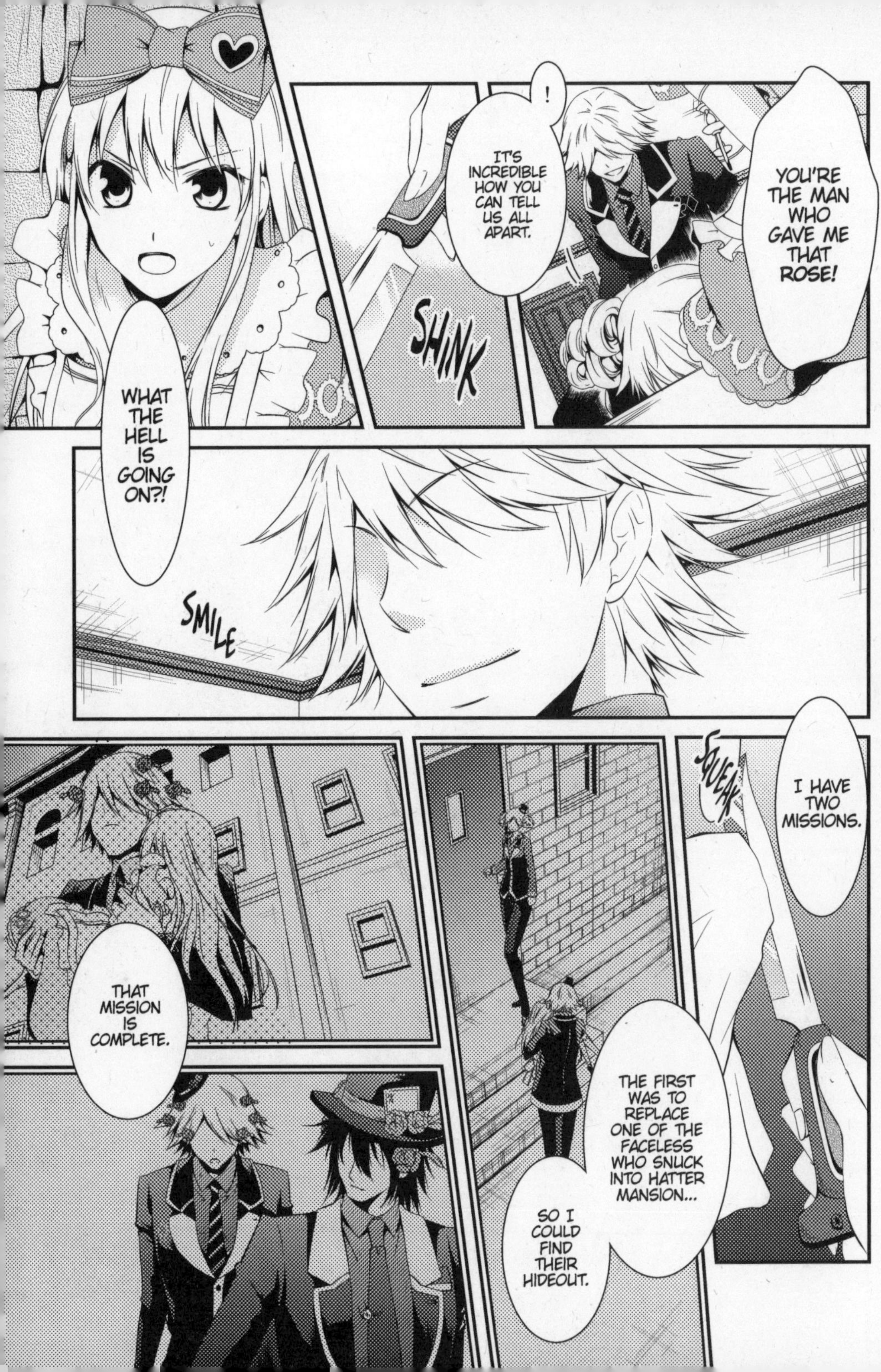
YOU'RE THE MAN WHO GAVE ME THAT ROSE!
!
IT'S INCREDIBLE HOW YOU CAN TELL US ALL APART.
SHINK
WHAT THE HELL IS GOING ON?!
SMILE
SQUEAK
I HAVE TWO MISSIONS.
THE FIRST WAS TO REPLACE ONE OF THE FACELESS WHO SNUCK INTO HATTER MANSION...
SO I COULD FIND THEIR HIDEOUT.
THAT MISSION IS COMPLETE.

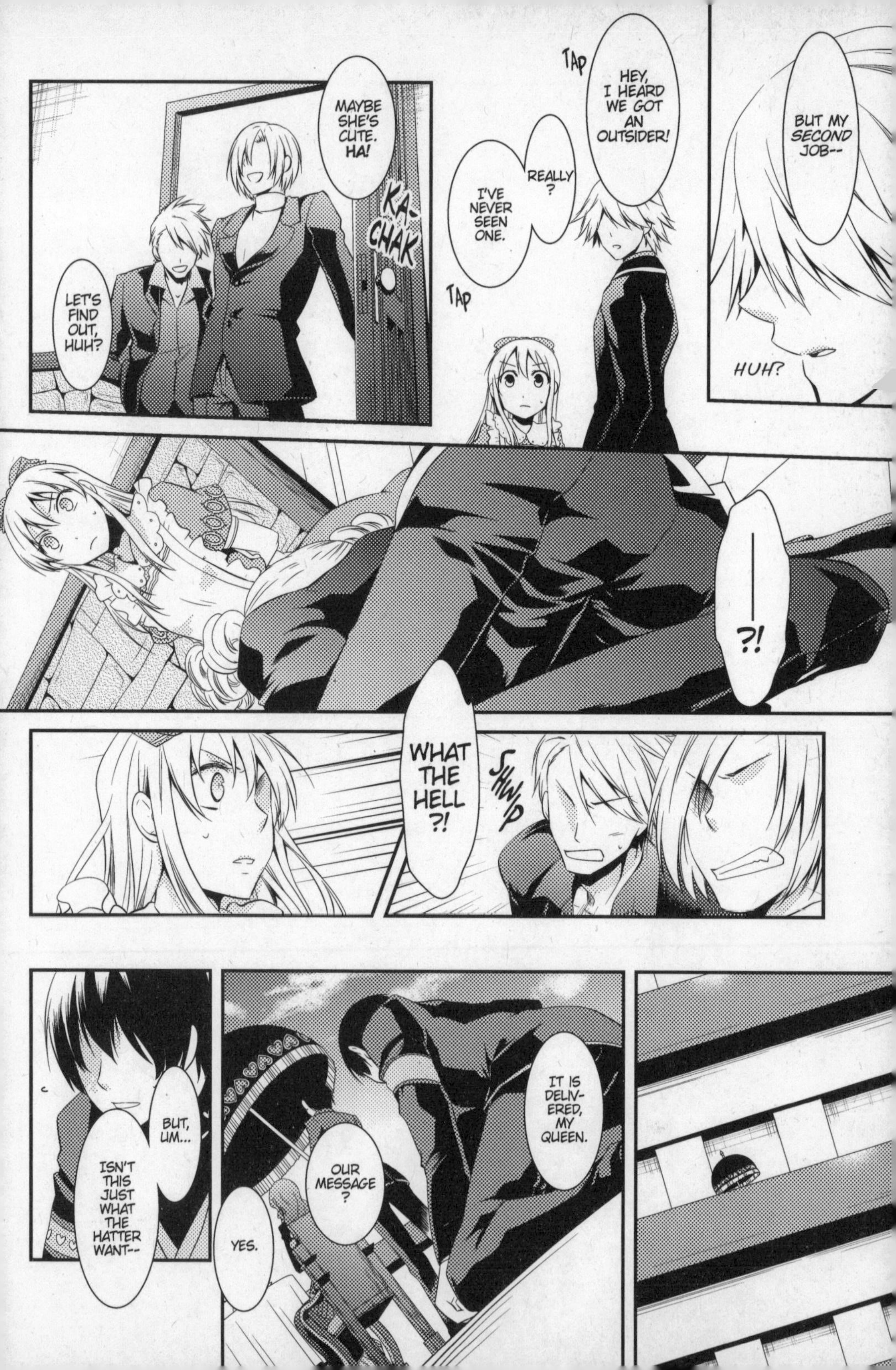
BUT MY SECOND JOB--
HUH?
TAP
HEY, I HEARD WE GOT AN OUTSIDER!
REALLY?
I'VE NEVER SEEN ONE.
TAP
MAYBE SHE'S CUTE. HA!
KA-CHAK
LET'S FIND OUT, HUH?
——?!
WHAT THE HELL?!
SHWIP
IT IS DELIVERED, MY QUEEN.
OUR MESSAGE?
YES.
BUT, UM...
ISN'T THIS JUST WHAT THE HATTER WANT--

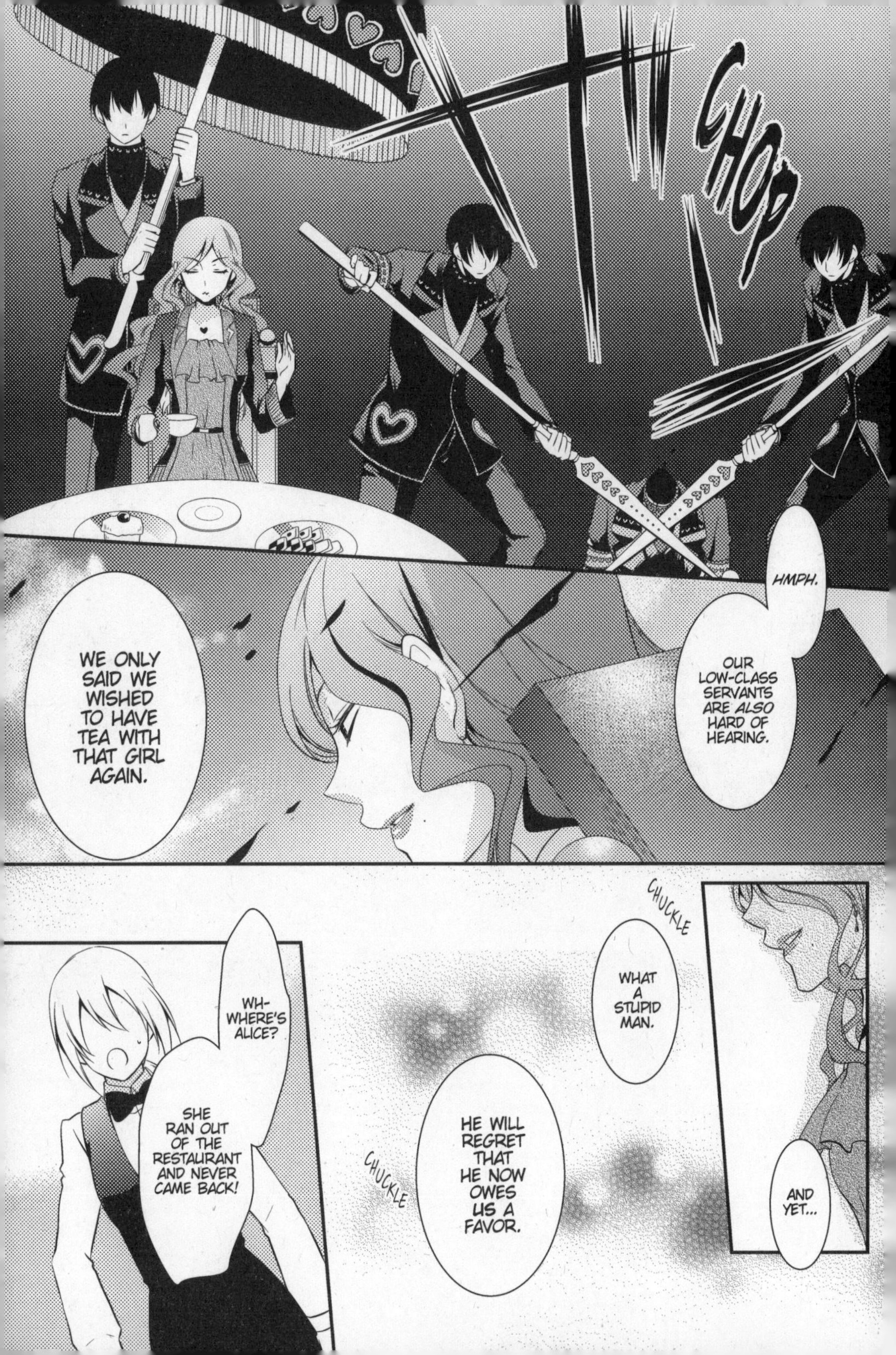
CHOP
HMPH.
OUR LOW-CLASS SERVANTS ARE ALSO HARD OF HEARING.
WE ONLY SAID WE WISHED TO HAVE TEA WITH THAT GIRL AGAIN.
CHUCKLE
WHAT A STUPID MAN.
HE WILL REGRET THAT HE NOW OWES US A FAVOR.
CHUCKLE
AND YET...
WH-WHERE'S ALICE?
SHE RAN OUT OF THE RESTAURANT AND NEVER CAME BACK!

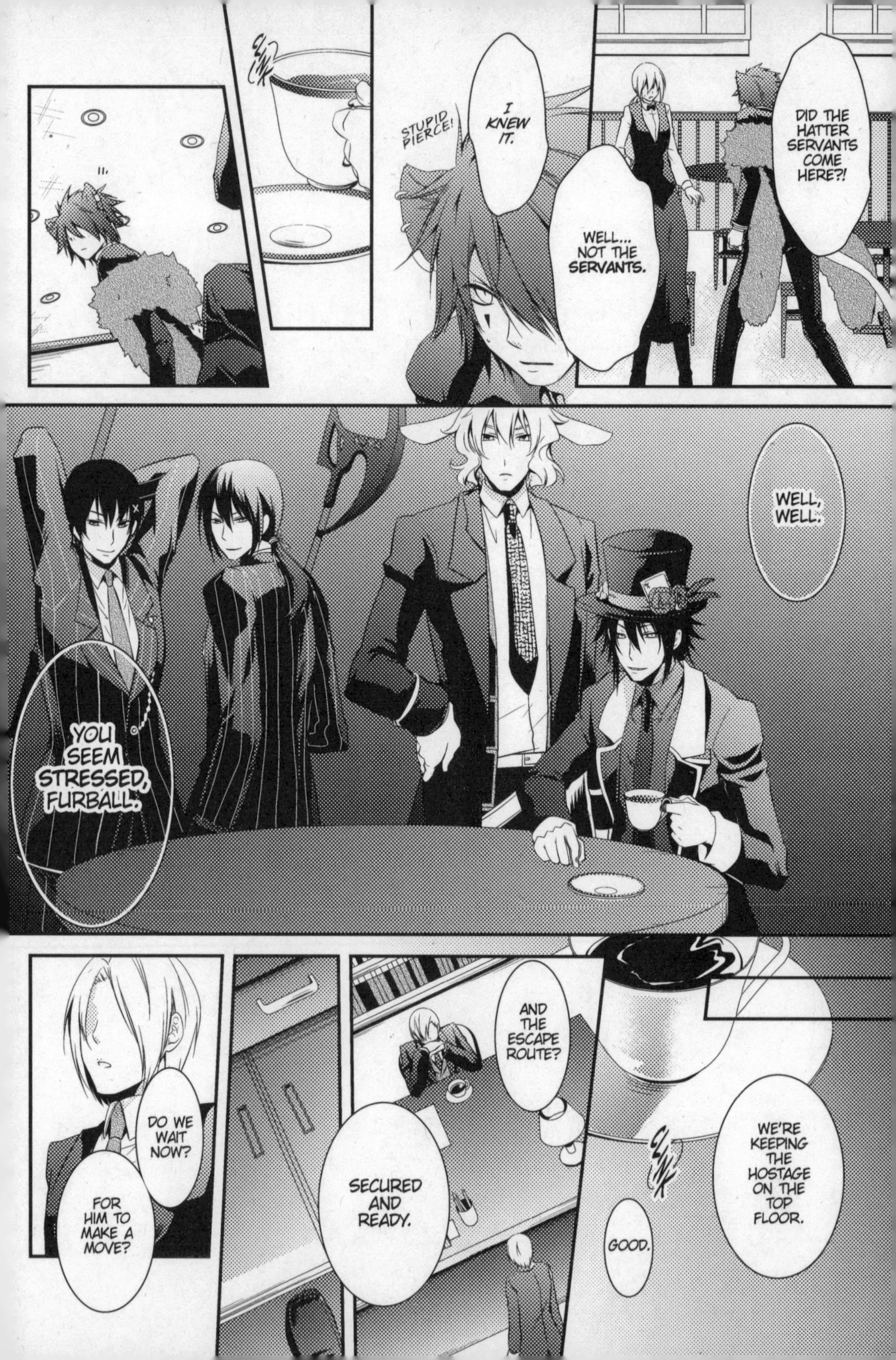
DID THE HATTER SERVANTS COME HERE?!
WELL... NOT THE SERVANTS.
I KNEW IT.
STUPID PIERCE!
CLINK
!!
WELL, WELL.
YOU SEEM STRESSED, FURBALL.
WE'RE KEEPING THE HOSTAGE ON THE TOP FLOOR.
GOOD.
CLINK
AND THE ESCAPE ROUTE?
SECURED AND READY.
DO WE WAIT NOW?
FOR HIM TO MAKE A MOVE?

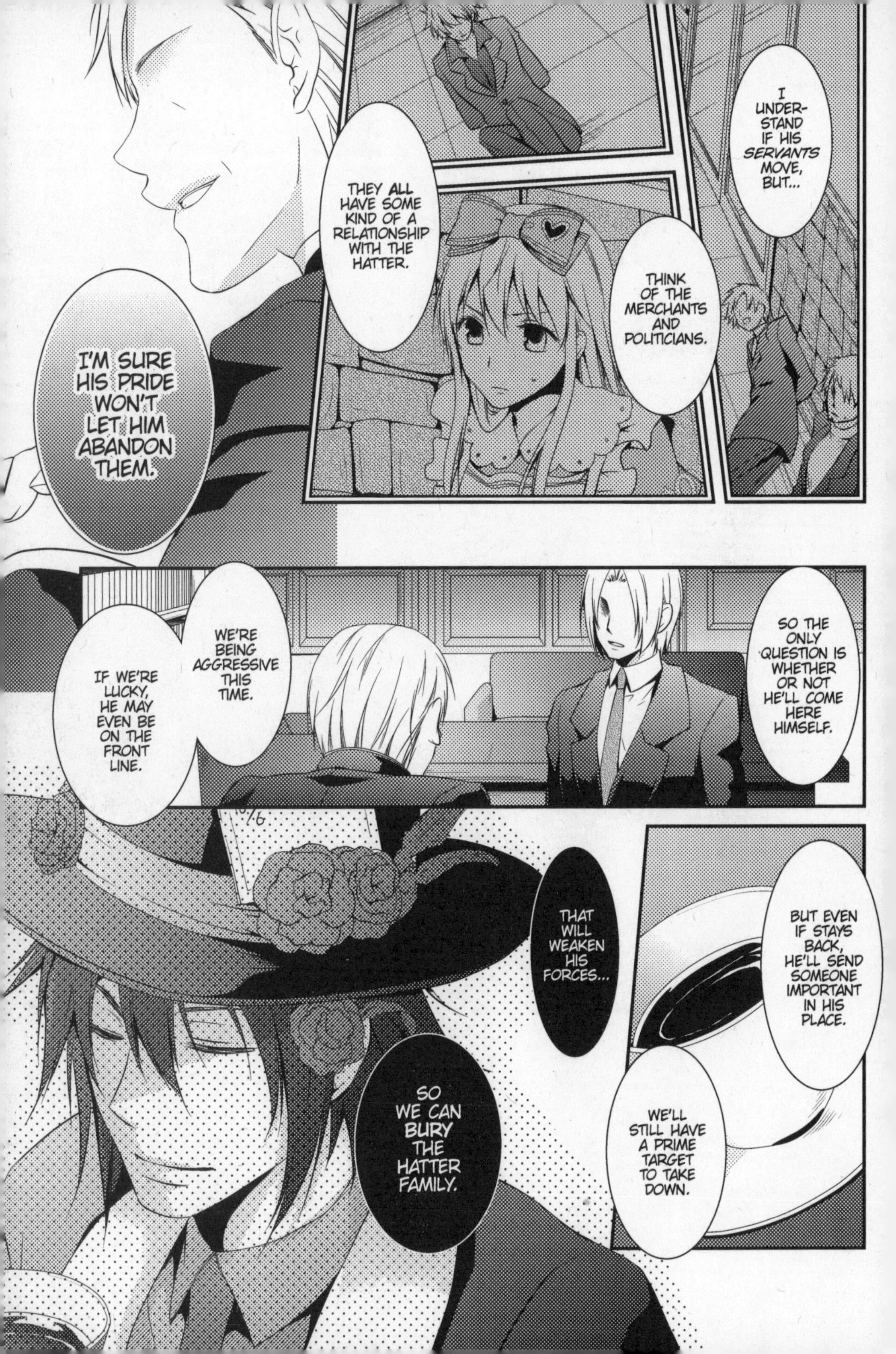
I UNDERSTAND IF HIS SERVANTS MOVE, BUT...
THINK OF THE MERCHANTS AND POLITICIANS.
THEY ALL HAVE SOME KIND OF A RELATIONSHIP WITH THE HATTER.
I'M SURE HIS PRIDE WON'T LET HIM ABANDON THEM.
SO THE ONLY QUESTION IS WHETHER OR NOT HE'LL COME HERE HIMSELF.
WE'RE BEING AGGRESSIVE THIS TIME.
IF WE'RE LUCKY, HE MAY EVEN BE ON THE FRONT LINE.
BUT EVEN IF STAYS BACK, HE'LL SEND SOMEONE IMPORTANT IN HIS PLACE.
WE'LL STILL HAVE A PRIME TARGET TO TAKE DOWN.
THAT WILL WEAKEN HIS FORCES...
SO WE CAN BURY THE HATTER FAMILY.

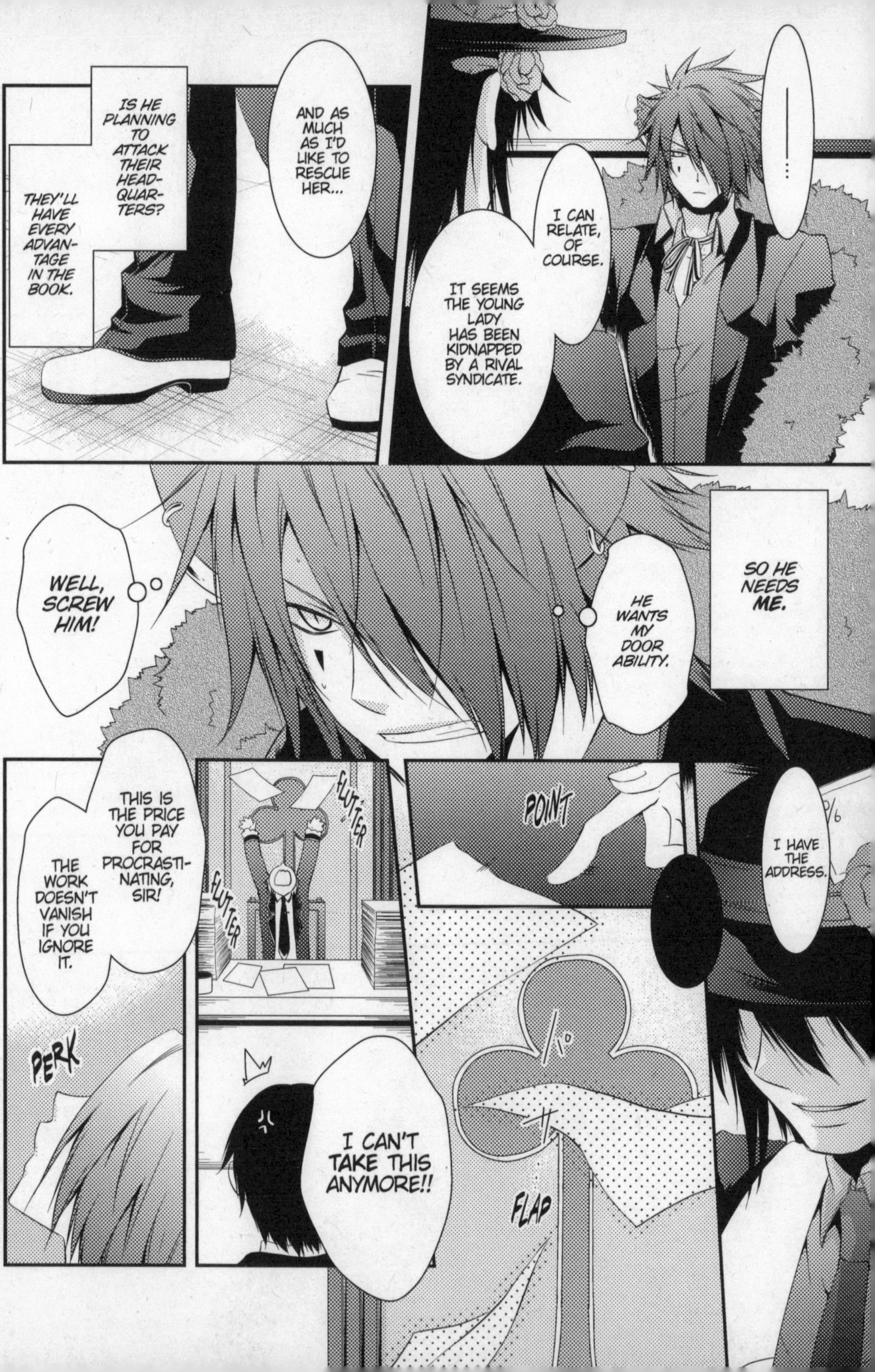
—......
I CAN RELATE, OF COURSE.
IT SEEMS THE YOUNG LADY HAS BEEN KIDNAPPED BY A RIVAL SYNDICATE.
AND AS MUCH AS I'D LIKE TO RESCUE HER...
IS HE PLANNING TO ATTACK THEIR HEAD-QUARTERS?
THEY'LL HAVE EVERY ADVANTAGE IN THE BOOK.
SO HE NEEDS ME.
HE WANTS MY DOOR ABILITY.
WELL, SCREW HIM!
I HAVE THE ADDRESS.
POINT
FLAP
THIS IS THE PRICE YOU PAY FOR PROCRASTINATING, SIR!
THE WORK DOESN'T VANISH IF YOU IGNORE IT.
FLUTTER
FLUTTER
I CAN'T TAKE THIS ANYMORE!!
PERK

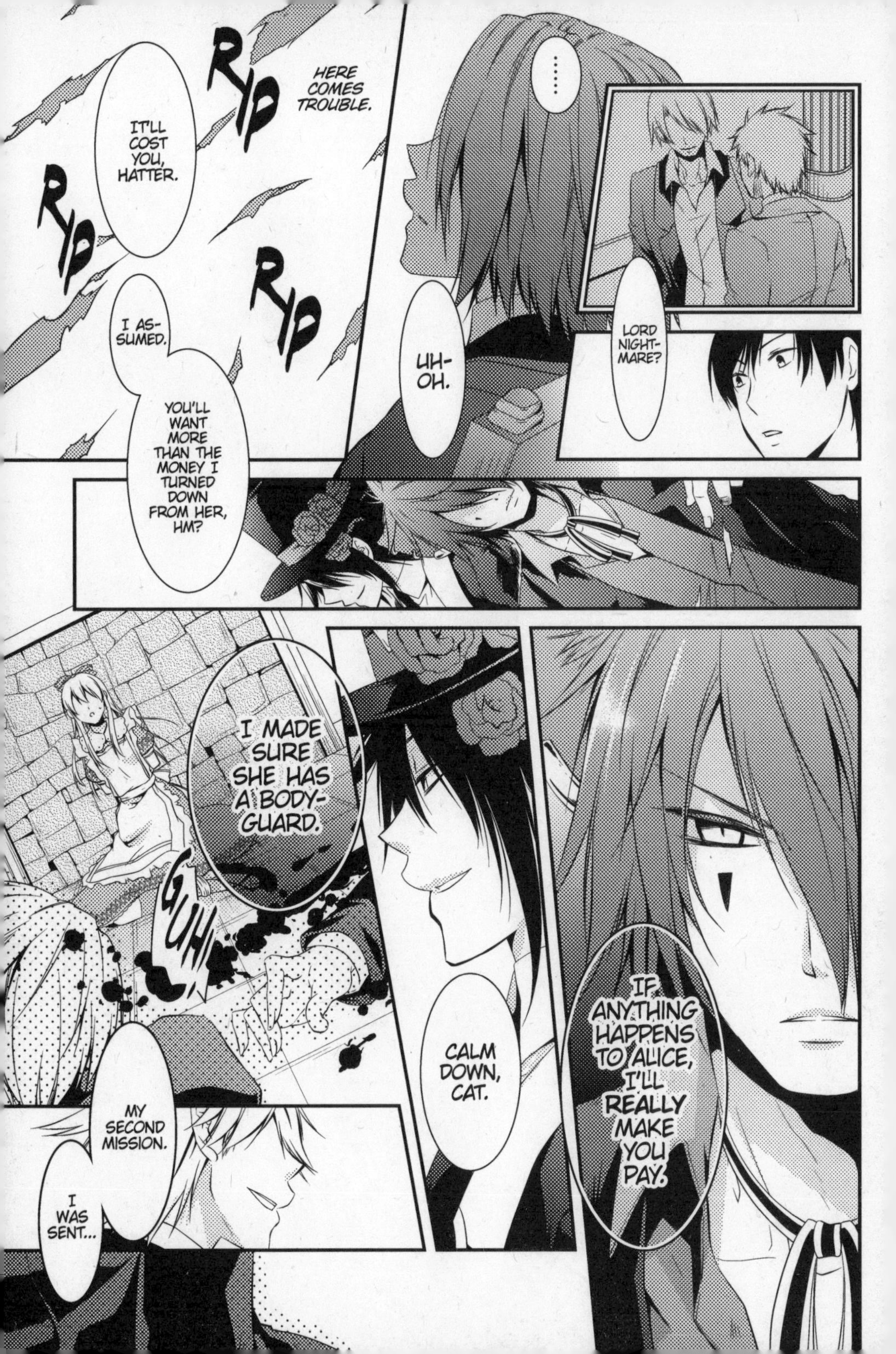

......
UH-OH.
LORD NIGHT-MARE?
HERE COMES TROUBLE.
IT'LL COST YOU, HATTER.
RIP
RIP
RIP
I AS-SUMED.
YOU'LL WANT MORE THAN THE MONEY I TURNED DOWN FROM HER, HM?
IF ANYTHING HAPPENS TO ALICE, I'LL REALLY MAKE YOU PAY.
I MADE SURE SHE HAS A BODY-GUARD.
CALM DOWN, CAT.
GUH!
MY SECOND MISSION.
I WAS SENT...

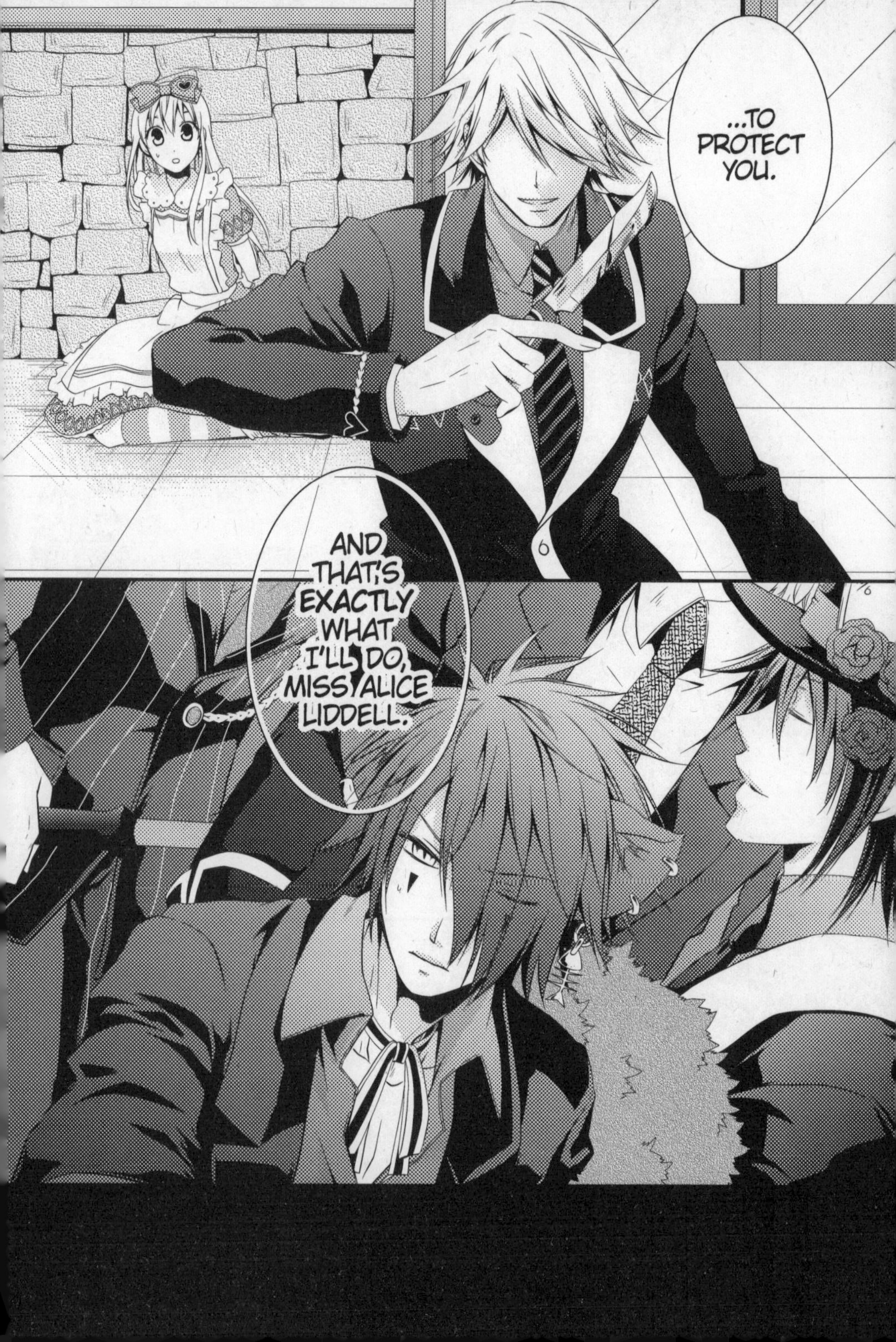
...TO PROTECT YOU.
AND THAT'S EXACTLY WHAT I'LL DO, MISS ALICE LIDDELL.

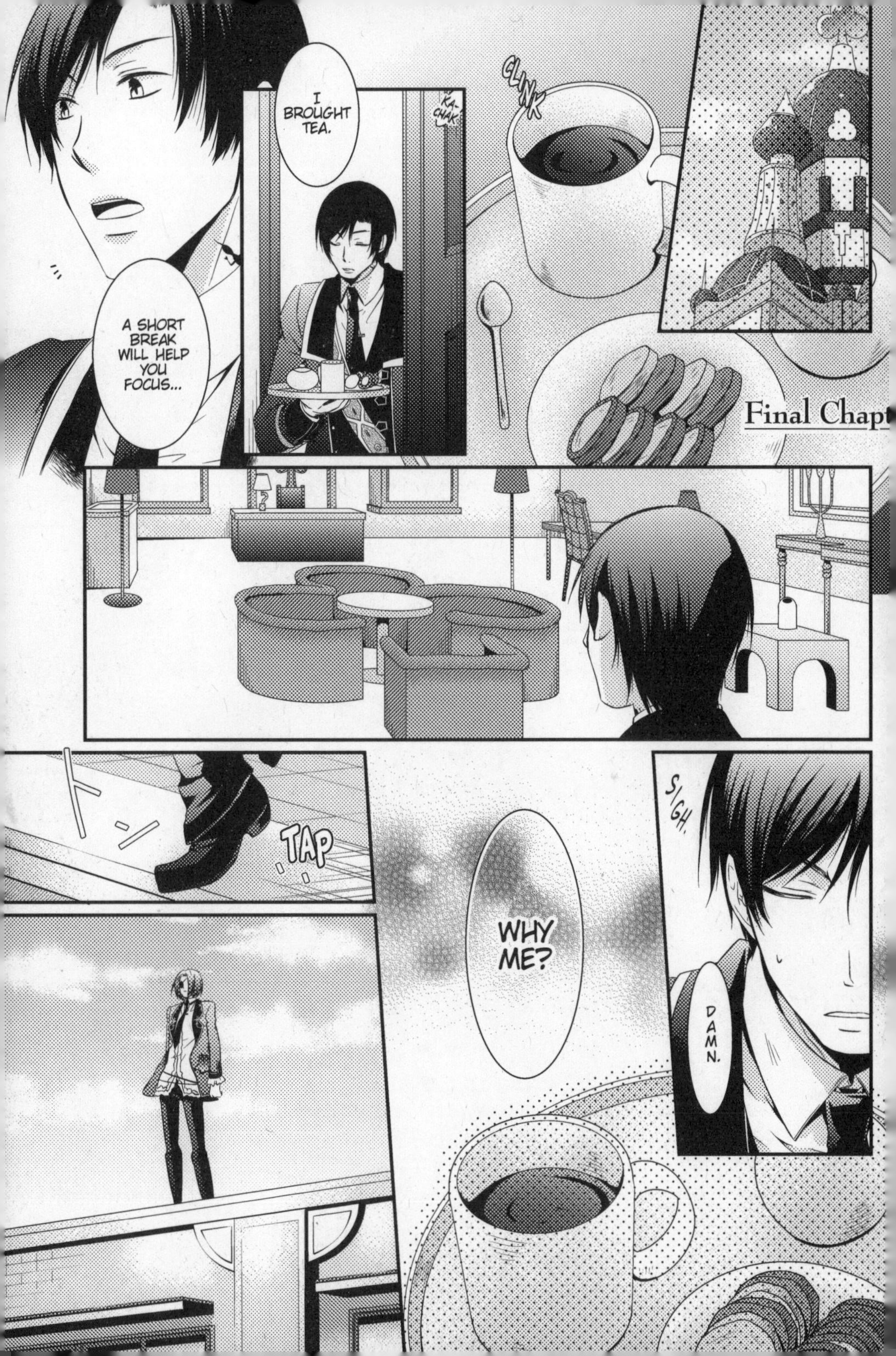
Final Chapt
CLINK
KA-CHAK
I BROUGHT TEA.
A SHORT BREAK WILL HELP YOU FOCUS...
SIGH.
DAMN.
WHY ME?
TAP

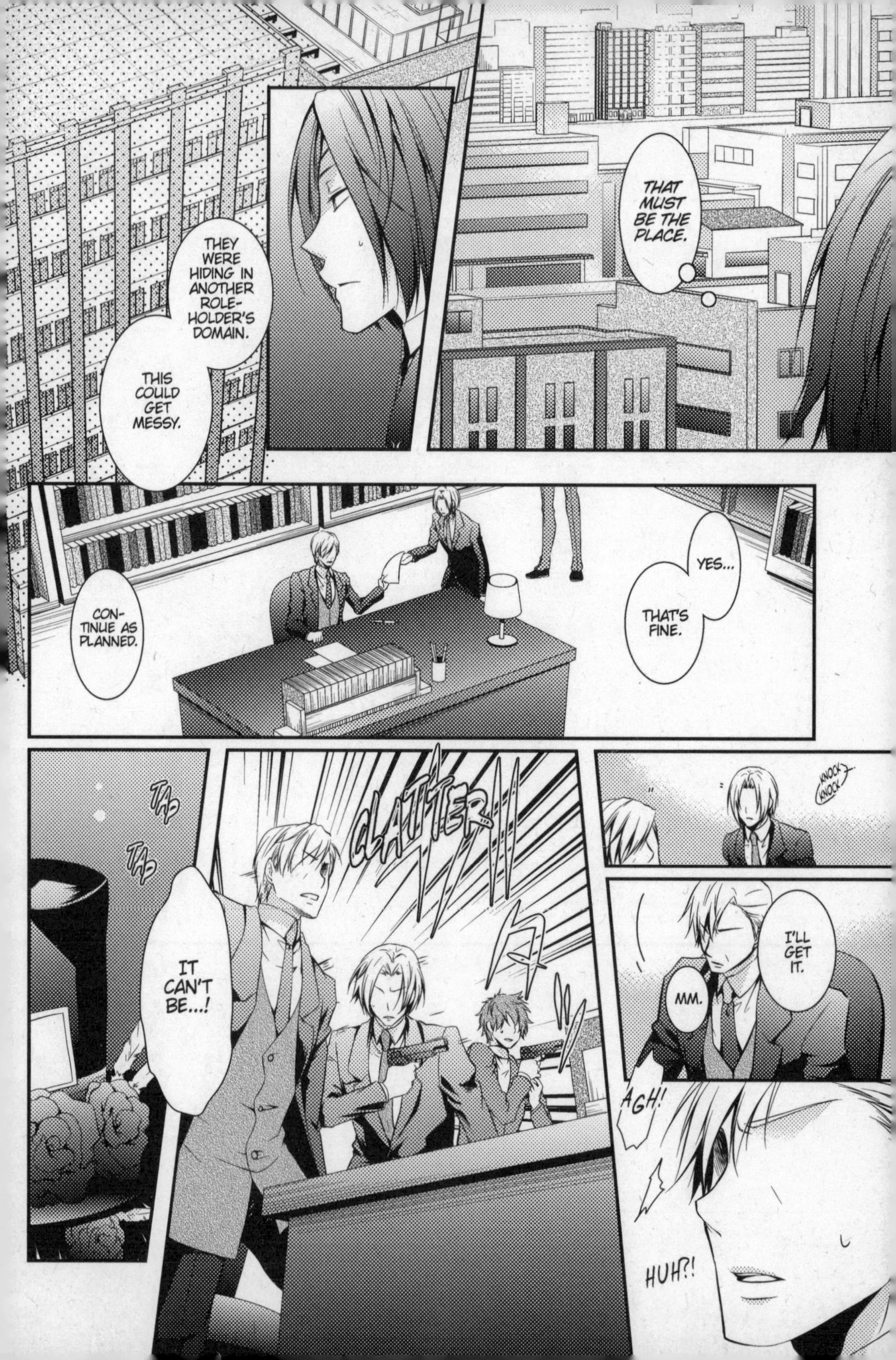
THAT MUST BE THE PLACE.
THEY WERE HIDING IN ANOTHER ROLE-HOLDER'S DOMAIN.
THIS COULD GET MESSY.
YES...
THAT'S FINE.
CONTINUE AS PLANNED.
KNOCK KNOCK
I'LL GET IT.
MM.
AGH!
HUH?!
CLATTER
TAP
TAP
IT CAN'T BE...!

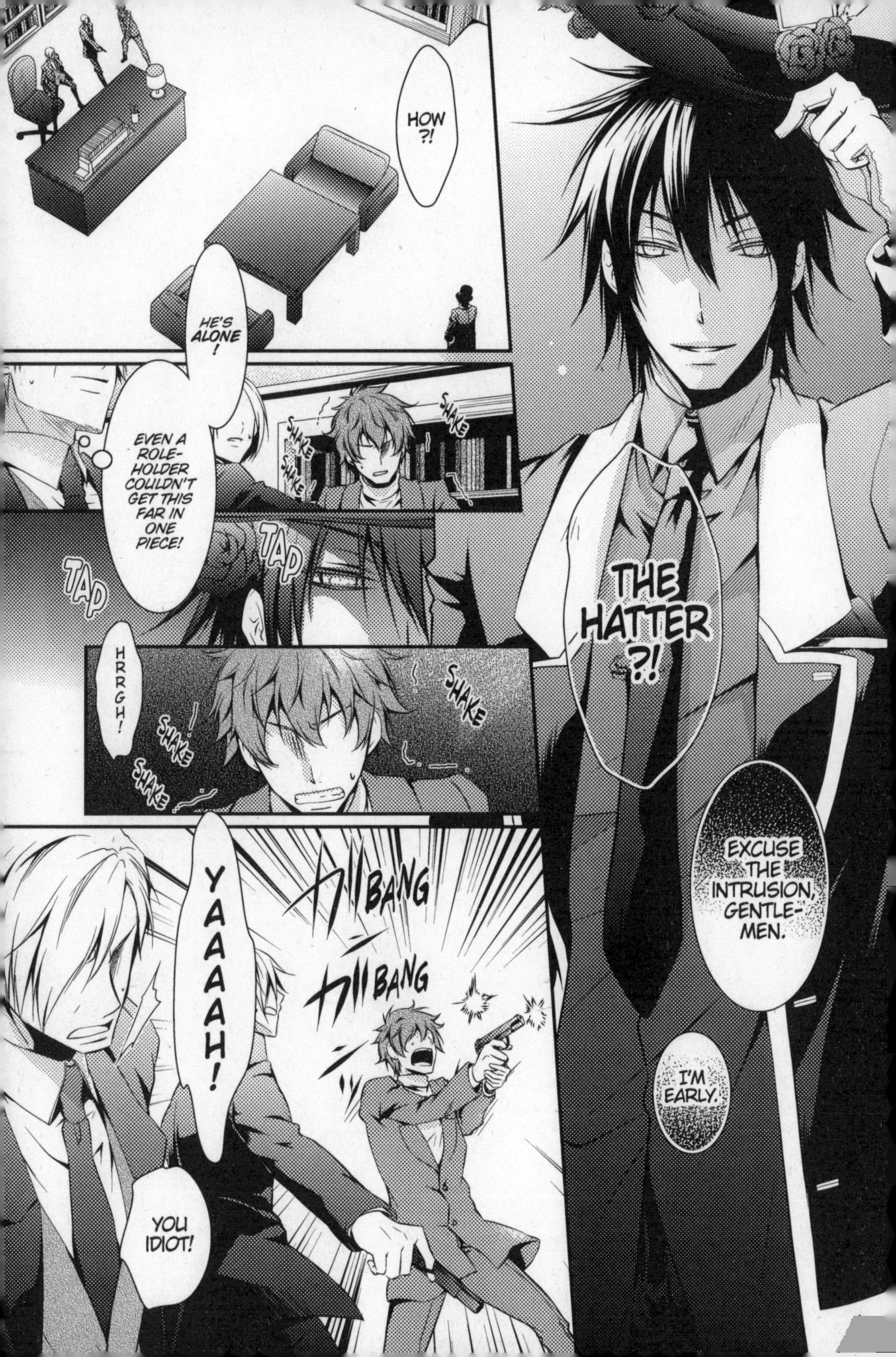
THE HATTER ?!
EXCUSE THE INTRUSION, GENTLE-MEN.
I'M EARLY.
HOW ?!
HE'S ALONE !
EVEN A ROLE-HOLDER COULDN'T GET THIS FAR IN ONE PIECE!
SHAKE
SHAKE
SHAKE
TAP
TAP
HRRGH!
SHAKE
SHAKE
SHAKE
YAAAAAH!
BANG
BANG
YOU IDIOT!

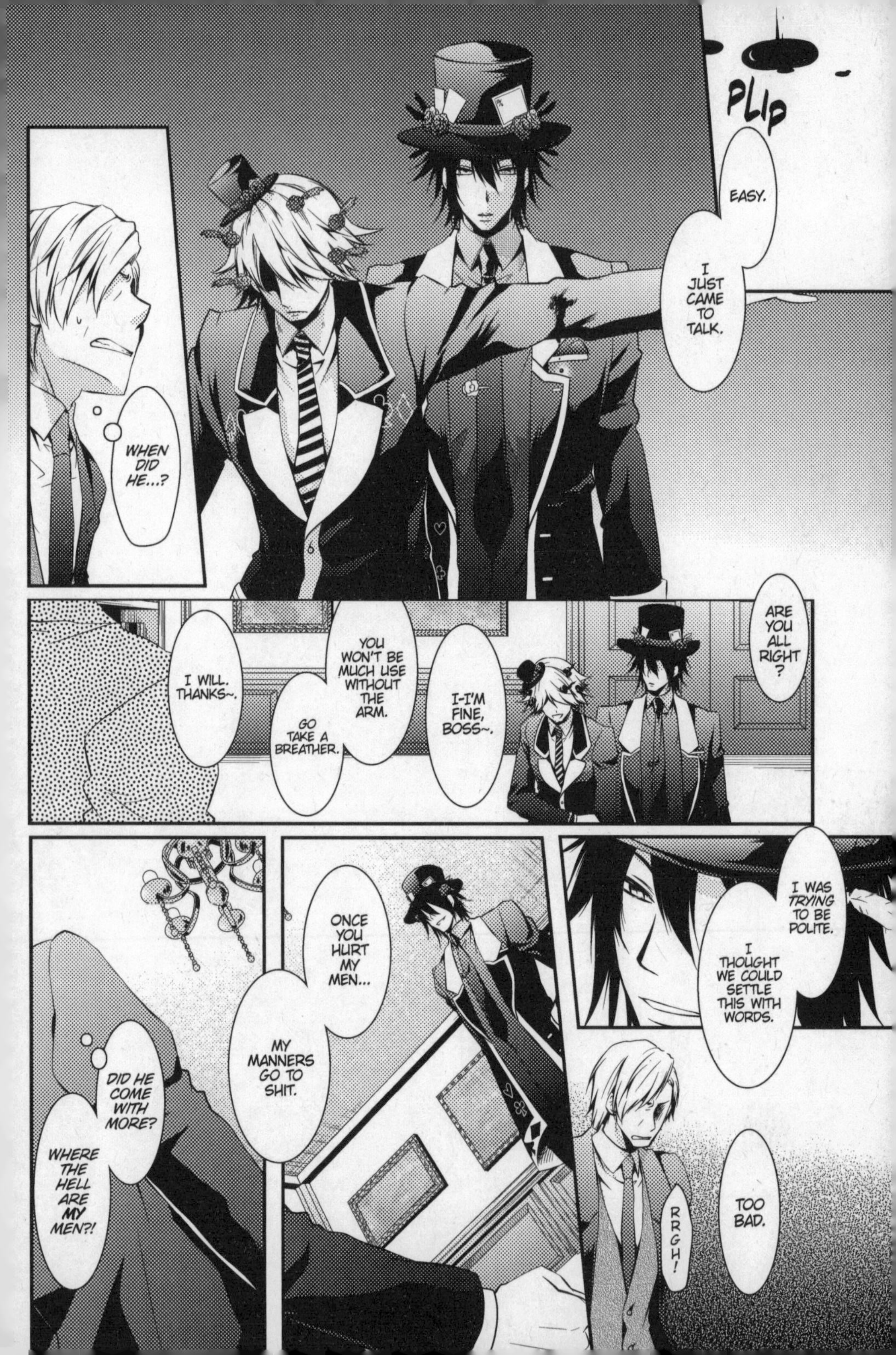
PLIP
EASY.
I JUST CAME TO TALK.
WHEN DID HE...?
ARE YOU ALL RIGHT?
I-I'M FINE, BOSS~.
YOU WON'T BE MUCH USE WITHOUT THE ARM.
GO TAKE A BREATHER.
I WILL. THANKS~.
I WAS TRYING TO BE POLITE.
I THOUGHT WE COULD SETTLE THIS WITH WORDS.
TOO BAD.
RRGH!
ONCE YOU HURT MY MEN...
MY MANNERS GO TO SHIT.
DID HE COME WITH MORE?
WHERE THE HELL ARE MY MEN?!

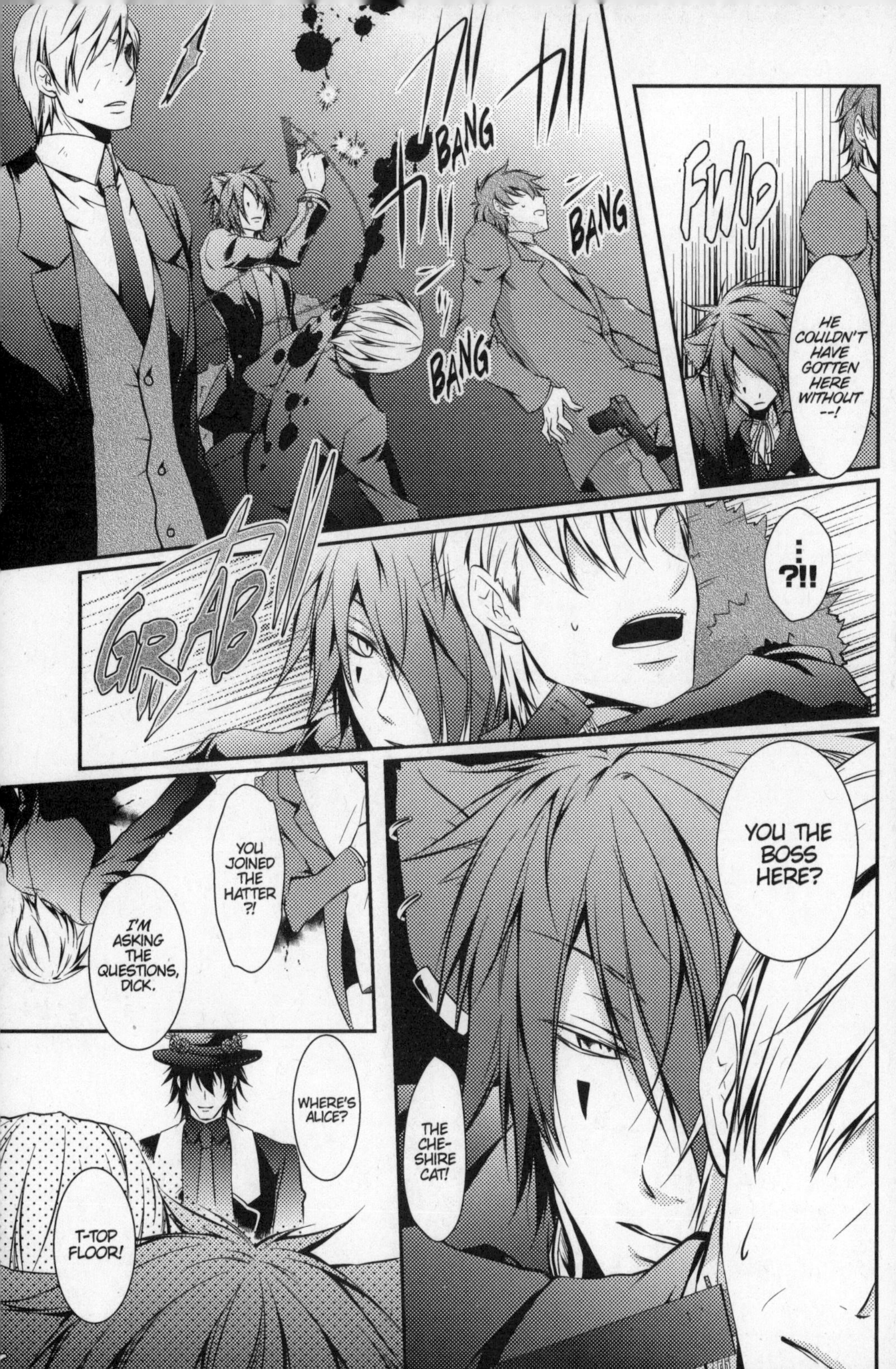
FWIP
HE COULDN'T HAVE GOTTEN HERE WITHOUT --!
BANG
BANG
BANG
...?!!
GRAB
YOU THE BOSS HERE?
THE CHE-SHIRE CAT!
YOU JOINED THE HATTER?!
I'M ASKING THE QUESTIONS, DICK.
WHERE'S ALICE?
T-TOP FLOOR!

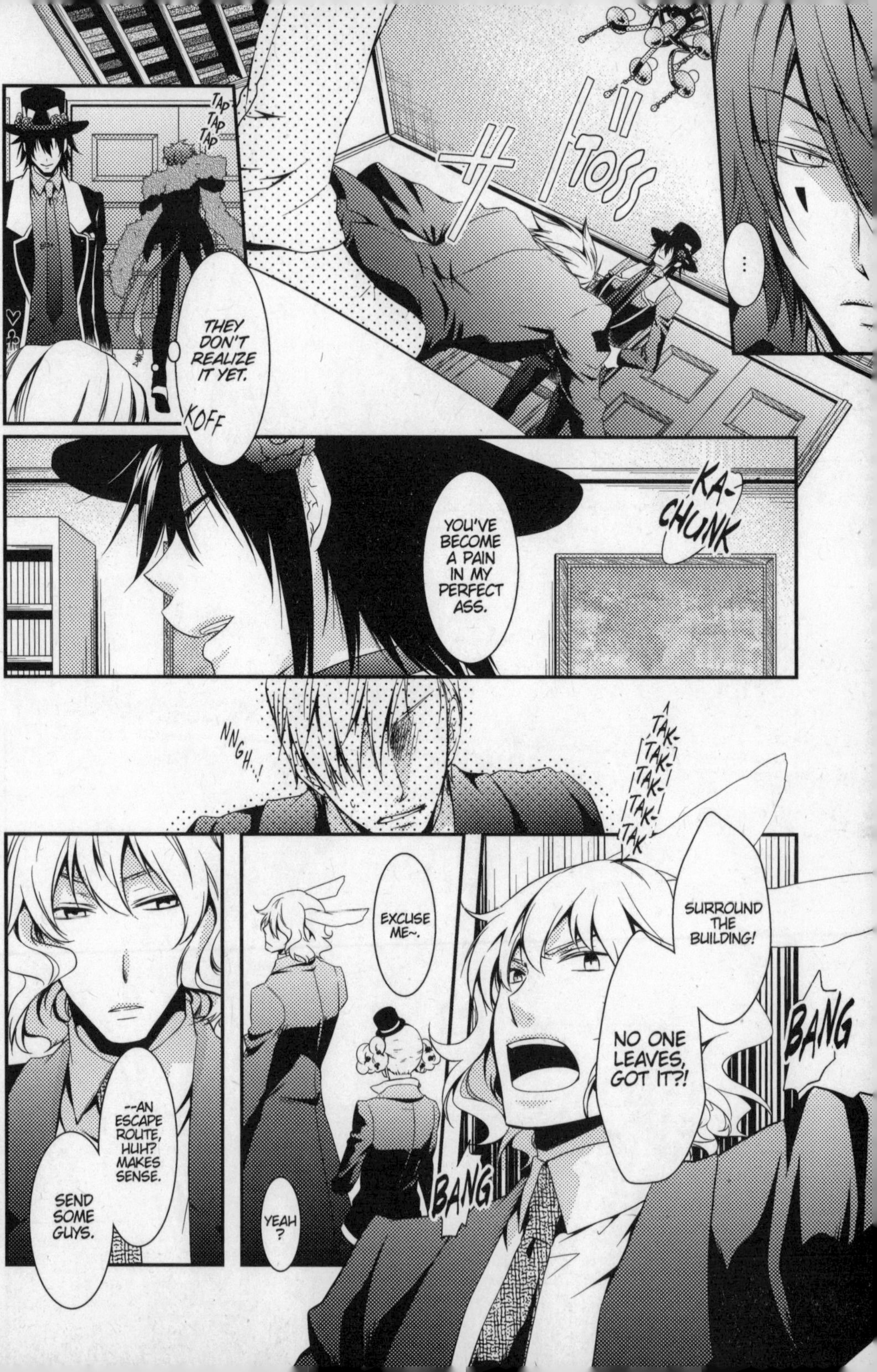
...
TOSS
TAP TAP TAP
THEY DON'T REALIZE IT YET.
KOFF
KA-CHUNK
YOU'VE BECOME A PAIN IN MY PERFECT ASS.
TAK-TAK-TAK-TAK-TAK
NNGH..!
SURROUND THE BUILDING!
NO ONE LEAVES, GOT IT?!
BANG
EXCUSE ME~.
BANG
YEAH?
--AN ESCAPE ROUTE, HUH? MAKES SENSE.
SEND SOME GUYS.

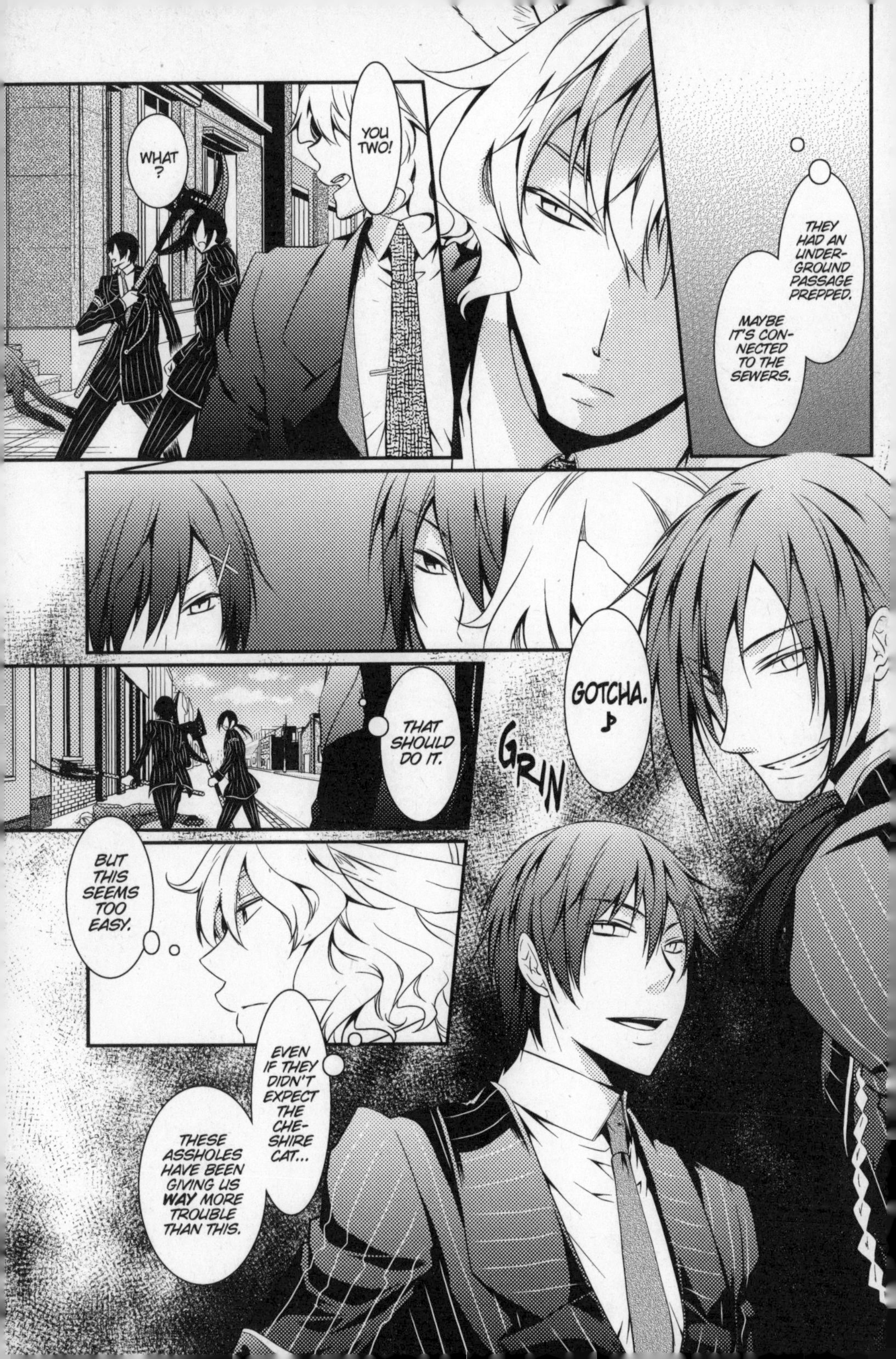
THEY HAD AN UNDER-GROUND PASSAGE PREPPED.
MAYBE IT'S CON-NECTED TO THE SEWERS.
YOU TWO!
WHAT?
THAT SHOULD DO IT.
BUT THIS SEEMS TOO EASY.
EVEN IF THEY DIDN'T EXPECT THE CHE-SHIRE CAT...
THESE ASSHOLES HAVE BEEN GIVING US **WAY** MORE TROUBLE THAN THIS.
GOTCHA. ♪
GRIN

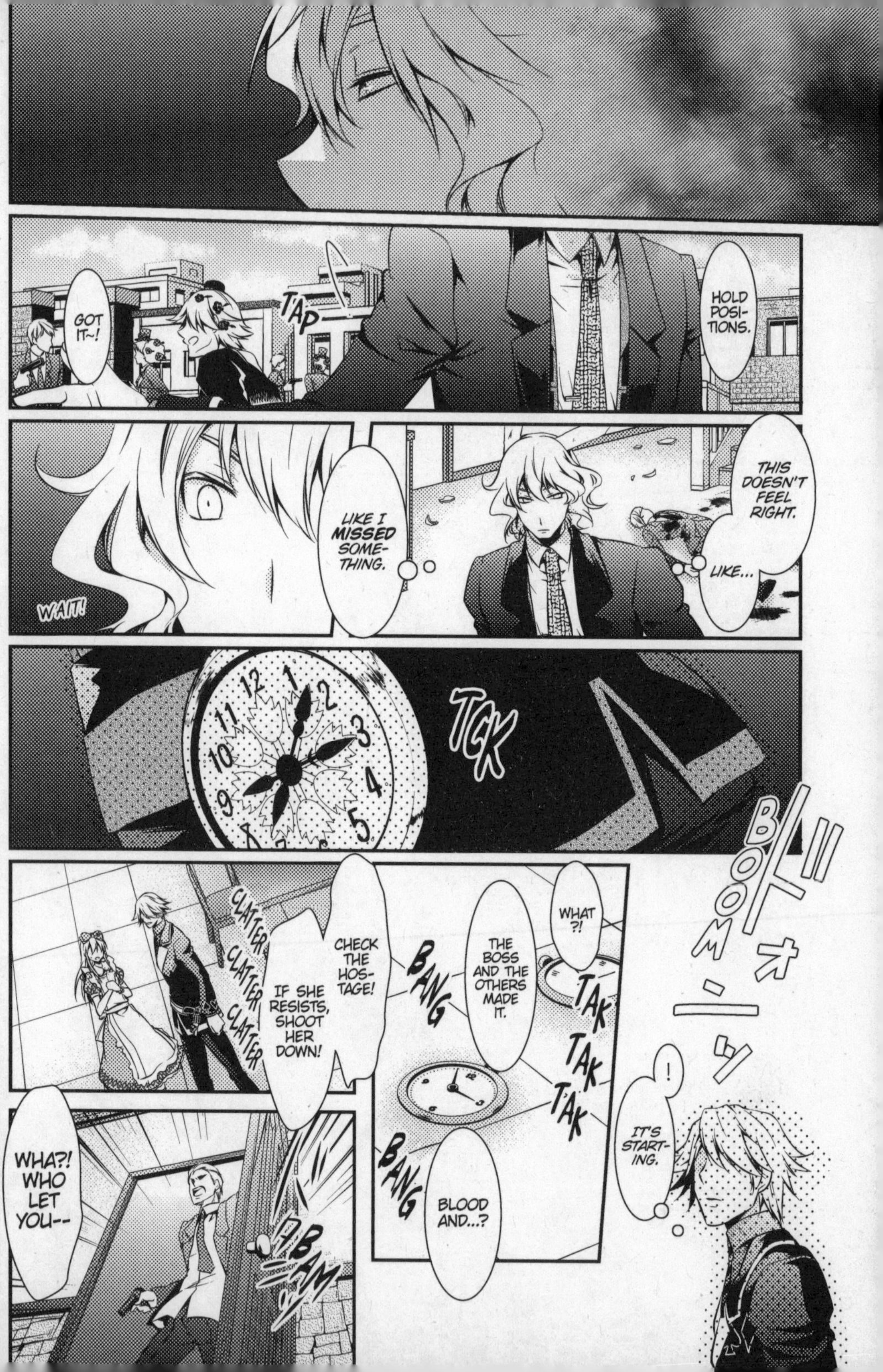
HOLD POSITIONS.
TAP
GOT IT~!
THIS DOESN'T FEEL RIGHT.
LIKE...
LIKE I MISSED SOMETHING.
WAIT!
TCK
BOOM
!
IT'S STARTING.
WHAT?!
THE BOSS AND THE OTHERS MADE IT.
TAK TAK TAK TAK
BANG
BANG
BLOOD AND...?
CHECK THE HOSTAGE!
IF SHE RESISTS, SHOOT HER DOWN!
CLATTER CLATTER CLATTER CLATTER
BAM
WHA?! WHO LET YOU--

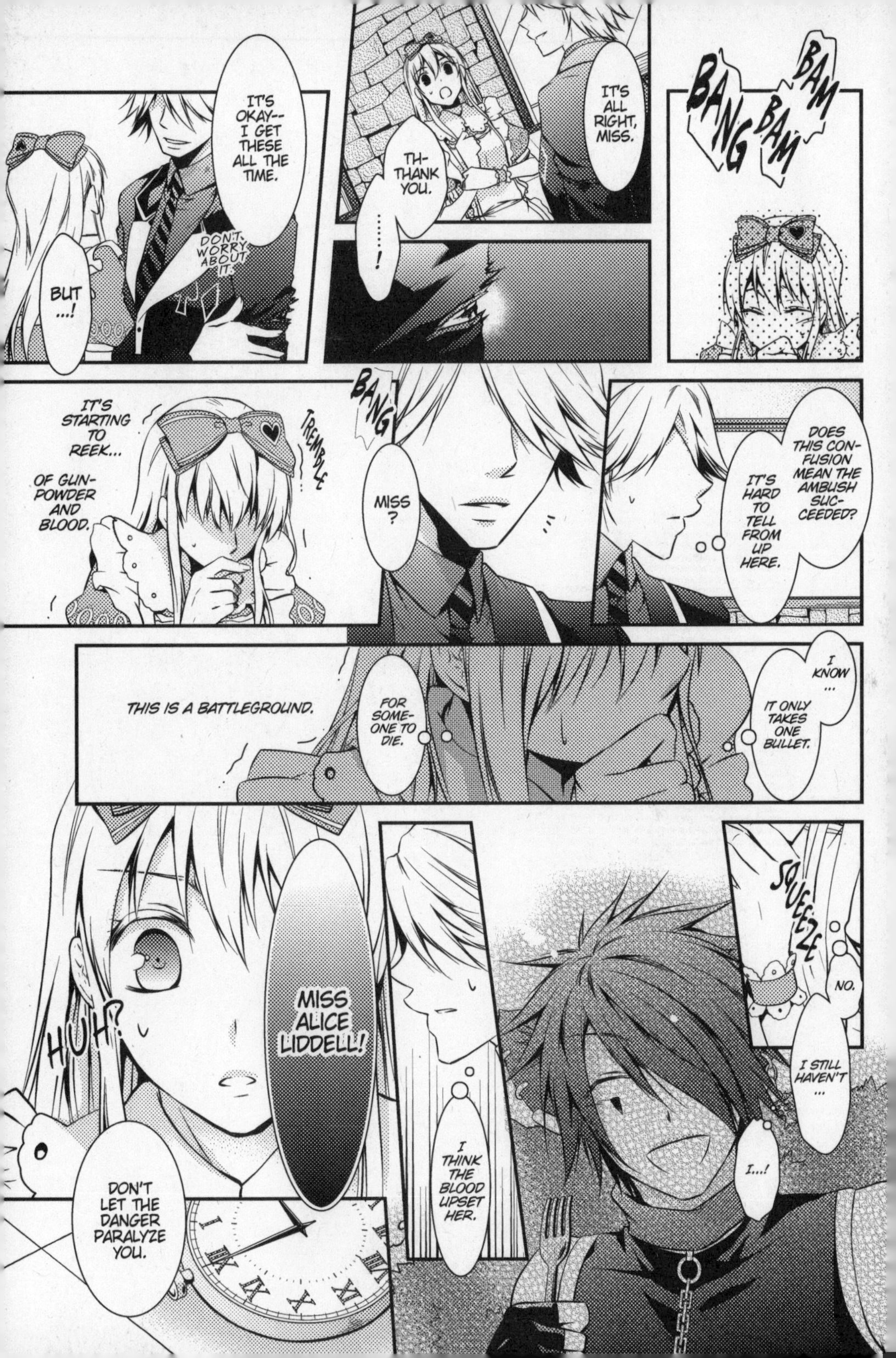
BANG
BAM
BAM
IT'S ALL RIGHT, MISS.
TH-THANK YOU.
.....!
IT'S OKAY-- I GET THESE ALL THE TIME.
DON'T WORRY ABOUT IT.
BUT ...!
DOES THIS CONFUSION MEAN THE AMBUSH SUC-CEEDED?
IT'S HARD TO TELL FROM UP HERE.
BANG
MISS?
TREMBLE
IT'S STARTING TO REEK...
OF GUN-POWDER AND BLOOD.
I KNOW ...
IT ONLY TAKES ONE BULLET.
FOR SOME-ONE TO DIE.
THIS IS A BATTLEGROUND.
SQUEEZE
NO.
I STILL HAVEN'T ...
I...!
MISS ALICE LIDDELL!
I THINK THE BLOOD UPSET HER.
HUH?
DON'T LET THE DANGER PARALYZE YOU.

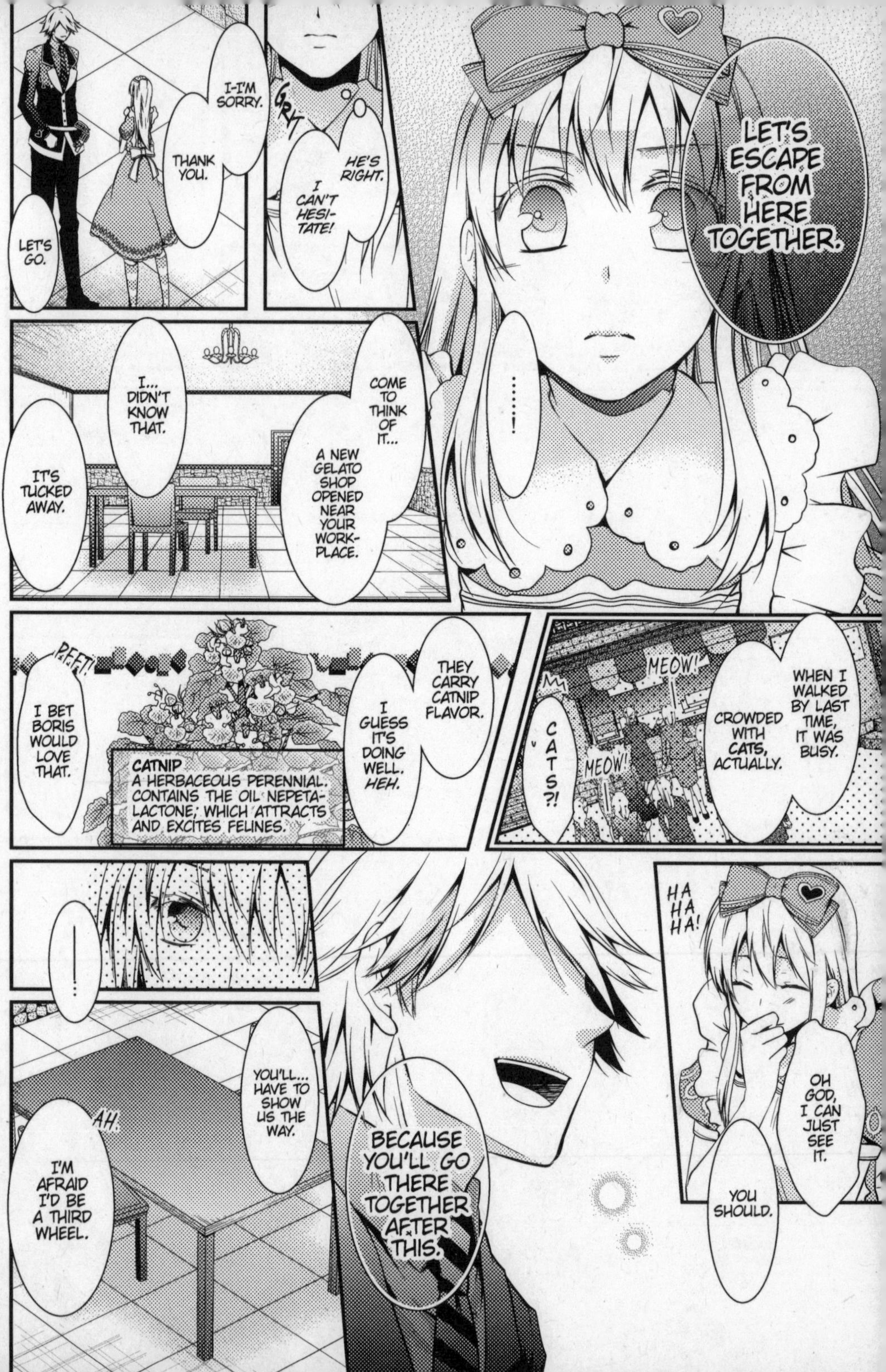
LET'S ESCAPE FROM HERE TOGETHER.
......!
HE'S RIGHT.
I CAN'T HESI-TATE!
GRRT
I-I'M SORRY.
THANK YOU.
LET'S GO.
COME TO THINK OF IT...
A NEW GELATO SHOP OPENED NEAR YOUR WORK-PLACE.
I... DIDN'T KNOW THAT.
IT'S TUCKED AWAY.
WHEN I WALKED BY LAST TIME, IT WAS BUSY.
CROWDED WITH CATS, ACTUALLY.
MEOW!
MEOW!
CATS?!
THEY CARRY CATNIP FLAVOR.
I GUESS IT'S DOING WELL. HEH.
PFFT!
I BET BORIS WOULD LOVE THAT.
CATNIP
A HERBACEOUS PERENNIAL. CONTAINS THE OIL NEPETA-LACTONE, WHICH ATTRACTS AND EXCITES FELINES.
HA HA HA HA!
OH GOD, I CAN JUST SEE IT.
YOU SHOULD.
BECAUSE YOU'LL GO THERE TOGETHER AFTER THIS.
YOU'LL... HAVE TO SHOW US THE WAY.
......!
AH.
I'M AFRAID I'D BE A THIRD WHEEL.

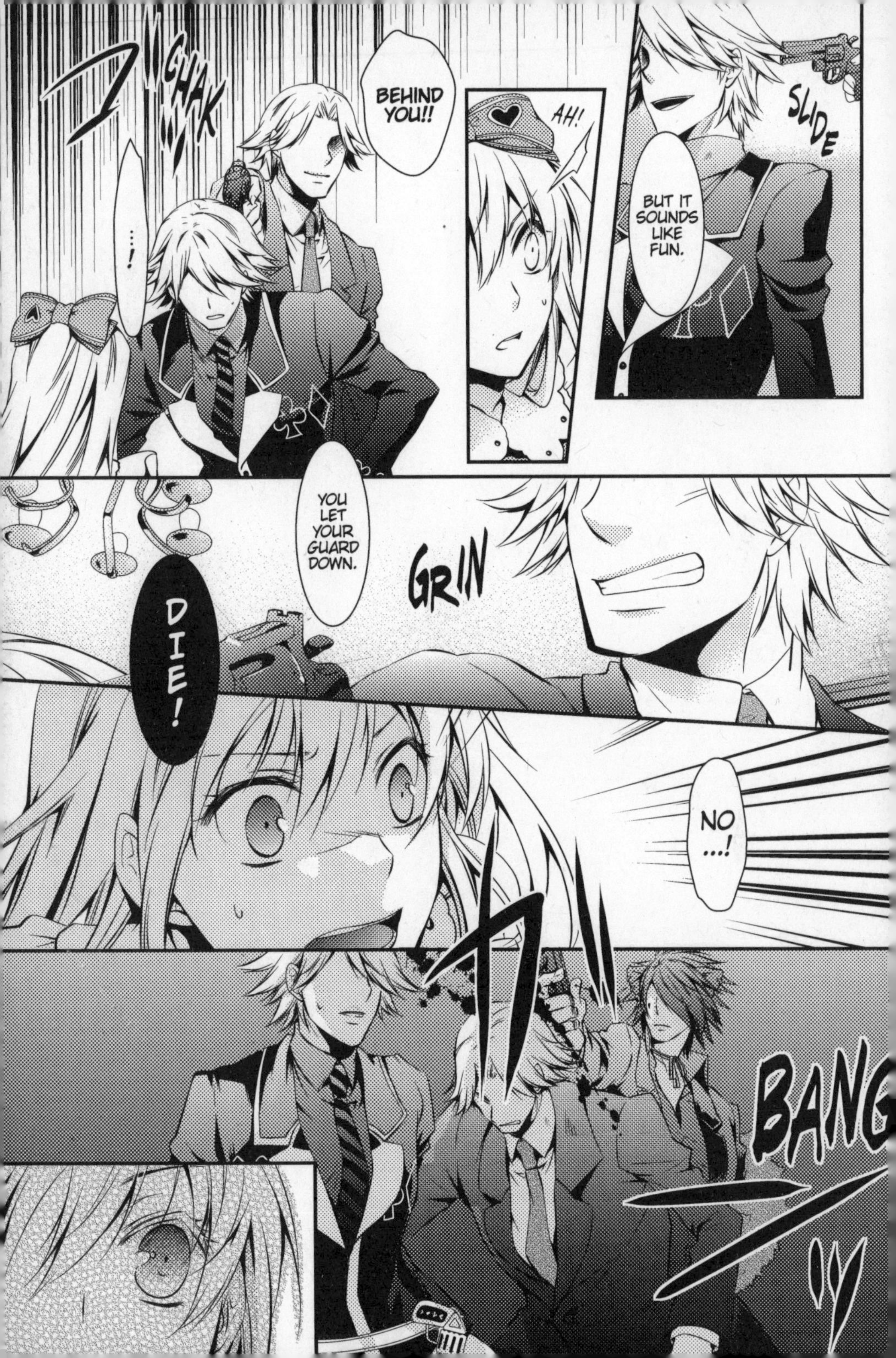
SLIDE
BUT IT SOUNDS LIKE FUN.
AH!
BEHIND YOU!!
CHAK
...!
GRIN
YOU LET YOUR GUARD DOWN.
DIE!
NO ...!
BANG

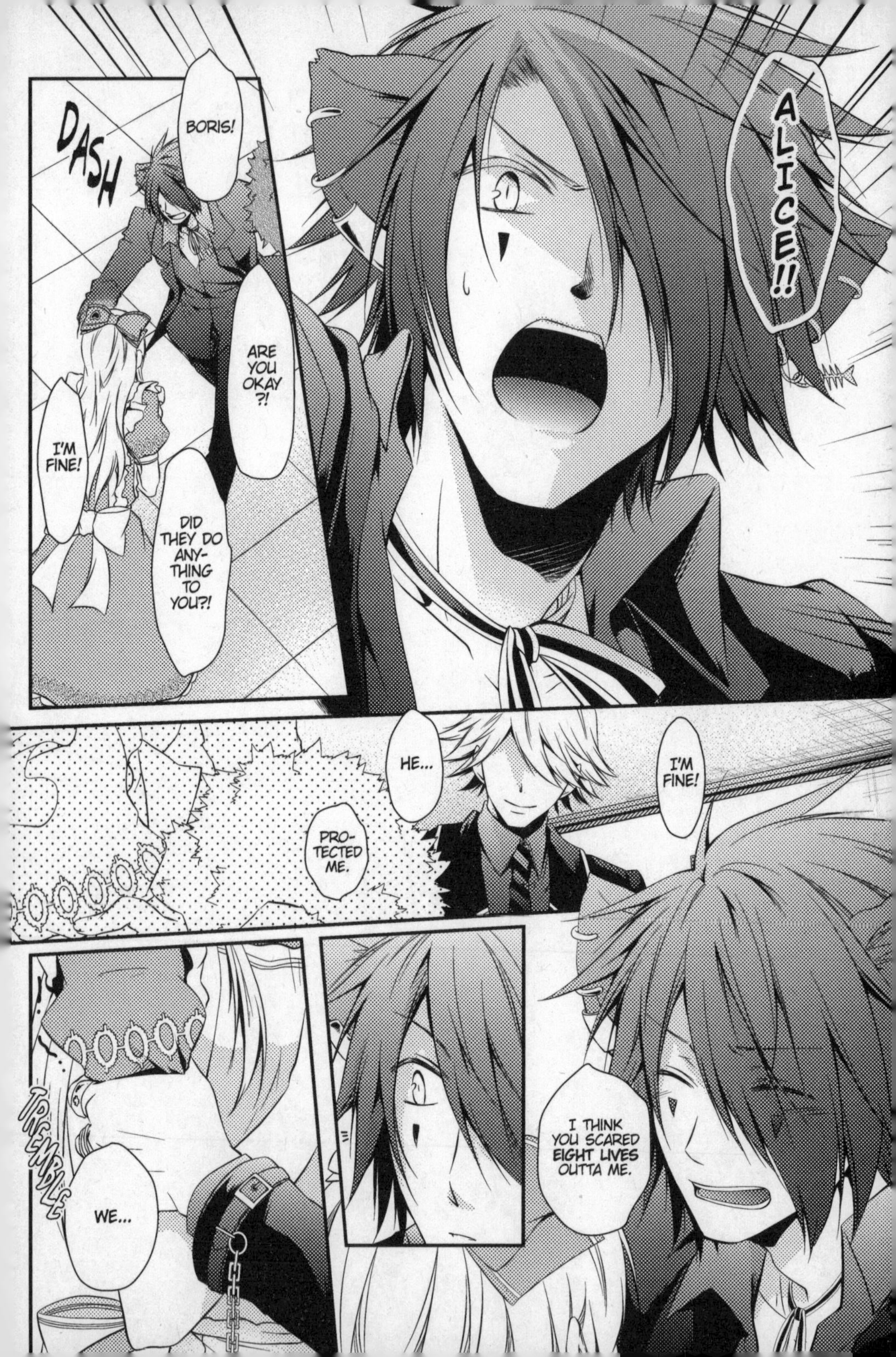
ALICE!!
BORIS!
DASH
ARE YOU OKAY?!
I'M FINE!
DID THEY DO ANY-THING TO YOU?!
I'M FINE!
HE...
PRO-TECTED ME.
I THINK YOU SCARED EIGHT LIVES OUTTA ME.
TREMBLE
WE...

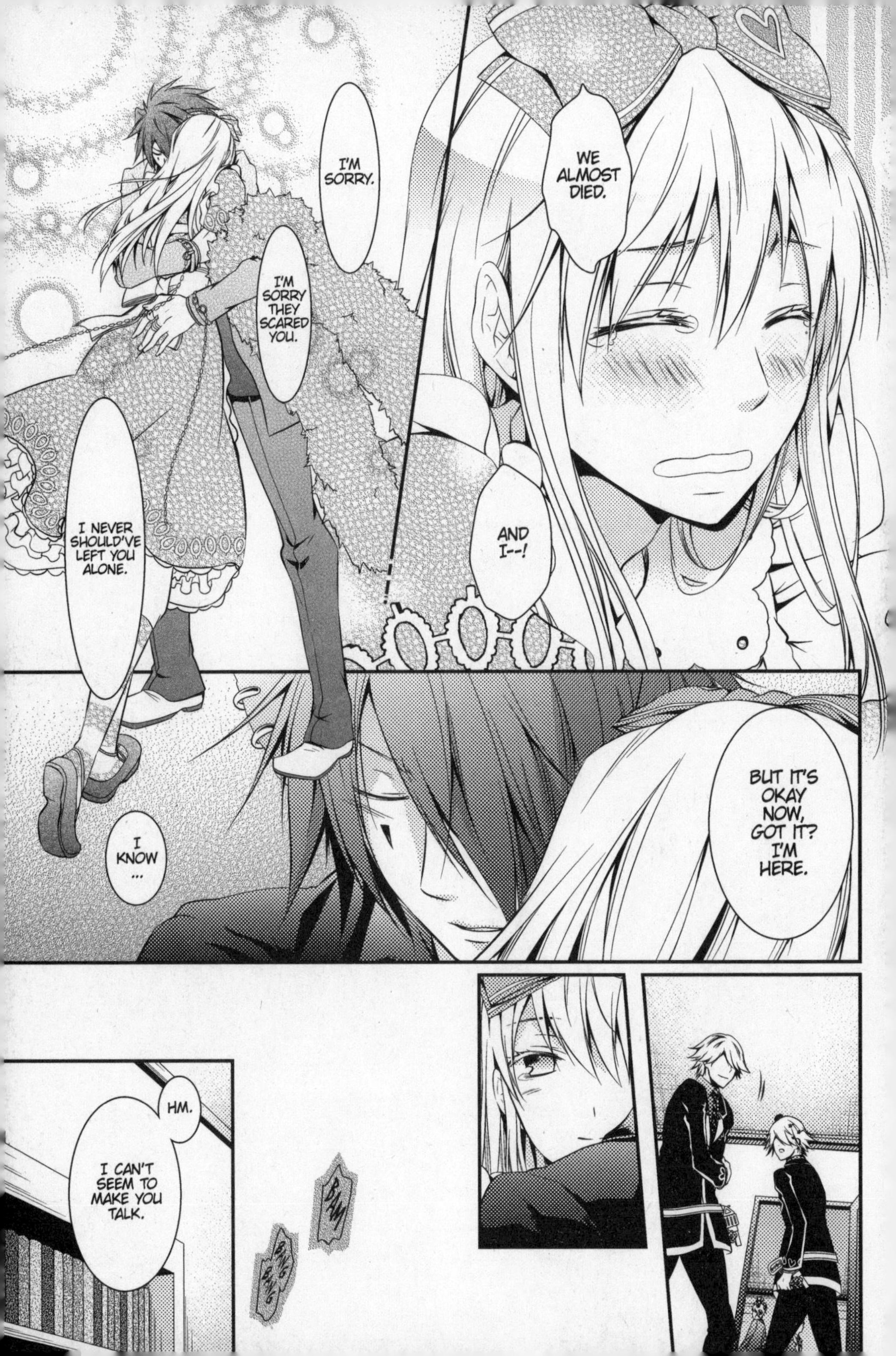
WE ALMOST DIED.
AND I--!
I'M SORRY.
I'M SORRY THEY SCARED YOU.
I NEVER SHOULD'VE LEFT YOU ALONE.
BUT IT'S OKAY NOW, GOT IT? I'M HERE.
I KNOW ...
HM.
I CAN'T SEEM TO MAKE YOU TALK.
BAM
BANG BANG

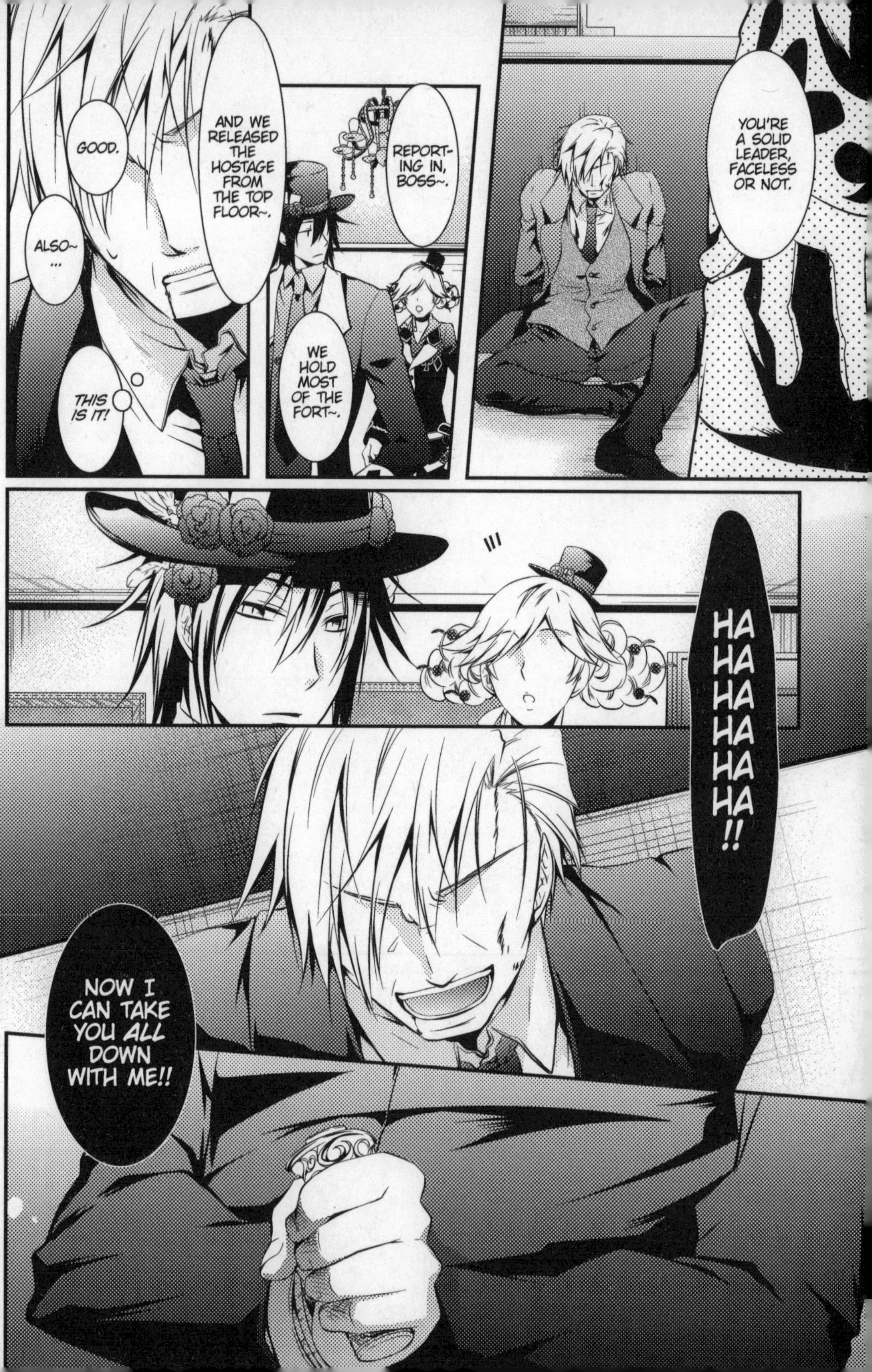
YOU'RE A SOLID LEADER, FACELESS OR NOT.
REPORTING IN, BOSS~.
WE HOLD MOST OF THE FORT~.
AND WE RELEASED THE HOSTAGE FROM THE TOP FLOOR~.
GOOD.
ALSO~ ...
THIS IS IT!
!!!
HA HA HA HA HA HA!!
NOW I CAN TAKE YOU ALL DOWN WITH ME!!

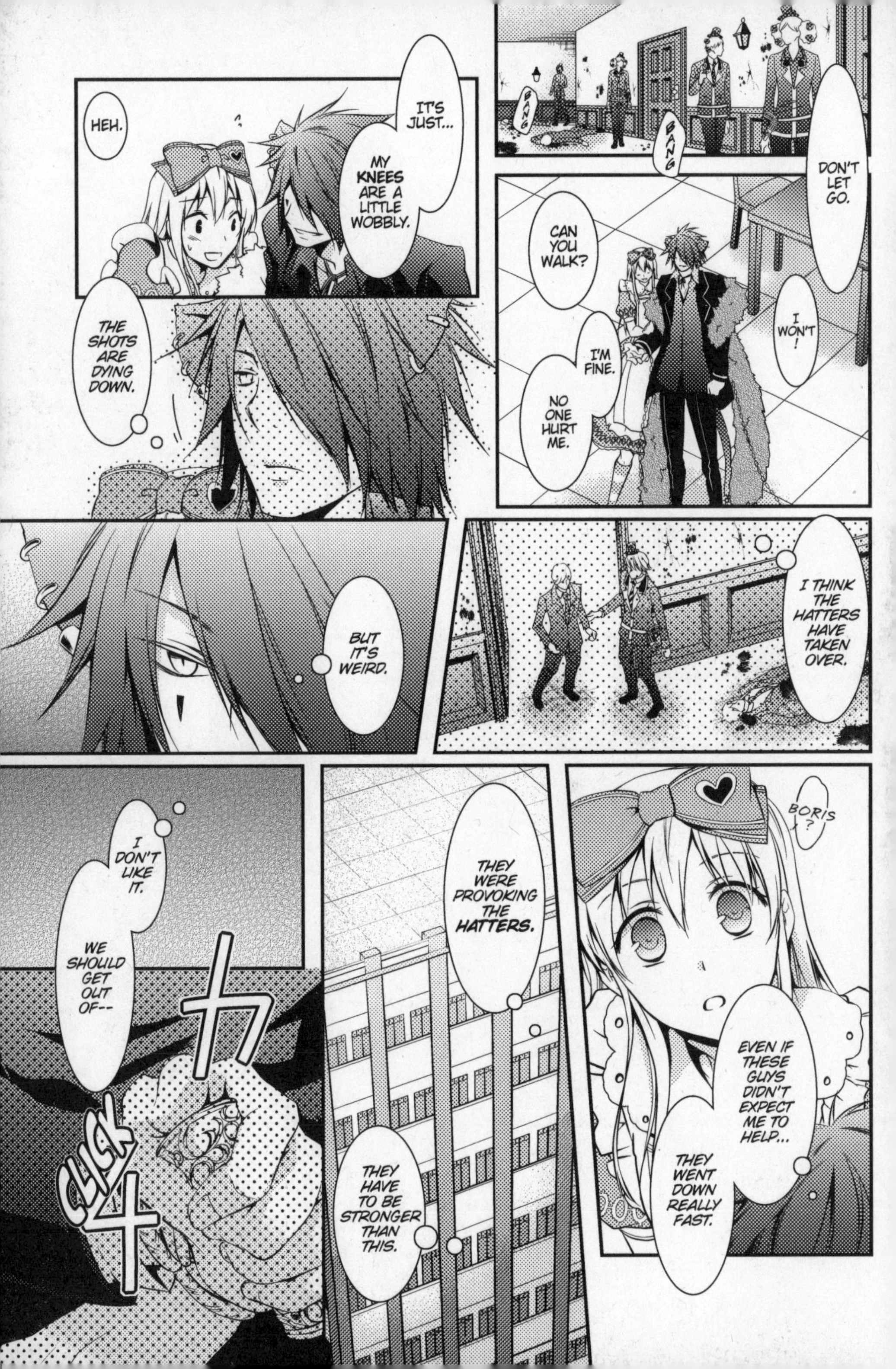
BANG
BANG
DON'T LET GO.
I WON'T!
CAN YOU WALK?
I'M FINE.
NO ONE HURT ME.
IT'S JUST...
MY KNEES ARE A LITTLE WOBBLY.
HEH.
THE SHOTS ARE DYING DOWN.
I THINK THE HATTERS HAVE TAKEN OVER.
BUT IT'S WEIRD.
BORIS?
EVEN IF THESE GUYS DIDN'T EXPECT ME TO HELP...
THEY WENT DOWN REALLY FAST.
THEY WERE PROVOKING THE HATTERS.
THEY HAVE TO BE STRONGER THAN THIS.
I DON'T LIKE IT.
WE SHOULD GET OUT OF--
カ
CLICK

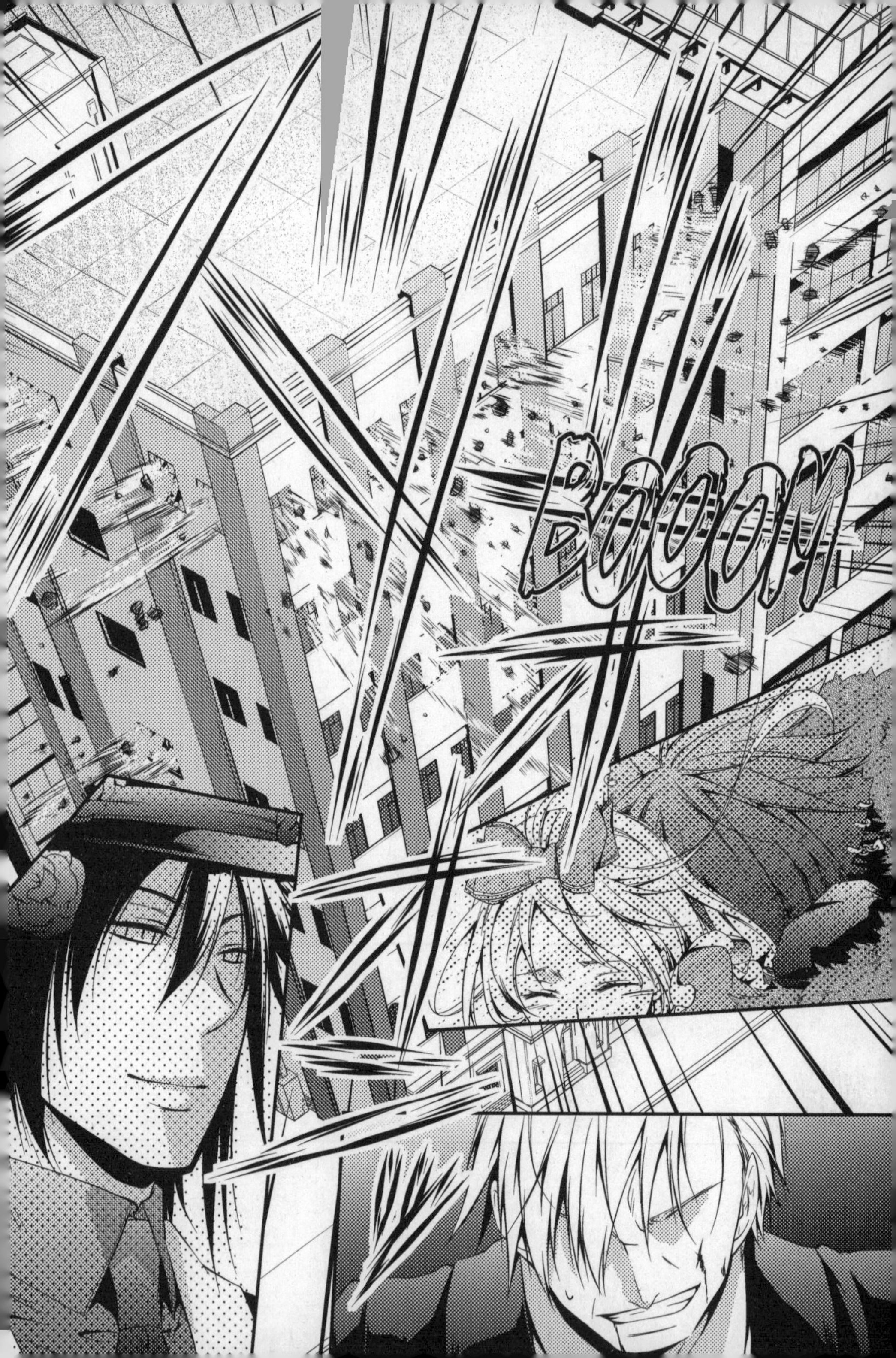
BOOOM

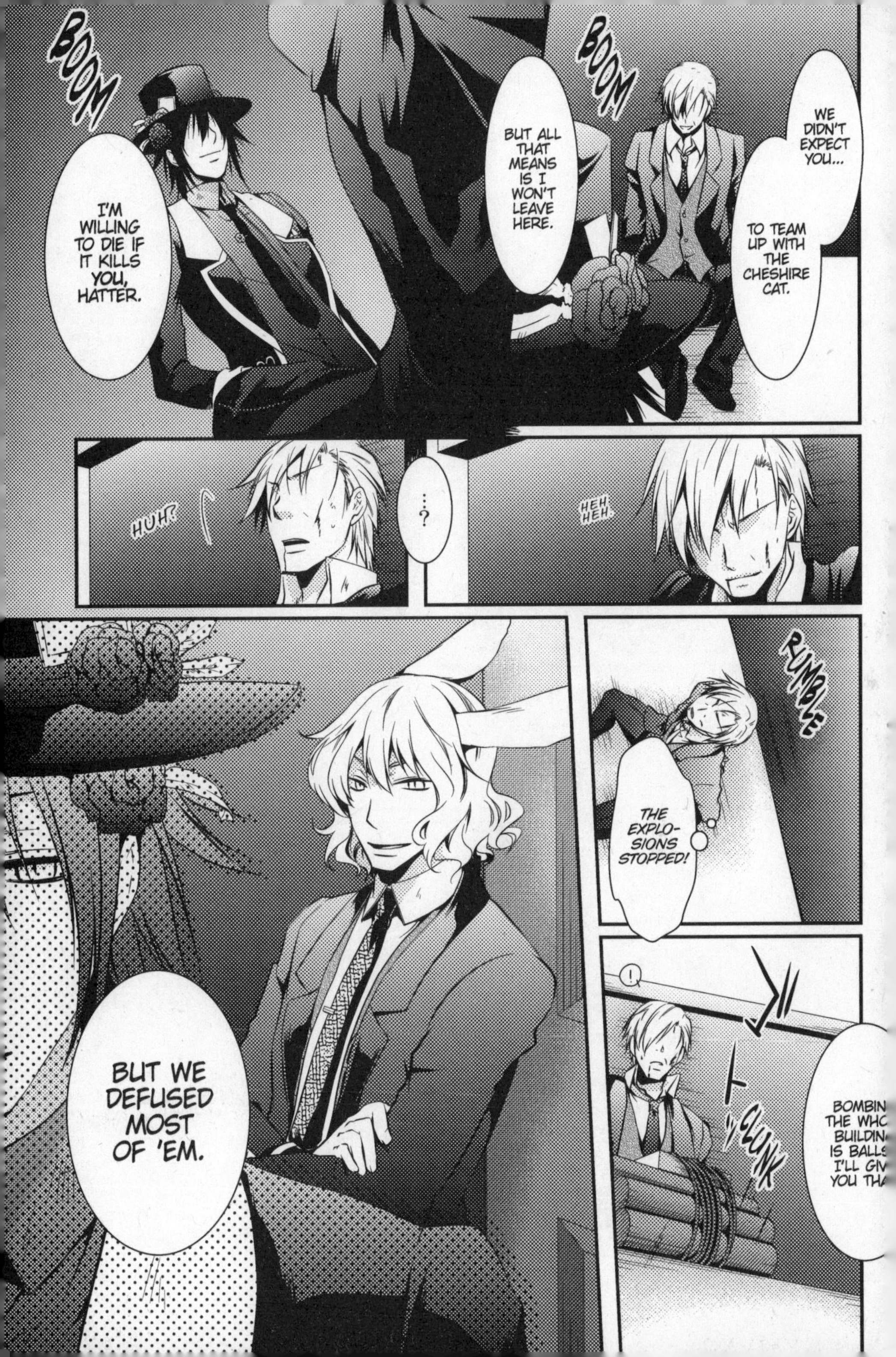

WE DIDN'T EXPECT YOU...
TO TEAM UP WITH THE CHESHIRE CAT.
BOOM
BUT ALL THAT MEANS IS I WON'T LEAVE HERE.
BOOM
I'M WILLING TO DIE IF IT KILLS YOU, HATTER.
HEH HEH
...?
HUH?
RUMBLE
THE EXPLOSIONS STOPPED!
BUT WE DEFUSED MOST OF 'EM.
!
CLUNK
BOMBIN THE WHO BUILDIN IS BALLS I'LL GIV YOU TH

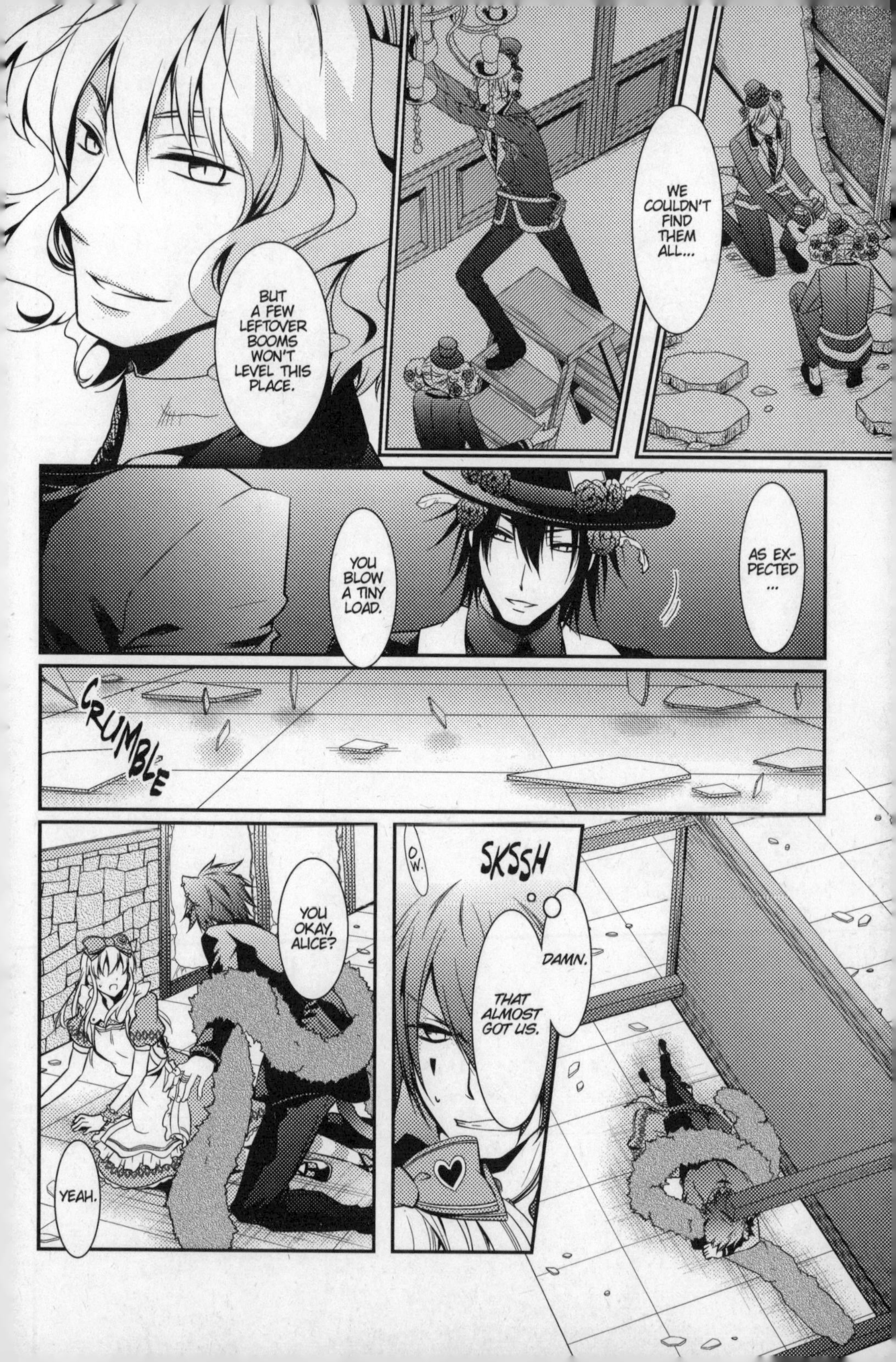
WE COULDN'T FIND THEM ALL...
BUT A FEW LEFTOVER BOOMS WON'T LEVEL THIS PLACE.
AS EX-PECTED...
YOU BLOW A TINY LOAD.
CRUMBLE
SKSSH
OW.
DAMN.
THAT ALMOST GOT US.
YOU OKAY, ALICE?
YEAH.

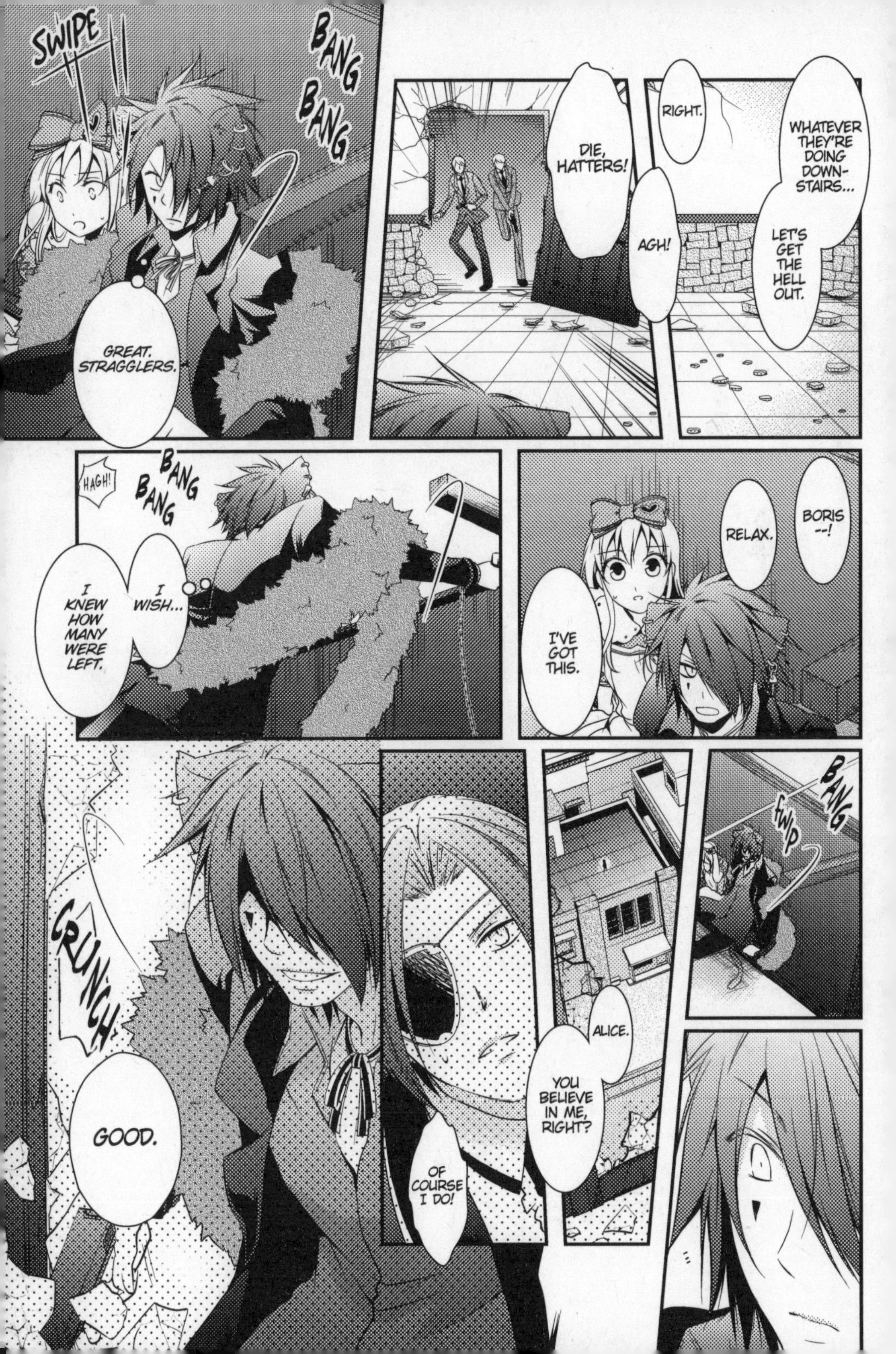

WHATEVER THEY'RE DOING DOWN-STAIRS...
LET'S GET THE HELL OUT.
RIGHT.
DIE, HATTERS!
AGH!
SWIPE
BANG BANG
GREAT. STRAGGLERS.
BORIS--!
RELAX.
I'VE GOT THIS.
BANG BANG
HAGH!
I WISH...
I KNEW HOW MANY WERE LEFT.
BANG
FWIP
...
ALICE.
YOU BELIEVE IN ME, RIGHT?
OF COURSE I DO!
CRUNCH
GOOD.

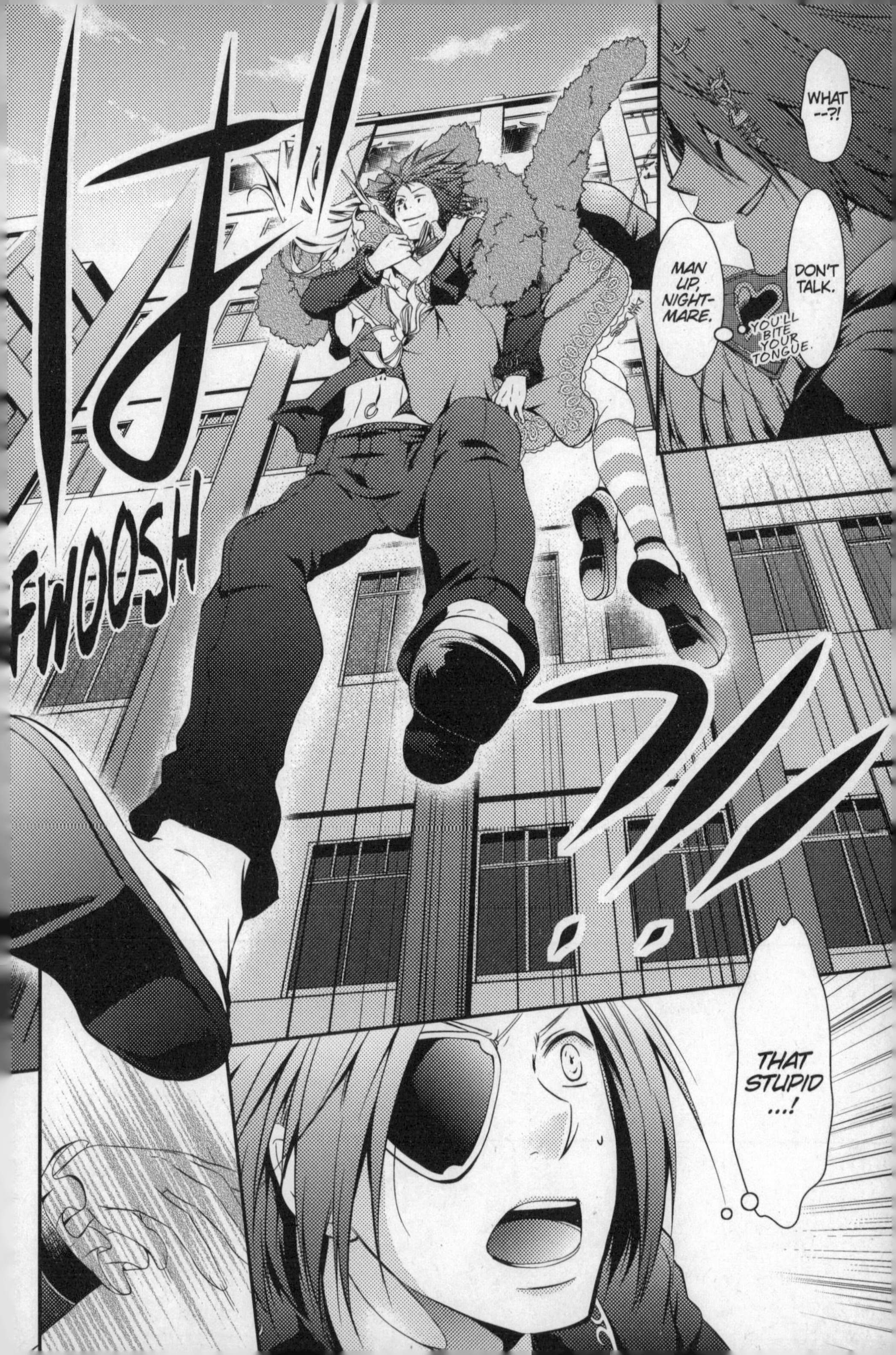
WHAT--?!
DON'T TALK.
YOU'LL BITE YOUR TONGUE.
MAN UP, NIGHT-MARE.
FWOOSH
THAT STUPID ...!

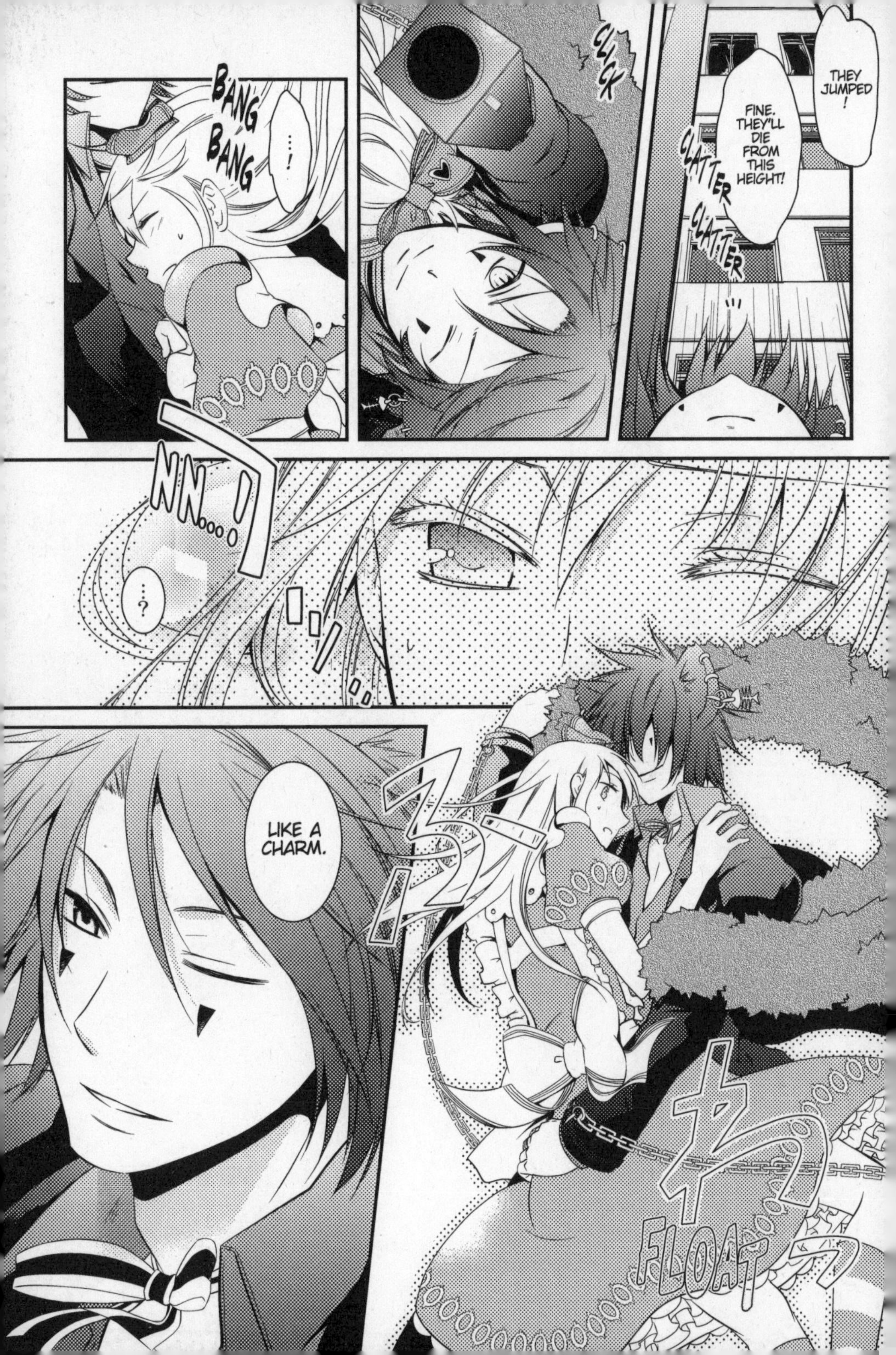
THEY JUMPED!
FINE. THEY'LL DIE FROM THIS HEIGHT!
CLATTER
CLATTER
CLATTER
CLICK
BANG
BANG
...!
NNN...OOO
...?
FLOAT
LIKE A CHARM.

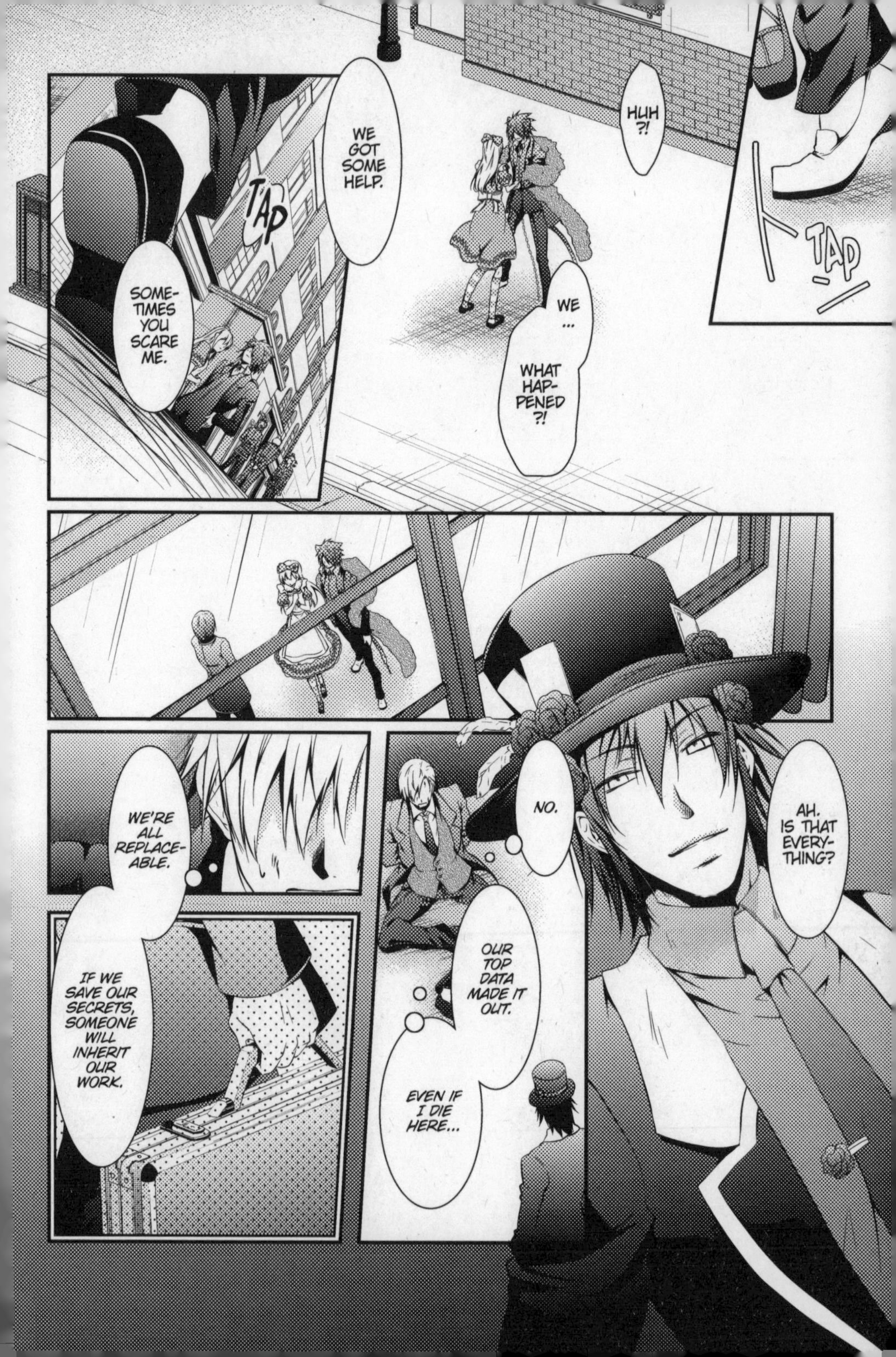
TAP
HUH ?!
WE ... WHAT HAP-PENED ?!
WE GOT SOME HELP.
TAP
SOME-TIMES YOU SCARE ME.
AH. IS THAT EVERY-THING?
NO.
OUR TOP DATA MADE IT OUT.
EVEN IF I DIE HERE...
WE'RE ALL REPLACE-ABLE.
IF WE SAVE OUR SECRETS, SOMEONE WILL INHERIT OUR WORK.

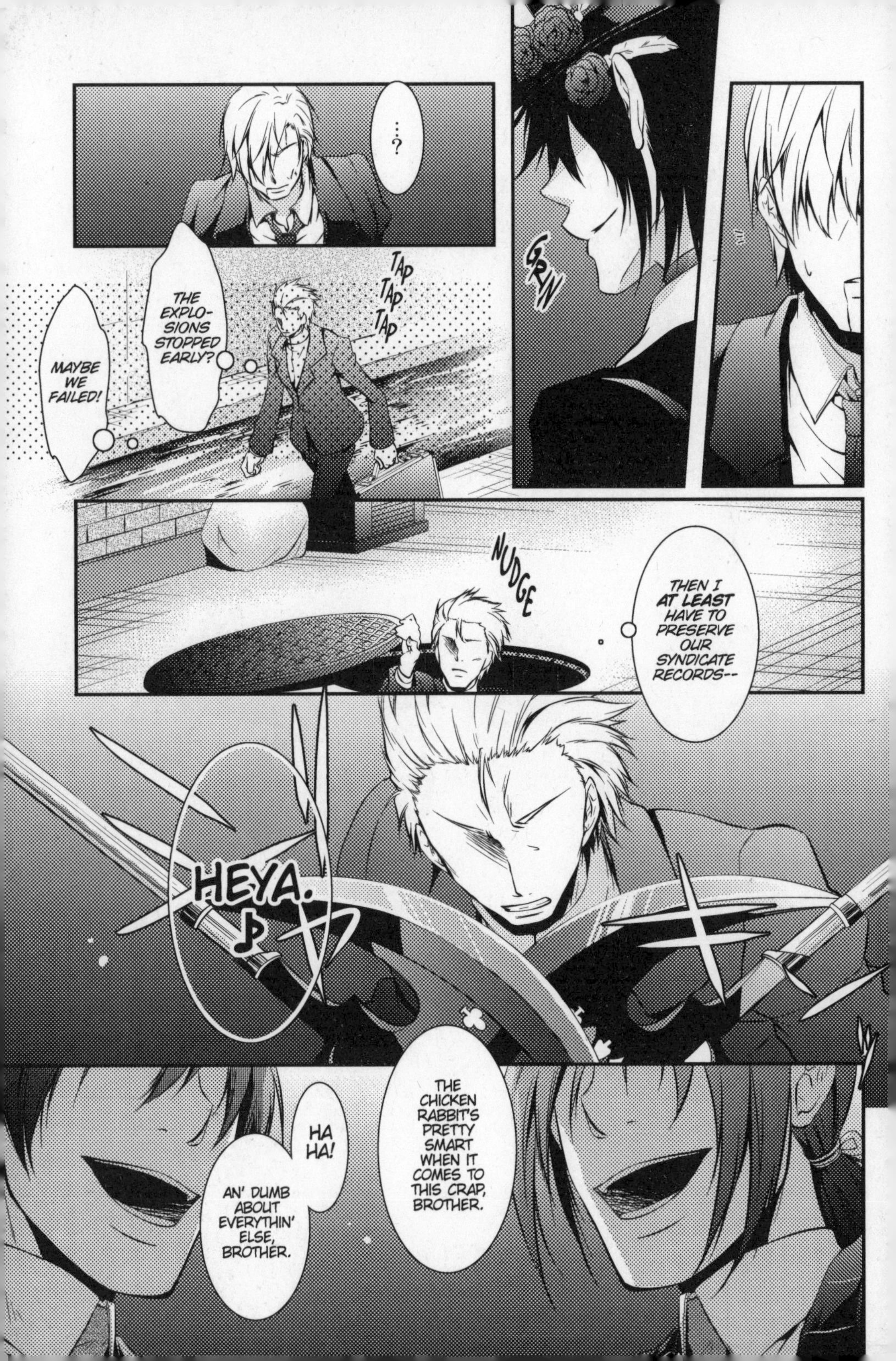
GRIN
...?
THE EXPLOSIONS STOPPED EARLY?
MAYBE WE FAILED!
TAP TAP TAP
NUDGE
THEN I AT LEAST HAVE TO PRESERVE OUR SYNDICATE RECORDS--
HEYA. ♪
THE CHICKEN RABBIT'S PRETTY SMART WHEN IT COMES TO THIS CRAP, BROTHER.
HA HA!
AN' DUMB ABOUT EVERYTHIN' ELSE, BROTHER.

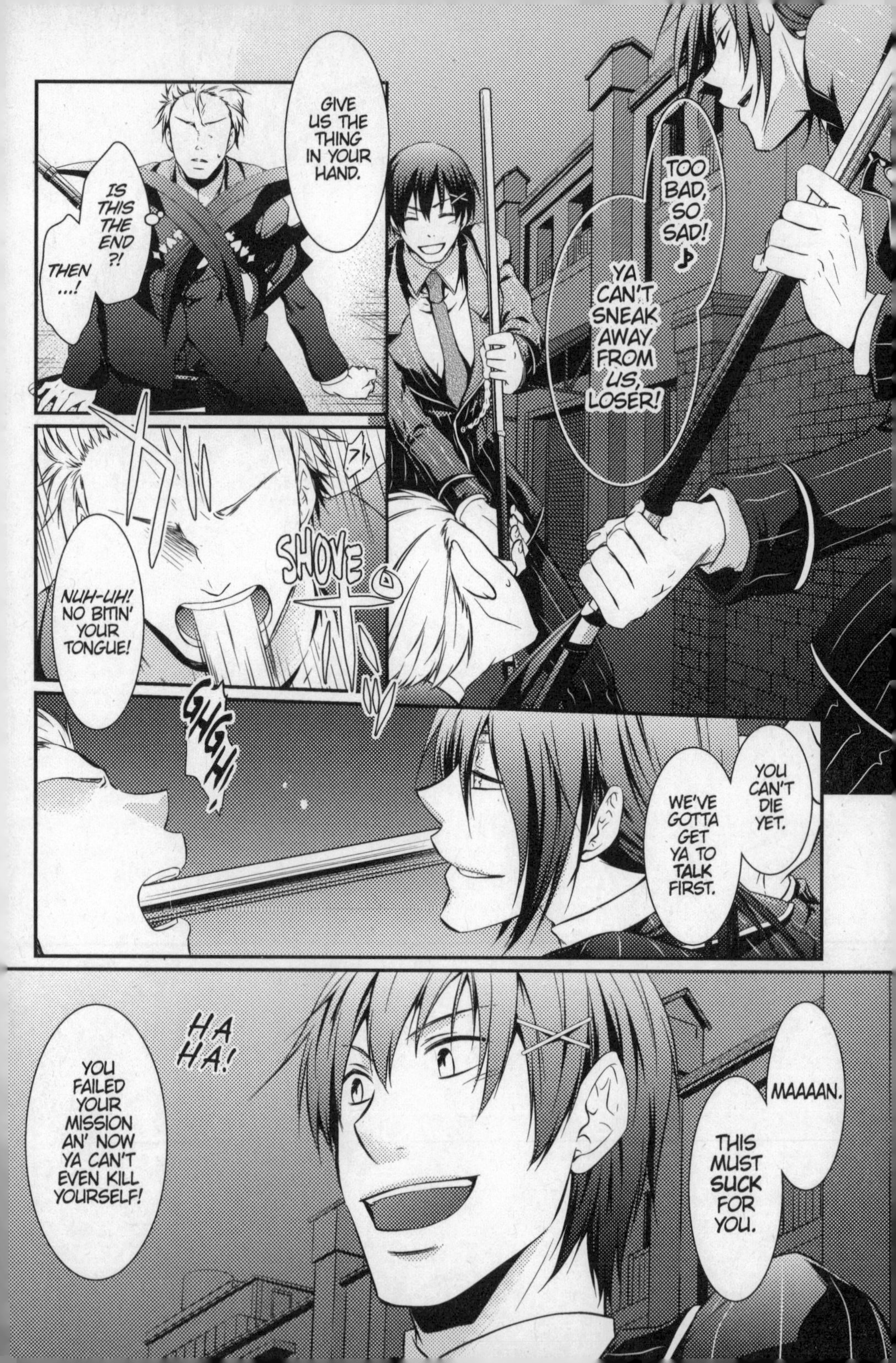
TOO BAD, SO SAD! ♪
YA CAN'T SNEAK AWAY FROM US, LOSER!
GIVE US THE THING IN YOUR HAND.
IS THIS THE END?!
THEN...!
NUH-UH! NO BITIN' YOUR TONGUE!
SHOVE
GHGH!
YOU CAN'T DIE YET.
WE'VE GOTTA GET YA TO TALK FIRST.
MAAAAN.
THIS MUST SUCK FOR YOU.
HA HA!
YOU FAILED YOUR MISSION AN' NOW YA CAN'T EVEN KILL YOURSELF!

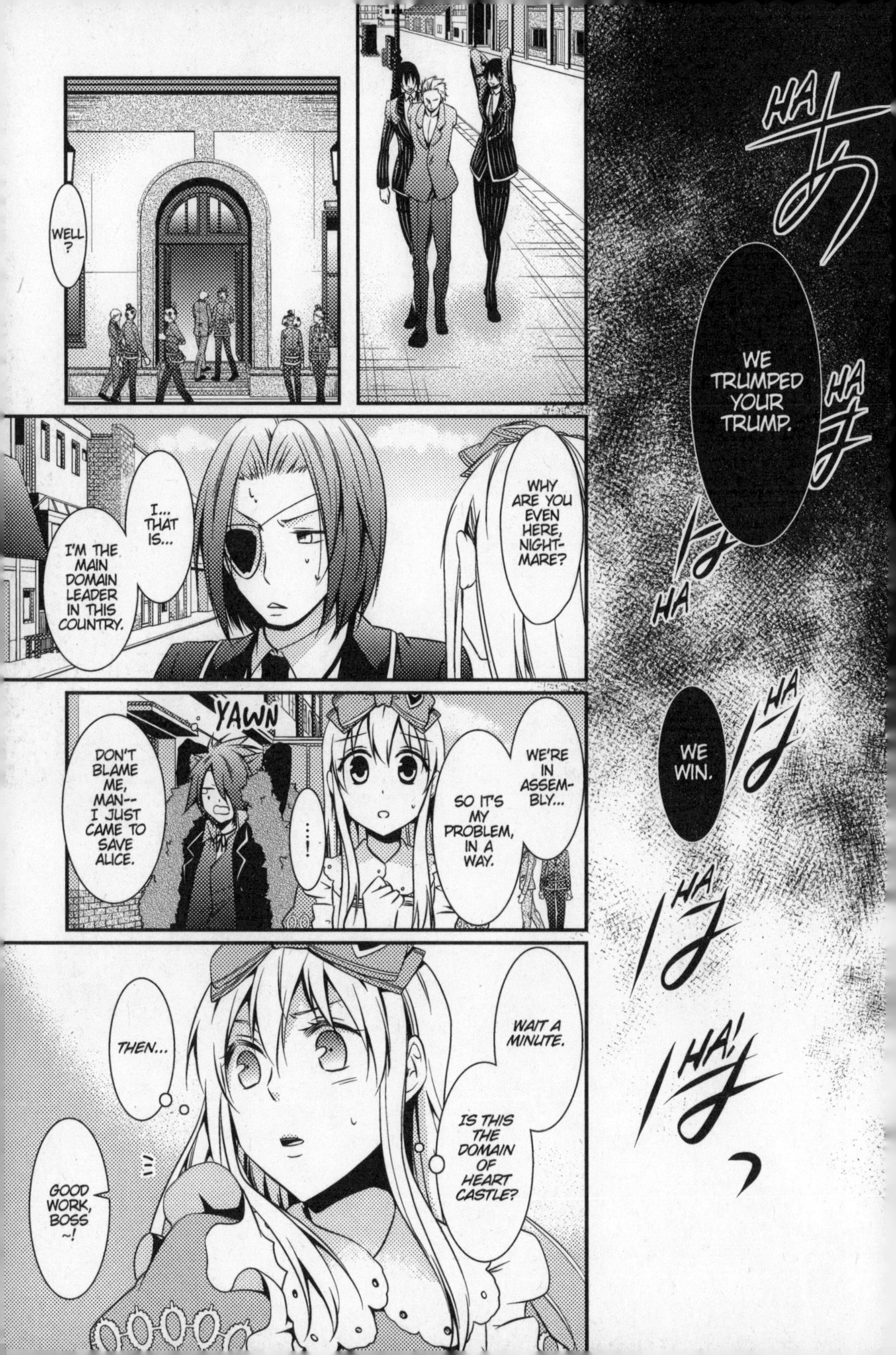
HA
WE TRUMPED YOUR TRUMP.
HA
HA
HA
WE WIN.
HA
HA
HA!
WELL?
WHY ARE YOU EVEN HERE, NIGHTMARE?
I... THAT IS...
I'M THE MAIN DOMAIN LEADER IN THIS COUNTRY.
WE'RE IN ASSEMBLY...
SO IT'S MY PROBLEM, IN A WAY.
...!
YAWN
DON'T BLAME ME, MAN-- I JUST CAME TO SAVE ALICE.
WAIT A MINUTE.
IS THIS THE DOMAIN OF HEART CASTLE?
THEN...
GOOD WORK, BOSS~!

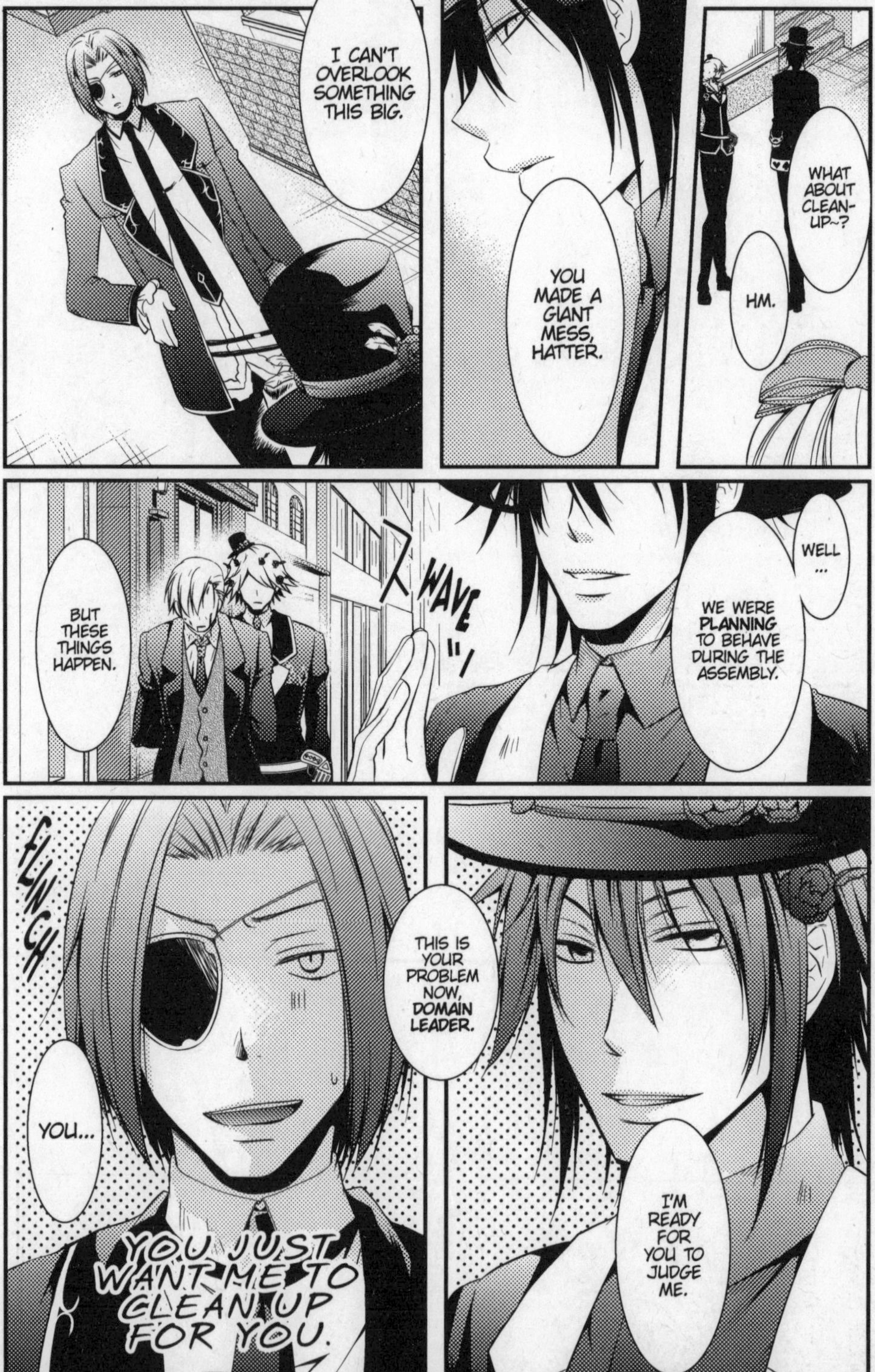
WHAT ABOUT CLEAN-UP~?
HM.
YOU MADE A GIANT MESS, HATTER.
I CAN'T OVERLOOK SOMETHING THIS BIG.
WELL ...
WE WERE PLANNING TO BEHAVE DURING THE ASSEMBLY.
WAVE
BUT THESE THINGS HAPPEN.
THIS IS YOUR PROBLEM NOW, DOMAIN LEADER.
I'M READY FOR YOU TO JUDGE ME.
FLINCH
YOU...
YOU JUST WANT ME TO CLEAN UP FOR YOU.

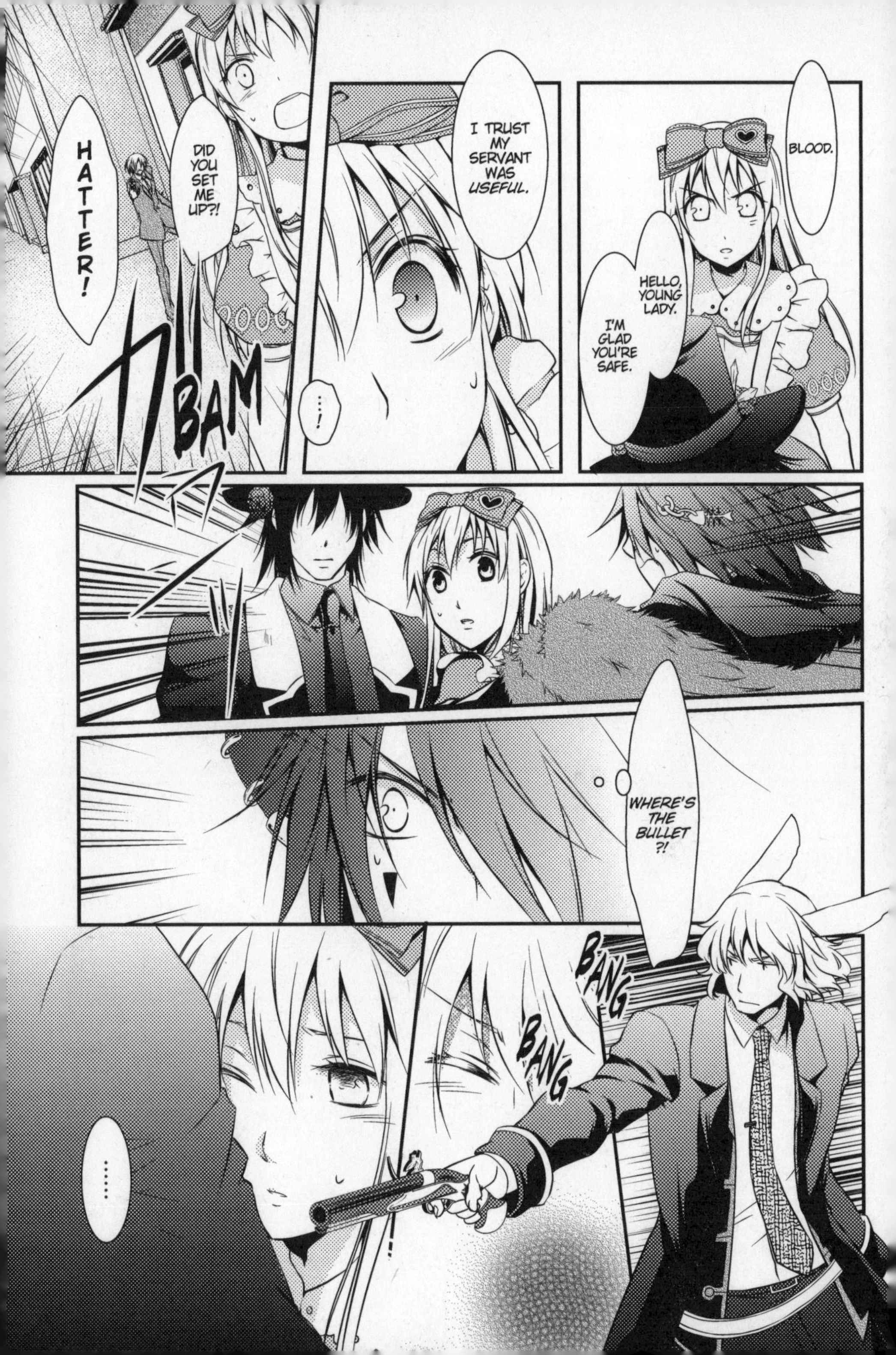
BLOOD.
HELLO, YOUNG LADY.
I'M GLAD YOU'RE SAFE.
I TRUST MY SERVANT WAS USEFUL.
...!
DID YOU SET ME UP?!
HATTER!
BAM
WHERE'S THE BULLET?!
BANG
BANG
......

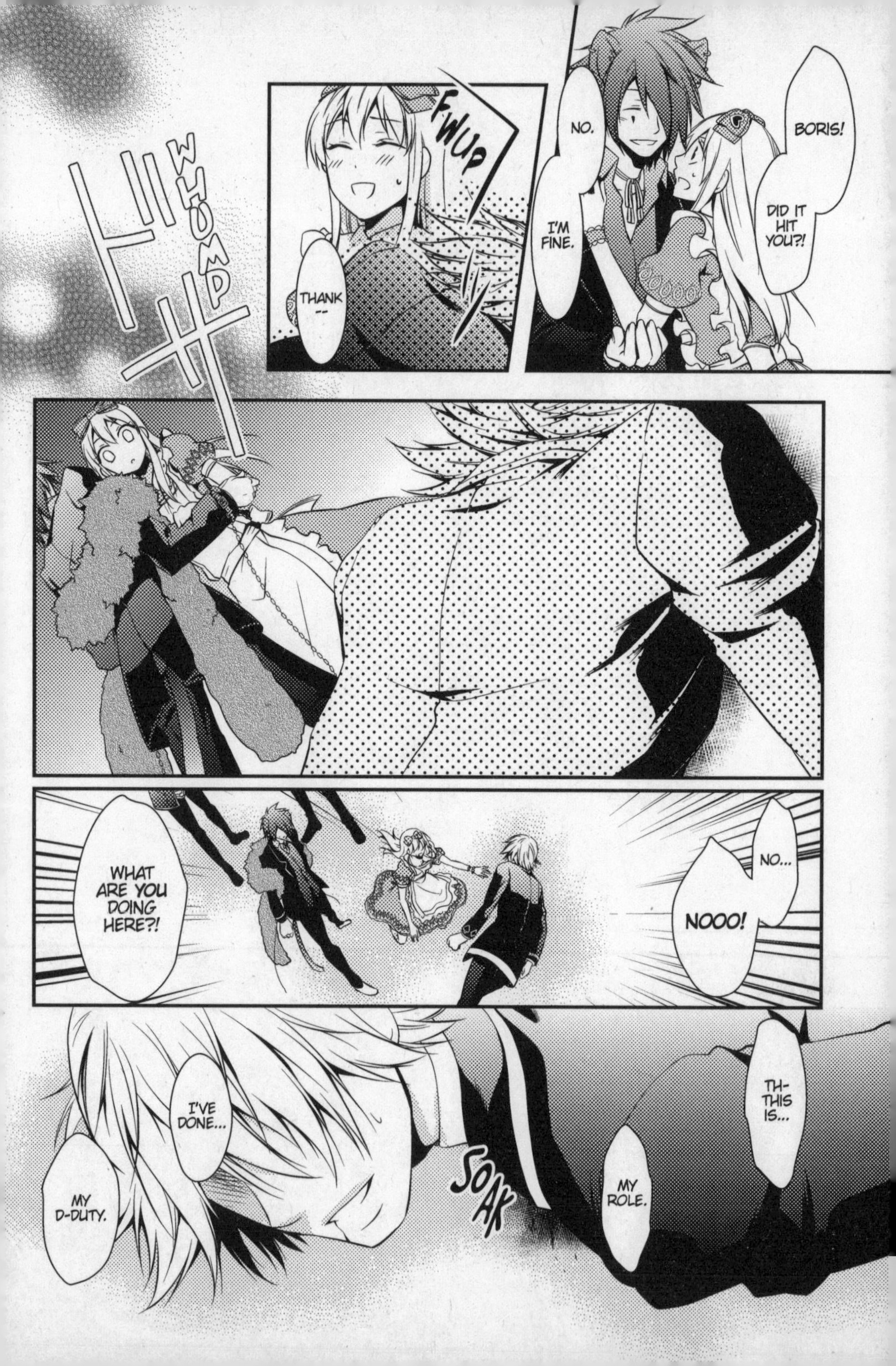
BORIS!
DID IT HIT YOU?!
NO.
I'M FINE.
FWUP
THANK--
WHUMP
NO...
NOOO!
WHAT ARE YOU DOING HERE?!
TH-THIS IS...
MY ROLE.
SOAK
I'VE DONE...
MY D-DUTY.

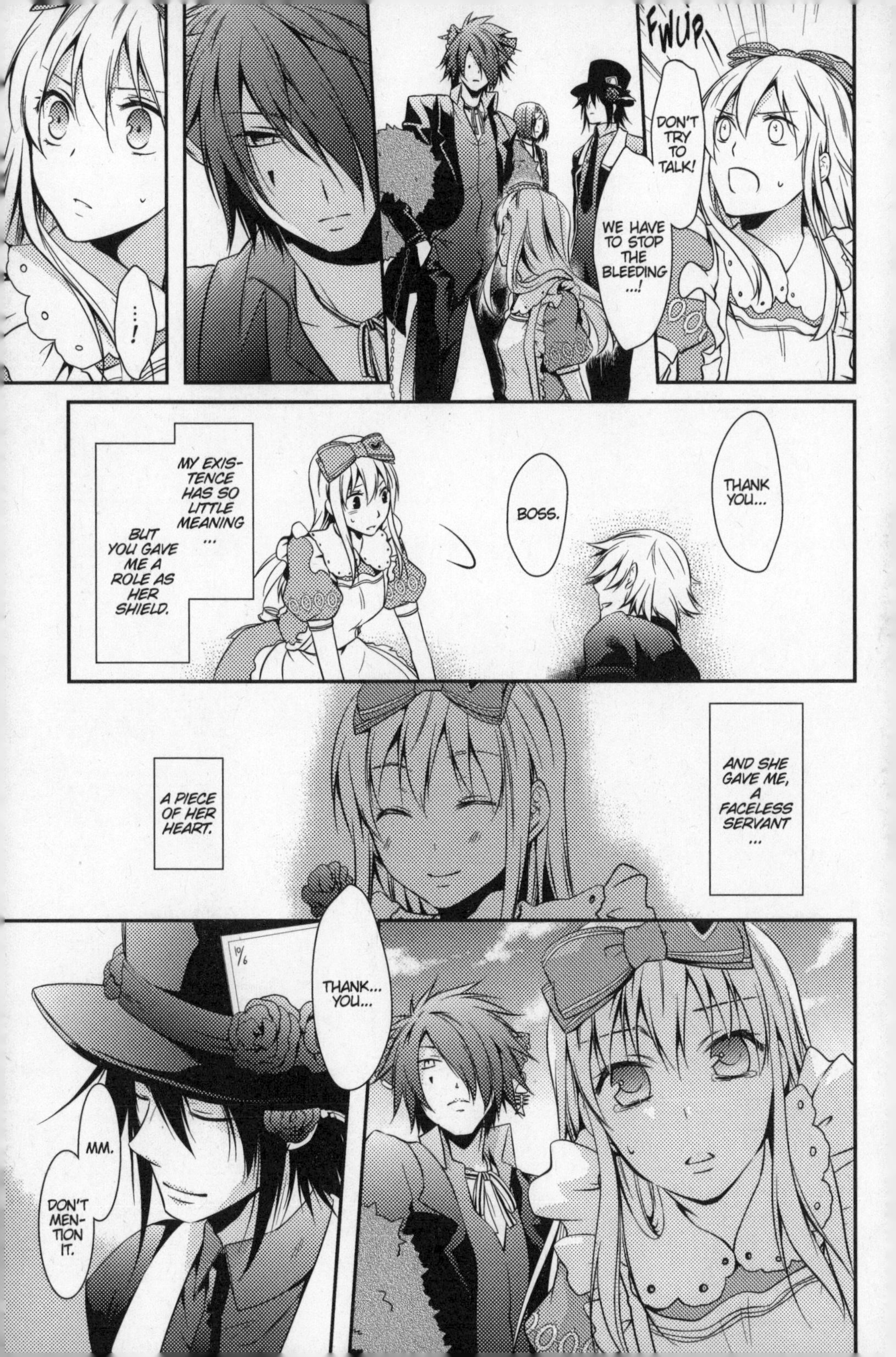
FWUP
DON'T TRY TO TALK!
WE HAVE TO STOP THE BLEEDING ...!
...!
THANK YOU...
BOSS.
MY EXISTENCE HAS SO LITTLE MEANING ...
BUT YOU GAVE ME A ROLE AS HER SHIELD.
AND SHE GAVE ME, A FACELESS SERVANT ...
A PIECE OF HER HEART.
THANK... YOU...
MM.
DON'T MENTION IT.

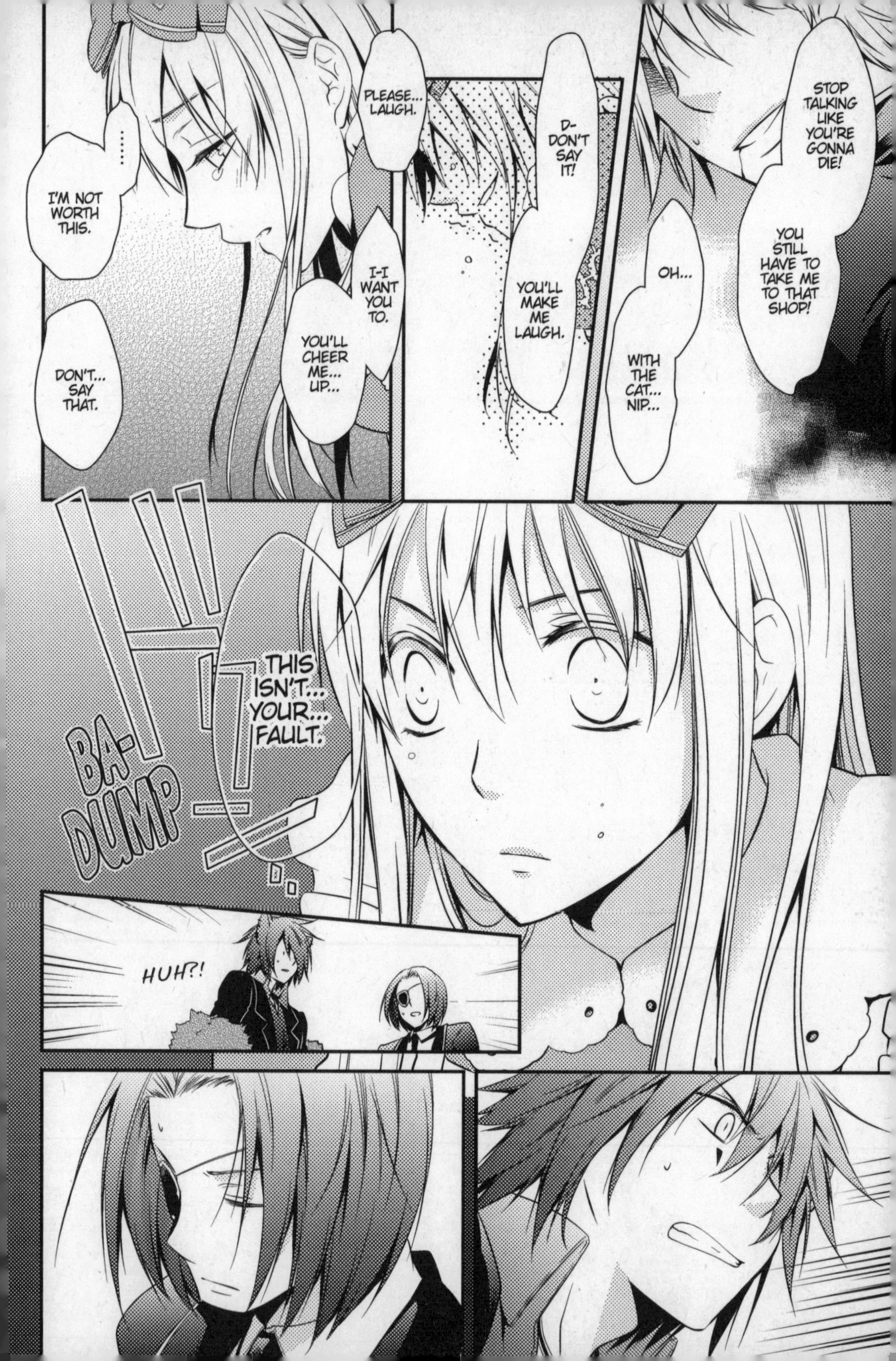
STOP TALKING LIKE YOU'RE GONNA DIE!
YOU STILL HAVE TO TAKE ME TO THAT SHOP!
OH...
WITH THE CAT... NIP...
D-DON'T SAY IT!
YOU'LL MAKE ME LAUGH.
PLEASE... LAUGH.
I-I WANT YOU TO.
YOU'LL CHEER ME... UP...
......
I'M NOT WORTH THIS.
DON'T... SAY THAT.
THIS ISN'T... YOUR... FAULT.
BA-DUMP
HUH?!

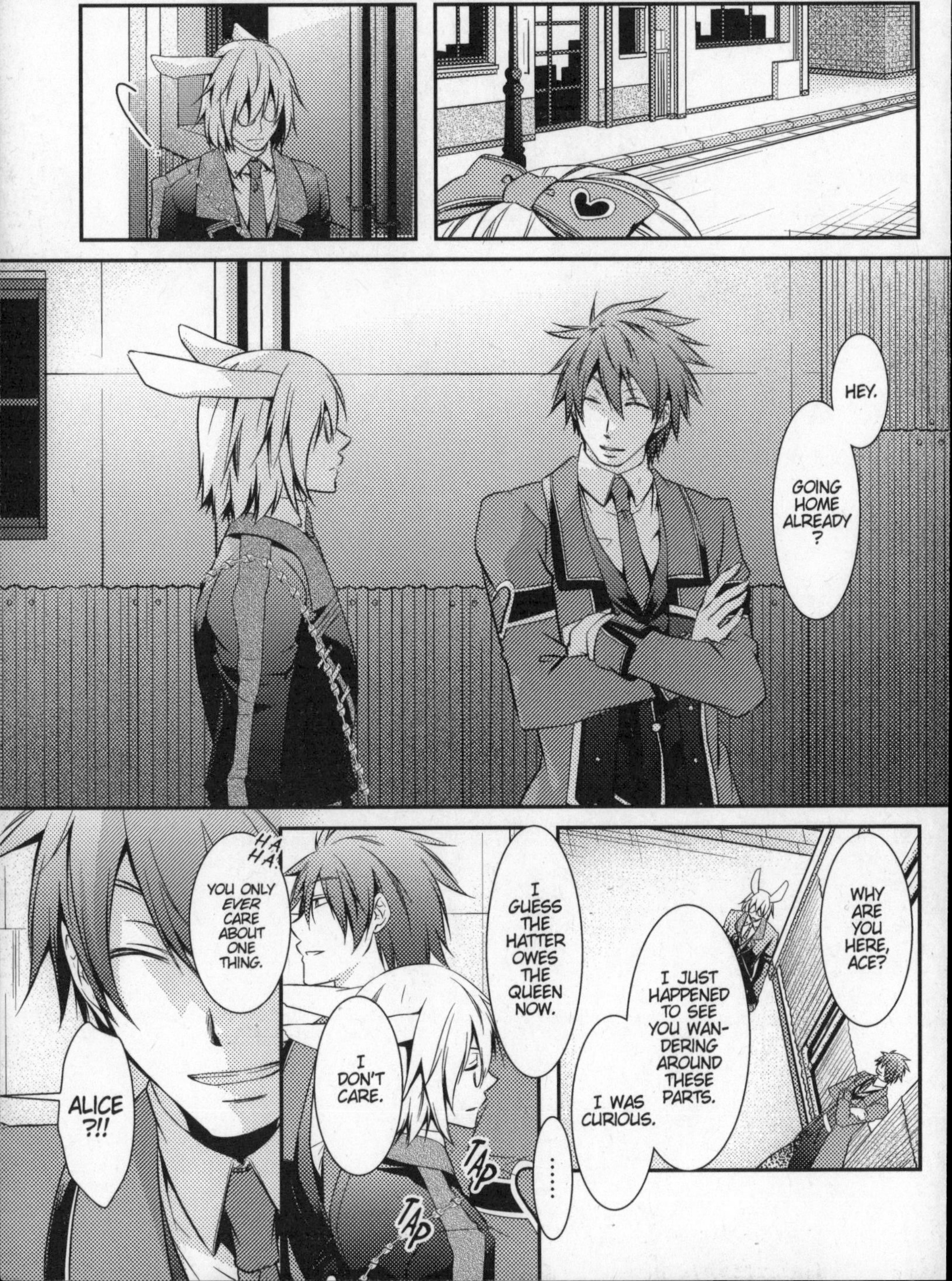
HEY.
GOING HOME ALREADY?
WHY ARE YOU HERE, ACE?
I JUST HAPPENED TO SEE YOU WAN-DERING AROUND THESE PARTS.
I WAS CURIOUS.
......
I GUESS THE HATTER OWES THE QUEEN NOW.
I DON'T CARE.
TAP
TAP
HA HA!
YOU ONLY EVER CARE ABOUT ONE THING.
ALICE?!!

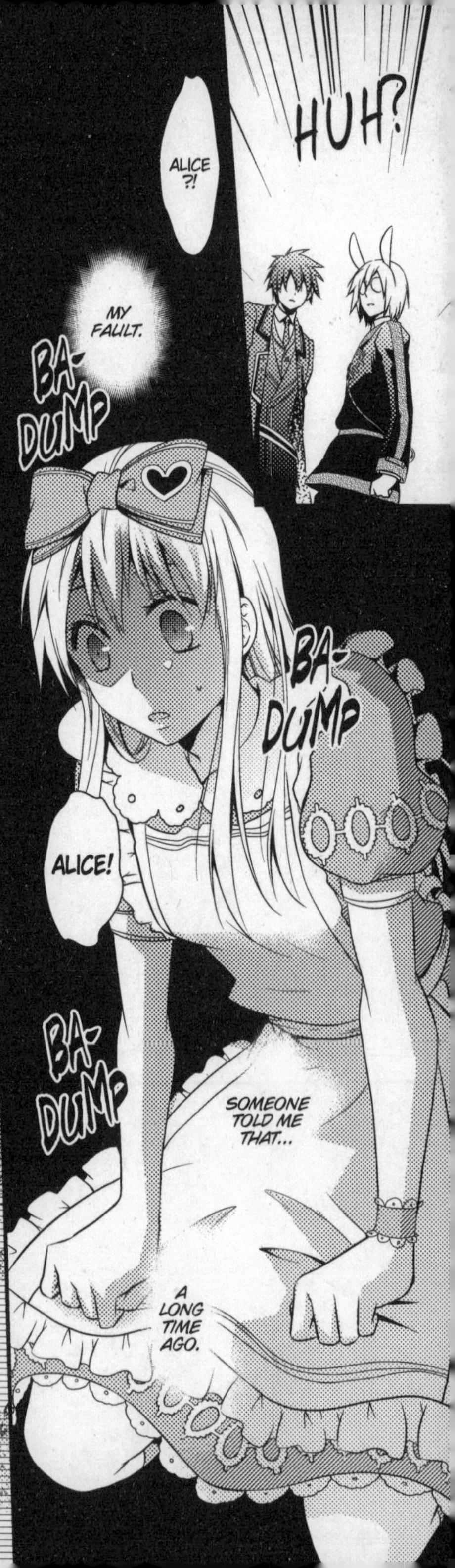
HUH?
ALICE ?!
MY FAULT.
BA-DUMP
BA-DUMP
ALICE!
BA-DUMP
SOMEONE TOLD ME THAT...
A LONG TIME AGO.
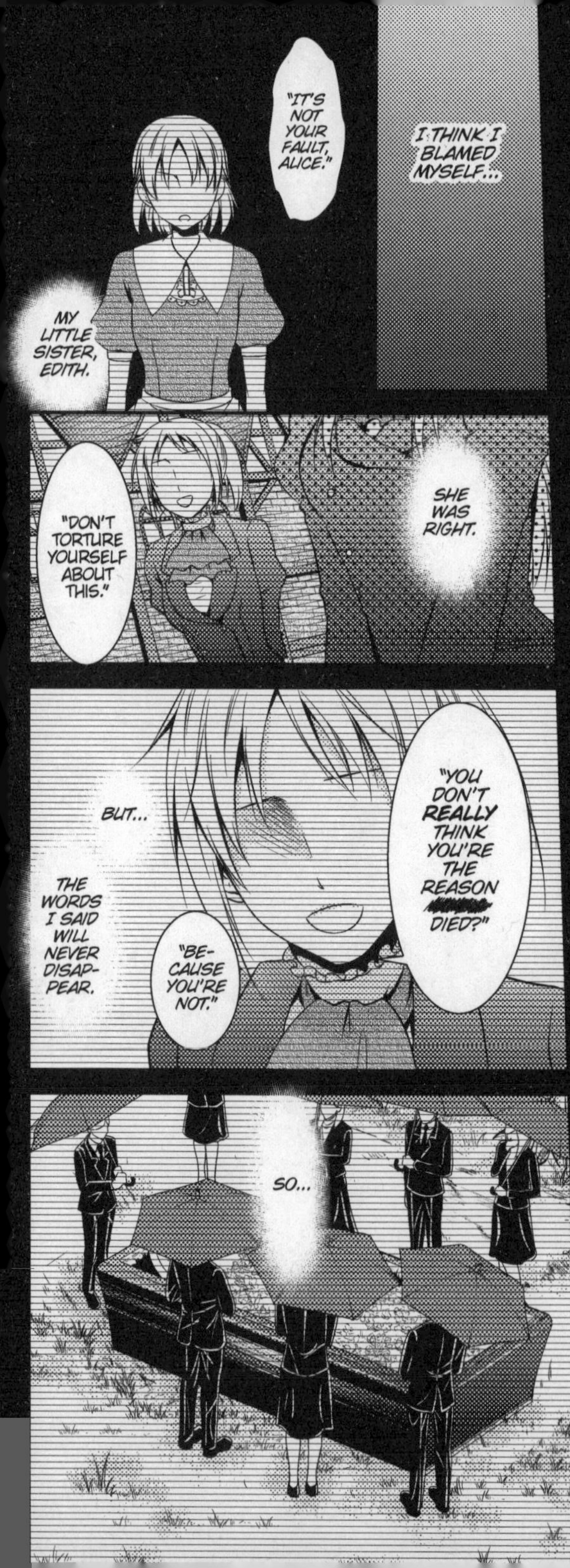
I THINK I BLAMED MYSELF...
"IT'S NOT YOUR FAULT, ALICE."
MY LITTLE SISTER, EDITH.
SHE WAS RIGHT.
"DON'T TORTURE YOURSELF ABOUT THIS."
"YOU DON'T REALLY THINK YOU'RE THE REASON [redacted] DIED?"
"BE-CAUSE YOU'RE NOT."
BUT...
THE WORDS I SAID WILL NEVER DISAP-PEAR.
SO...

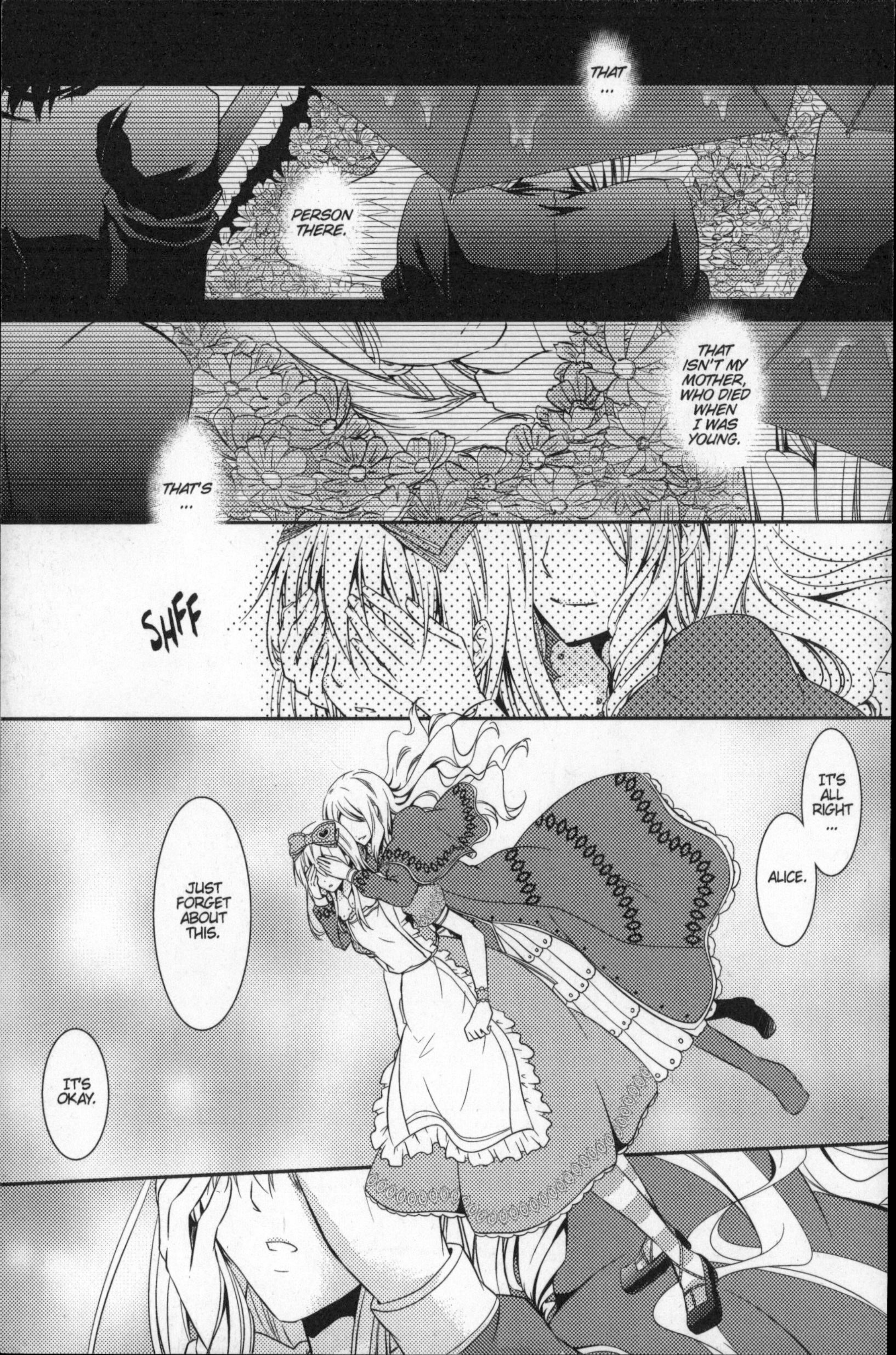
THAT ...
PERSON THERE.
THAT ISN'T MY MOTHER, WHO DIED WHEN I WAS YOUNG.
THAT'S ...
SHFF
IT'S ALL RIGHT ...
ALICE.
JUST FORGET ABOUT THIS.
IT'S OKAY.

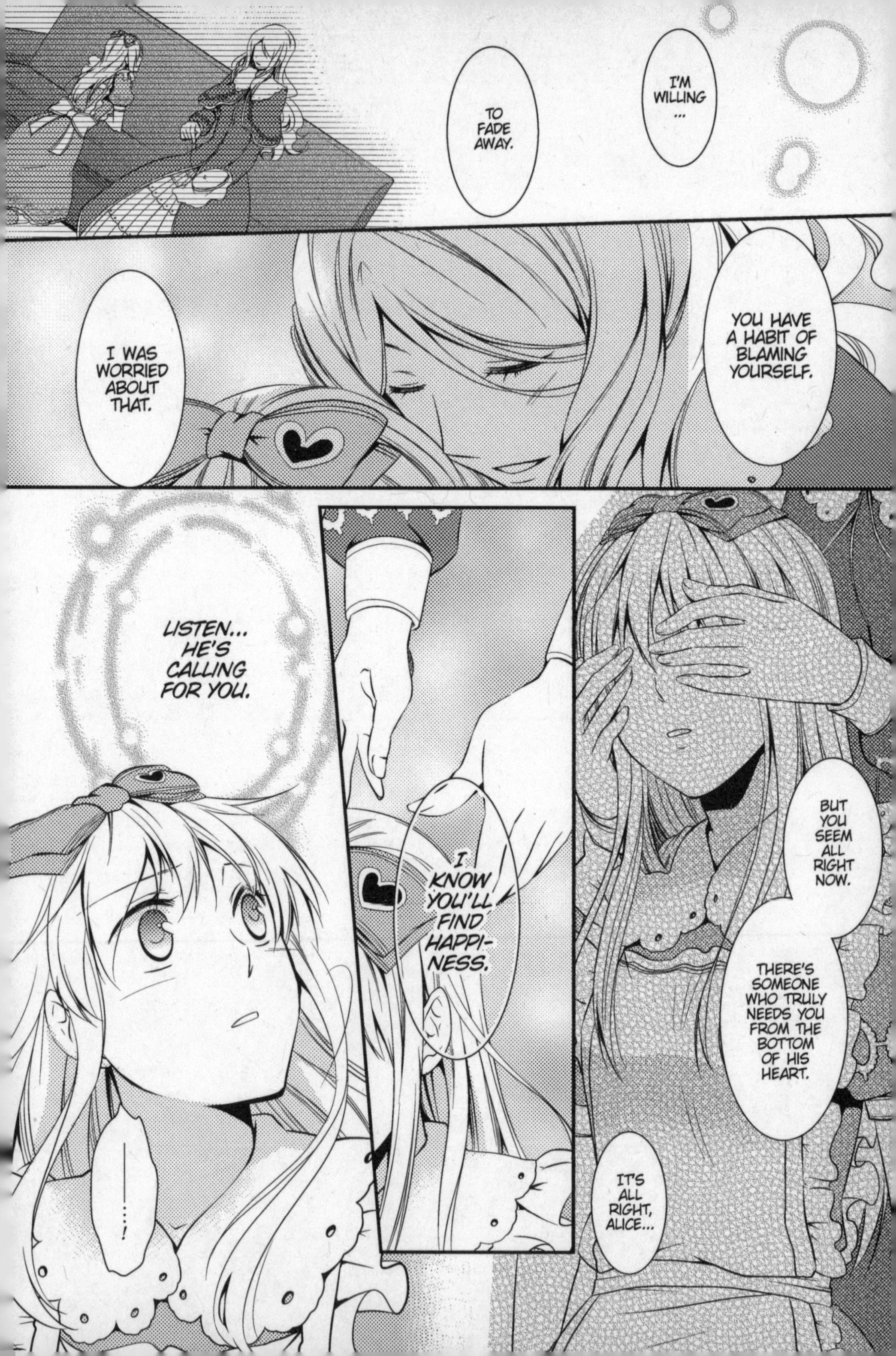
I'M WILLING ...
TO FADE AWAY.
YOU HAVE A HABIT OF BLAMING YOURSELF.
I WAS WORRIED ABOUT THAT.
BUT YOU SEEM ALL RIGHT NOW.
THERE'S SOMEONE WHO TRULY NEEDS YOU FROM THE BOTTOM OF HIS HEART.
IT'S ALL RIGHT, ALICE...
I KNOW YOU'LL FIND HAPPINESS.
LISTEN... HE'S CALLING FOR YOU.
......!

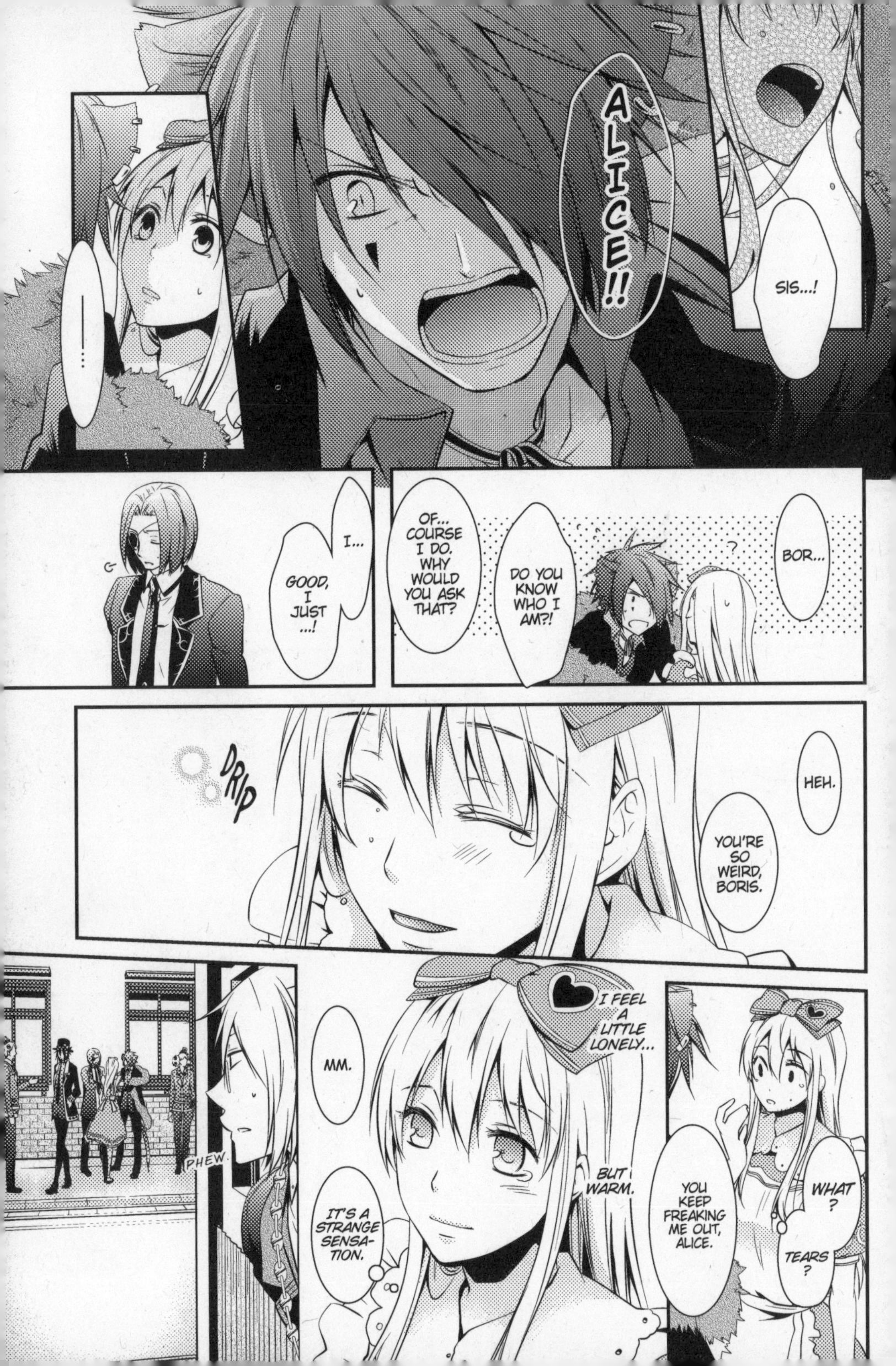
SIS...!
ALICE!!
......
BOR...
DO YOU KNOW WHO I AM?!
OF... COURSE I DO. WHY WOULD YOU ASK THAT?
I...
GOOD, I JUST ...!
HEH.
YOU'RE SO WEIRD, BORIS.
DRIP
WHAT?
TEARS?
YOU KEEP FREAKING ME OUT, ALICE.
I FEEL A LITTLE LONELY...
BUT WARM.
MM.
IT'S A STRANGE SENSA-TION.
PHEW.

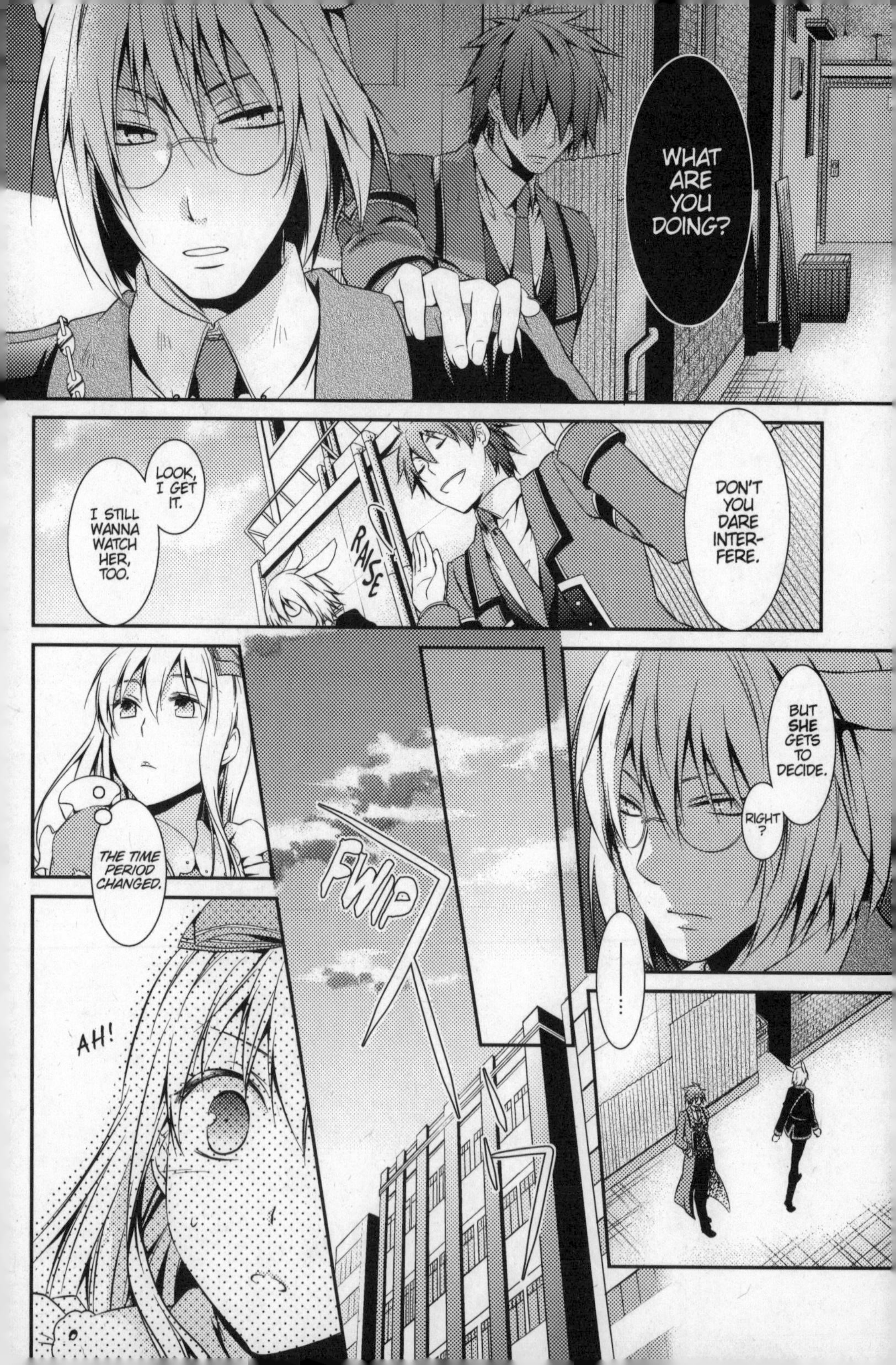

WHAT ARE YOU DOING?
DON'T YOU DARE INTER-FERE.
RAISE
LOOK, I GET IT.
I STILL WANNA WATCH HER, TOO.
BUT SHE GETS TO DECIDE.
RIGHT?
......
FWIP
THE TIME PERIOD CHANGED.
AH!

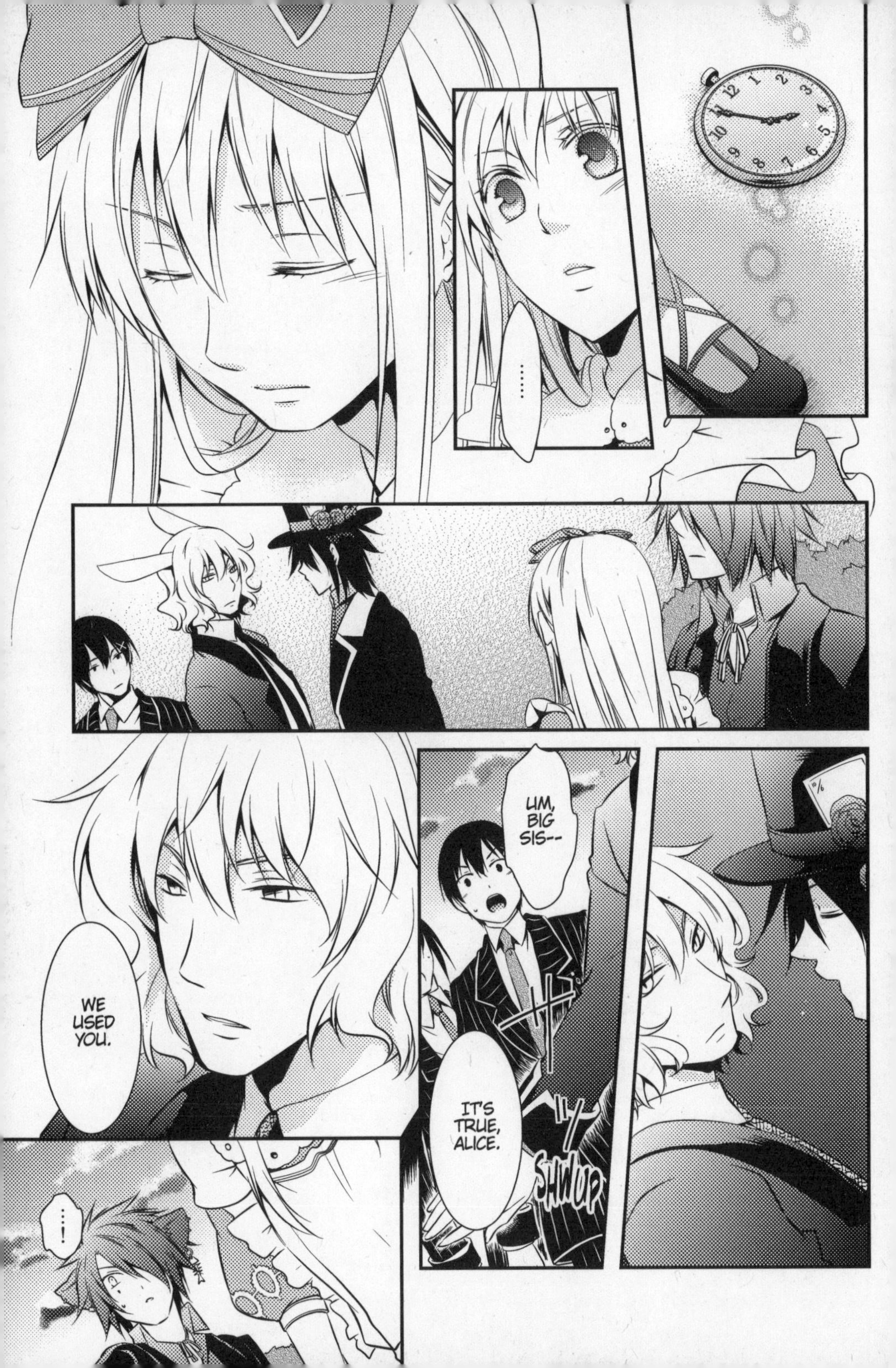
......
UM, BIG SIS--
IT'S TRUE, ALICE.
SHWOP
WE USED YOU.
...!

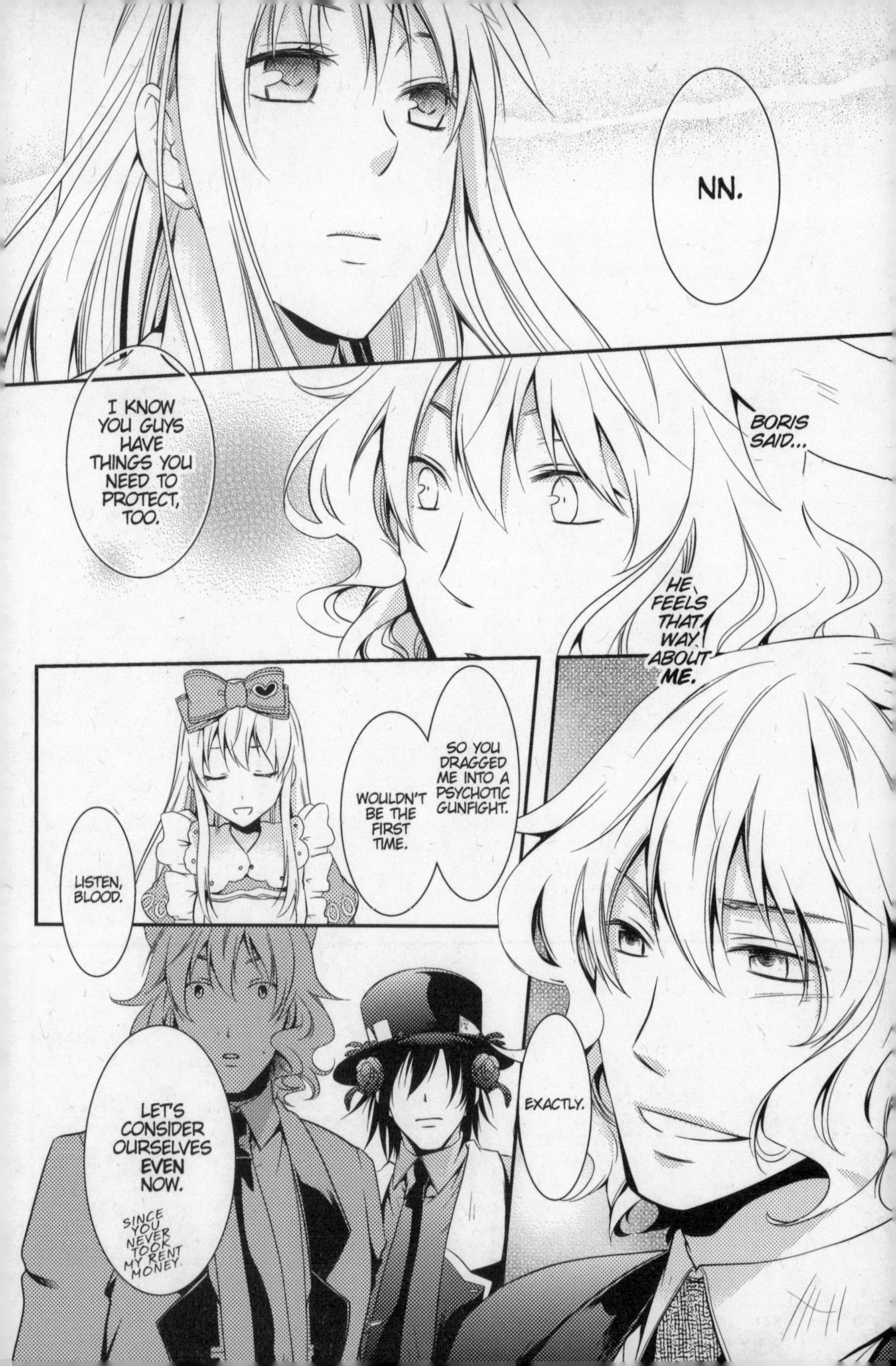
NN.
BORIS SAID...
HE FEELS THAT WAY ABOUT ME.
I KNOW YOU GUYS HAVE THINGS YOU NEED TO PROTECT, TOO.
SO YOU DRAGGED ME INTO A PSYCHOTIC GUNFIGHT.
WOULDN'T BE THE FIRST TIME.
LISTEN, BLOOD.
LET'S CONSIDER OURSELVES EVEN NOW.
SINCE YOU NEVER TOOK MY RENT MONEY.
EXACTLY.

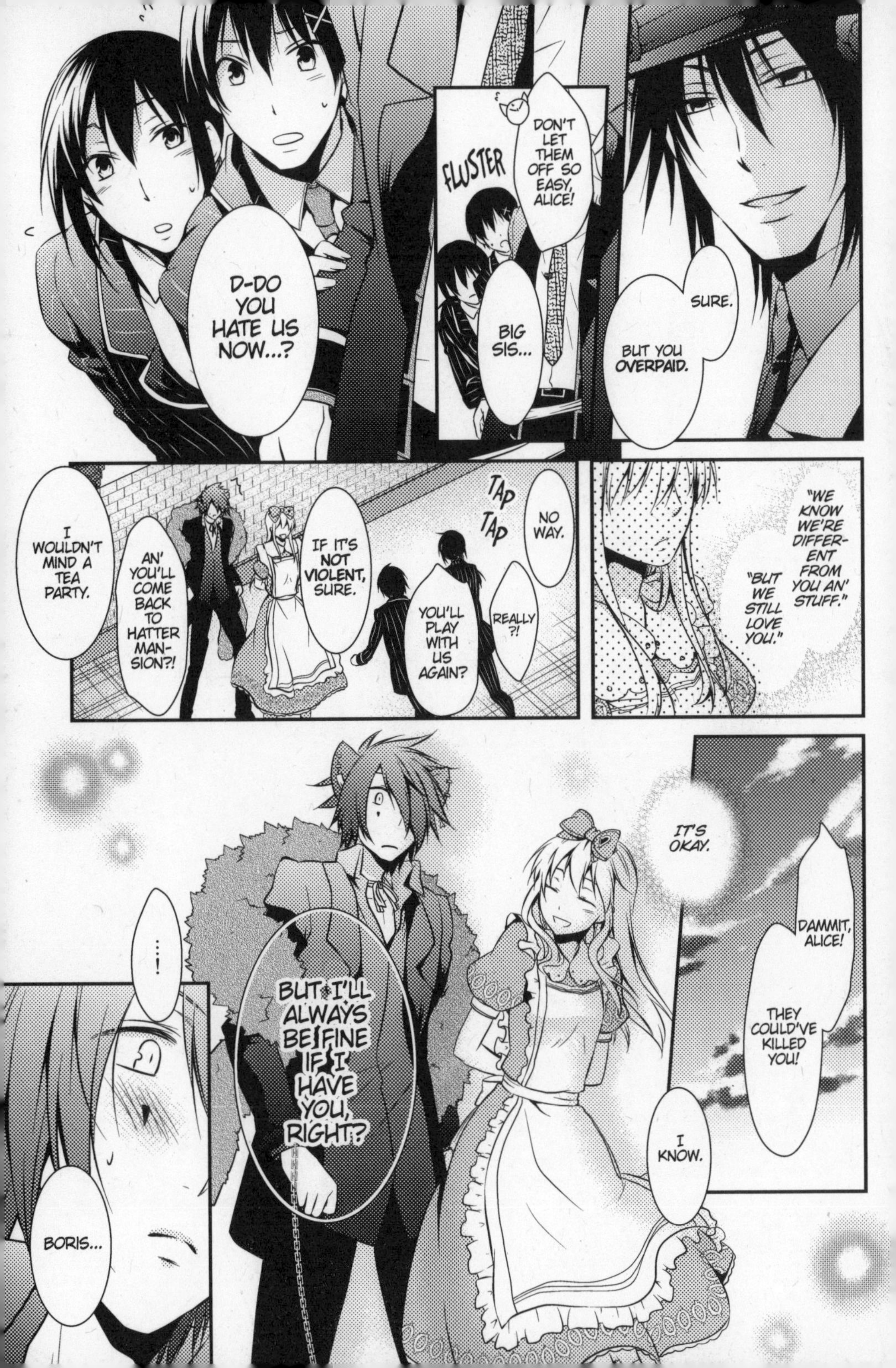
SURE.
BUT YOU OVERPAID.
DON'T LET THEM OFF SO EASY, ALICE!
FLUSTER
BIG SIS...
D-DO YOU HATE US NOW...?
"WE KNOW WE'RE DIFFER-ENT FROM YOU AN' STUFF."
"BUT WE STILL LOVE YOU."
TAP TAP
NO WAY.
REALLY?!
YOU'LL PLAY WITH US AGAIN?
IF IT'S NOT VIOLENT, SURE.
AN' YOU'LL COME BACK TO HATTER MAN-SION?!
I WOULDN'T MIND A TEA PARTY.
IT'S OKAY.
DAMMIT, ALICE!
THEY COULD'VE KILLED YOU!
I KNOW.
...!
BUT I'LL ALWAYS BE FINE IF I HAVE YOU, RIGHT?
BORIS...

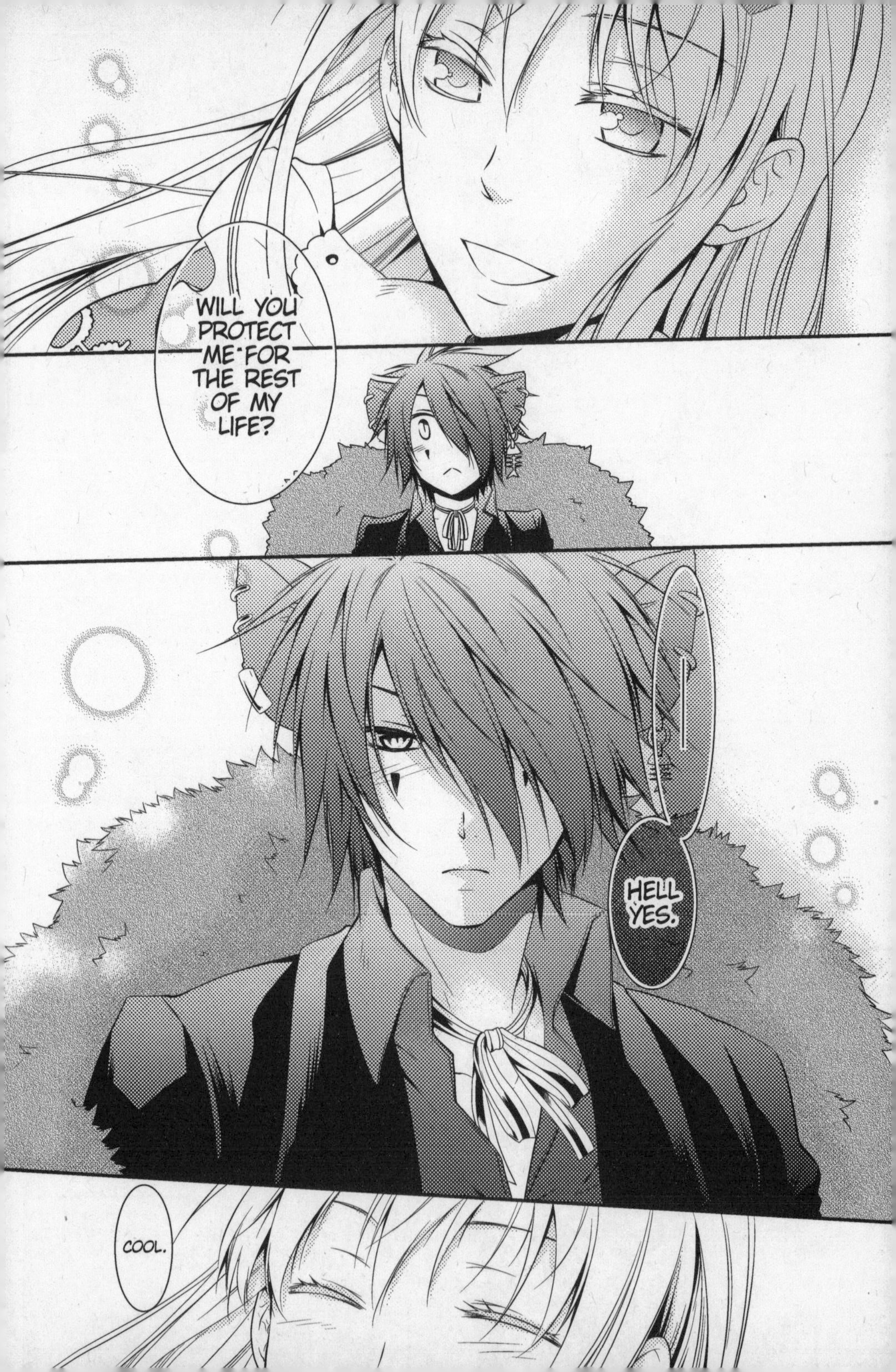
WILL YOU PROTECT ME FOR THE REST OF MY LIFE?
......
HELL YES.
COOL.

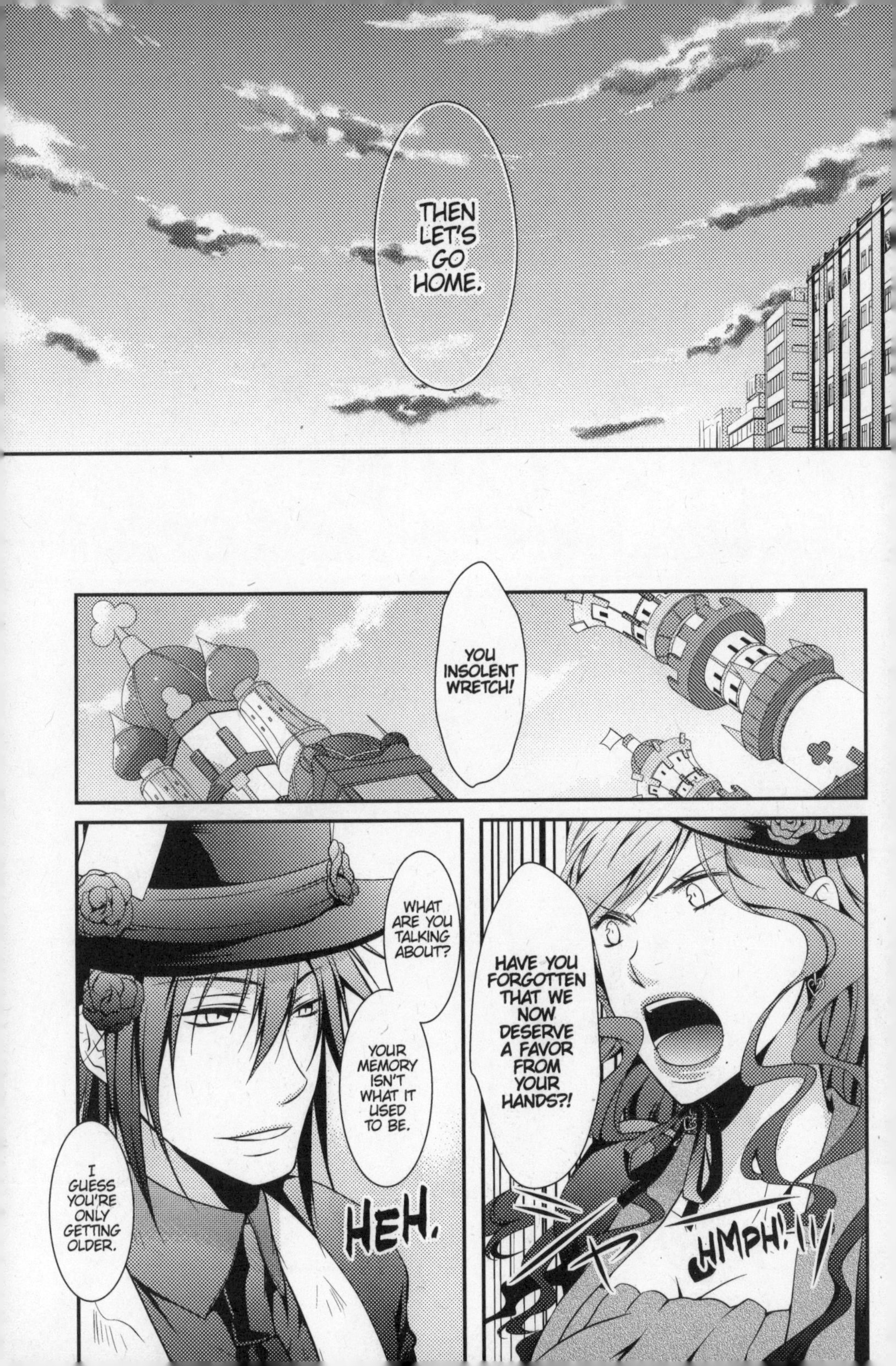
THEN LET'S GO HOME.
YOU INSOLENT WRETCH!
HAVE YOU FORGOTTEN THAT WE NOW DESERVE A FAVOR FROM YOUR HANDS?!
HMPH!
WHAT ARE YOU TALKING ABOUT?
YOUR MEMORY ISN'T WHAT IT USED TO BE.
I GUESS YOU'RE ONLY GETTING OLDER.
HEH.

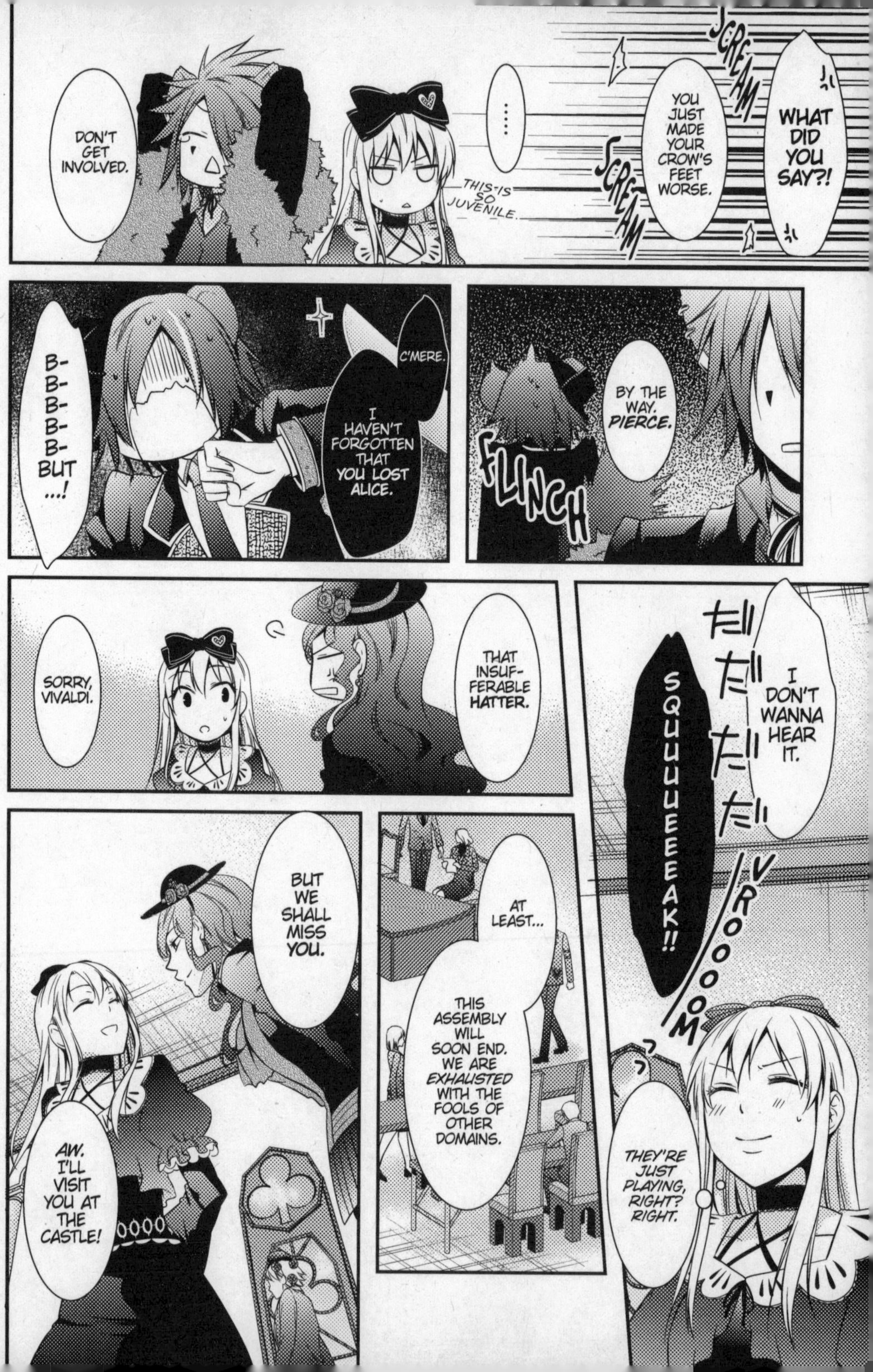

WHAT DID YOU SAY?!
YOU JUST MADE YOUR CROW'S FEET WORSE.
SCREAM
SCREAM
......
THIS IS SO JUVENILE.
DON'T GET INVOLVED.
BY THE WAY. PIERCE.
FLINCH
C'MERE.
I HAVEN'T FORGOTTEN THAT YOU LOST ALICE.
B-B-B-B-B-BUT ...!
I DON'T WANNA HEAR IT.
SQUUUUEEEAK!!
VROOOOOOM
THEY'RE JUST PLAYING, RIGHT? RIGHT.
THAT INSUFFERABLE HATTER.
SORRY, VIVALDI.
AT LEAST...
THIS ASSEMBLY WILL SOON END. WE ARE EXHAUSTED WITH THE FOOLS OF OTHER DOMAINS.
BUT WE SHALL MISS YOU.
AW. I'LL VISIT YOU AT THE CASTLE!

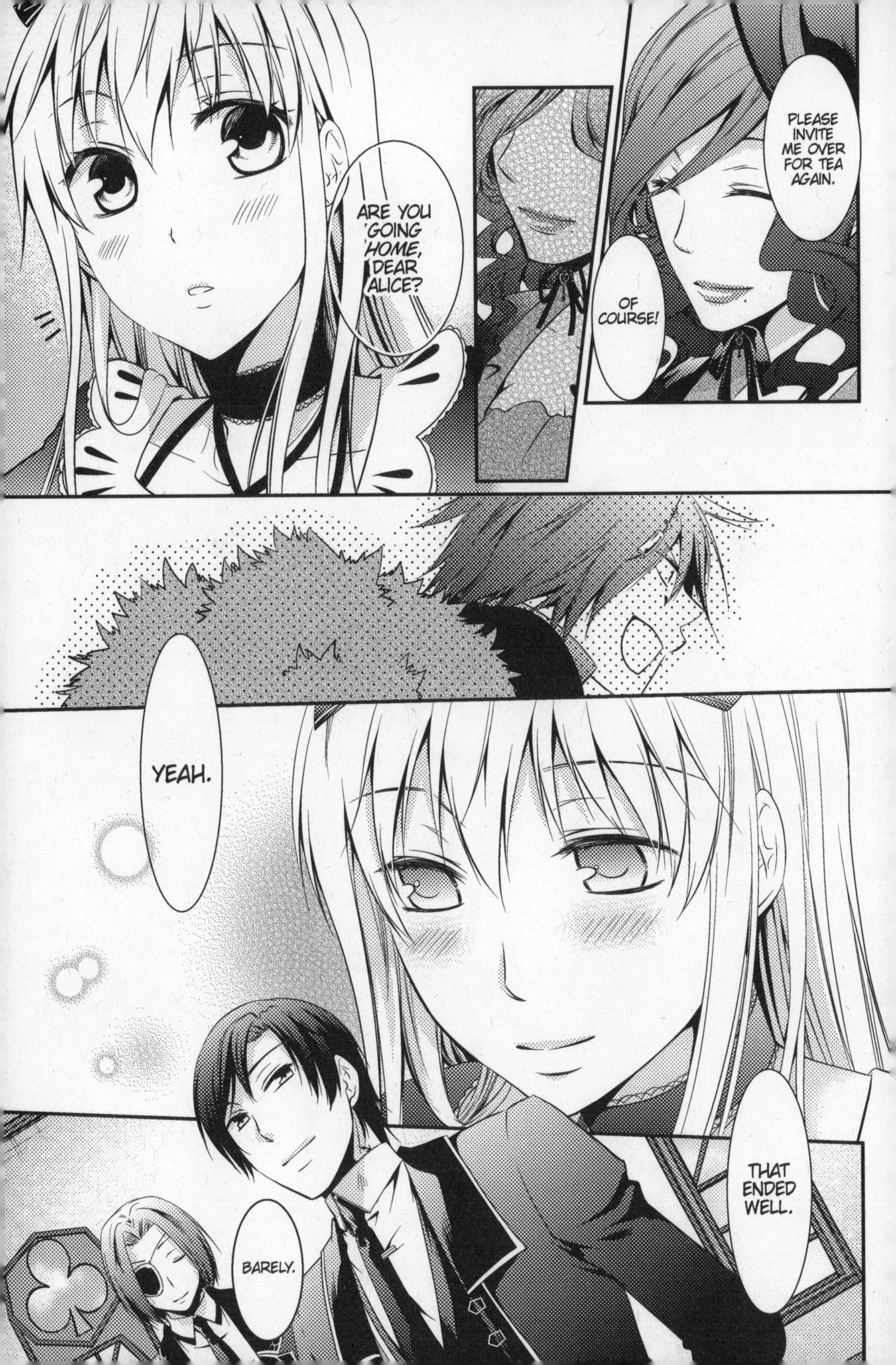
PLEASE INVITE ME OVER FOR TEA AGAIN.
OF COURSE!
ARE YOU GOING HOME, DEAR ALICE?
YEAH.
THAT ENDED WELL.
BARELY.

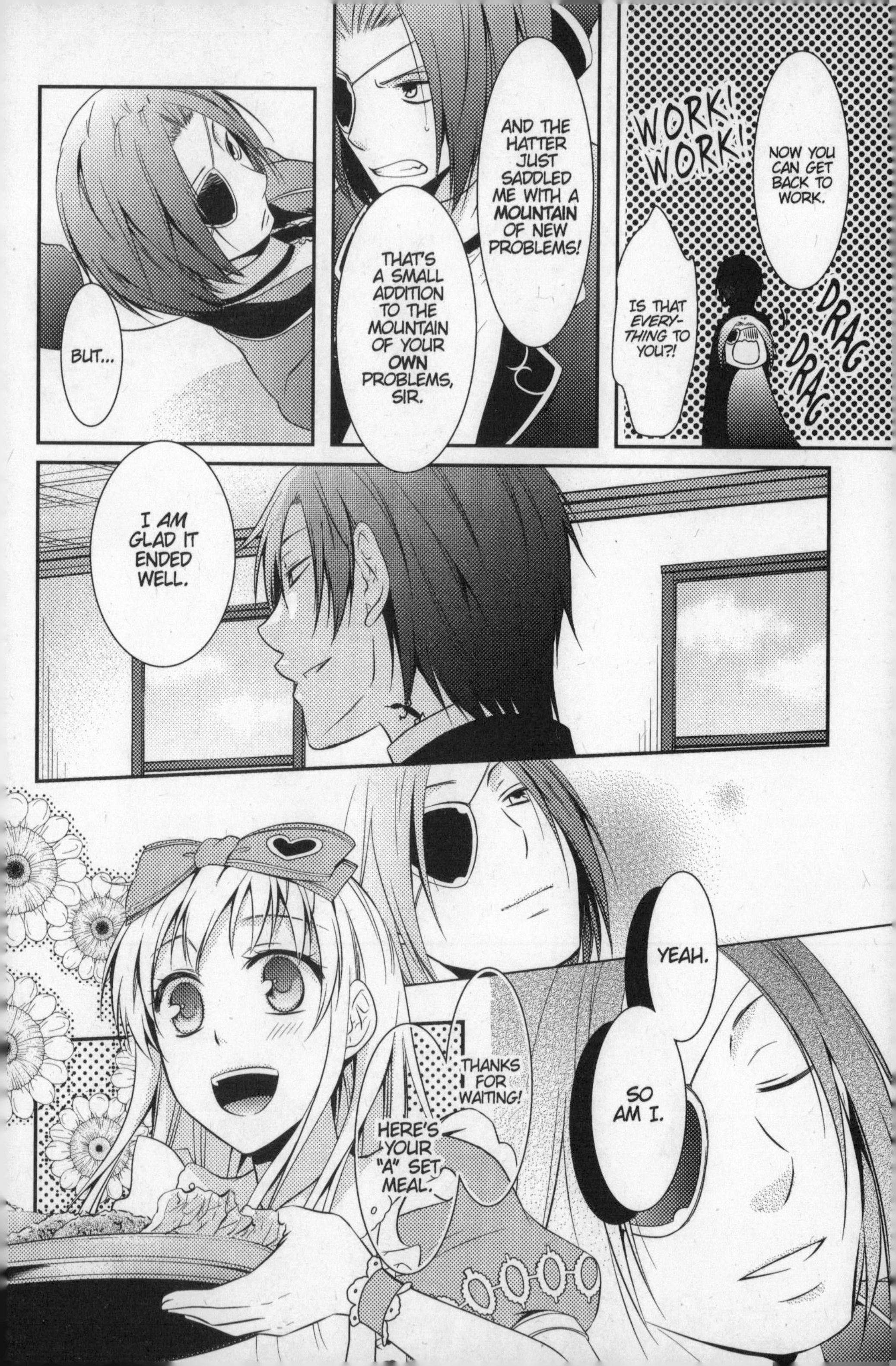
NOW YOU CAN GET BACK TO WORK.
WORK! WORK!
IS THAT EVERYTHING TO YOU?!
DRAG DRAG
AND THE HATTER JUST SADDLED ME WITH A MOUNTAIN OF NEW PROBLEMS!
THAT'S A SMALL ADDITION TO THE MOUNTAIN OF YOUR OWN PROBLEMS, SIR.
BUT...
I AM GLAD IT ENDED WELL.
YEAH.
SO AM I.
THANKS FOR WAITING!
HERE'S YOUR "A" SET MEAL.

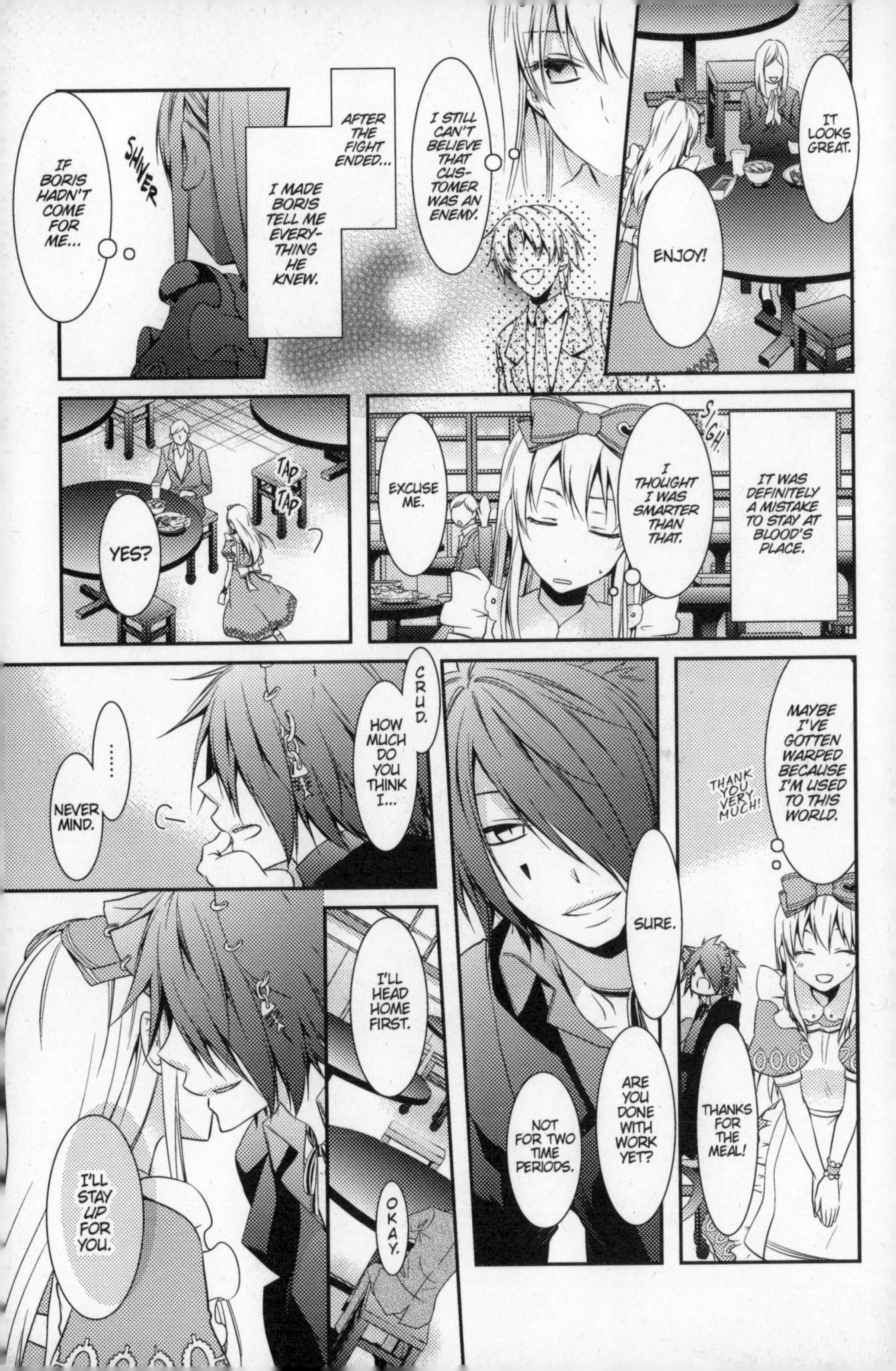
IT LOOKS GREAT.
ENJOY!
I STILL CAN'T BELIEVE THAT CUS-TOMER WAS AN ENEMY.
AFTER THE FIGHT ENDED...
I MADE BORIS TELL ME EVERY-THING HE KNEW.
SHIVER
IF BORIS HADN'T COME FOR ME...
SIGH
IT WAS DEFINITELY A MISTAKE TO STAY AT BLOOD'S PLACE.
I THOUGHT I WAS SMARTER THAN THAT.
EXCUSE ME.
TAP TAP
YES?
MAYBE I'VE GOTTEN WARPED BECAUSE I'M USED TO THIS WORLD.
THANK YOU, VERY MUCH!
THANKS FOR THE MEAL!
SURE.
ARE YOU DONE WITH WORK YET?
NOT FOR TWO TIME PERIODS.
CRUD.
HOW MUCH DO YOU THINK I...
......
NEVER MIND.
I'LL HEAD HOME FIRST.
OKAY.
I'LL STAY UP FOR YOU.

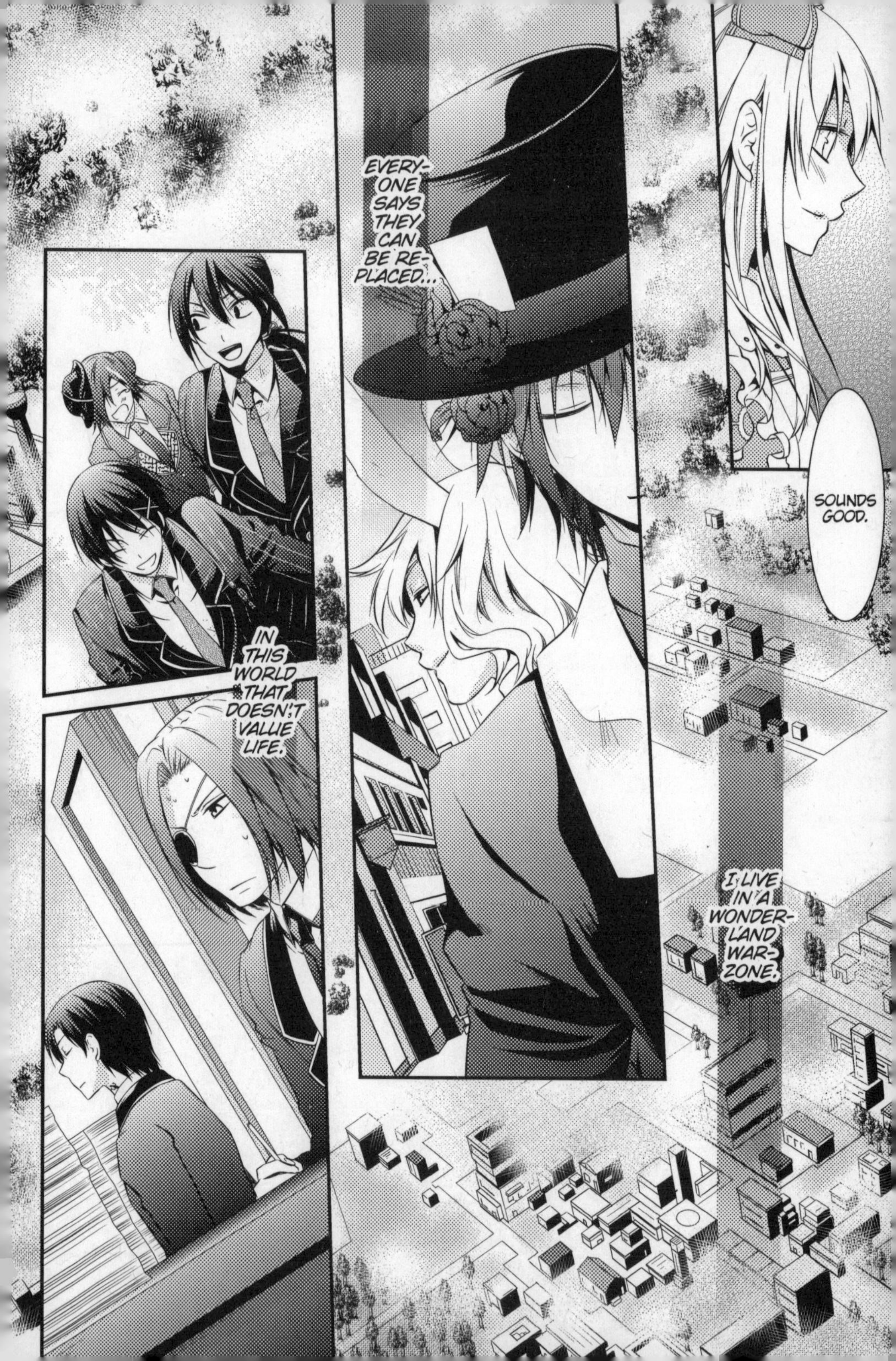
SOUNDS GOOD.
I LIVE IN A WONDER-LAND WAR-ZONE.
EVERY-ONE SAYS THEY CAN BE RE-PLACED...
IN THIS WORLD THAT DOESN'T VALUE LIFE.

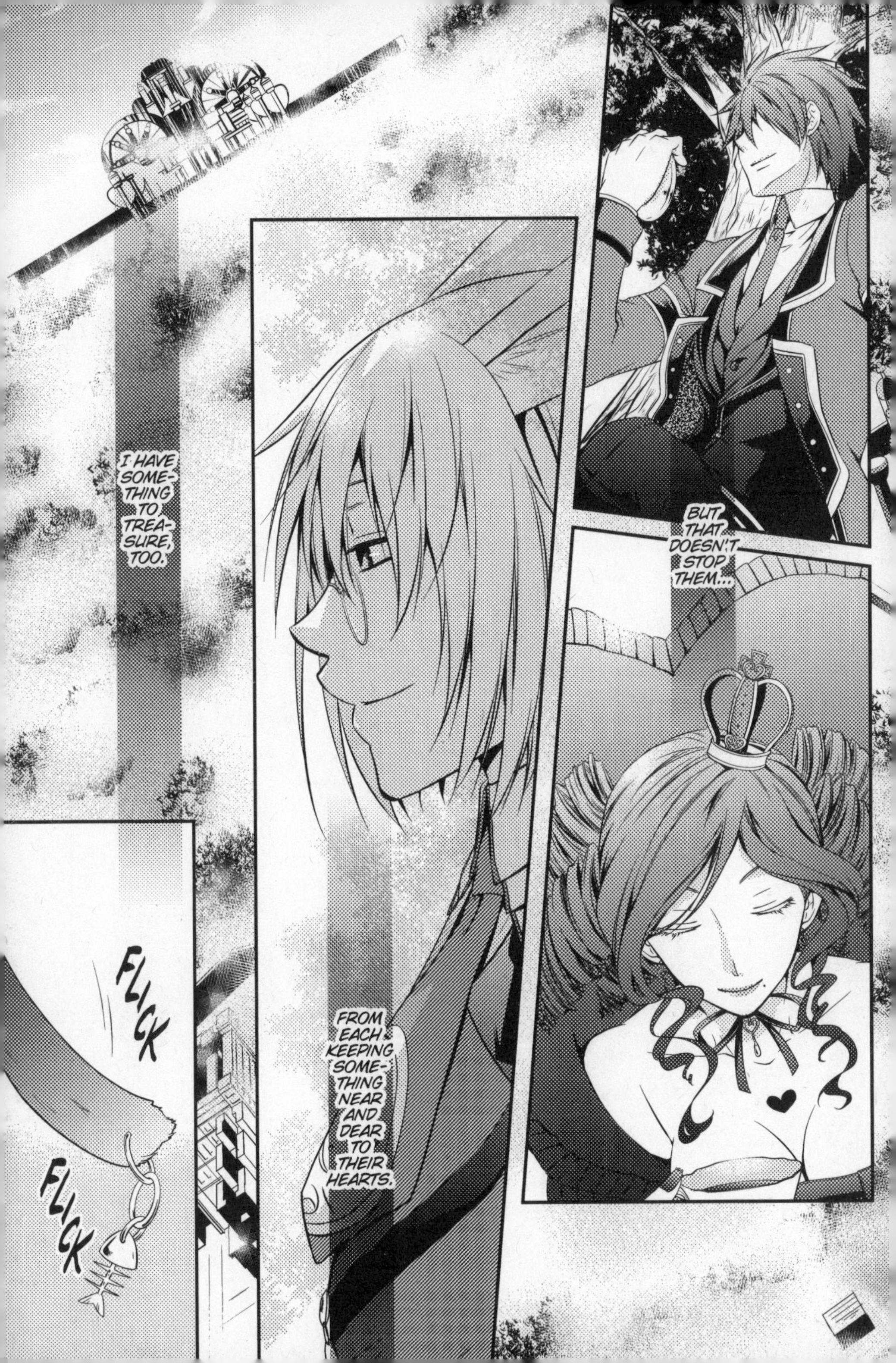
BUT THAT DOESN'T STOP THEM...
FROM EACH KEEPING SOME-THING NEAR AND DEAR TO THEIR HEARTS.
I HAVE SOME-THING TO TREA-SURE, TOO.
FLICK
FLICK

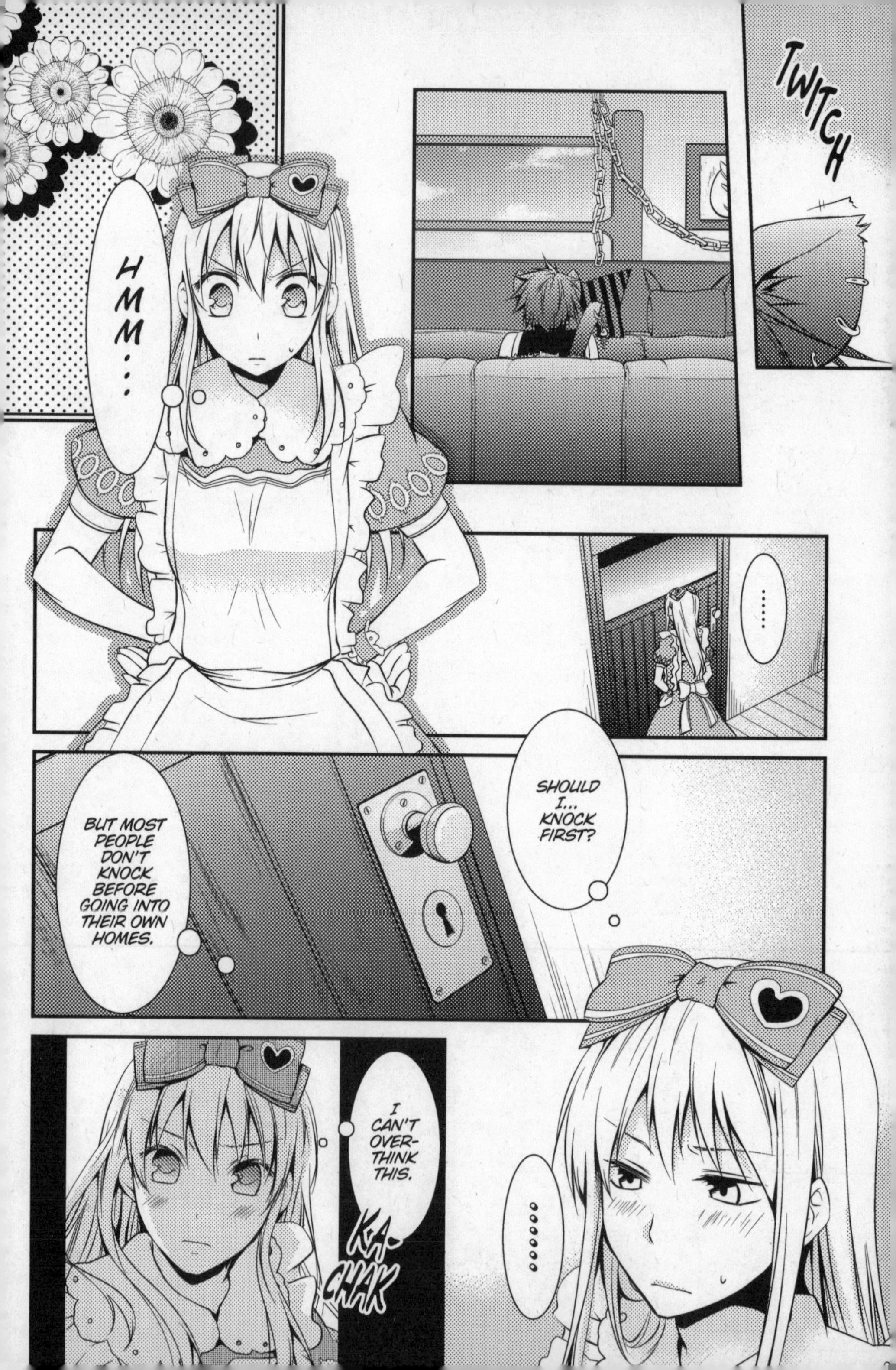
TWITCH
HMM...
......
SHOULD I... KNOCK FIRST?
BUT MOST PEOPLE DON'T KNOCK BEFORE GOING INTO THEIR OWN HOMES.
......
I CAN'T OVER-THINK THIS.
KA-CHAK

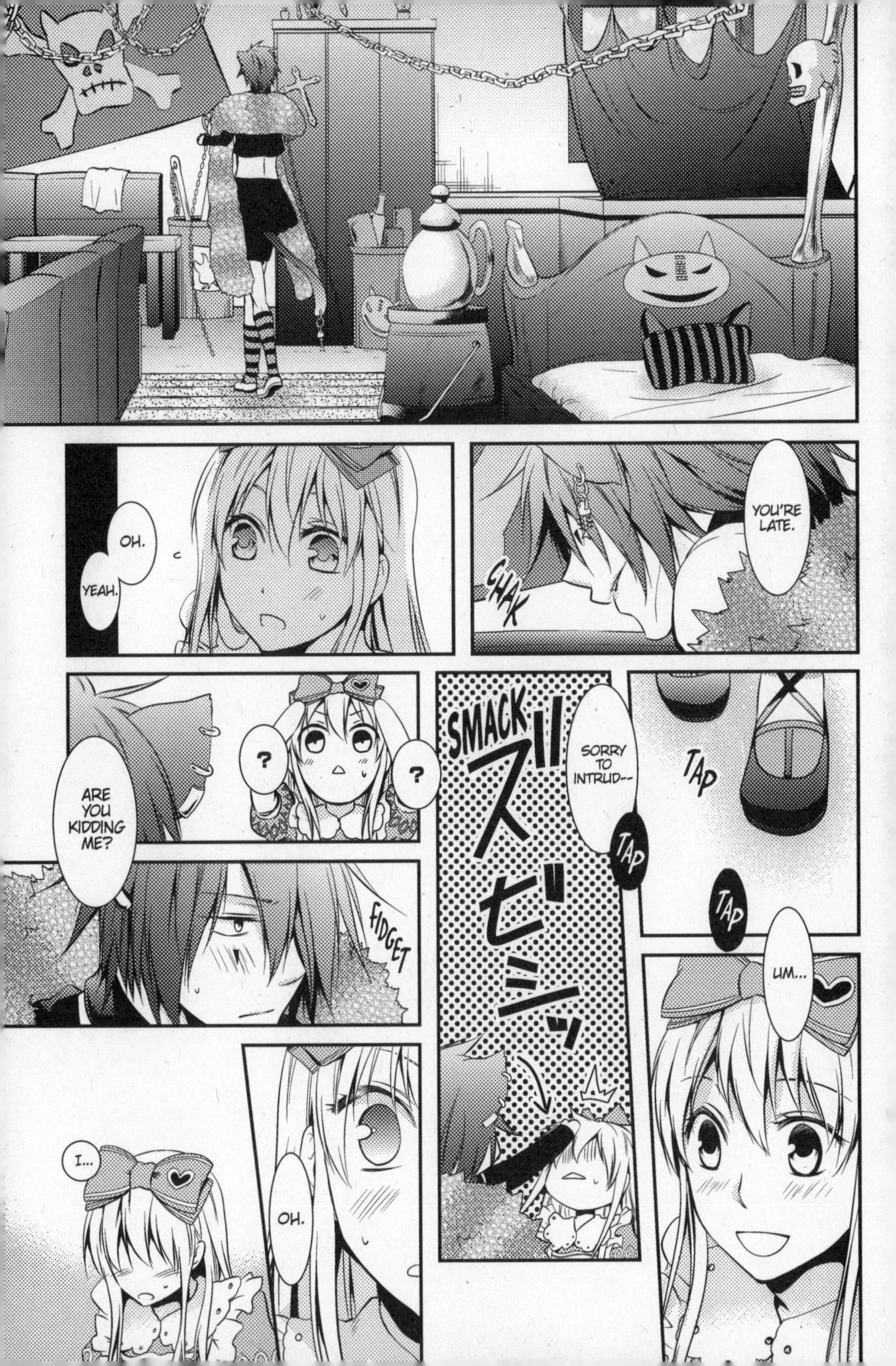

YOU'RE LATE.
CHAK
OH.
YEAH.
TAP
TAP
TAP
UM...
SORRY TO INTRUD--
SMACK
?
?
ARE YOU KIDDING ME?
FIDGET
OH.
I...

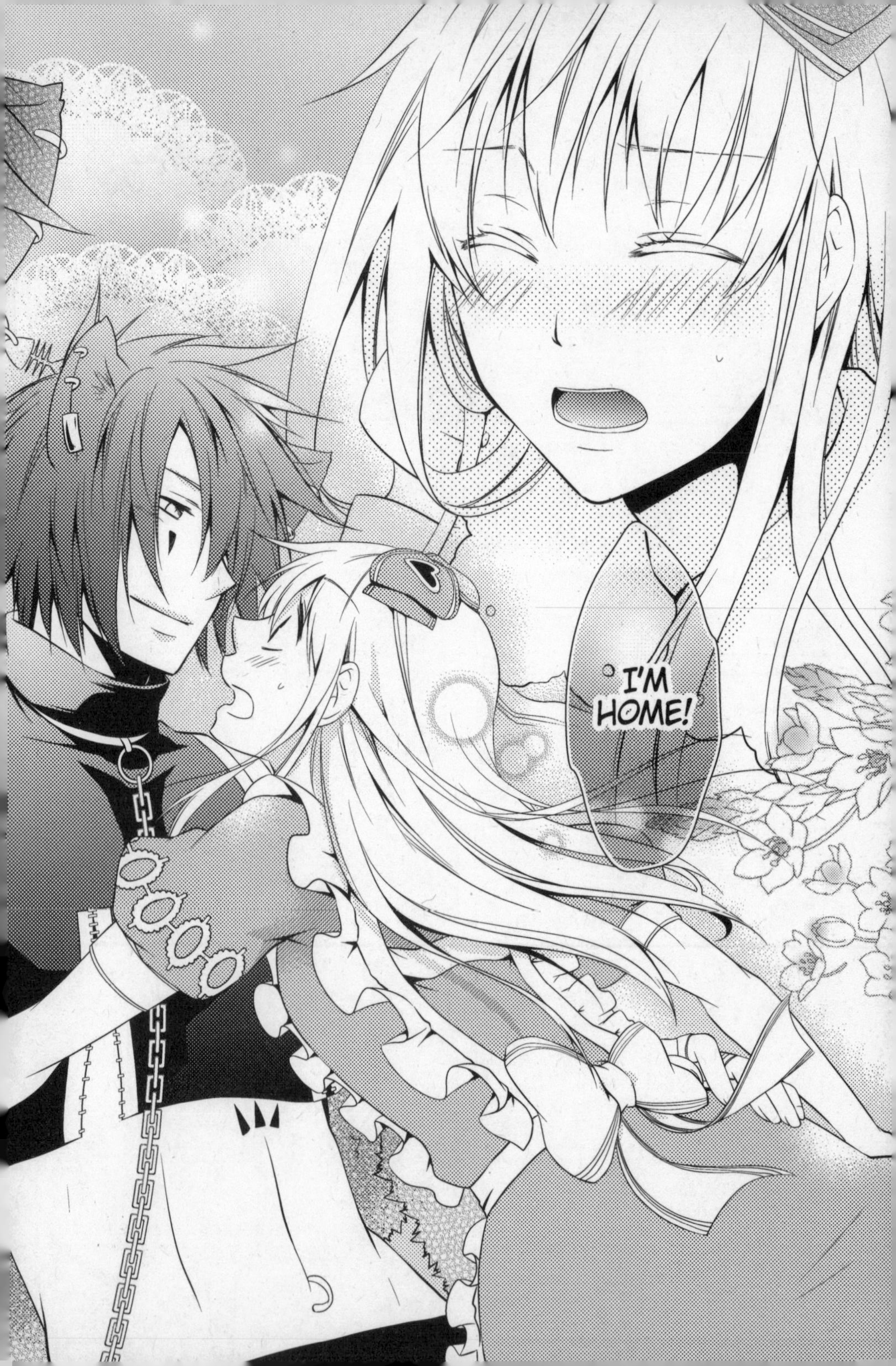
I'M HOME!

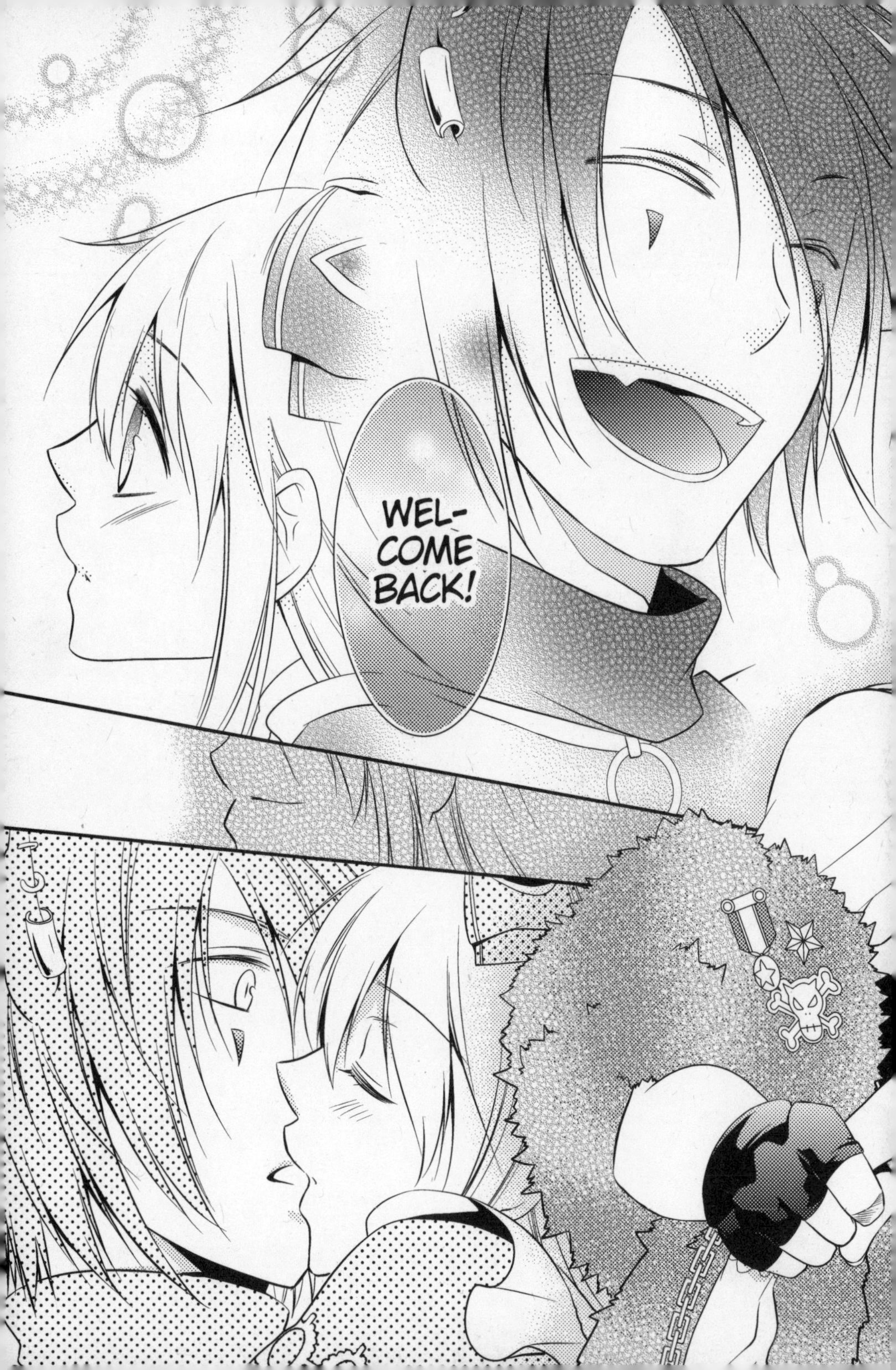
WEL-
COME
BACK!

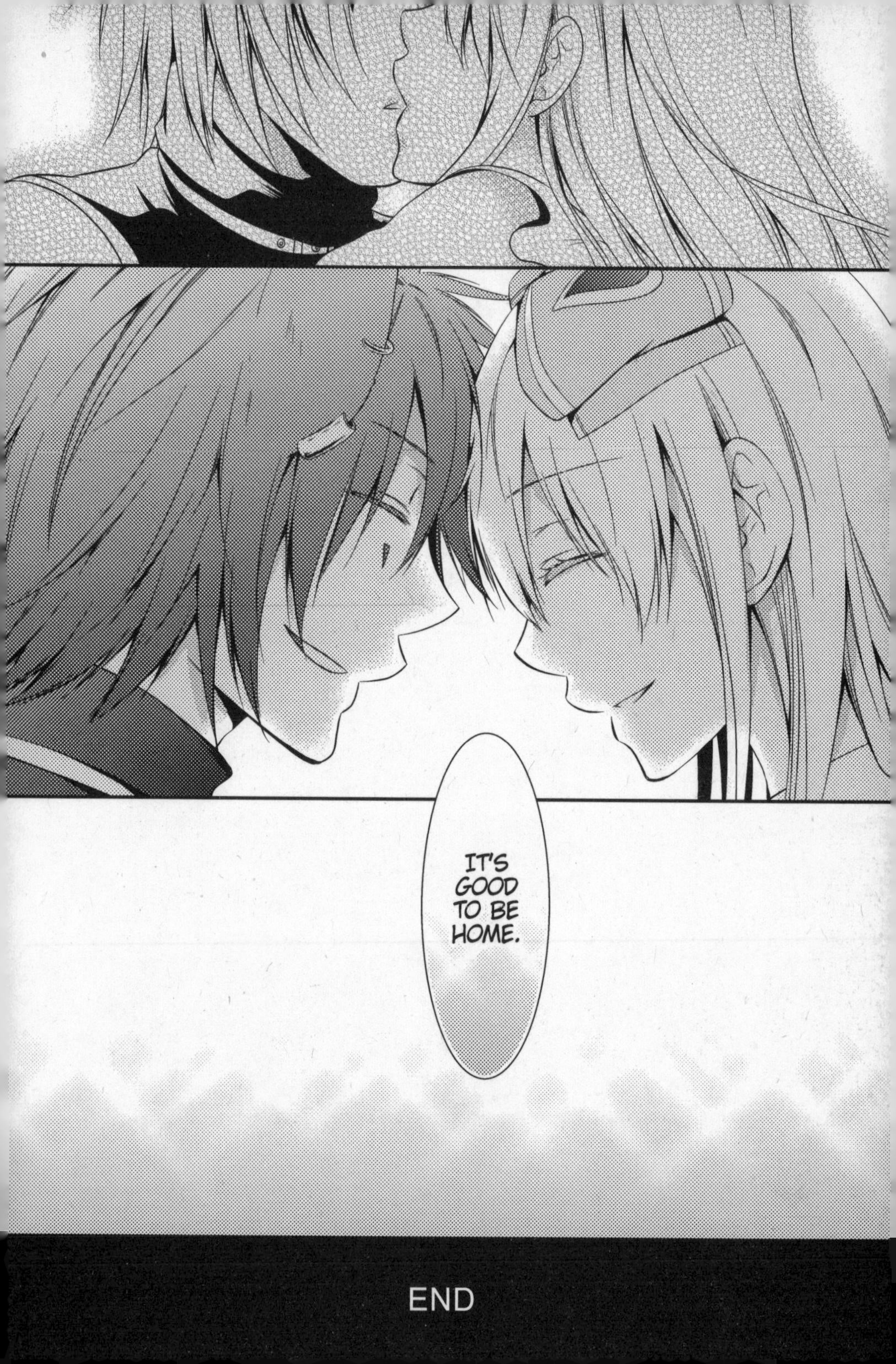
IT'S GOOD TO BE HOME.
END

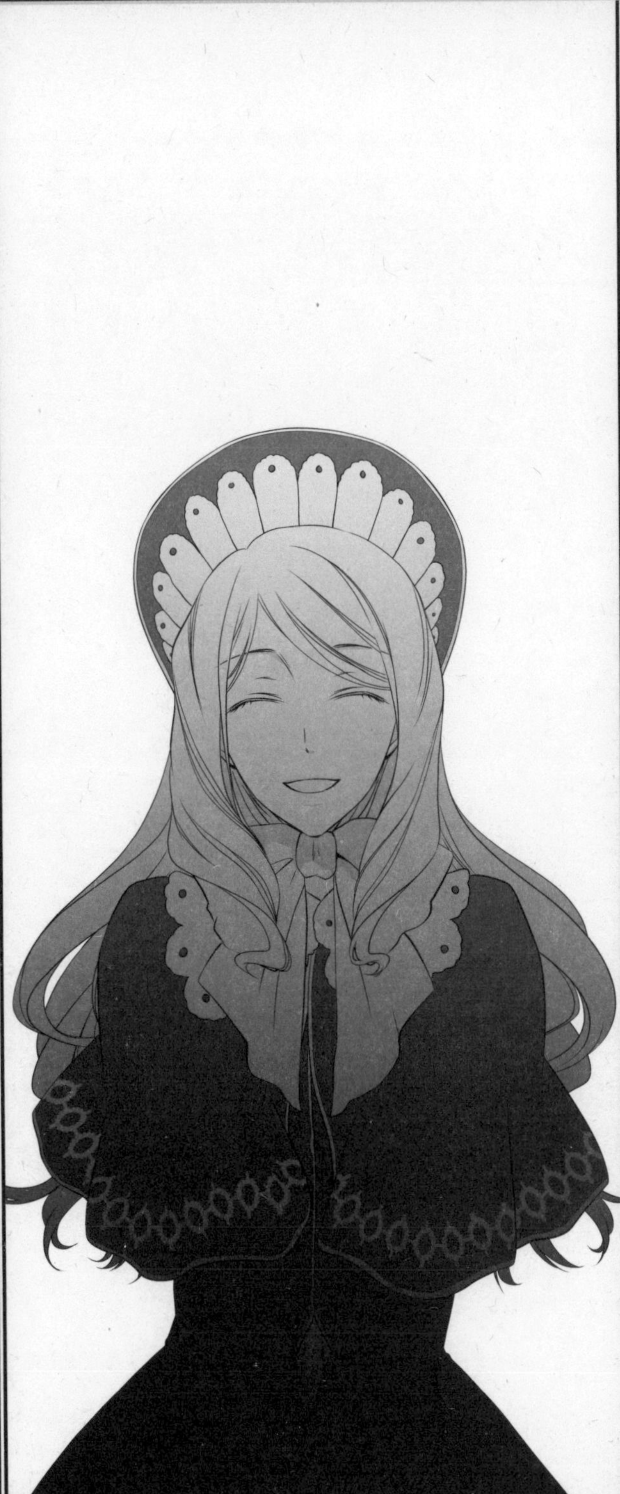

QuinRoseBox

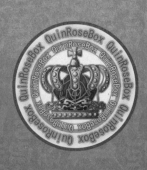

Alice in the Country of Hearts

ハートの国のアリス

~Wonderful Wonder World~

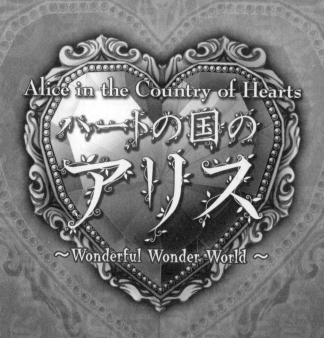

- STORY -

This is a love adventure game. It is based on *Alice in Wonderland,* but evolves into a completely different story.

The main character is far from a romantic. In fact, she's especially sick of love relationships.

She's pulled (against her will) into the dangerous Country of Hearts, which is not as peaceful as the name makes it sound. The Hatters are a mafia family and even the employees of the Amusement Park carry weapons.

The leaders of the three domains are constantly trying to kill each other. Many of the skirmishes are the result of territory grabs by three major powers trying to control more land: the Hatter, the Queen of Hearts, and Gowland.

After drinking some strange medicine (again, against her will), the main character is unable to return to her world. She quickly decides that she's trapped in a dream and allows herself to enjoy(?) the extraordinary experience she's been thrown into.

What territory will she stay with and who will she interact with to get herself home?
And will this girl, so jaded about love, fall into a relationship she doesn't expect?

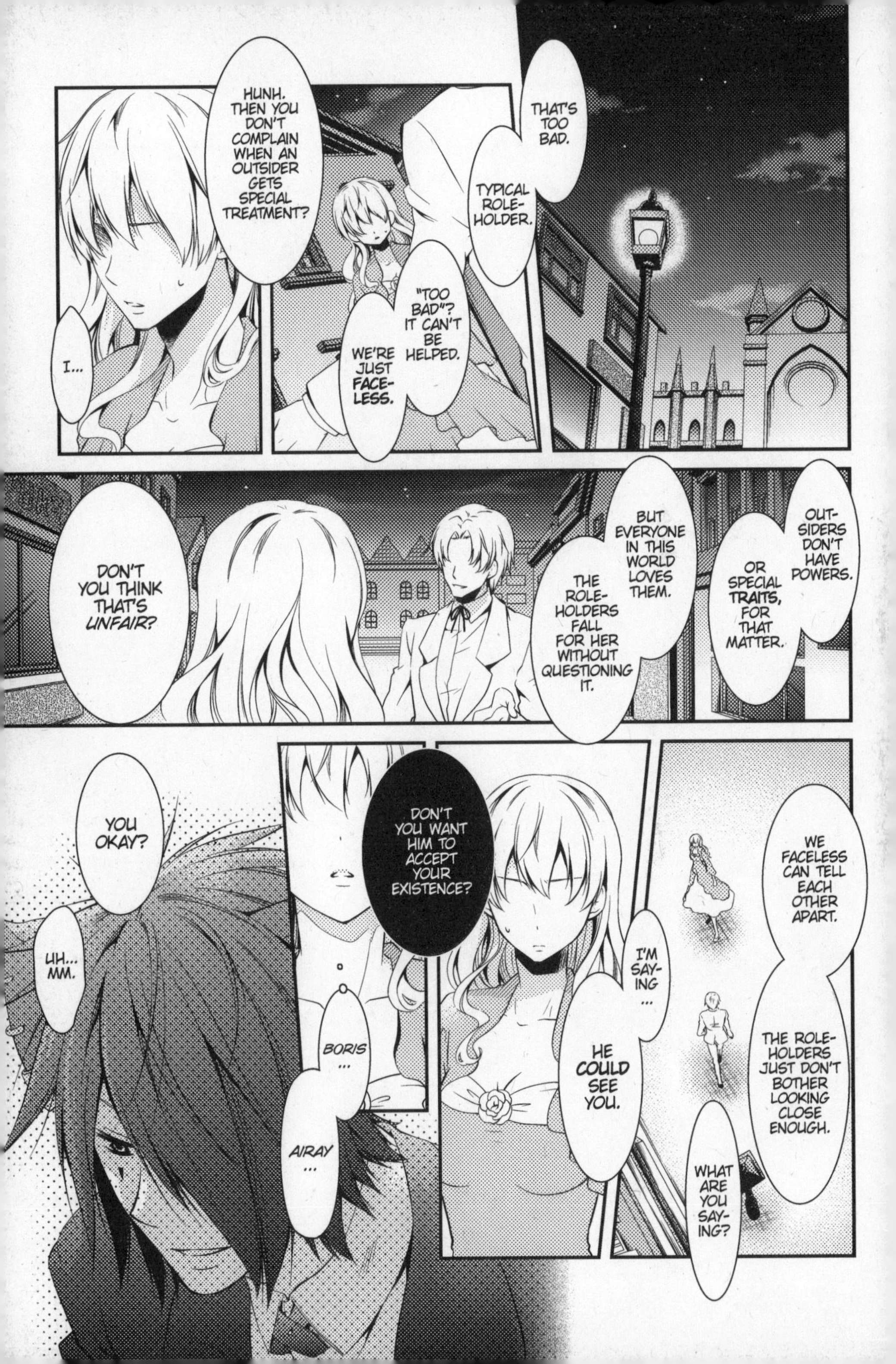
THAT'S TOO BAD.
TYPICAL ROLE-HOLDER.
HUNH. THEN YOU DON'T COMPLAIN WHEN AN OUTSIDER GETS SPECIAL TREATMENT?
"TOO BAD"? IT CAN'T BE HELPED.
WE'RE JUST **FACELESS.**
I...
OUTSIDERS DON'T HAVE POWERS.
OR SPECIAL **TRAITS,** FOR THAT MATTER.
BUT EVERYONE IN THIS WORLD LOVES THEM.
THE ROLE-HOLDERS FALL FOR HER WITHOUT QUESTIONING IT.
DON'T YOU THINK THAT'S *UNFAIR?*
WE FACELESS CAN TELL EACH OTHER APART.
THE ROLE-HOLDERS JUST DON'T BOTHER LOOKING CLOSE ENOUGH.
WHAT ARE YOU SAYING?
I'M SAYING...
HE **COULD** SEE YOU.
DON'T YOU WANT HIM TO ACCEPT YOUR EXISTENCE?
YOU OKAY?
UH... MM.
BORIS...
AIRAY...

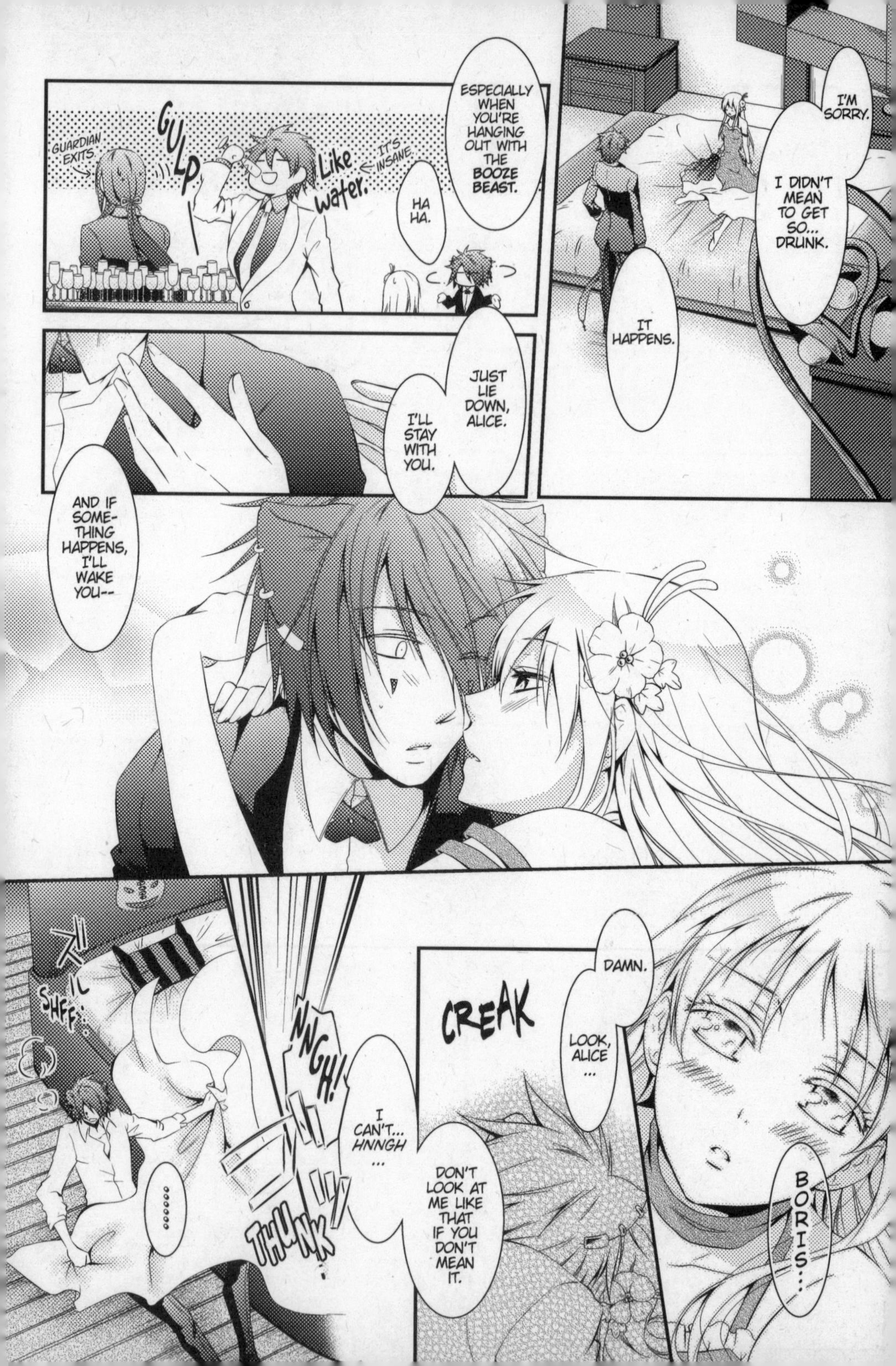

I'M SORRY.
I DIDN'T MEAN TO GET SO... DRUNK.
IT HAPPENS.
ESPECIALLY WHEN YOU'RE HANGING OUT WITH THE BOOZE BEAST.
HA HA.
IT'S INSANE
Like water.
GULP
GUARDIAN EXITS.
JUST LIE DOWN, ALICE.
I'LL STAY WITH YOU.
AND IF SOMETHING HAPPENS, I'LL WAKE YOU--
DAMN.
BORIS...
LOOK, ALICE...
CREAK
DON'T LOOK AT ME LIKE THAT IF YOU DON'T MEAN IT.
I CAN'T... HNNGH...
HNNGH!
THUNK
SHFF
.....

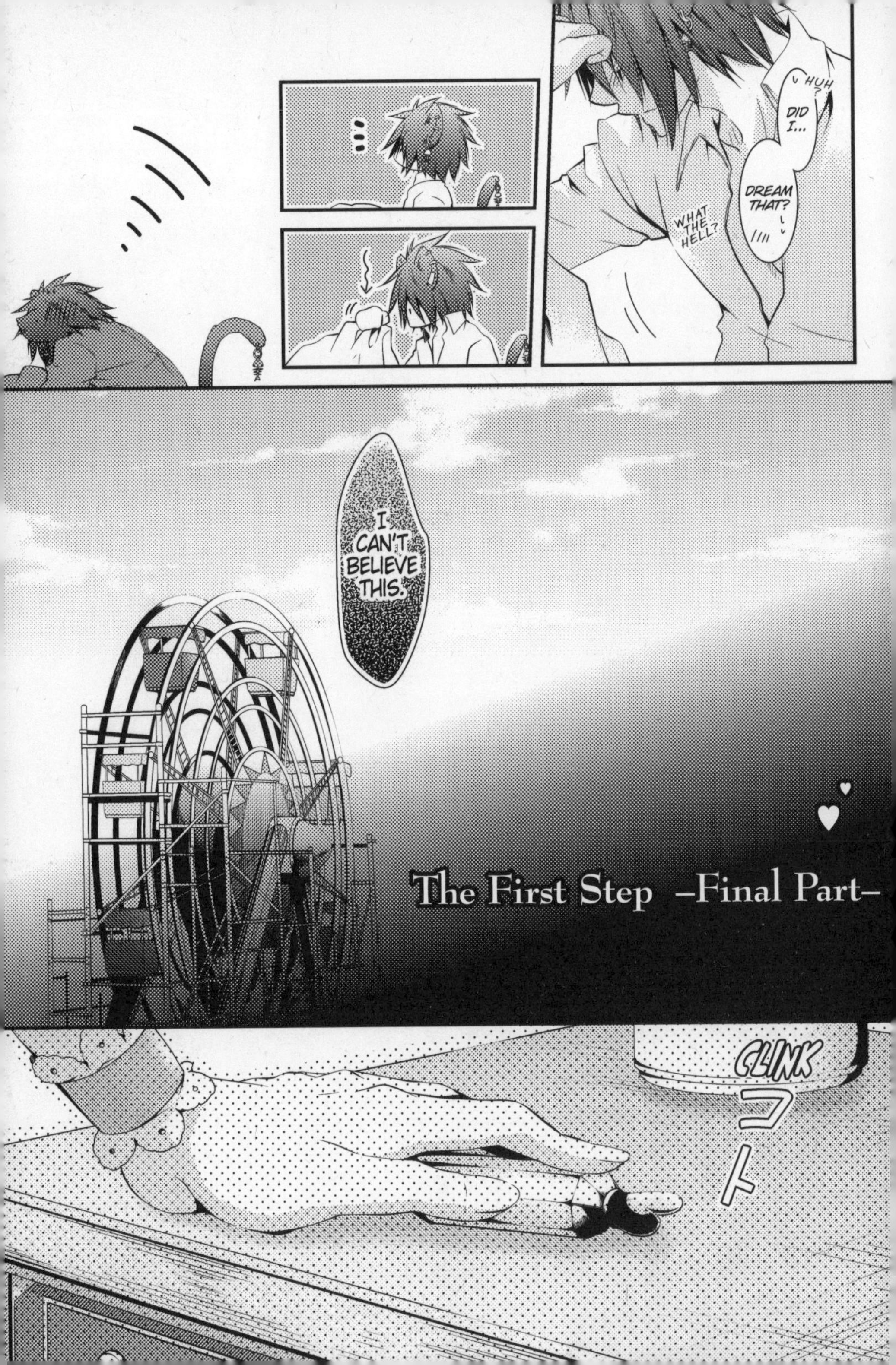
HUH?
DID I...
DREAM THAT?
WHAT THE HELL?
...
I CAN'T BELIEVE THIS.
The First Step –Final Part–
CLINK
コト

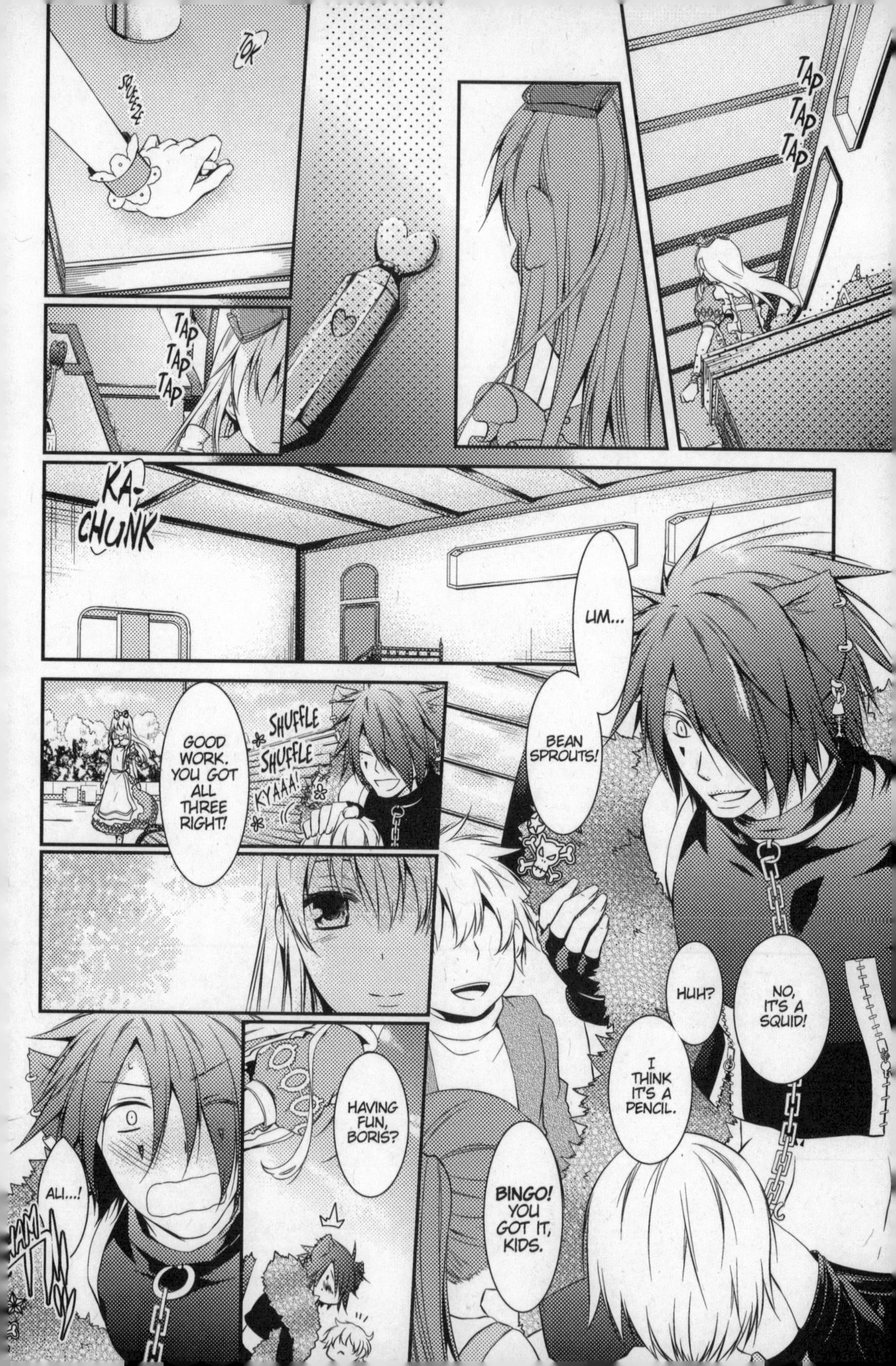
TAP
TAP
TAP
TOK
SQUEEZE
TAP
TAP
TAP
KA-CHUNK
UM...
BEAN SPROUTS!
GOOD WORK. YOU GOT ALL THREE RIGHT!
SHUFFLE
SHUFFLE
KYAAA!
NO, IT'S A SQUID!
HUH?
I THINK IT'S A PENCIL.
BINGO! YOU GOT IT, KIDS.
HAVING FUN, BORIS?
ALI...!

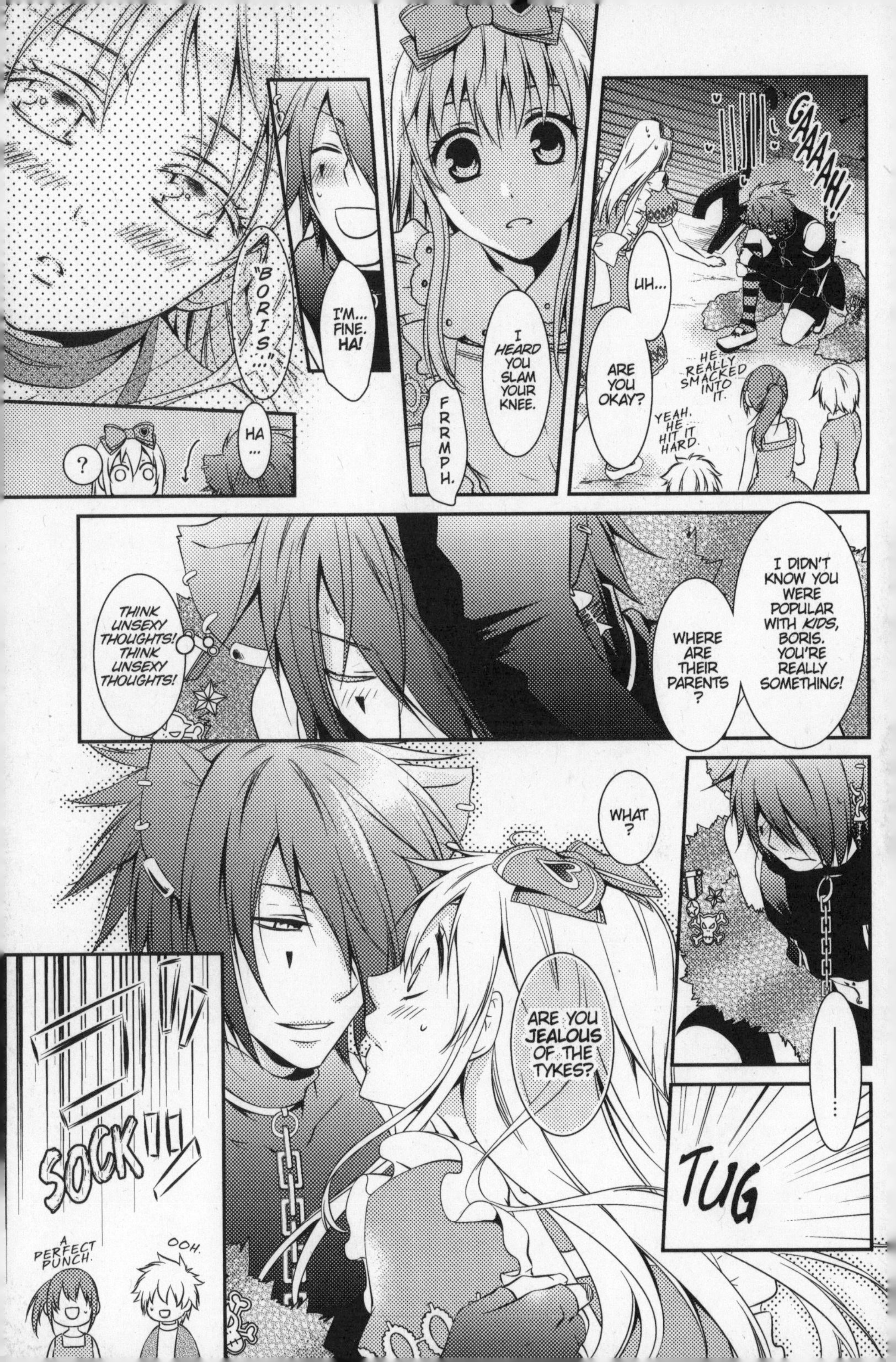
GAAAAH!
UH... ARE YOU OKAY?
HE REALLY SMACKED INTO IT.
YEAH, HE HIT IT HARD.
I HEARD YOU SLAM YOUR KNEE.
FRRMPH.
I'M... FINE. HA!
"BORIS..."
HA...
?
I DIDN'T KNOW YOU WERE POPULAR WITH KIDS, BORIS. YOU'RE REALLY SOMETHING!
WHERE ARE THEIR PARENTS?
THINK UNSEXY THOUGHTS! THINK UNSEXY THOUGHTS!
...
TUG
WHAT?
ARE YOU JEALOUS OF THE TYKES?
SOCK!!
OOH.
A PERFECT PUNCH.

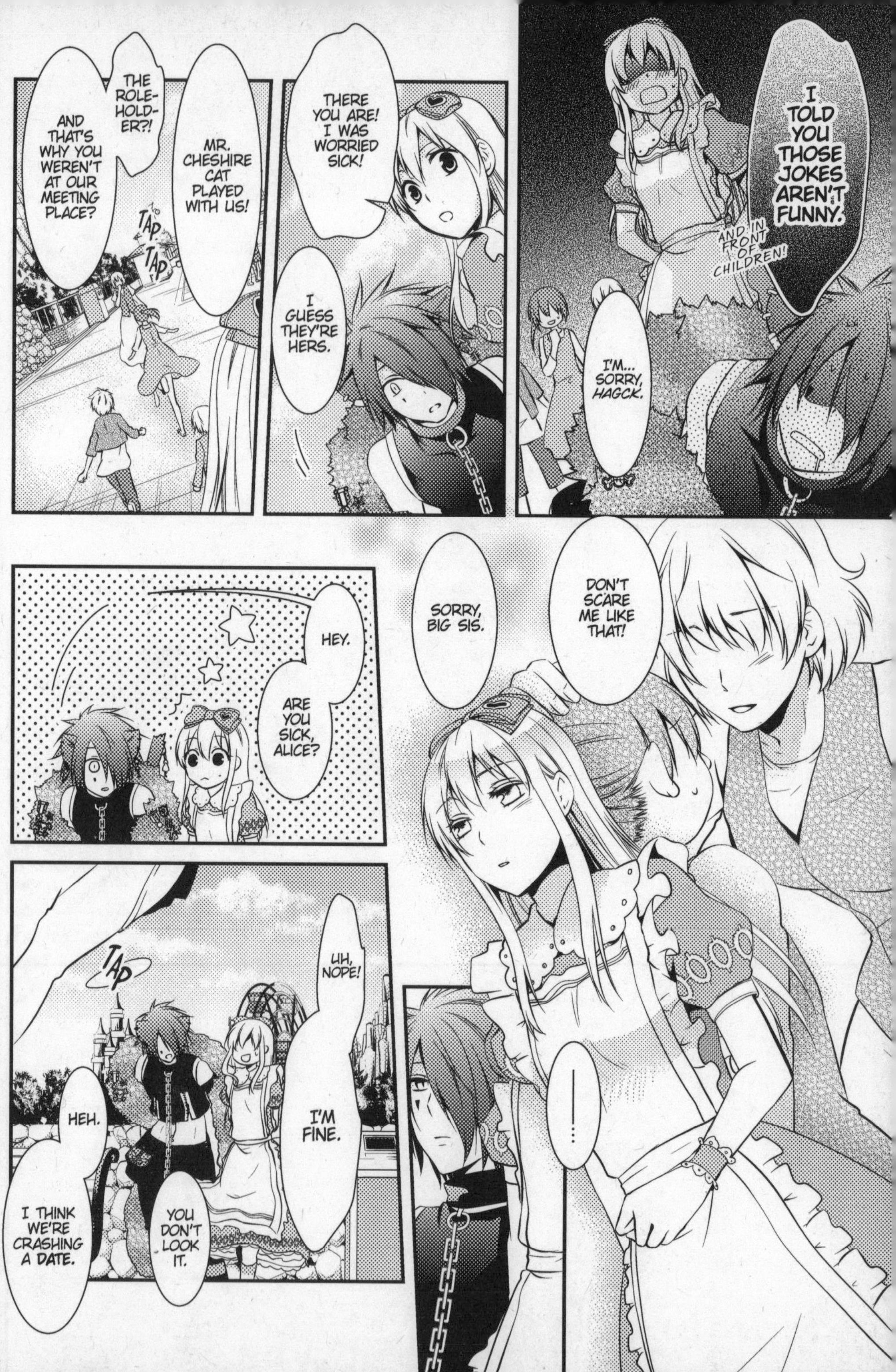

I TOLD YOU THOSE JOKES AREN'T FUNNY.
AND IN FRONT OF CHILDREN!
I'M... SORRY, HAGCK.
THERE YOU ARE! I WAS WORRIED SICK!
I GUESS THEY'RE HERS.
MR. CHESHIRE CAT PLAYED WITH US!
THE ROLE-HOLDER?!
AND THAT'S WHY YOU WEREN'T AT OUR MEETING PLACE?
TAP TAP
DON'T SCARE ME LIKE THAT!
SORRY, BIG SIS.
......
HEY.
ARE YOU SICK, ALICE?
TAP
UH, NOPE!
I'M FINE.
HEH.
YOU DON'T LOOK IT.
I THINK WE'RE CRASHING A DATE.

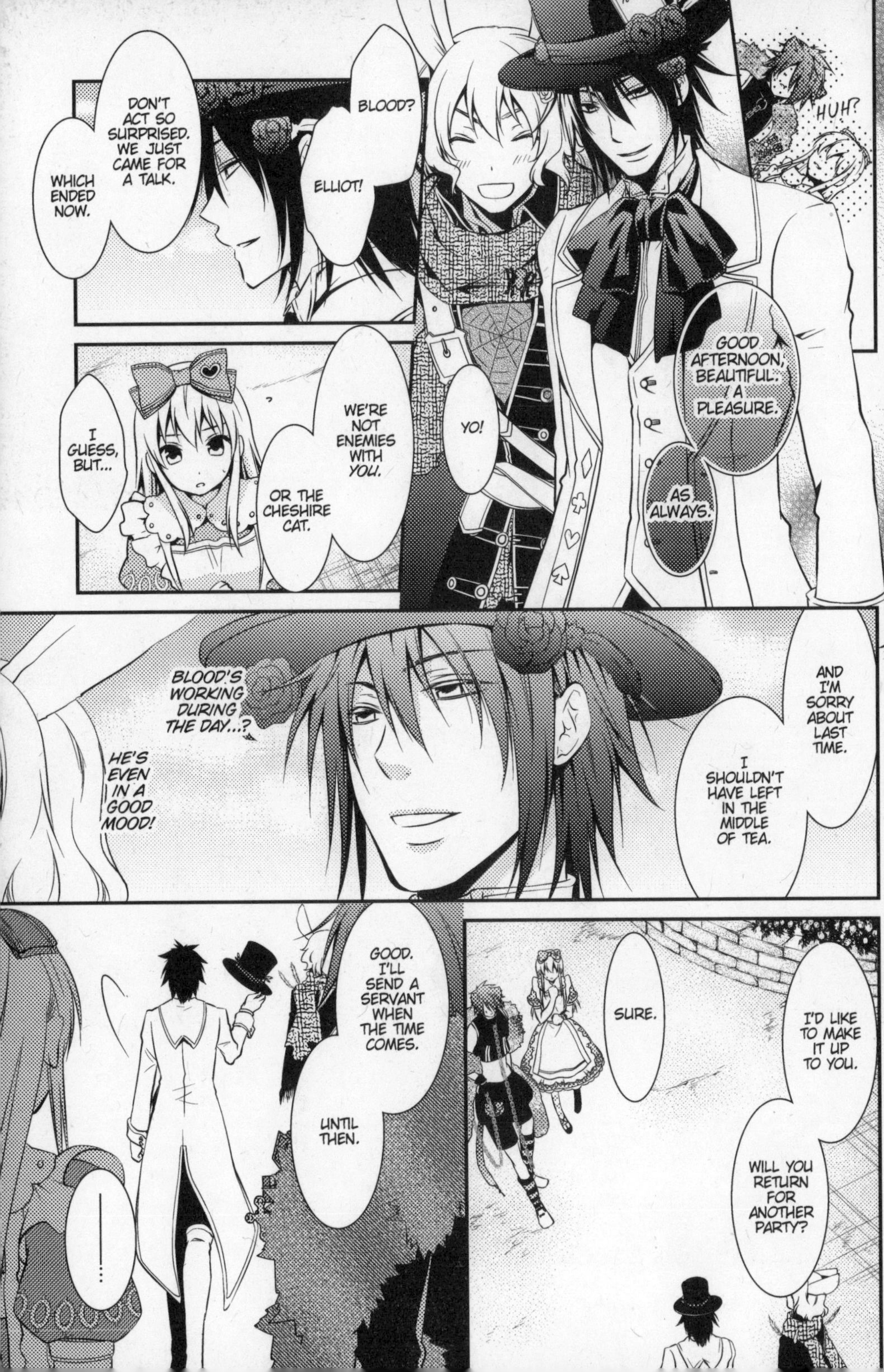
HUH?
BLOOD?
ELLIOT!
GOOD AFTERNOON, BEAUTIFUL. A PLEASURE.
AS ALWAYS.
YO!
DON'T ACT SO SURPRISED. WE JUST CAME FOR A TALK.
WHICH ENDED NOW.
WE'RE NOT ENEMIES WITH *YOU*.
OR THE CHESHIRE CAT.
I GUESS, BUT...
AND I'M SORRY ABOUT LAST TIME.
I SHOULDN'T HAVE LEFT IN THE MIDDLE OF TEA.
BLOOD'S WORKING DURING THE DAY...?
HE'S EVEN IN A GOOD MOOD!
I'D LIKE TO MAKE IT UP TO YOU.
WILL YOU RETURN FOR ANOTHER PARTY?
SURE.
GOOD. I'LL SEND A SERVANT WHEN THE TIME COMES.
UNTIL THEN.
......

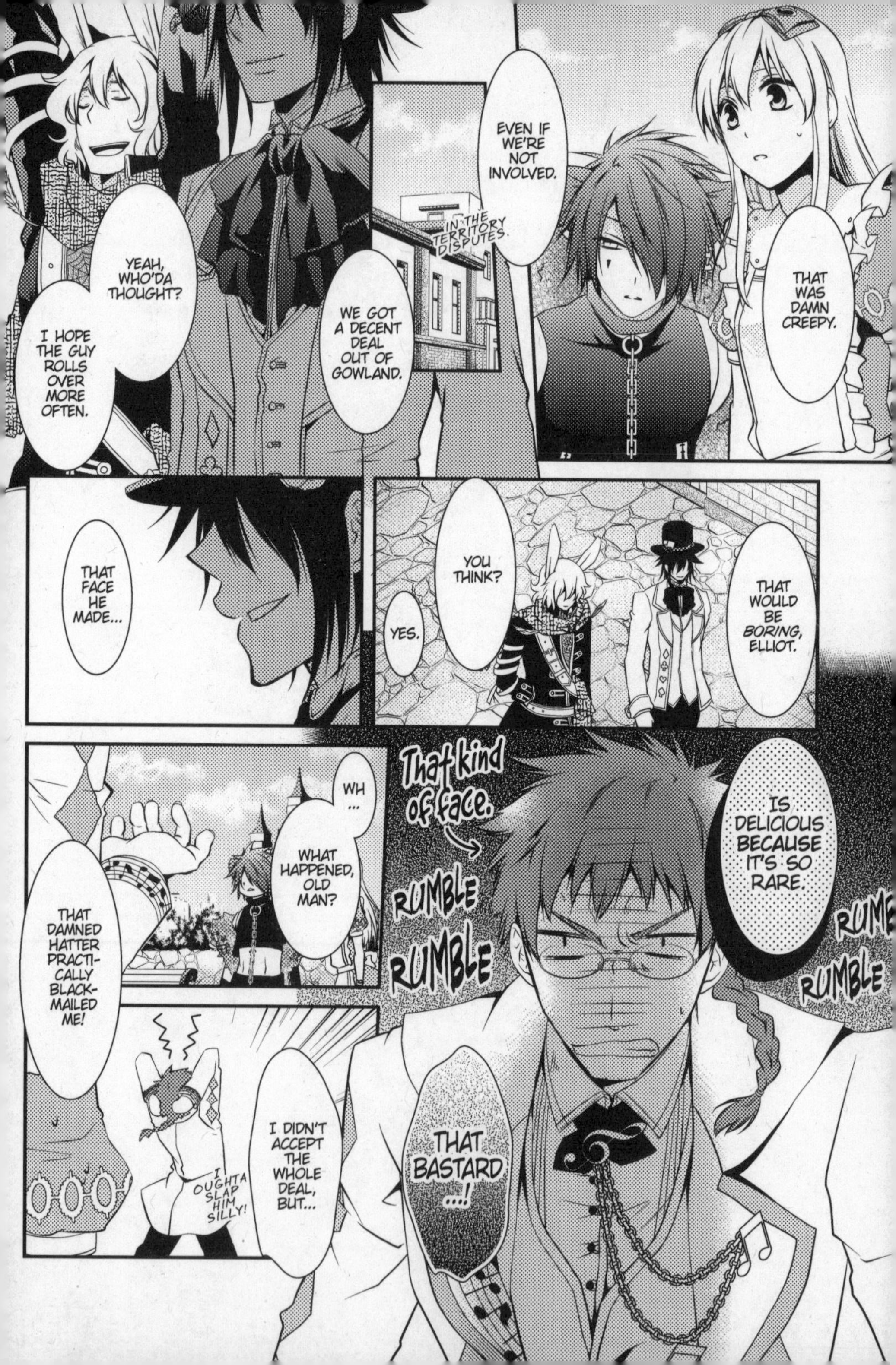
THAT WAS DAMN CREEPY.
EVEN IF WE'RE NOT INVOLVED.
IN THE TERRITORY DISPUTES.
WE GOT A DECENT DEAL OUT OF GOWLAND.
YEAH, WHO'DA THOUGHT?
I HOPE THE GUY ROLLS OVER MORE OFTEN.
THAT WOULD BE BORING, ELLIOT.
YOU THINK?
YES.
THAT FACE HE MADE...
That kind of face.
IS DELICIOUS BECAUSE IT'S SO RARE.
RUMBLE
RUMBLE
RUMB
RUMBLE
WH...
WHAT HAPPENED, OLD MAN?
THAT DAMNED HATTER PRACTICALLY BLACKMAILED ME!
I DIDN'T ACCEPT THE WHOLE DEAL, BUT...
I OUGHTA SLAP HIM SILLY!
THAT BASTARD...!

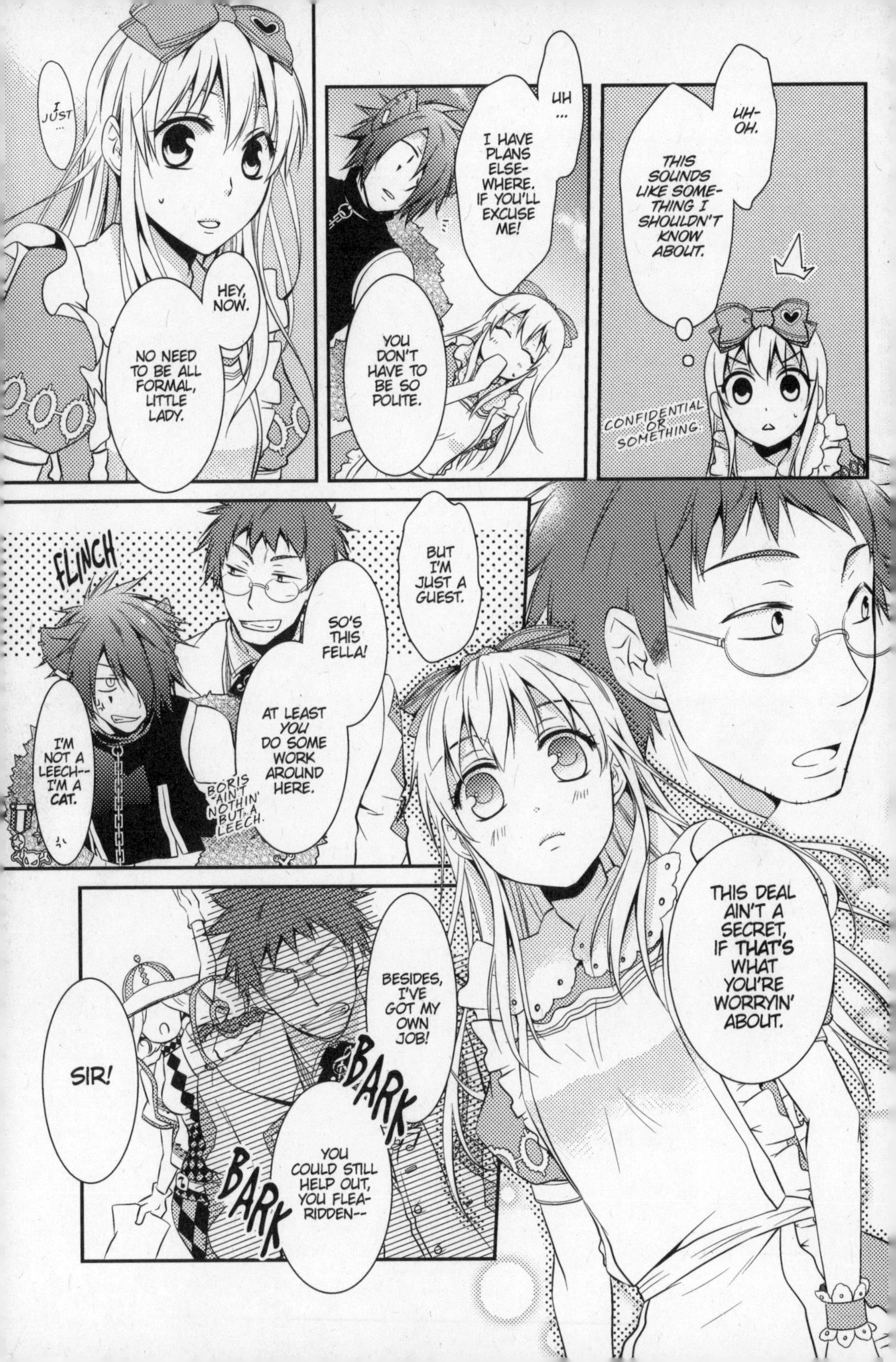
UH-OH.
THIS SOUNDS LIKE SOME-THING I SHOULDN'T KNOW ABOUT.
CONFIDENTIAL OR SOMETHING.
UH ...
I HAVE PLANS ELSE-WHERE. IF YOU'LL EXCUSE ME!
YOU DON'T HAVE TO BE SO POLITE.
I JUST ...
HEY, NOW.
NO NEED TO BE ALL FORMAL, LITTLE LADY.
THIS DEAL AIN'T A SECRET, IF THAT'S WHAT YOU'RE WORRYIN' ABOUT.
BUT I'M JUST A GUEST.
SO'S THIS FELLA!
AT LEAST YOU DO SOME WORK AROUND HERE.
BORIS AIN'T NOTHIN' BUT A LEECH.
FLINCH
I'M NOT A LEECH-- I'M A CAT.
BESIDES, I'VE GOT MY OWN JOB!
BARK
BARK
YOU COULD STILL HELP OUT, YOU FLEA-RIDDEN--
SIR!

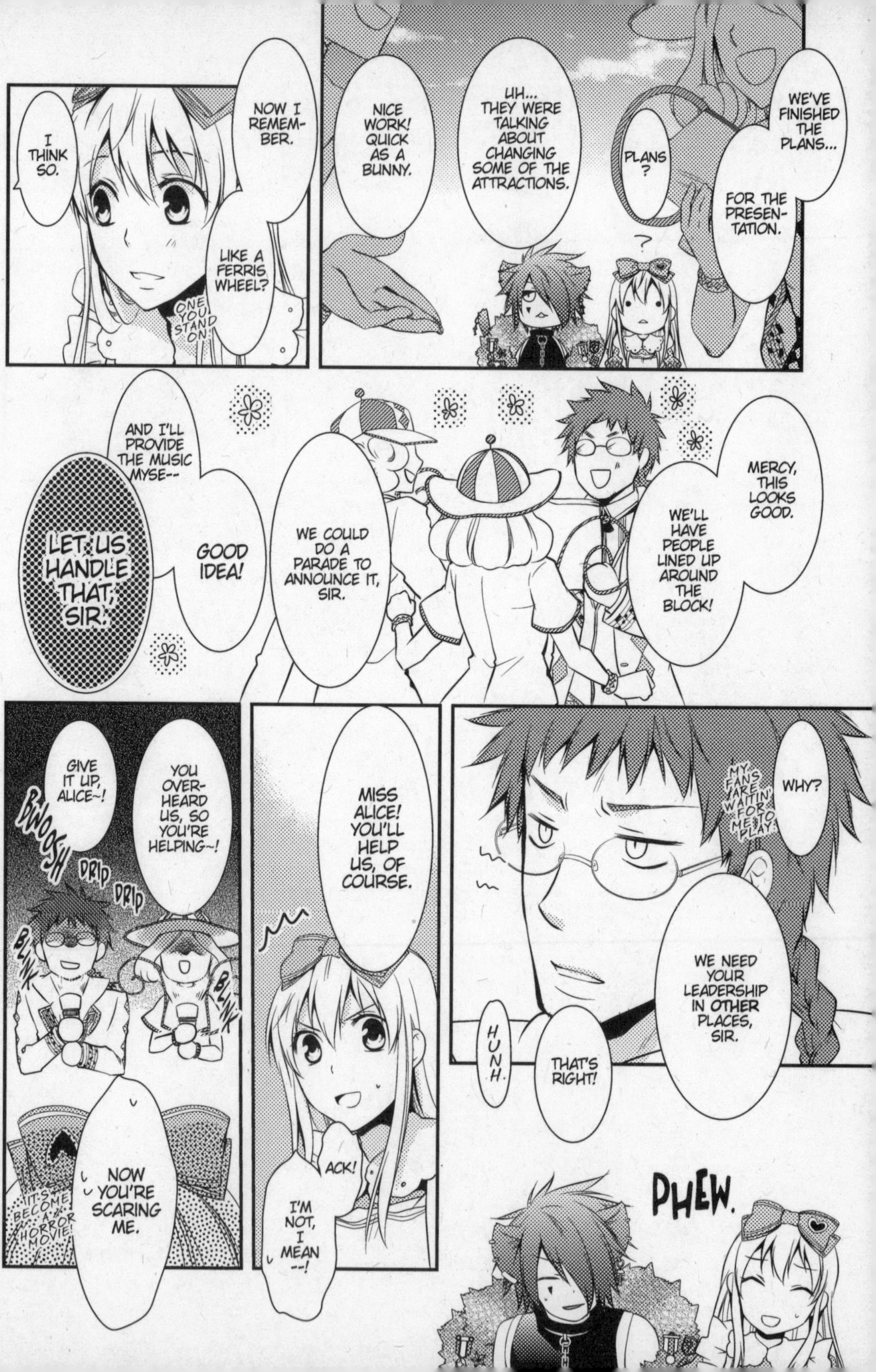
WE'VE FINISHED THE PLANS...
FOR THE PRESENTATION.
PLANS?
UH... THEY WERE TALKING ABOUT CHANGING SOME OF THE ATTRACTIONS.
NICE WORK! QUICK AS A BUNNY.
NOW I REMEMBER.
LIKE A FERRIS WHEEL?
ONE YOU STAND ON!
I THINK SO.
MERCY, THIS LOOKS GOOD.
WE'LL HAVE PEOPLE LINED UP AROUND THE BLOCK!
WE COULD DO A PARADE TO ANNOUNCE IT, SIR.
GOOD IDEA!
AND I'LL PROVIDE THE MUSIC MYSE--
LET US HANDLE THAT, SIR.
WHY?
MY FANS ARE WAITIN' FOR ME TO PLAY!
WE NEED YOUR LEADERSHIP IN OTHER PLACES, SIR.
THAT'S RIGHT!
HUNH.
PHEW.
MISS ALICE! YOU'LL HELP US, OF COURSE.
ACK!
I'M NOT, I MEAN --!
YOU OVERHEARD US, SO YOU'RE HELPING~!
GIVE IT UP, ALICE~!
BWOOSH
DRIP
DRIP
BLINK
BLINK
NOW YOU'RE SCARING ME.
IT'S BECOME A HORROR MOVIE!

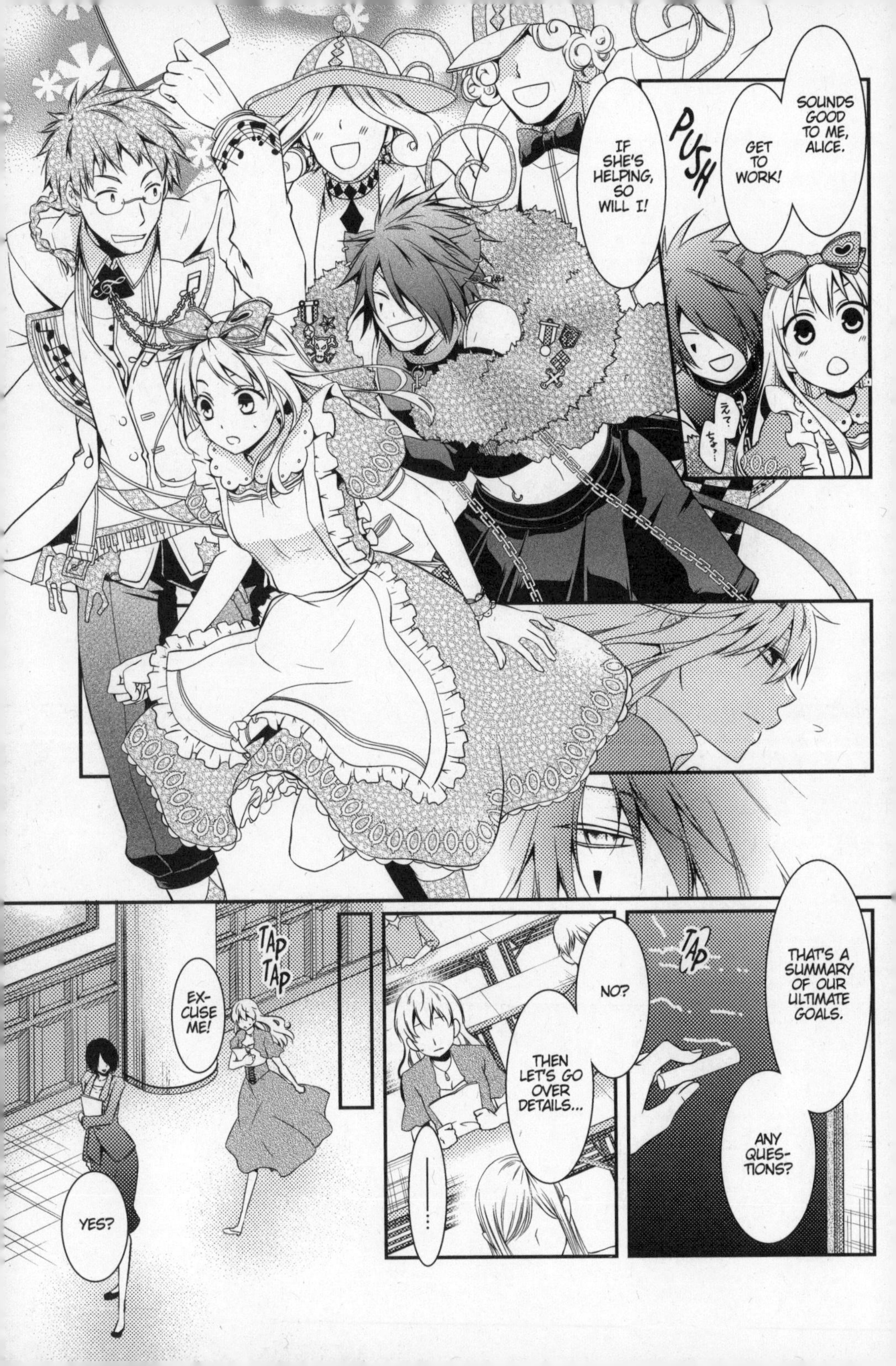
SOUNDS GOOD TO ME, ALICE.
GET TO WORK!
PUSH
IF SHE'S HELPING, SO WILL I!
えて・ちょっ…
THAT'S A SUMMARY OF OUR ULTIMATE GOALS.
TAP
ANY QUES-TIONS?
NO?
THEN LET'S GO OVER DETAILS...
......
TAP TAP
EX-CUSE ME!
YES?

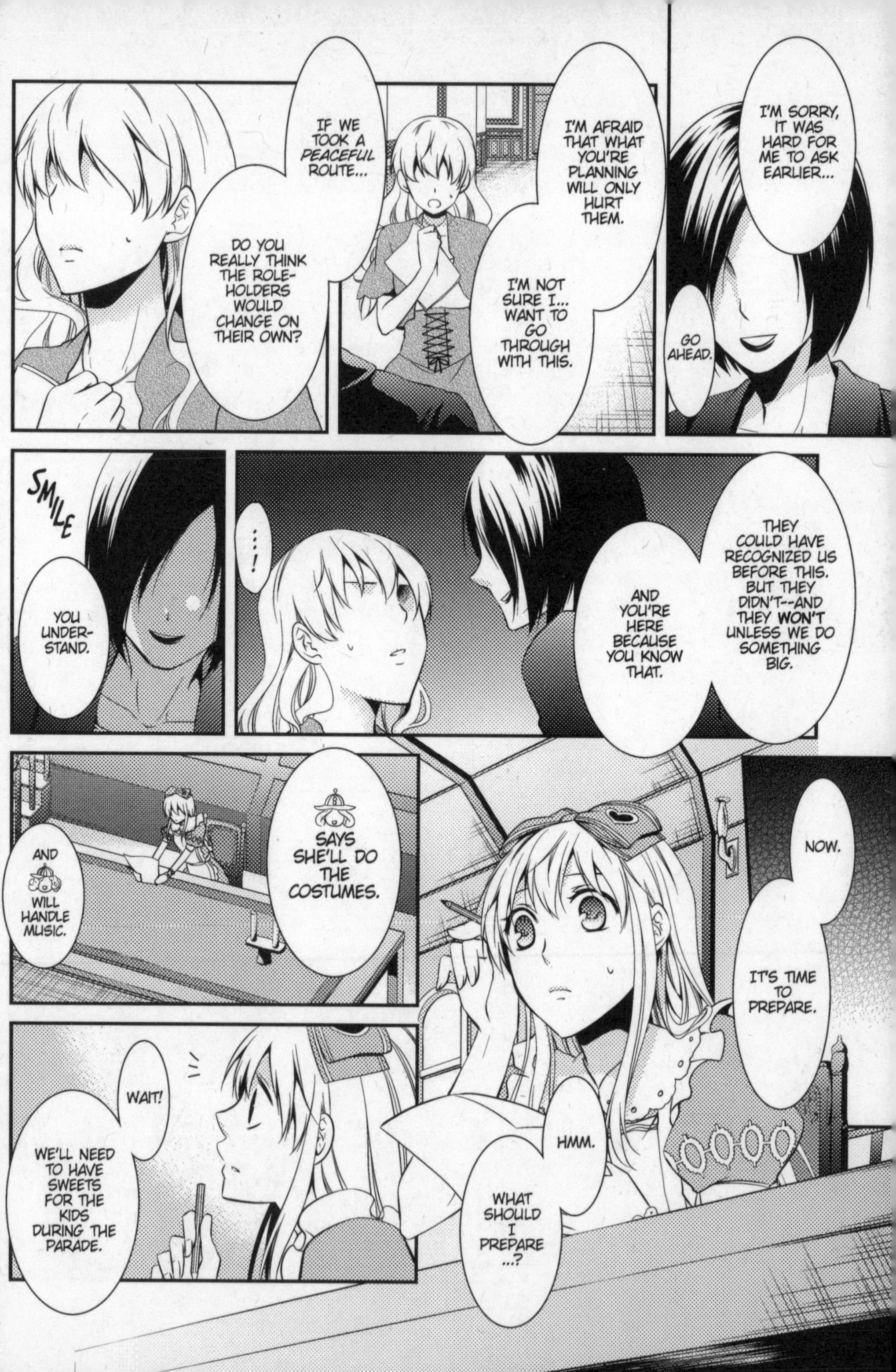
I'M SORRY, IT WAS HARD FOR ME TO ASK EARLIER...
GO AHEAD.
I'M AFRAID THAT WHAT YOU'RE PLANNING WILL ONLY HURT THEM.
I'M NOT SURE I... WANT TO GO THROUGH WITH THIS.
IF WE TOOK A *PEACEFUL* ROUTE...
DO YOU REALLY THINK THE ROLE-HOLDERS WOULD CHANGE ON THEIR OWN?
THEY COULD HAVE RECOGNIZED US BEFORE THIS. BUT THEY DIDN'T--AND THEY **WON'T** UNLESS WE DO SOMETHING BIG.
AND YOU'RE HERE BECAUSE YOU KNOW THAT.
...!
SMILE
YOU UNDER-STAND.
NOW.
IT'S TIME TO PREPARE.
SAYS SHE'LL DO THE COSTUMES.
AND WILL HANDLE MUSIC.
HMM.
WHAT SHOULD I PREPARE ...?
WAIT!
WE'LL NEED TO HAVE SWEETS FOR THE KIDS DURING THE PARADE.

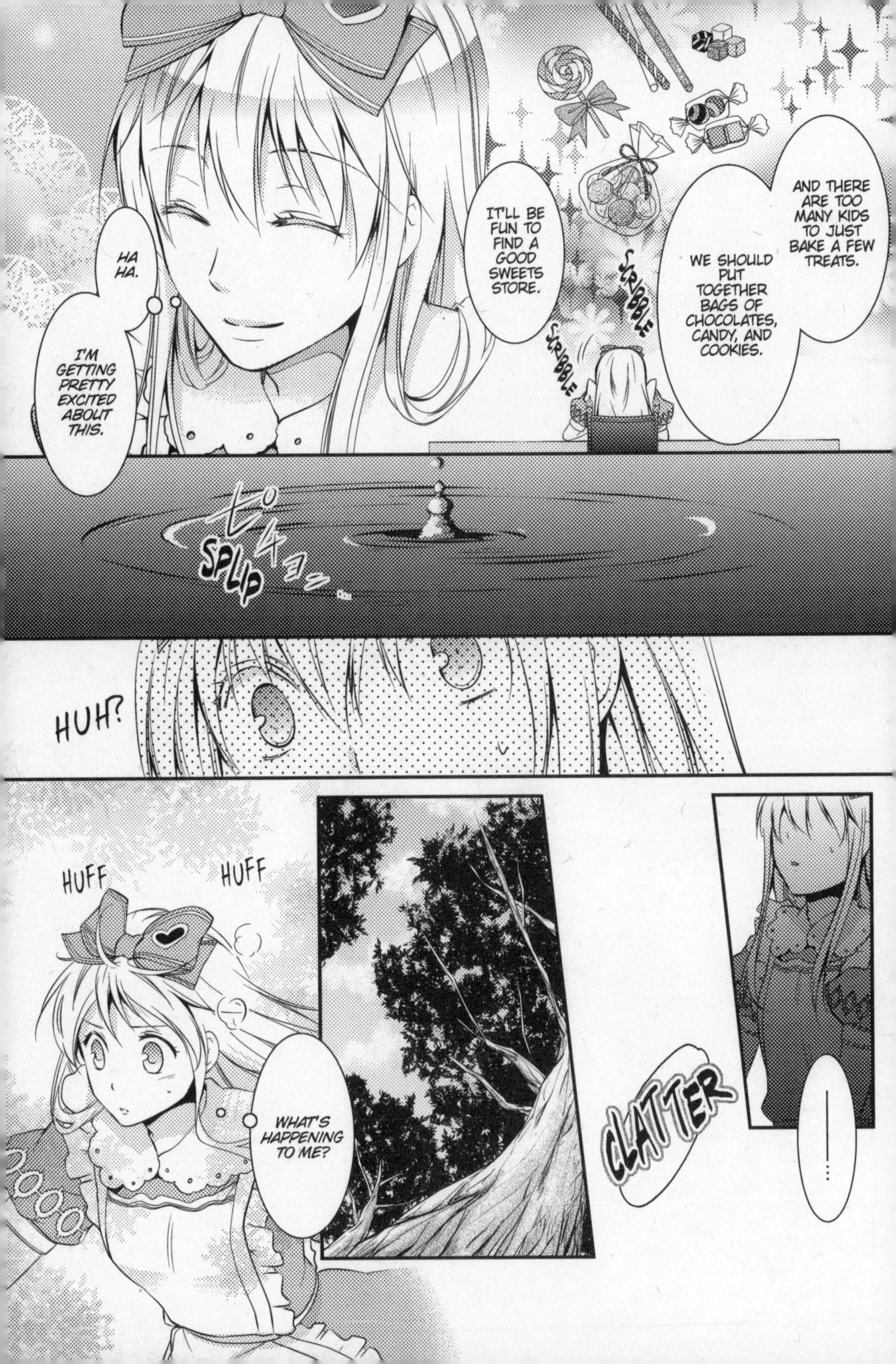
AND THERE ARE TOO MANY KIDS TO JUST BAKE A FEW TREATS.
WE SHOULD PUT TOGETHER BAGS OF CHOCOLATES, CANDY, AND COOKIES.
SCRIBBLE
SCRIBBLE
IT'LL BE FUN TO FIND A GOOD SWEETS STORE.
HA HA.
I'M GETTING PRETTY EXCITED ABOUT THIS.
SPLIP
HUH?
......
CLATTER
HUFF
HUFF
WHAT'S HAPPENING TO ME?

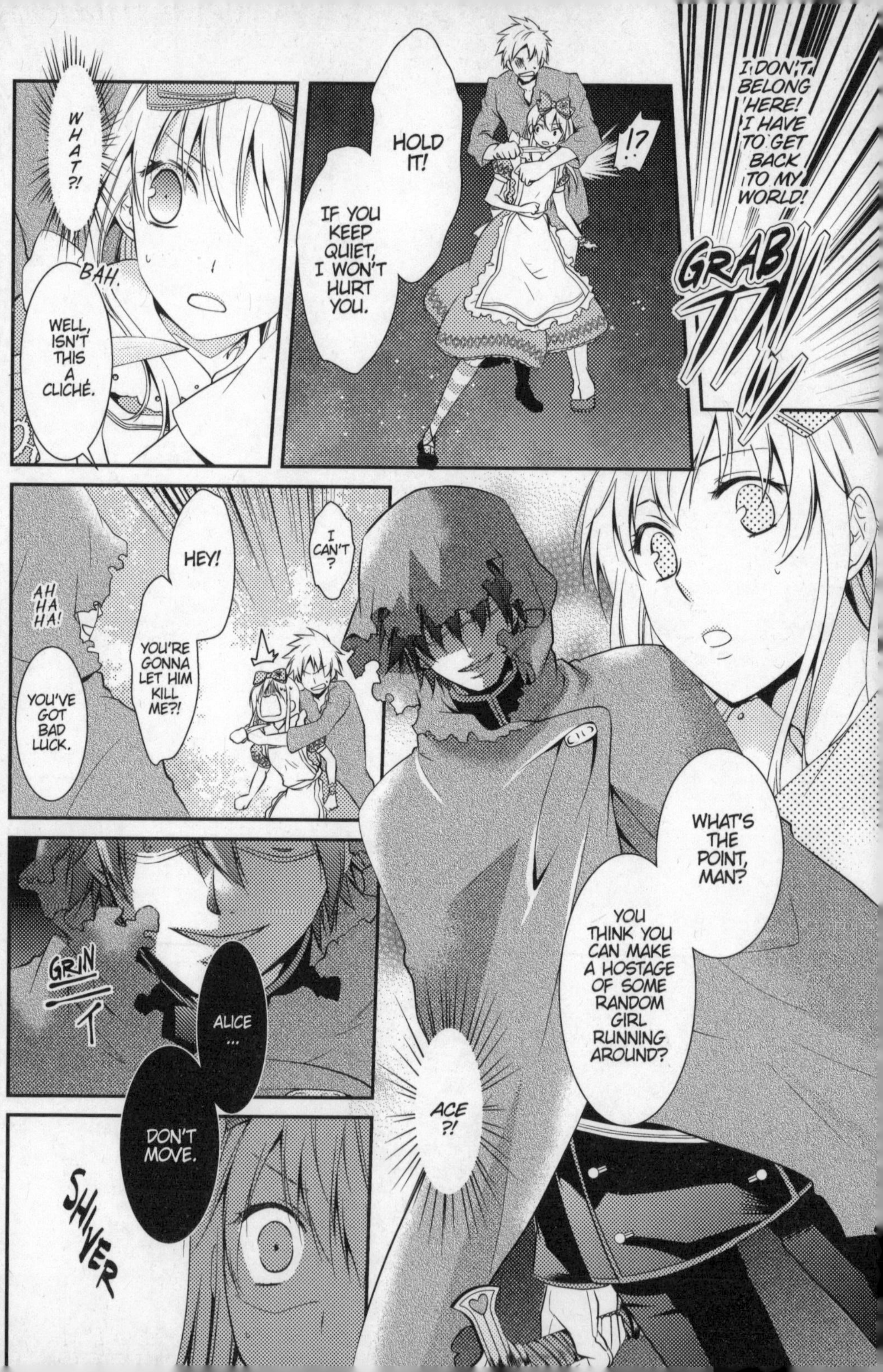
I DON'T BELONG HERE! I HAVE TO GET BACK TO MY WORLD!
GRAB
!?
HOLD IT!
IF YOU KEEP QUIET, I WON'T HURT YOU.
WHAT?!
BAH.
WELL, ISN'T THIS A CLICHÉ.
WHAT'S THE POINT, MAN?
YOU THINK YOU CAN MAKE A HOSTAGE OF SOME RANDOM GIRL RUNNING AROUND?
ACE?!
I CAN'T?
HEY!
YOU'RE GONNA LET HIM KILL ME?!
AH HA HA!
YOU'VE GOT BAD LUCK.
GRIN
ALICE...
DON'T MOVE.
SHIVER

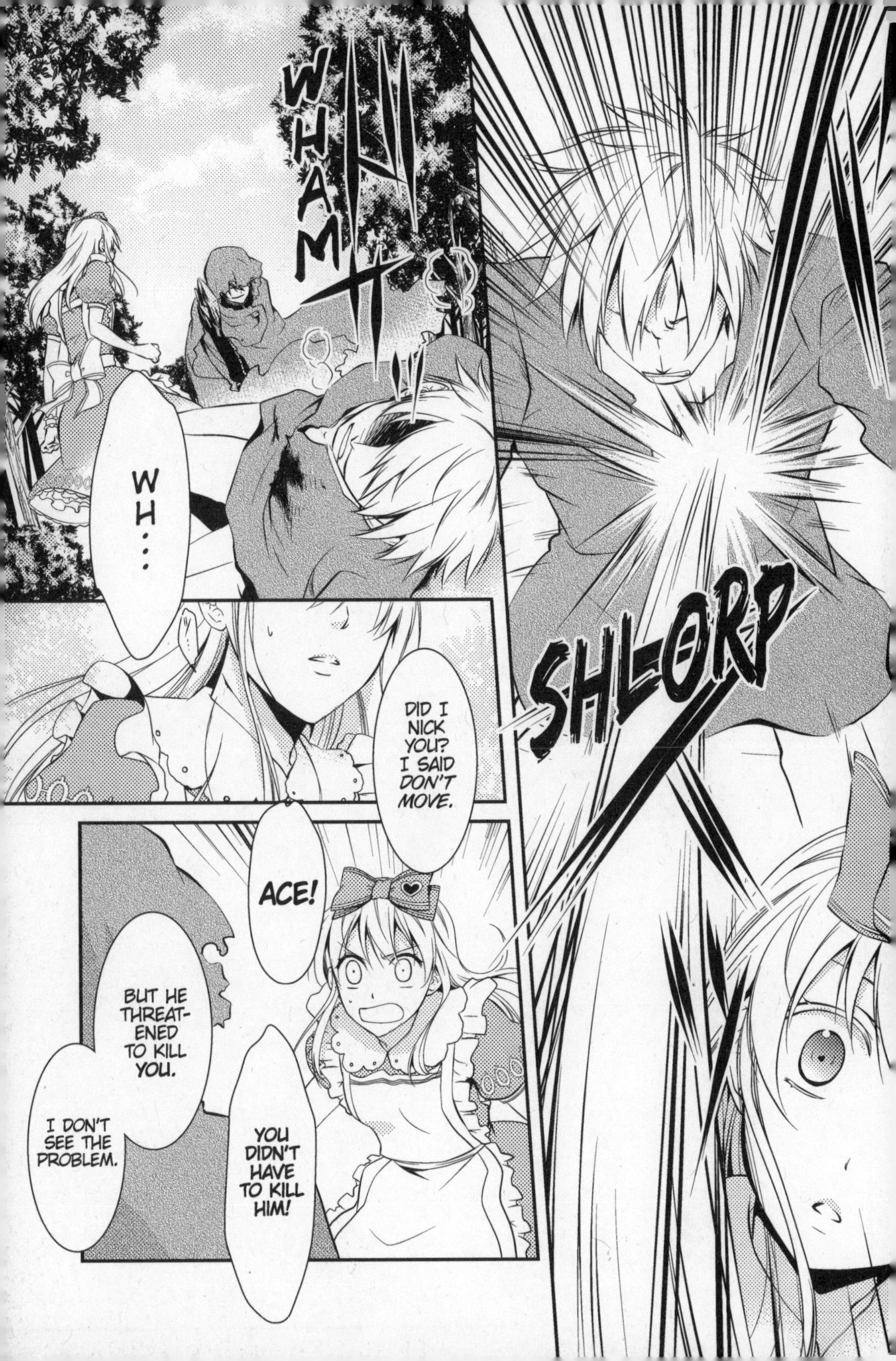
SHLORP
WHAM
WH...
DID I NICK YOU? I SAID DON'T MOVE.
ACE!
YOU DIDN'T HAVE TO KILL HIM!
BUT HE THREAT-ENED TO KILL YOU.
I DON'T SEE THE PROBLEM.

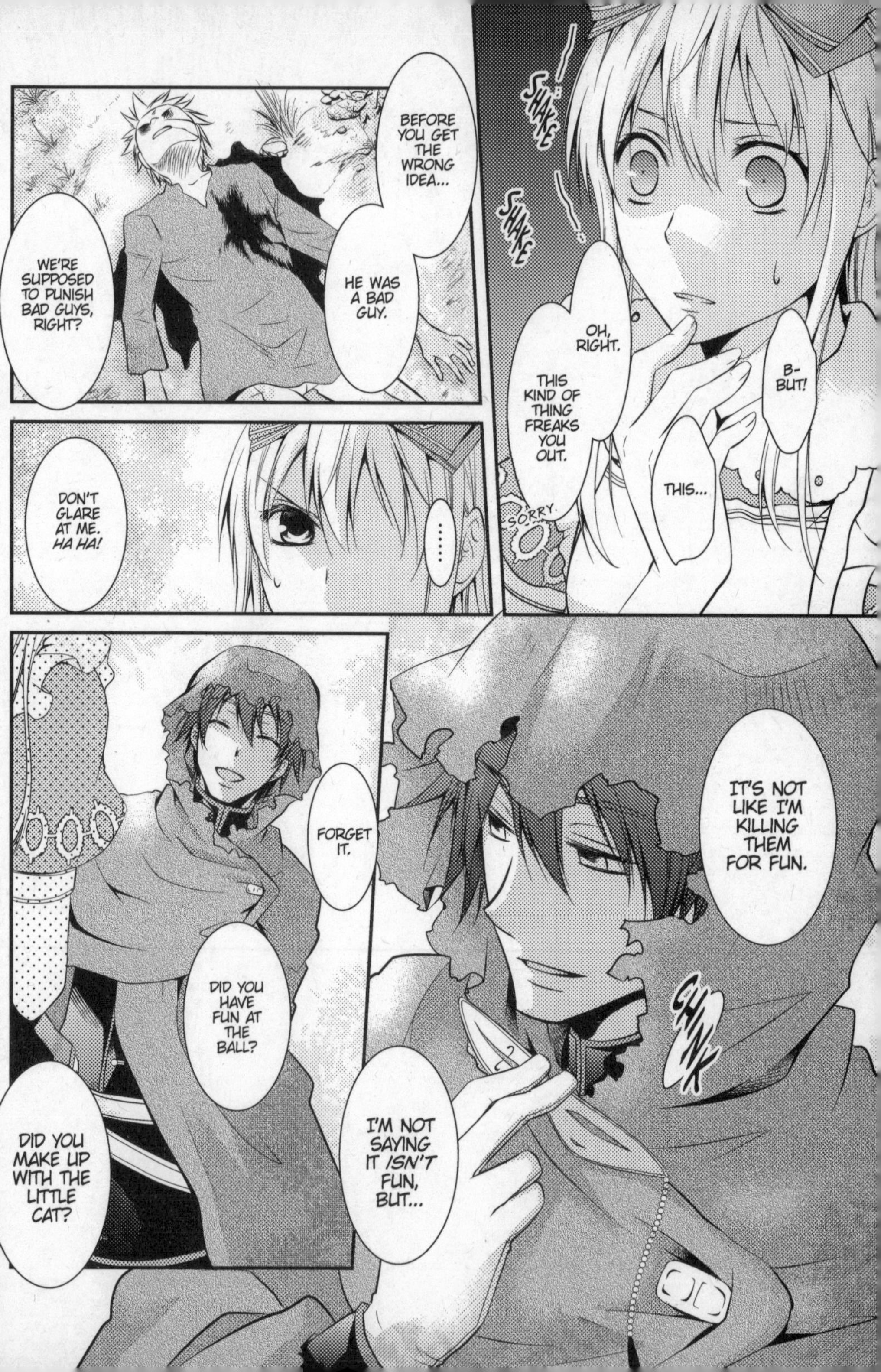
SHAKE
SHAKE
B-BUT!
THIS...
OH, RIGHT.
THIS KIND OF THING FREAKS YOU OUT.
SORRY.
BEFORE YOU GET THE WRONG IDEA...
HE WAS A BAD GUY.
WE'RE SUPPOSED TO PUNISH BAD GUYS, RIGHT?
......
DON'T GLARE AT ME. *HA HA!*
IT'S NOT LIKE I'M KILLING THEM FOR FUN.
CHINK
I'M NOT SAYING IT *ISN'T* FUN, BUT...
FORGET IT.
DID YOU HAVE FUN AT THE BALL?
DID YOU MAKE UP WITH THE LITTLE CAT?

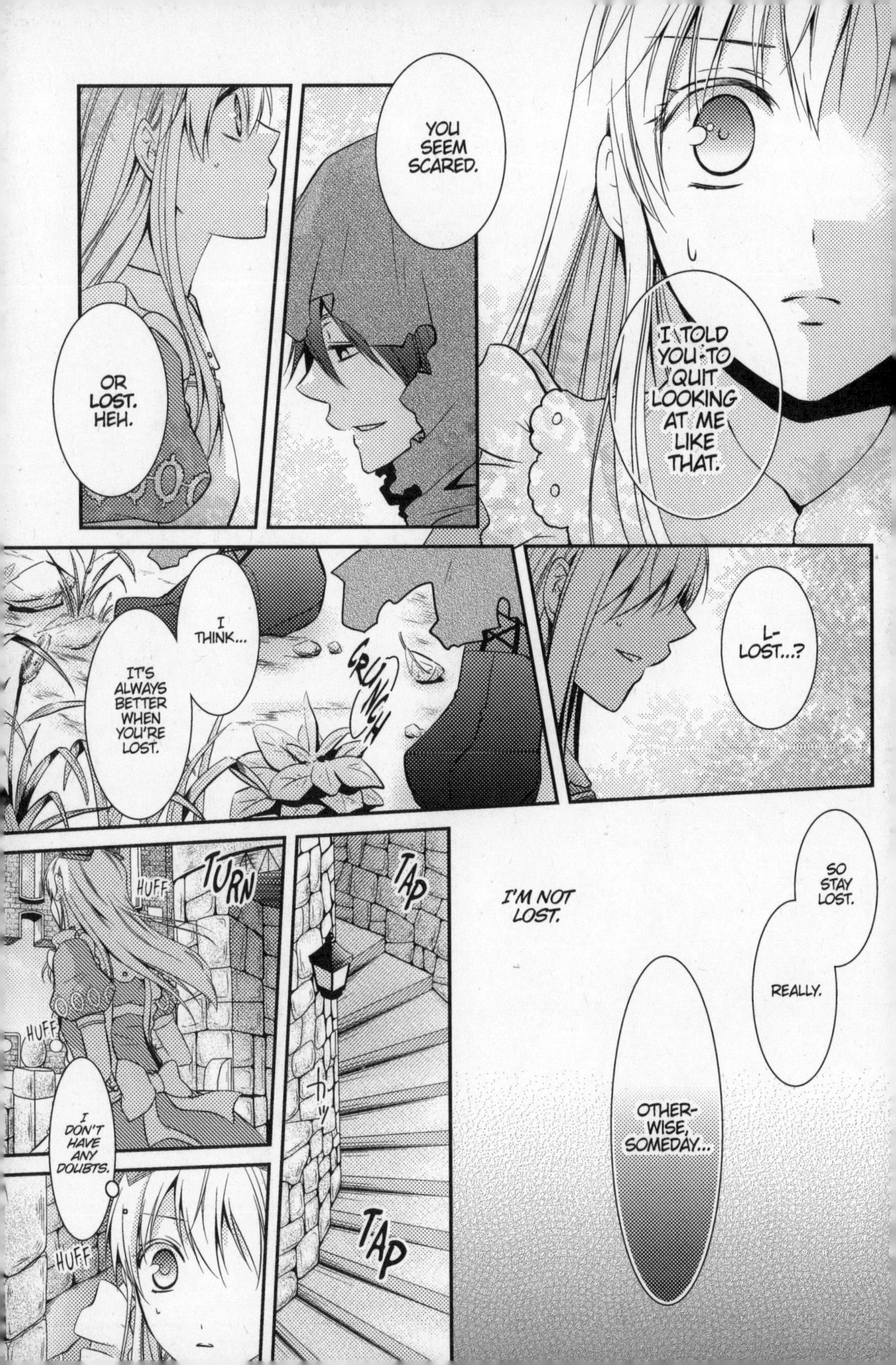

I TOLD YOU TO QUIT LOOKING AT ME LIKE THAT.
YOU SEEM SCARED.
OR LOST. HEH.
L-LOST...?
GRUNCH
I THINK...
IT'S ALWAYS BETTER WHEN YOU'RE LOST.
SO STAY LOST.
REALLY.
OTHER-WISE, SOMEDAY...
I'M NOT LOST.
TAP
TAP
TURN
HUFF
HUFF
I DON'T HAVE ANY DOUBTS.
HUFF

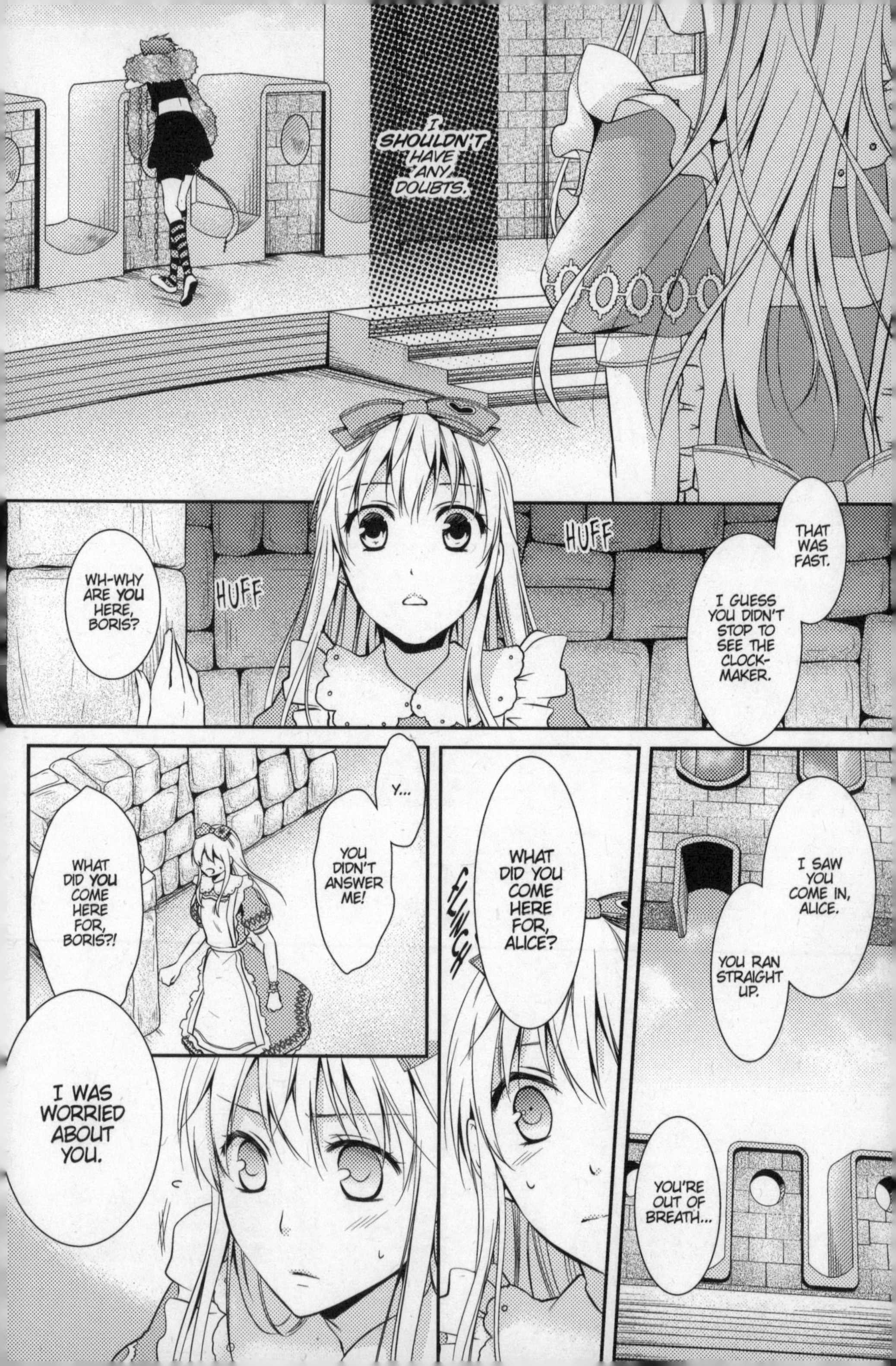
I SHOULDN'T HAVE ANY DOUBTS.
THAT WAS FAST.
I GUESS YOU DIDN'T STOP TO SEE THE CLOCK-MAKER.
HUFF
HUFF
WH-WHY ARE YOU HERE, BORIS?
I SAW YOU COME IN, ALICE.
YOU RAN STRAIGHT UP.
WHAT DID YOU COME HERE FOR, ALICE?
FLINCH
Y...
YOU DIDN'T ANSWER ME!
WHAT DID YOU COME HERE FOR, BORIS?!
YOU'RE OUT OF BREATH...
I WAS WORRIED ABOUT YOU.

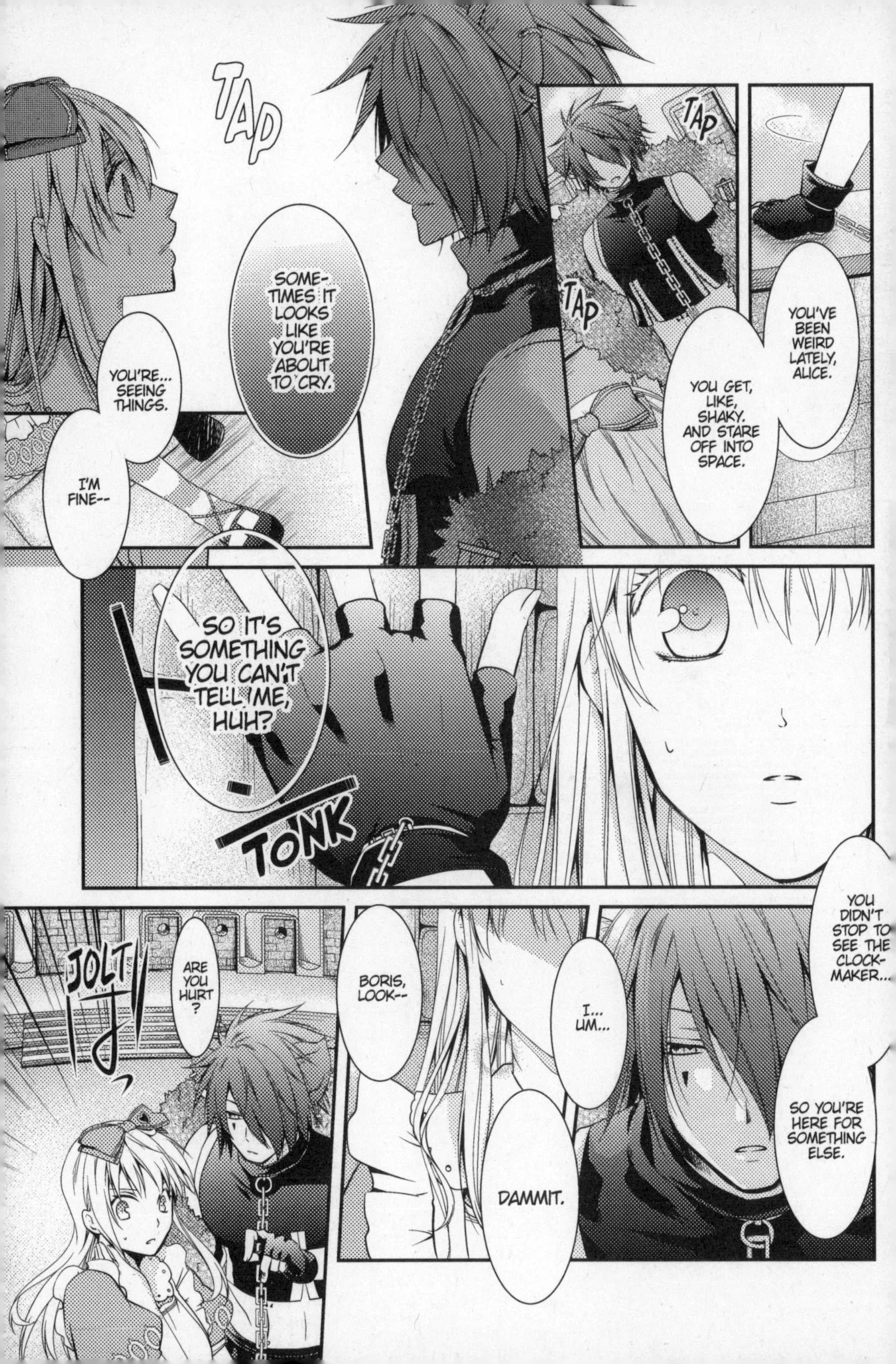
YOU'VE BEEN WEIRD LATELY, ALICE.
TAP
TAP
YOU GET, LIKE, SHAKY. AND STARE OFF INTO SPACE.
TAP
SOME-TIMES IT LOOKS LIKE YOU'RE ABOUT TO CRY.
YOU'RE... SEEING THINGS.
I'M FINE--
SO IT'S SOMETHING YOU CAN'T TELL ME, HUH?
TONK
YOU DIDN'T STOP TO SEE THE CLOCK-MAKER...
SO YOU'RE HERE FOR SOMETHING ELSE.
I... UM...
DAMMIT.
BORIS, LOOK--
ARE YOU HURT?
JOLT

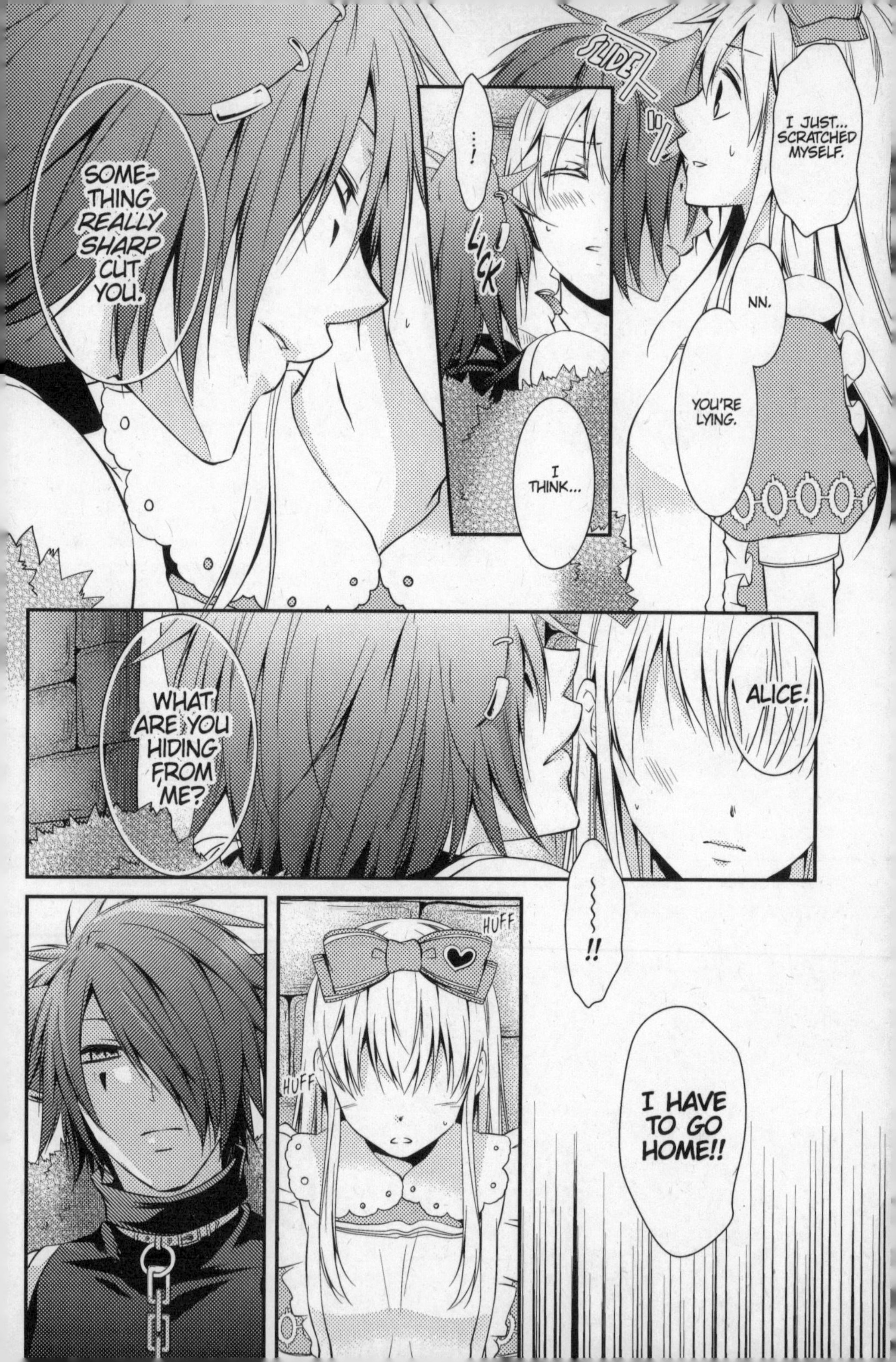
SLIDE
I JUST... SCRATCHED MYSELF.
NN.
YOU'RE LYING.
...!
LICK
I THINK...
SOME-THING REALLY SHARP CUT YOU.
ALICE.
WHAT ARE YOU HIDING FROM ME?
...!!
HUFF
HUFF
I HAVE TO GO HOME!!

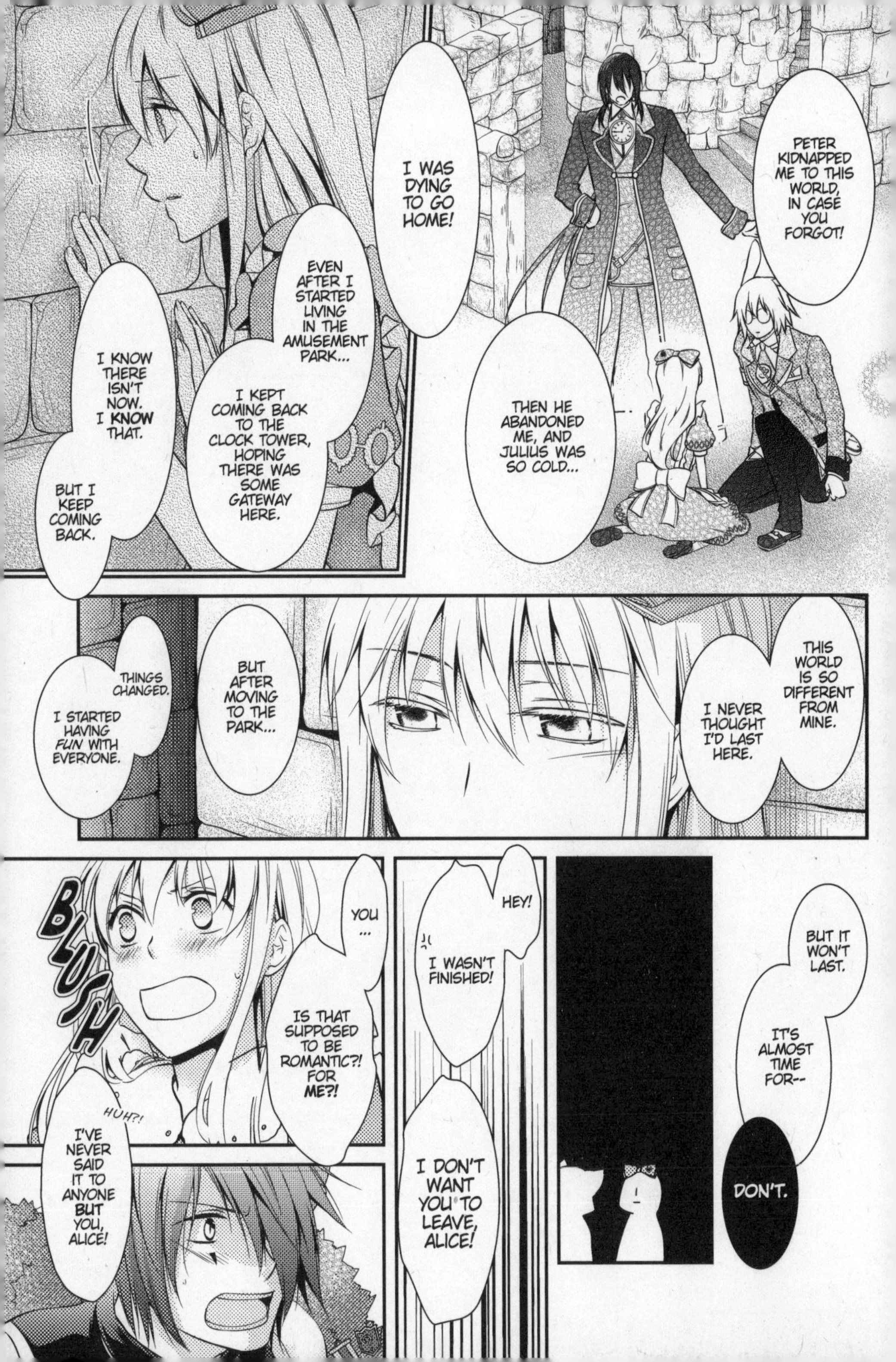
PETER KIDNAPPED ME TO THIS WORLD, IN CASE YOU FORGOT!
I WAS DYING TO GO HOME!
THEN HE ABANDONED ME, AND JULIUS WAS SO COLD...
EVEN AFTER I STARTED LIVING IN THE AMUSEMENT PARK...
I KEPT COMING BACK TO THE CLOCK TOWER, HOPING THERE WAS SOME GATEWAY HERE.
I KNOW THERE ISN'T NOW. I **KNOW** THAT.
BUT I KEEP COMING BACK.
THIS WORLD IS SO DIFFERENT FROM MINE.
I NEVER THOUGHT I'D LAST HERE.
BUT AFTER MOVING TO THE PARK...
THINGS CHANGED.
I STARTED HAVING *FUN* WITH EVERYONE.
BUT IT WON'T LAST.
IT'S ALMOST TIME FOR--
DON'T.
HEY!
I WASN'T FINISHED!
I DON'T WANT YOU TO LEAVE, ALICE!
YOU ...
IS THAT SUPPOSED TO BE ROMANTIC?! FOR **ME**?!
BLUSH
HUH?!
I'VE NEVER SAID IT TO ANYONE **BUT** YOU, ALICE!

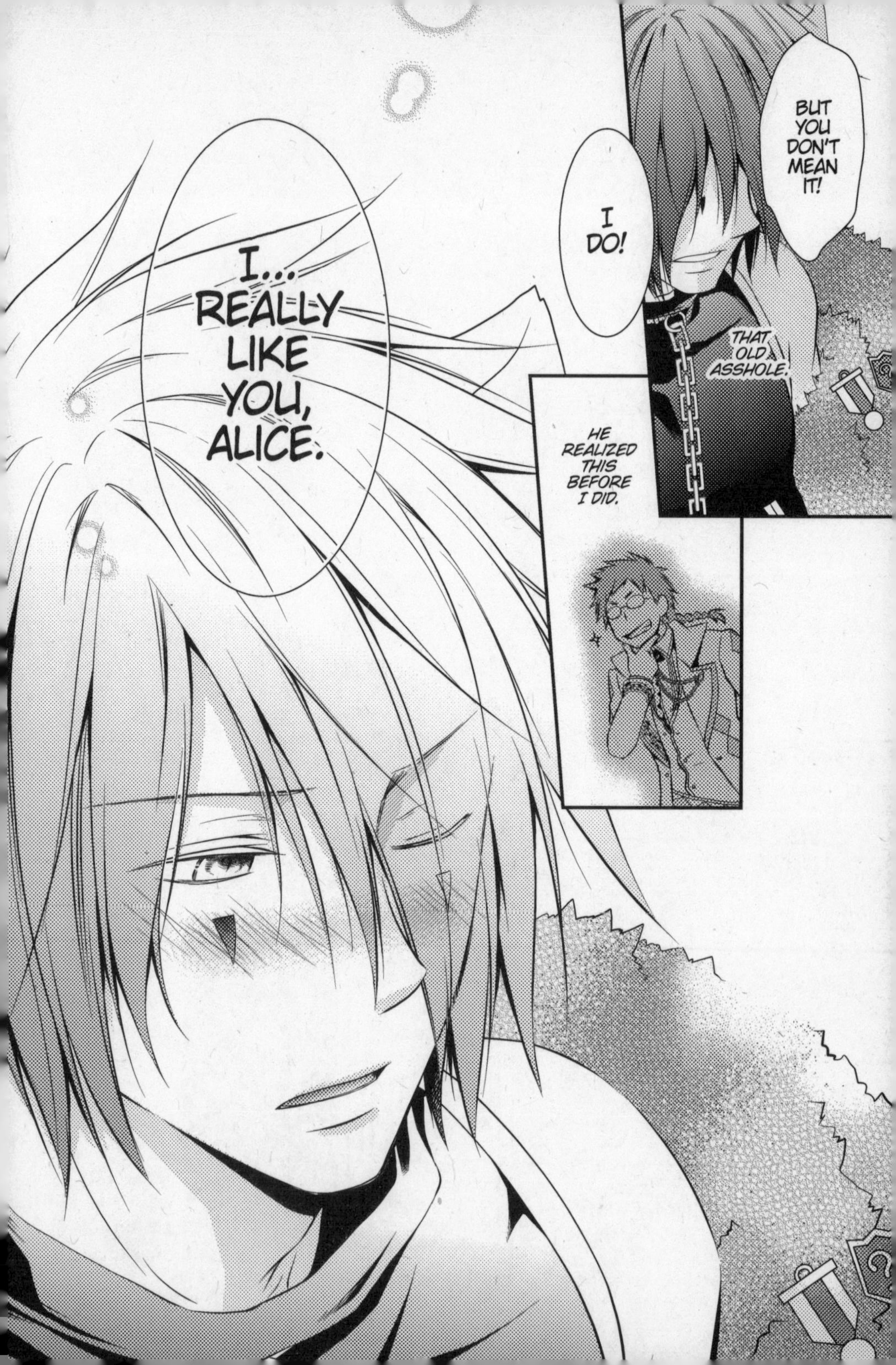
BUT YOU DON'T MEAN IT!
I DO!
THAT OLD ASSHOLE.
HE REALIZED THIS BEFORE I DID.
I... REALLY LIKE YOU, ALICE.

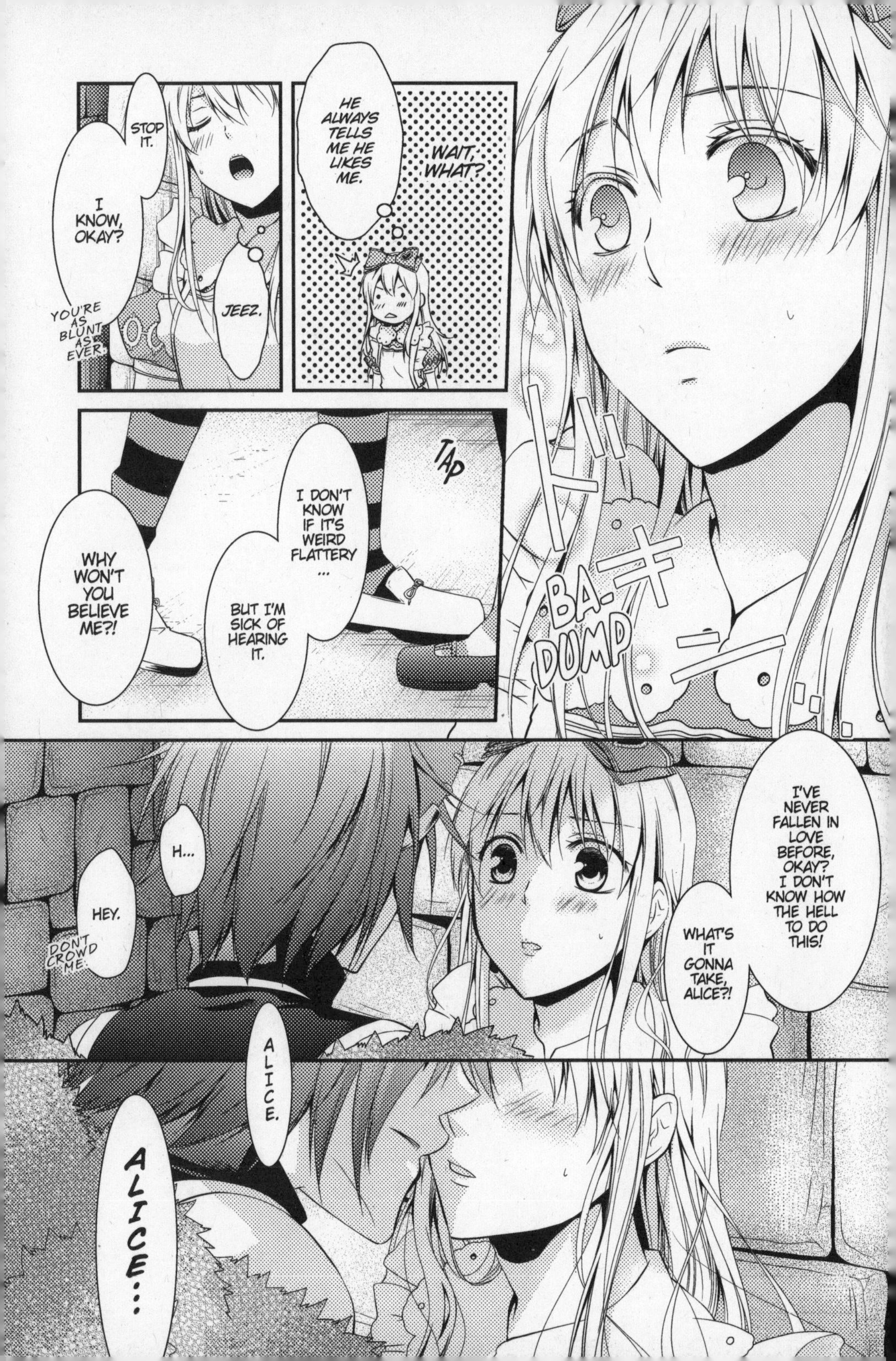
BA-DUMP
HE ALWAYS TELLS ME HE LIKES ME.
WAIT, WHAT?
STOP IT.
I KNOW, OKAY?
JEEZ.
YOU'RE AS BLUNT AS EVER.
TAP
I DON'T KNOW IF IT'S WEIRD FLATTERY...
BUT I'M SICK OF HEARING IT.
WHY WON'T YOU BELIEVE ME?!
I'VE NEVER FALLEN IN LOVE BEFORE, OKAY? I DON'T KNOW HOW THE HELL TO DO THIS!
WHAT'S IT GONNA TAKE, ALICE?!
H...
HEY.
DON'T CROWD ME.
ALICE.
ALICE...

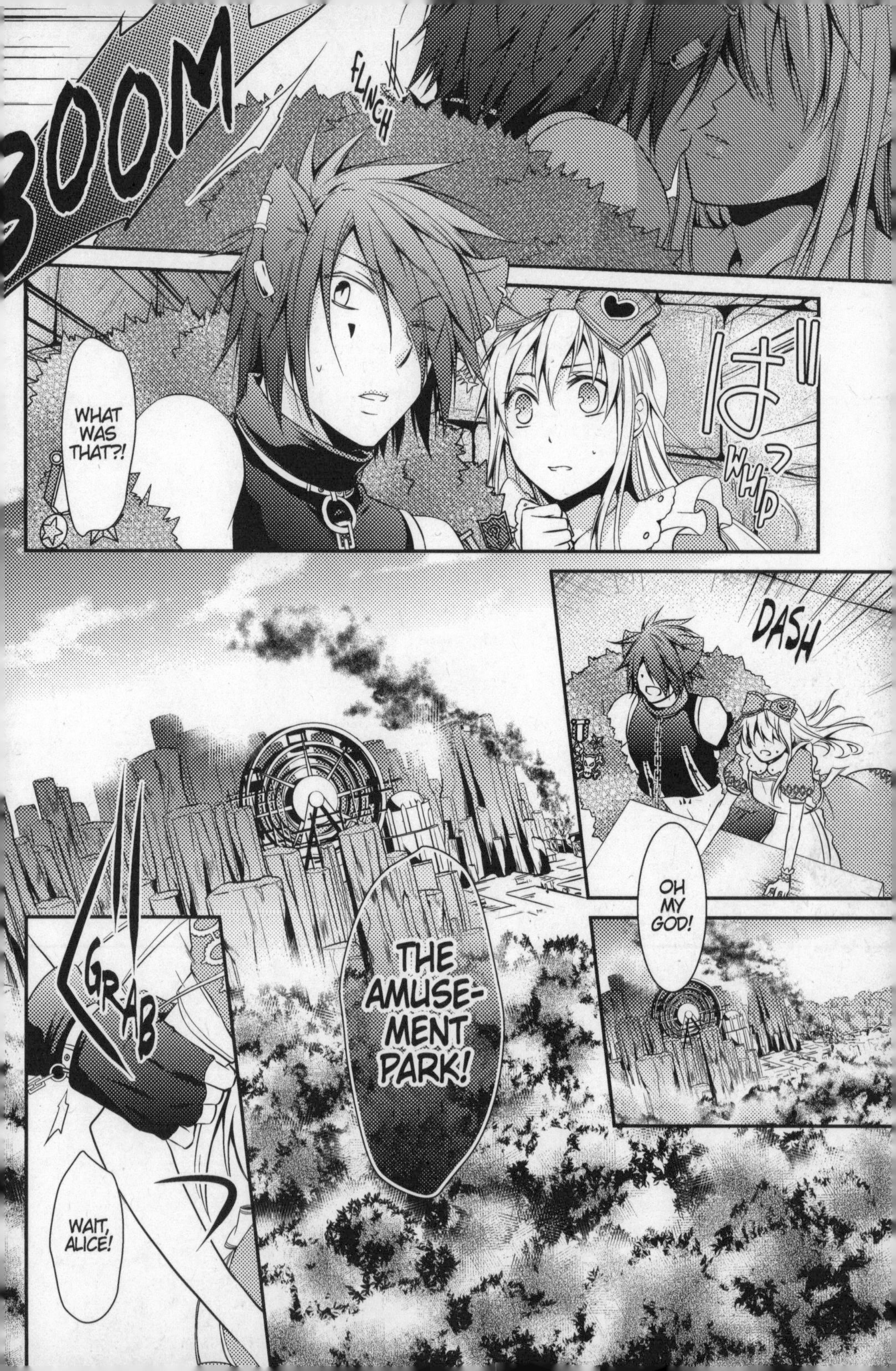
FLINCH
BOOM
はっ
WHIP
WHAT WAS THAT?!
DASH
OH MY GOD!
THE AMUSE-MENT PARK!
GRAB
WAIT, ALICE!

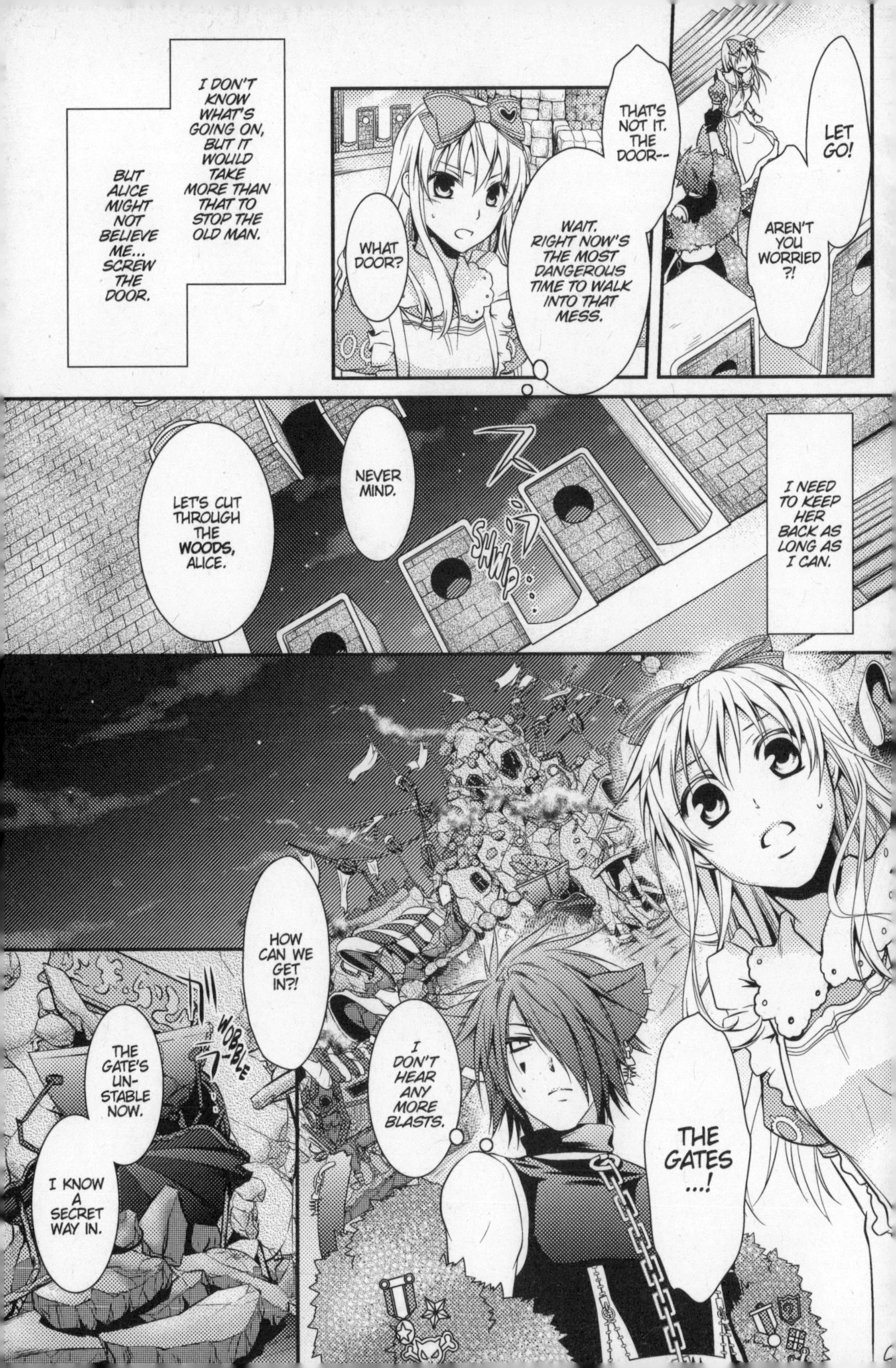
LET GO!
AREN'T YOU WORRIED?!
THAT'S NOT IT. THE DOOR--
WAIT. RIGHT NOW'S THE MOST DANGEROUS TIME TO WALK INTO THAT MESS.
WHAT DOOR?
I DON'T KNOW WHAT'S GOING ON, BUT IT WOULD TAKE MORE THAN THAT TO STOP THE OLD MAN.
BUT ALICE MIGHT NOT BELIEVE ME... SCREW THE DOOR.
I NEED TO KEEP HER BACK AS LONG AS I CAN.
SHWIP...
NEVER MIND.
LET'S CUT THROUGH THE WOODS, ALICE.
THE GATES...!
I DON'T HEAR ANY MORE BLASTS.
HOW CAN WE GET IN?!
WOBBLE-BBLE
THE GATE'S UN-STABLE NOW.
I KNOW A SECRET WAY IN.

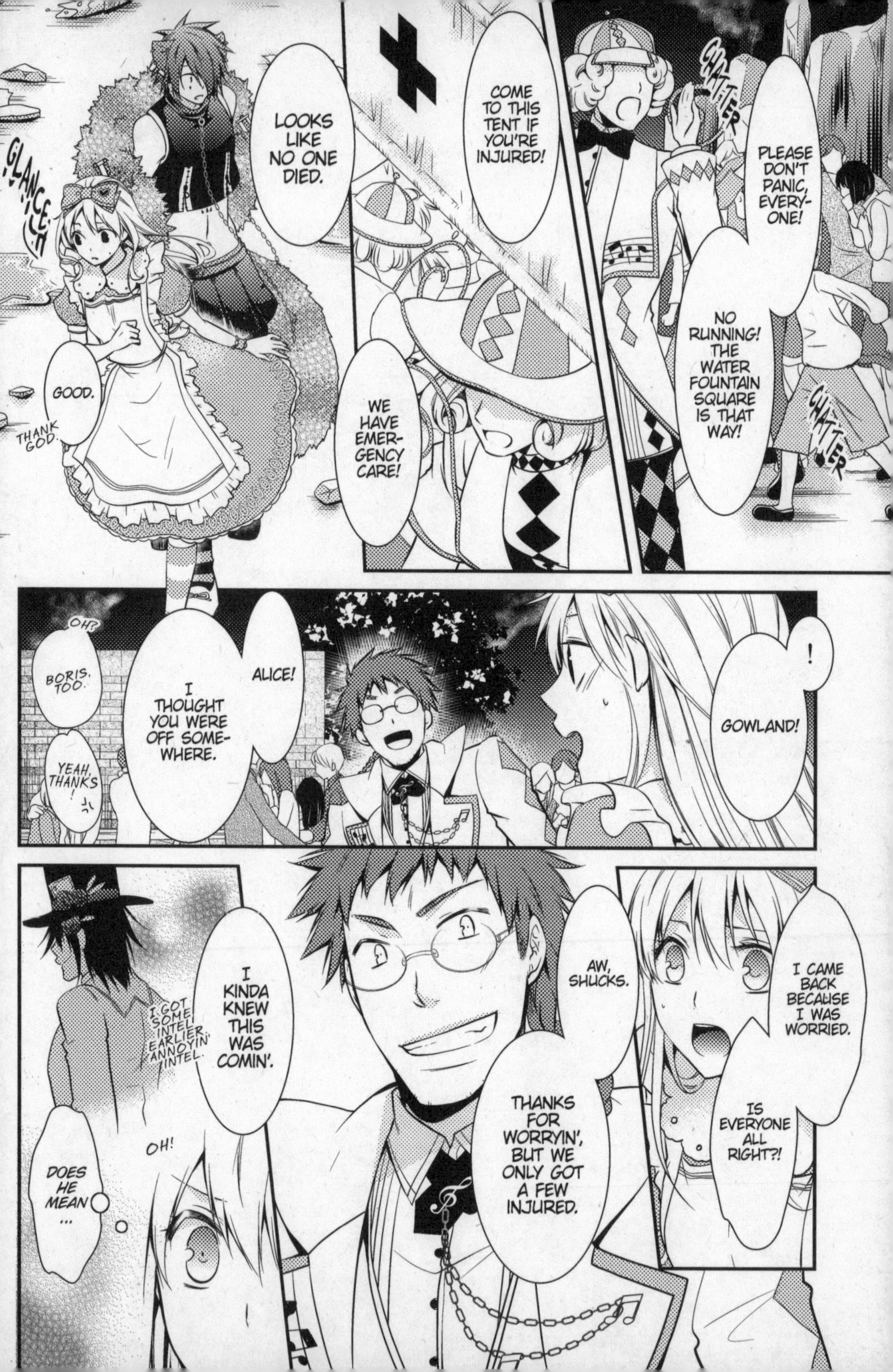
PLEASE DON'T PANIC, EVERYONE!
CHATTER
NO RUNNING! THE WATER FOUNTAIN SQUARE IS THAT WAY!
CHATTER
COME TO THIS TENT IF YOU'RE INJURED!
WE HAVE EMERGENCY CARE!
LOOKS LIKE NO ONE DIED.
GLANCE
GOOD.
THANK GOD.
!
GOWLAND!
ALICE!
I THOUGHT YOU WERE OFF SOMEWHERE.
OH?
BORIS, TOO.
YEAH, THANKS!
I CAME BACK BECAUSE I WAS WORRIED.
IS EVERYONE ALL RIGHT?!
AW, SHUCKS.
THANKS FOR WORRYIN', BUT WE ONLY GOT A FEW INJURED.
I KINDA KNEW THIS WAS COMIN'.
I GOT SOME INTEL EARLIER. ANNOYIN' INTEL.
OH!
DOES HE MEAN ...

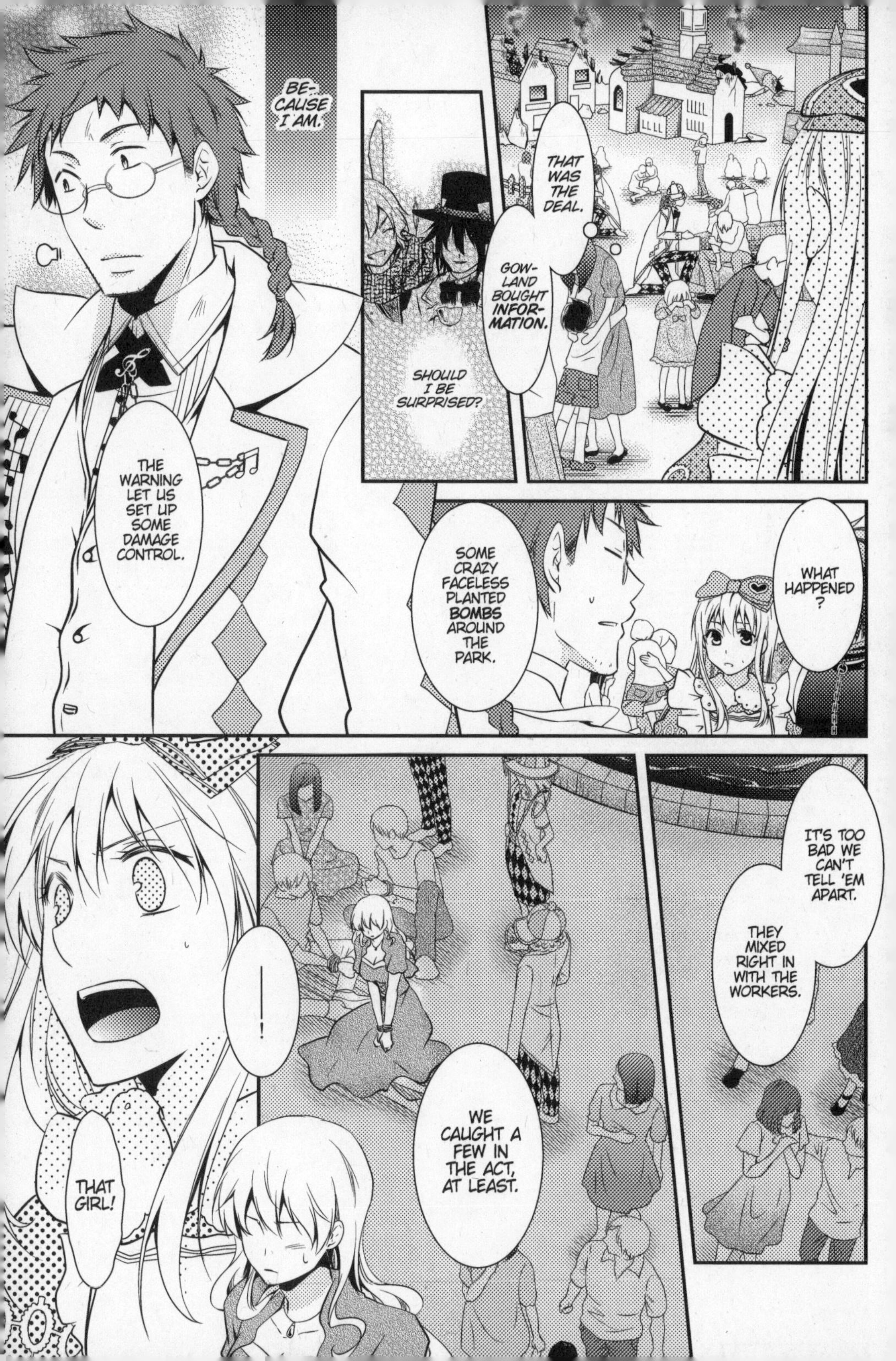
THAT WAS THE DEAL.
GOW-LAND BOUGHT INFORMATION.
SHOULD I BE SURPRISED?
WHAT HAPPENED?
SOME CRAZY FACELESS PLANTED BOMBS AROUND THE PARK.
BE-CAUSE I AM.
THE WARNING LET US SET UP SOME DAMAGE CONTROL.
IT'S TOO BAD WE CAN'T TELL 'EM APART.
THEY MIXED RIGHT IN WITH THE WORKERS.
WE CAUGHT A FEW IN THE ACT, AT LEAST.
!
THAT GIRL!

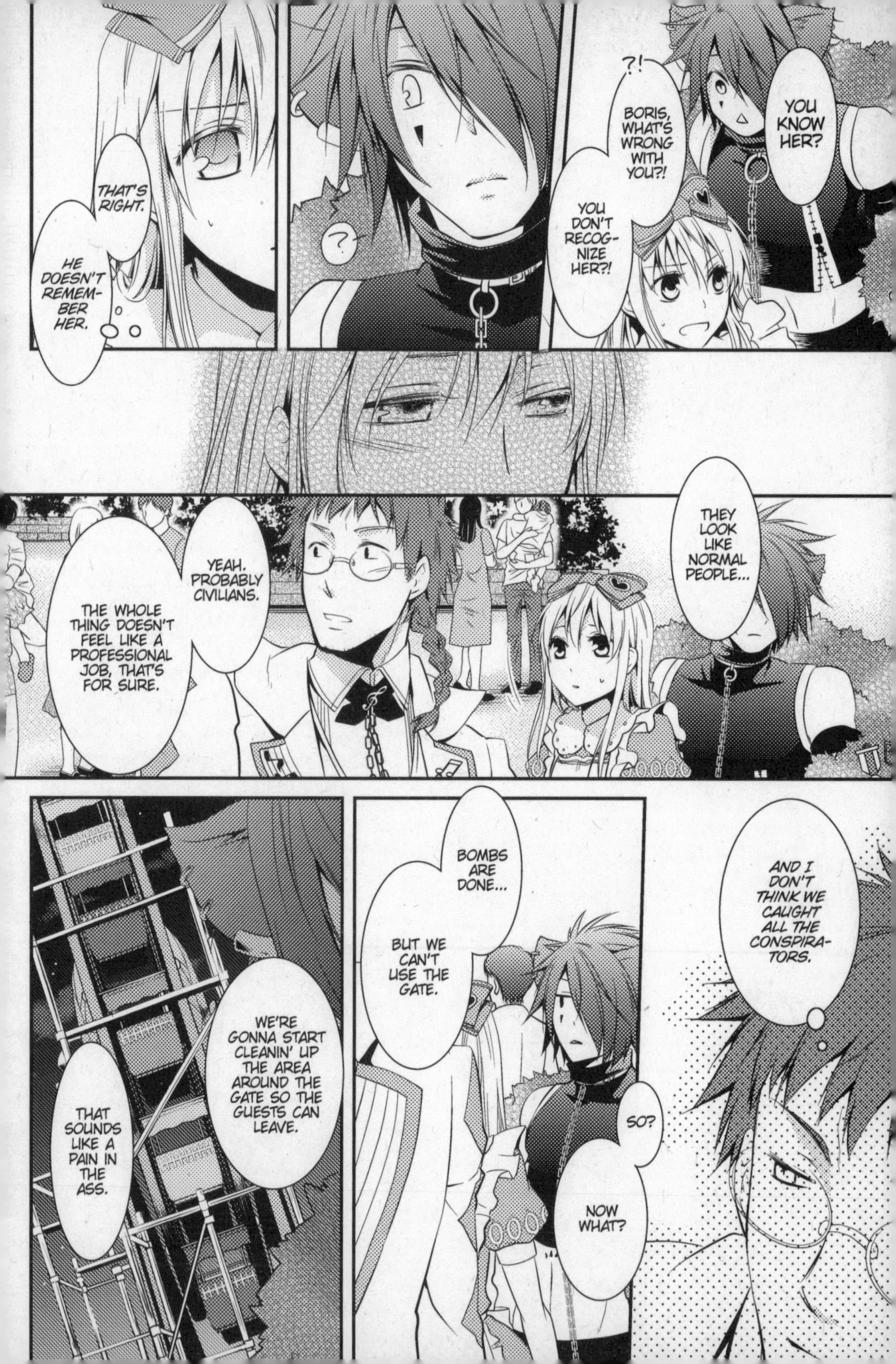
YOU KNOW HER?
?!
BORIS, WHAT'S WRONG WITH YOU?!
YOU DON'T RECOGNIZE HER?!
?
THAT'S RIGHT.
HE DOESN'T REMEMBER HER.
THEY LOOK LIKE NORMAL PEOPLE...
YEAH. PROBABLY CIVILIANS.
THE WHOLE THING DOESN'T FEEL LIKE A PROFESSIONAL JOB, THAT'S FOR SURE.
AND I DON'T THINK WE CAUGHT ALL THE CONSPIRATORS.
BOMBS ARE DONE...
BUT WE CAN'T USE THE GATE.
SO?
NOW WHAT?
WE'RE GONNA START CLEANIN' UP THE AREA AROUND THE GATE SO THE GUESTS CAN LEAVE.
THAT SOUNDS LIKE A PAIN IN THE ASS.

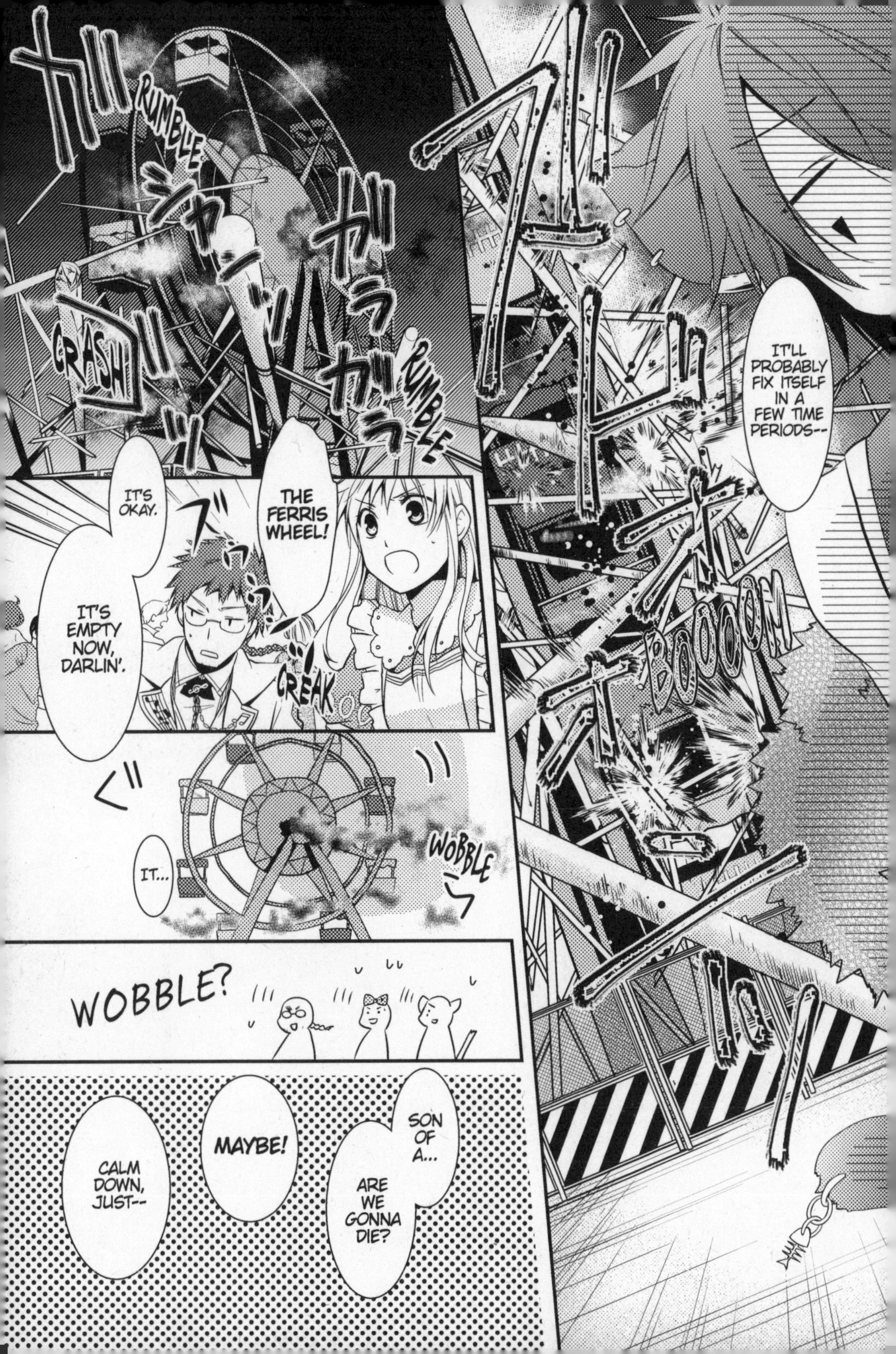
IT'LL PROBABLY FIX ITSELF IN A FEW TIME PERIODS--
BOOOOOM
RUMBLE
RUMBLE
CRASH
THE FERRIS WHEEL!
IT'S OKAY.
IT'S EMPTY NOW, DARLIN'.
CREAK
WOBBLE
IT...
WOBBLE?
SON OF A...
ARE WE GONNA DIE?
MAYBE!
CALM DOWN, JUST--

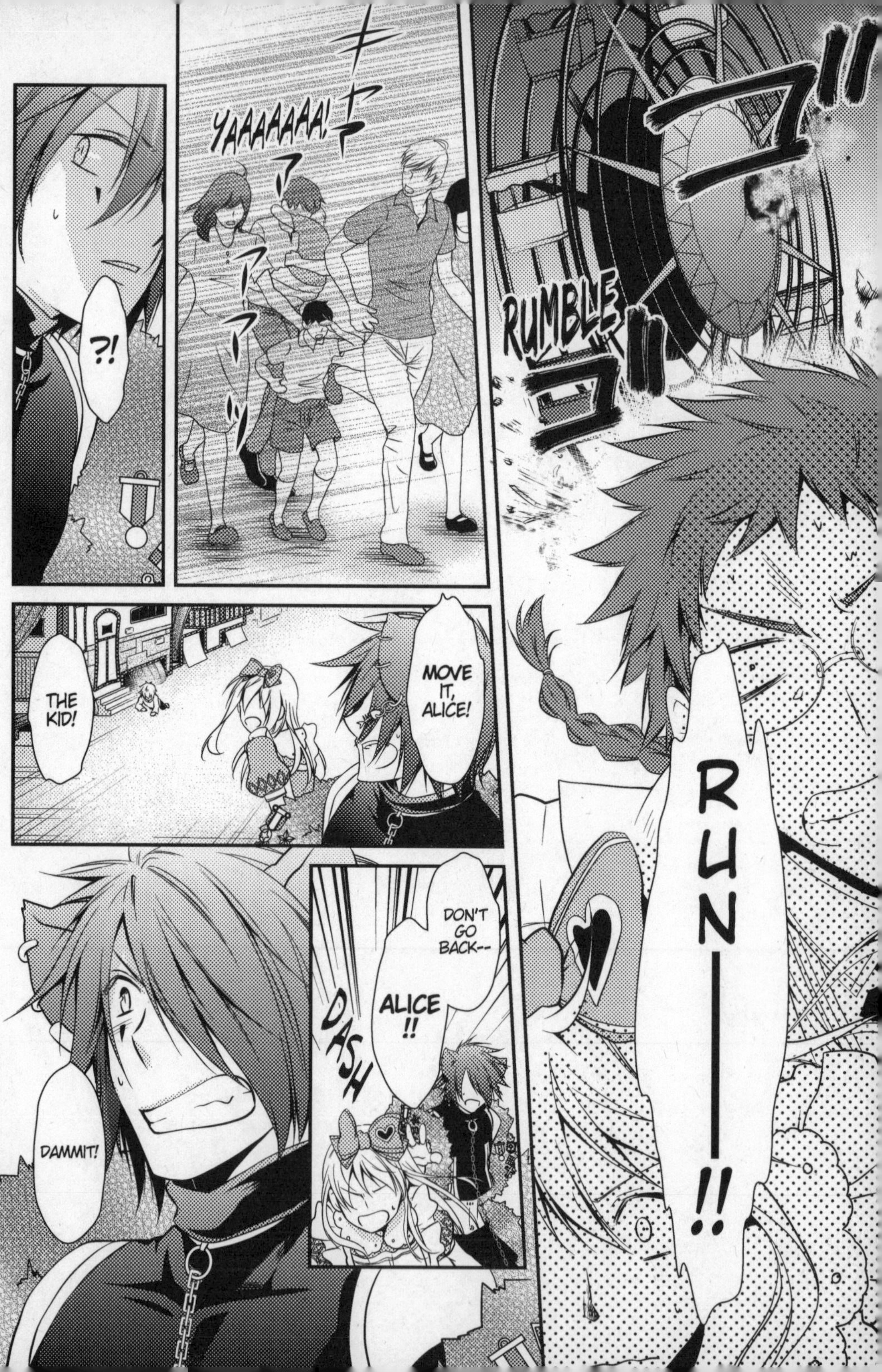
RUMBLE
RUN——!!
YAAAAAAA!
?!
MOVE IT, ALICE!
THE KID!
DON'T GO BACK--
ALICE!!
DASH
DAMMIT!

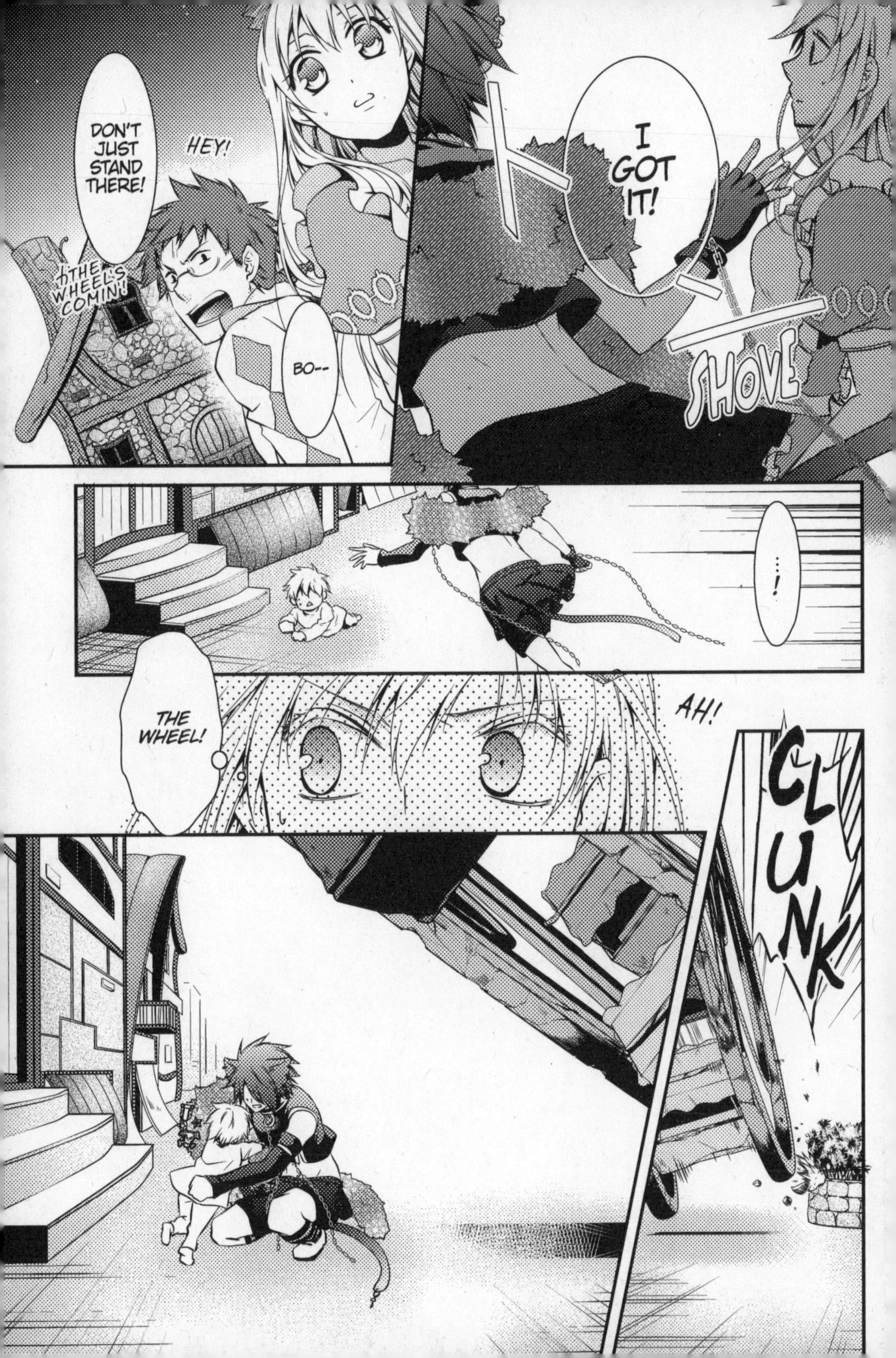
I GOT IT!
SHOVE
HEY!
DON'T JUST STAND THERE!
THE WHEEL'S COMIN'!
BO--
...!
AH!
THE WHEEL!
CLUNK

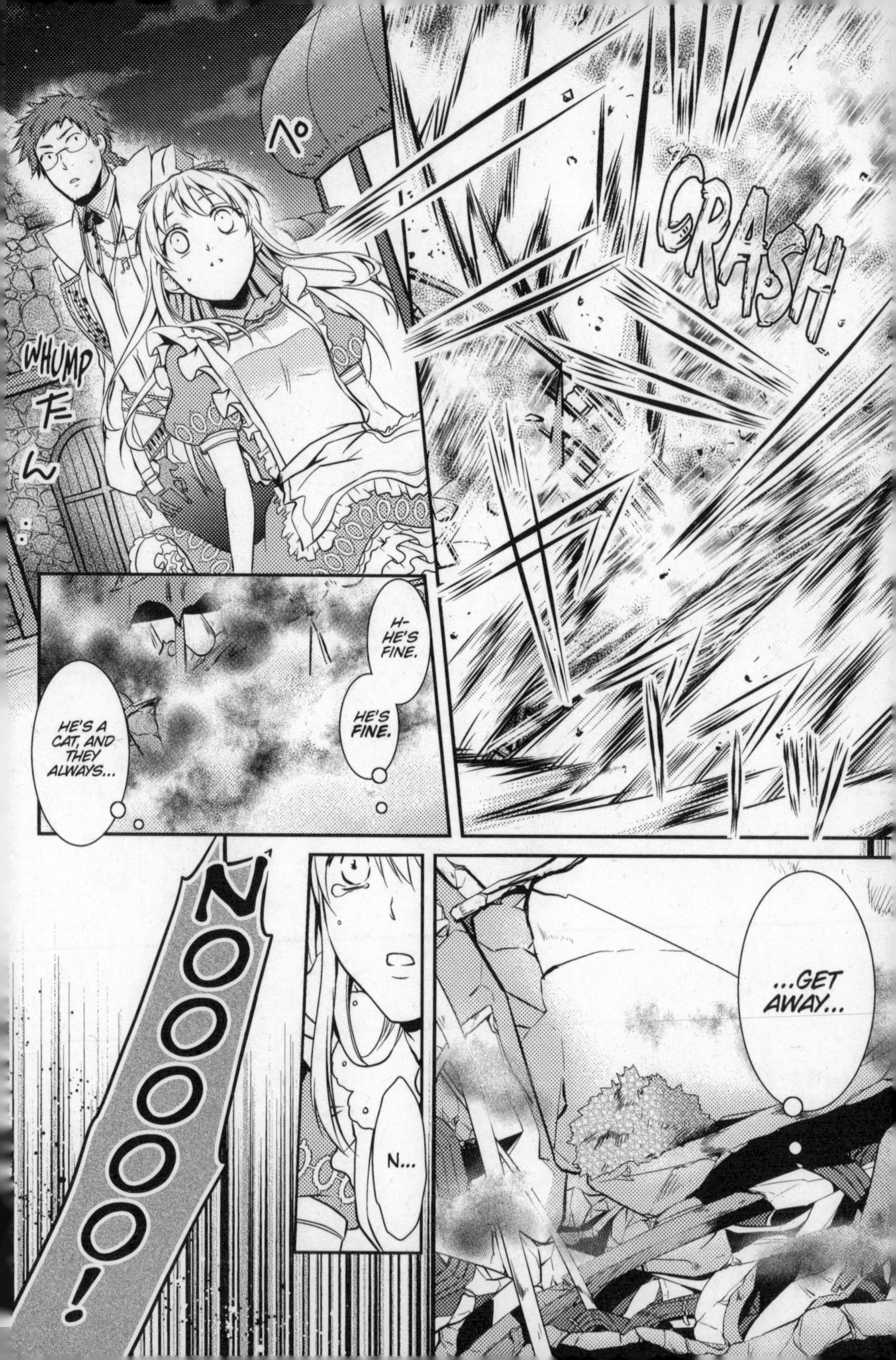
CRASH
ぺ
WHUMP
ドん
H-HE'S FINE.
HE'S FINE.
HE'S A CAT, AND THEY ALWAYS...
...GET AWAY...
N...
NOOOOOOO!

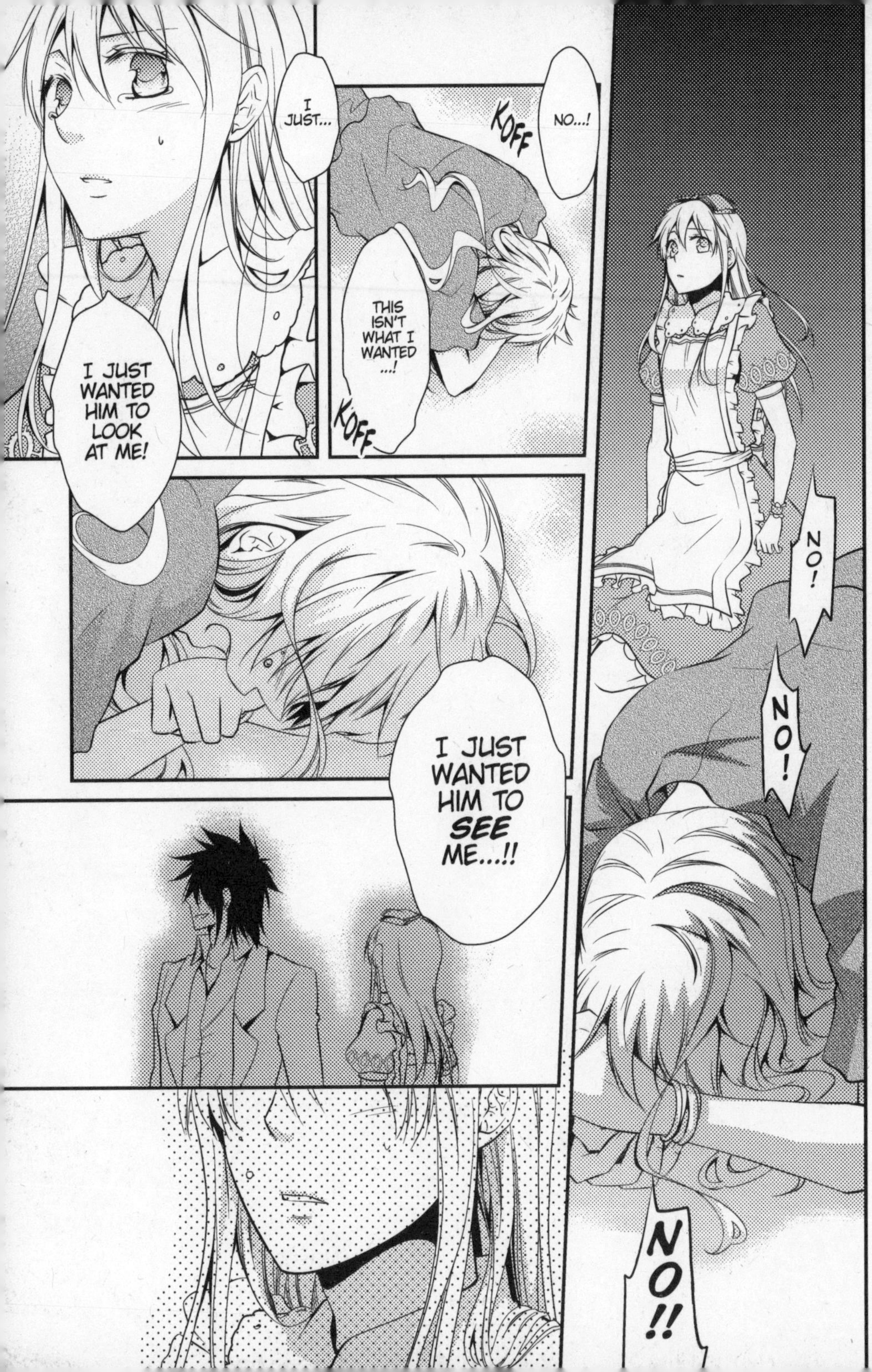
NO!
NO!
NO!!
NO...!
KOFF
I JUST...
THIS ISN'T WHAT I WANTED ...!
KOFF
I JUST WANTED HIM TO LOOK AT ME!
I JUST WANTED HIM TO *SEE* ME...!!

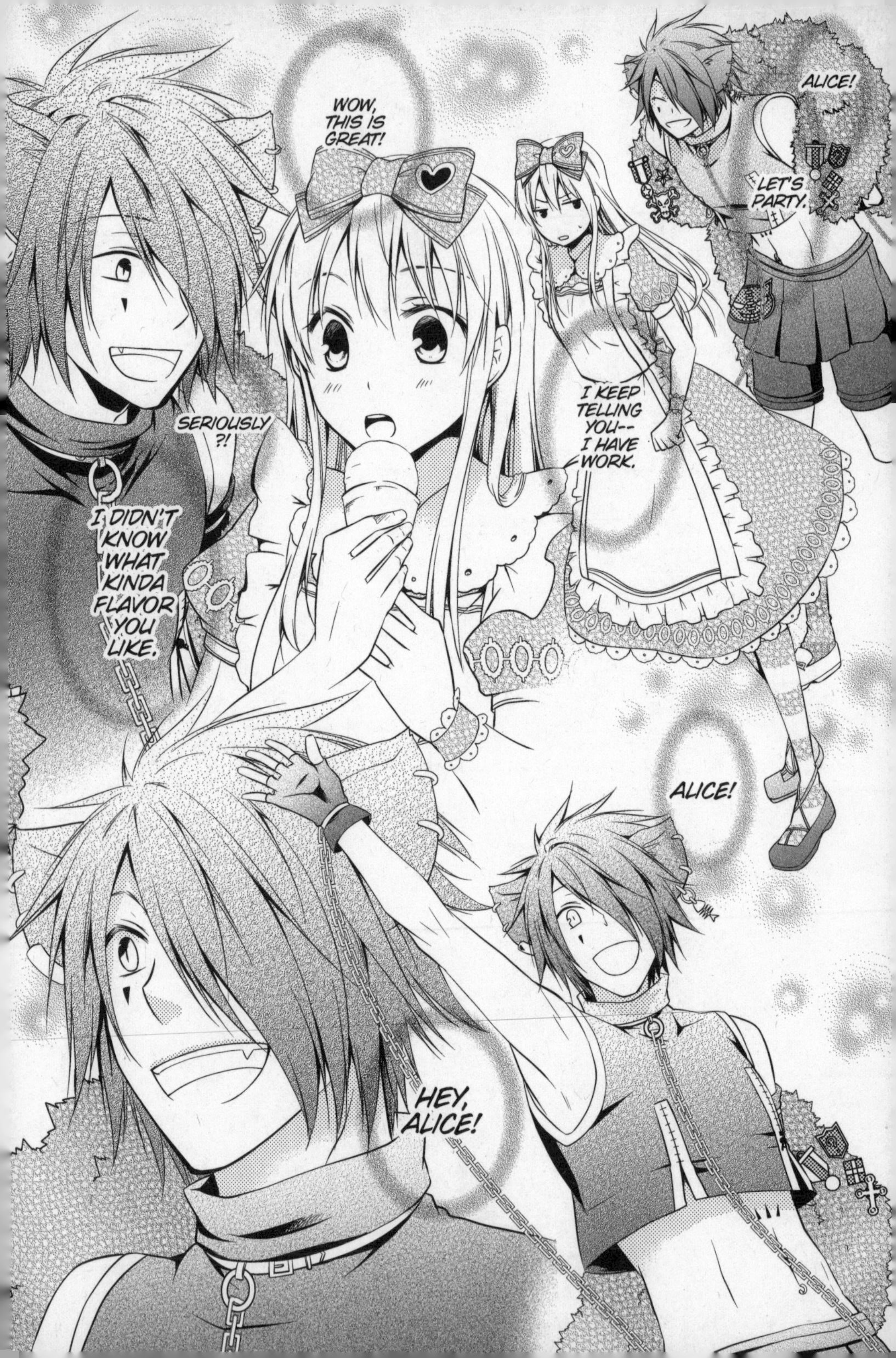
ALICE!
LET'S PARTY.
I KEEP TELLING YOU-- I HAVE WORK.
WOW, THIS IS GREAT!
SERIOUSLY?!
I DIDN'T KNOW WHAT KINDA FLAVOR YOU LIKE.
ALICE!
HEY, ALICE!

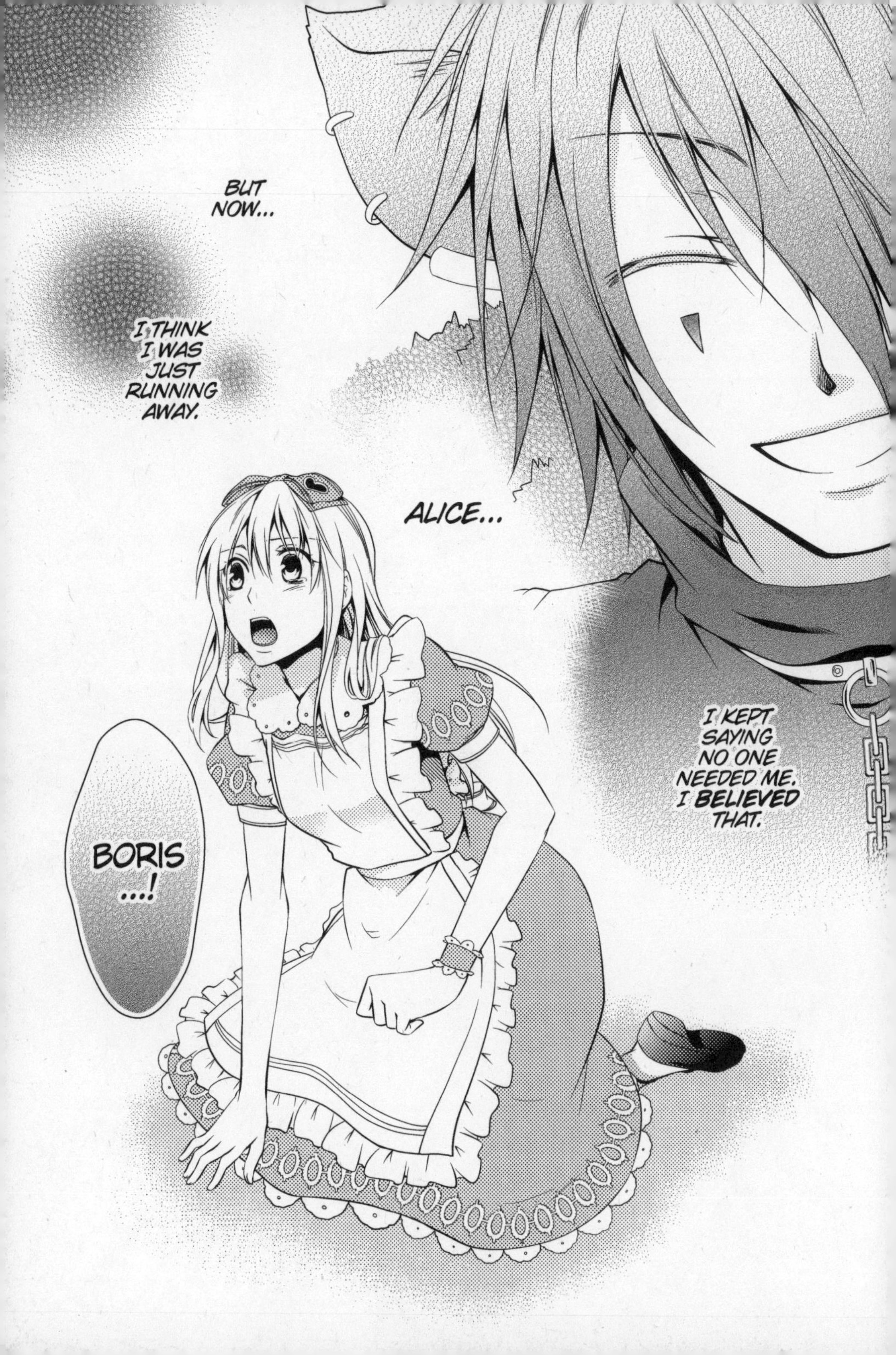
I KEPT SAYING NO ONE NEEDED ME. I BELIEVED THAT.
BUT NOW...
I THINK I WAS JUST RUNNING AWAY.
ALICE...
BORIS ...!

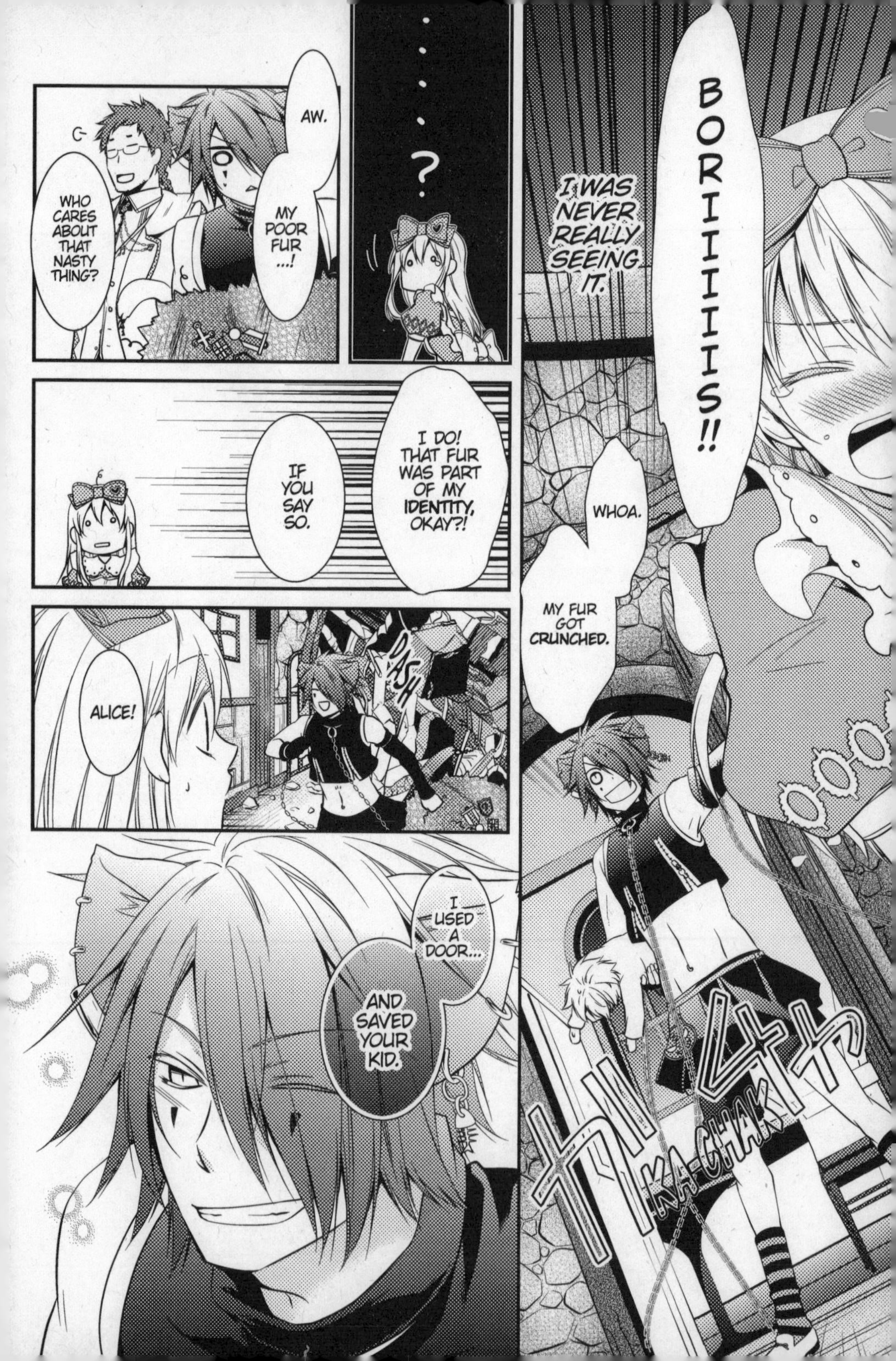
BORIIIIIS!!
I WAS NEVER REALLY SEEING IT.
WHOA.
MY FUR GOT CRUNCHED.
KA-CHAK
. . . . ?
AW.
MY POOR FUR ...!
WHO CARES ABOUT THAT NASTY THING?
I DO! THAT FUR WAS PART OF MY IDENTITY, OKAY?!
IF YOU SAY SO.
DASH
ALICE!
I USED A DOOR...
AND SAVED YOUR KID.

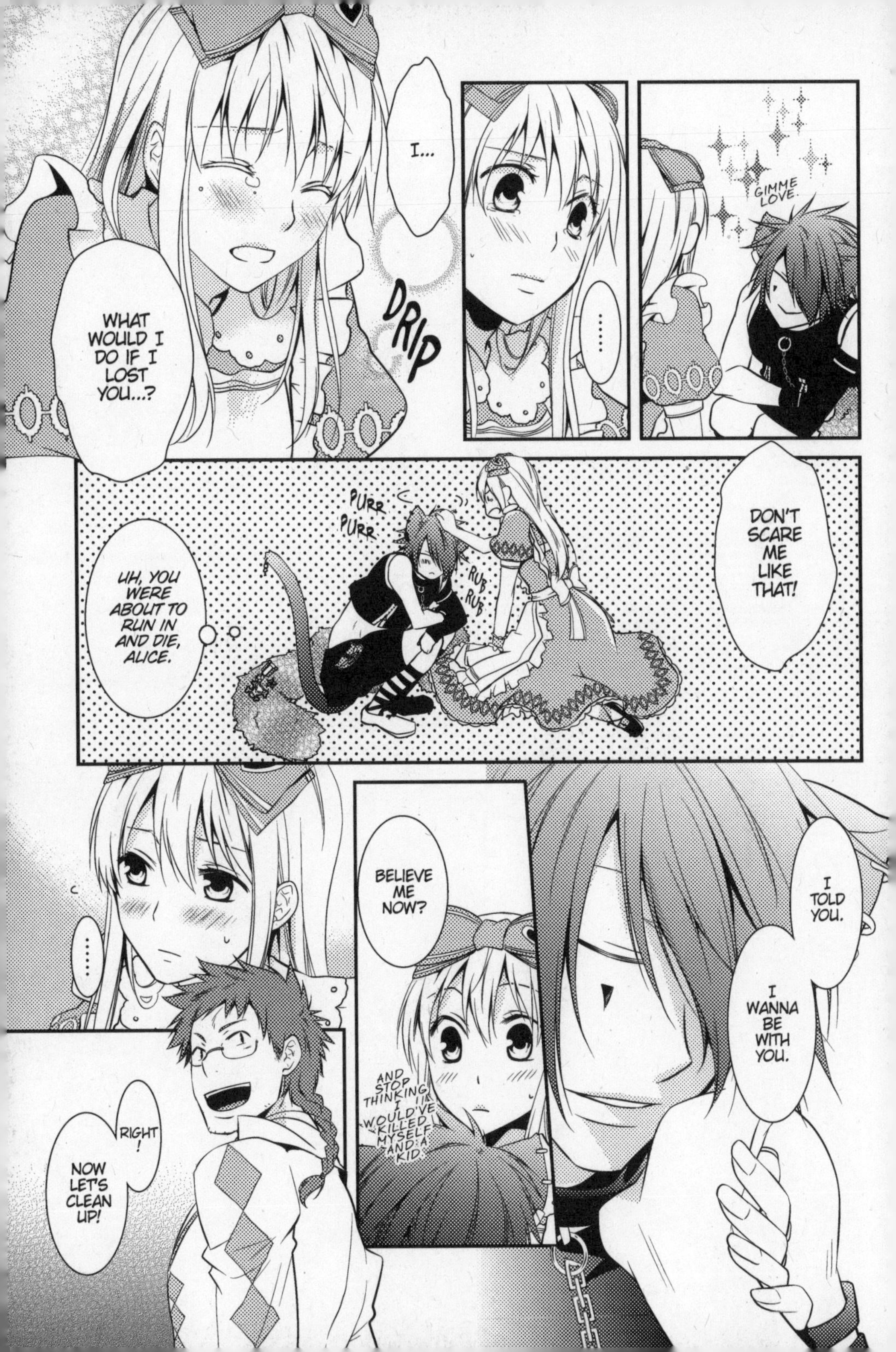
GIMME LOVE.
......
I...
DRIP
WHAT WOULD I DO IF I LOST YOU...?
DON'T SCARE ME LIKE THAT!
PURR PURR
RUB RUB
UH, YOU WERE ABOUT TO RUN IN AND DIE, ALICE.
I TOLD YOU.
I WANNA BE WITH YOU.
BELIEVE ME NOW?
AND STOP THINKING I WOULD'VE KILLED MYSELF AND A KID.
......
RIGHT! NOW LET'S CLEAN UP!

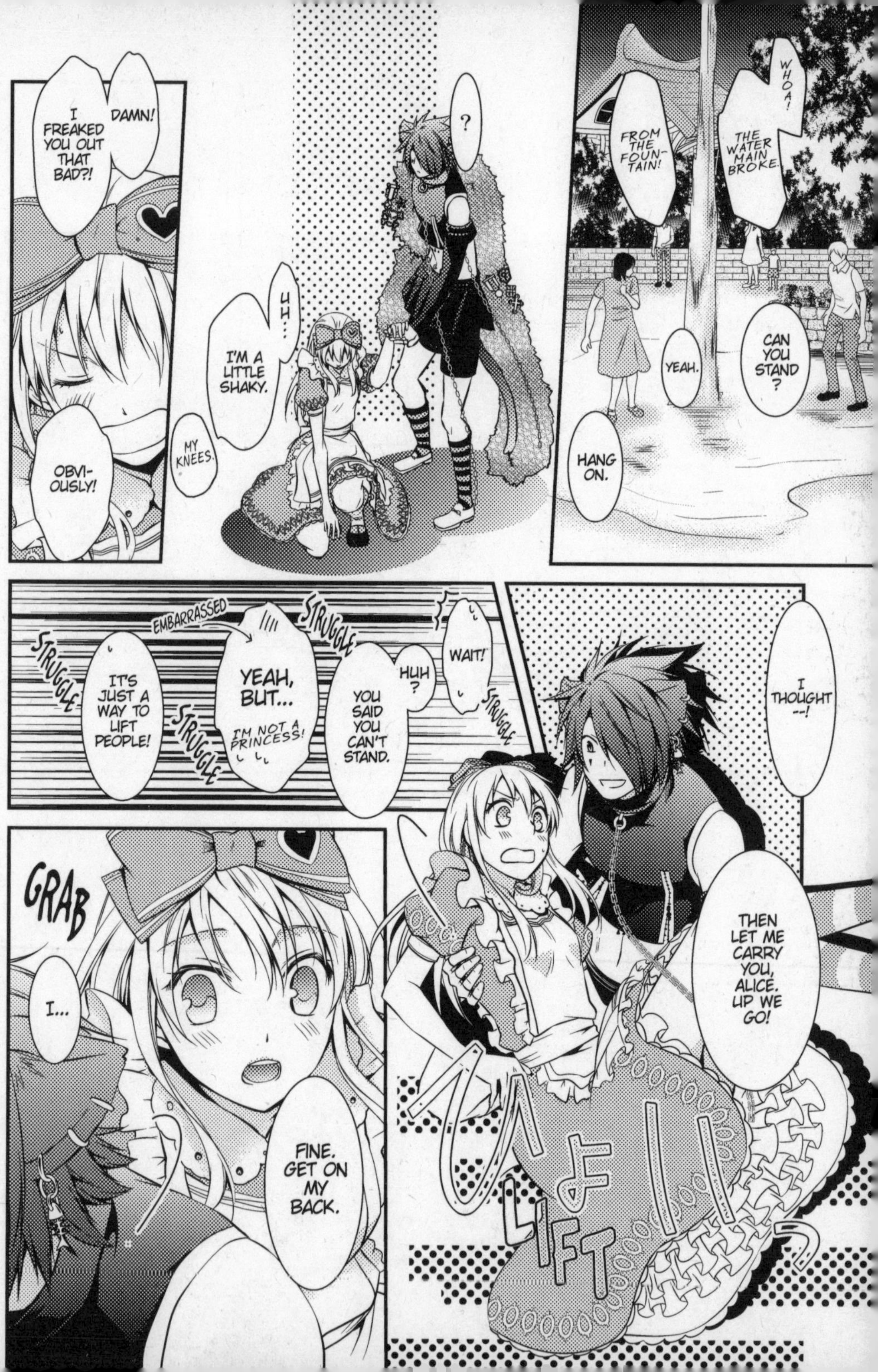
WHOA! THE WATER MAIN BROKE.
FROM THE FOUN-TAIN!
CAN YOU STAND?
YEAH.
HANG ON.
?
UH...
I'M A LITTLE SHAKY.
MY KNEES.
DAMN!
I FREAKED YOU OUT THAT BAD?!
OBVI-OUSLY!
I THOUGHT--!
THEN LET ME CARRY YOU, ALICE. UP WE GO!
LIFT
WAIT!
HUH?
YOU SAID YOU CAN'T STAND.
STRUGGLE
YEAH, BUT...
I'M NOT A PRINCESS!
EMBARRASSED
STRUGGLE
IT'S JUST A WAY TO LIFT PEOPLE!
STRUGGLE
STRUGGLE
GRAB
I...
FINE. GET ON MY BACK.

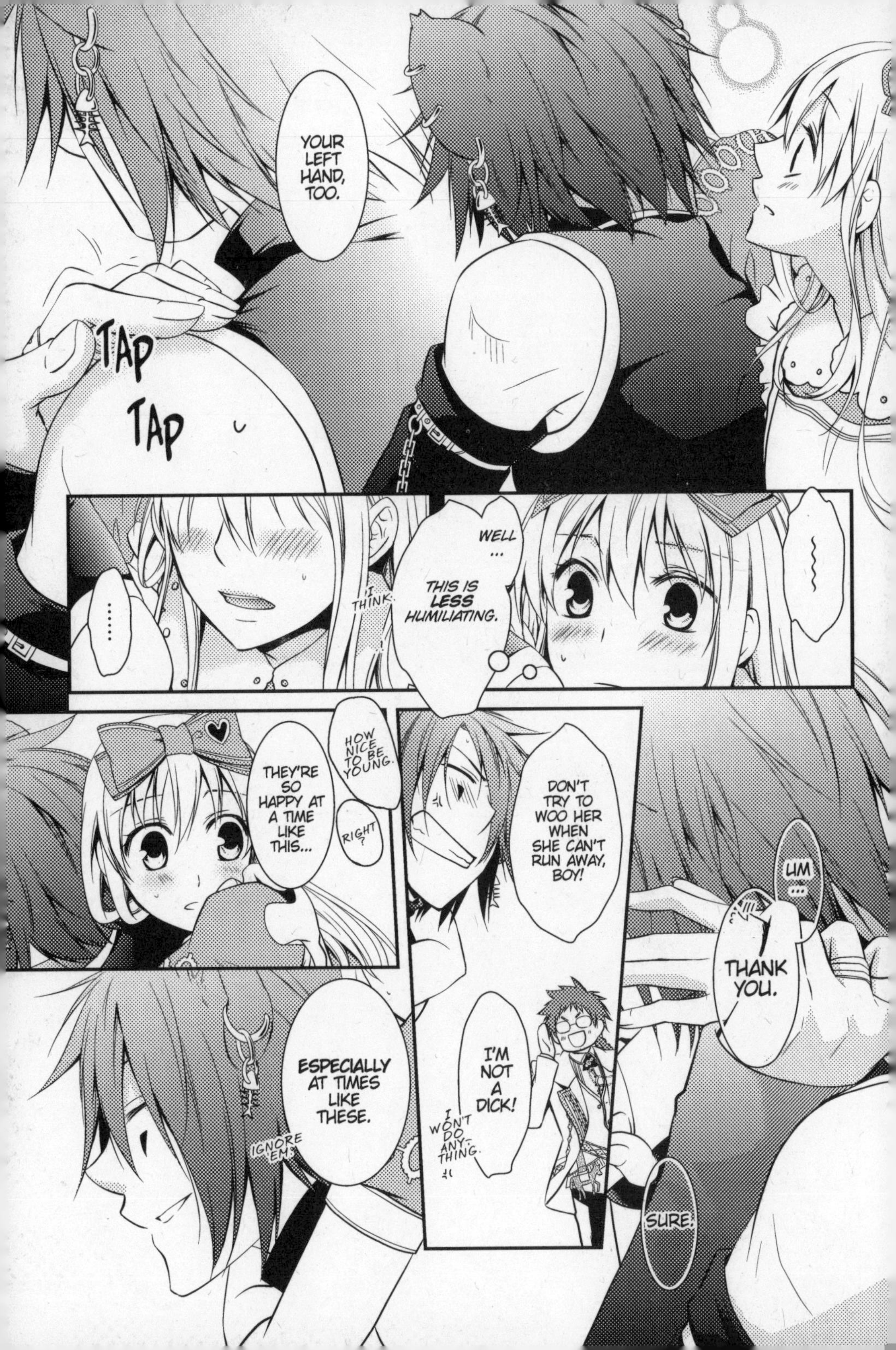

YOUR LEFT HAND, TOO.
TAP
TAP
WELL...
THIS IS LESS HUMILIATING.
I THINK.
......
UM...
THANK YOU.
DON'T TRY TO WOO HER WHEN SHE CAN'T RUN AWAY, BOY!
HOW NICE TO BE YOUNG.
THEY'RE SO HAPPY AT A TIME LIKE THIS...
RIGHT?
SURE.
I'M NOT A DICK!
I WON'T DO ANYTHING.
ESPECIALLY AT TIMES LIKE THESE.
IGNORE 'EM.

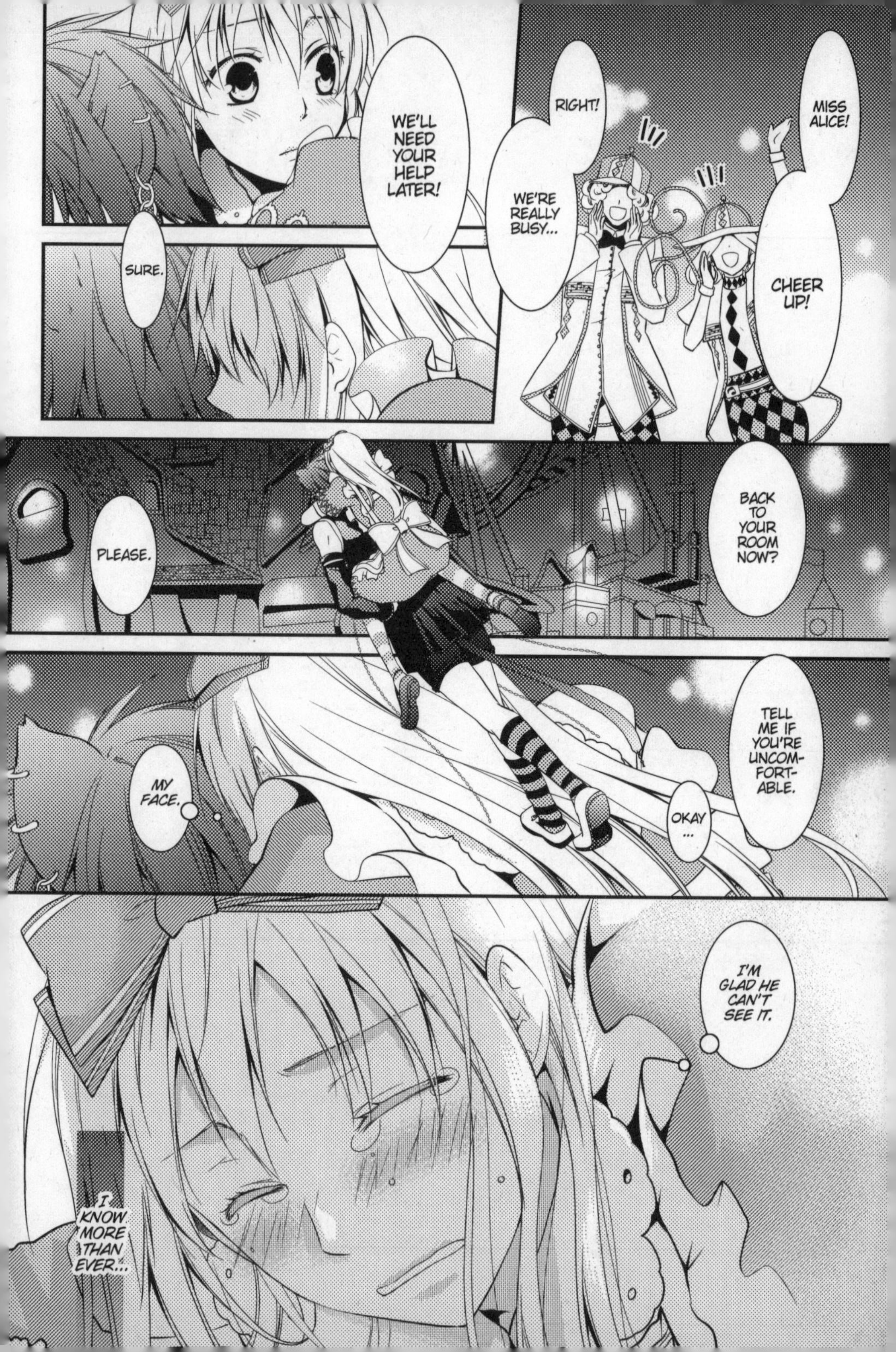
MISS ALICE!
CHEER UP!
RIGHT!
WE'RE REALLY BUSY...
WE'LL NEED YOUR HELP LATER!
SURE.
BACK TO YOUR ROOM NOW?
PLEASE.
TELL ME IF YOU'RE UNCOM-FORT-ABLE.
OKAY...
MY FACE.
I'M GLAD HE CAN'T SEE IT.
I KNOW MORE THAN EVER...

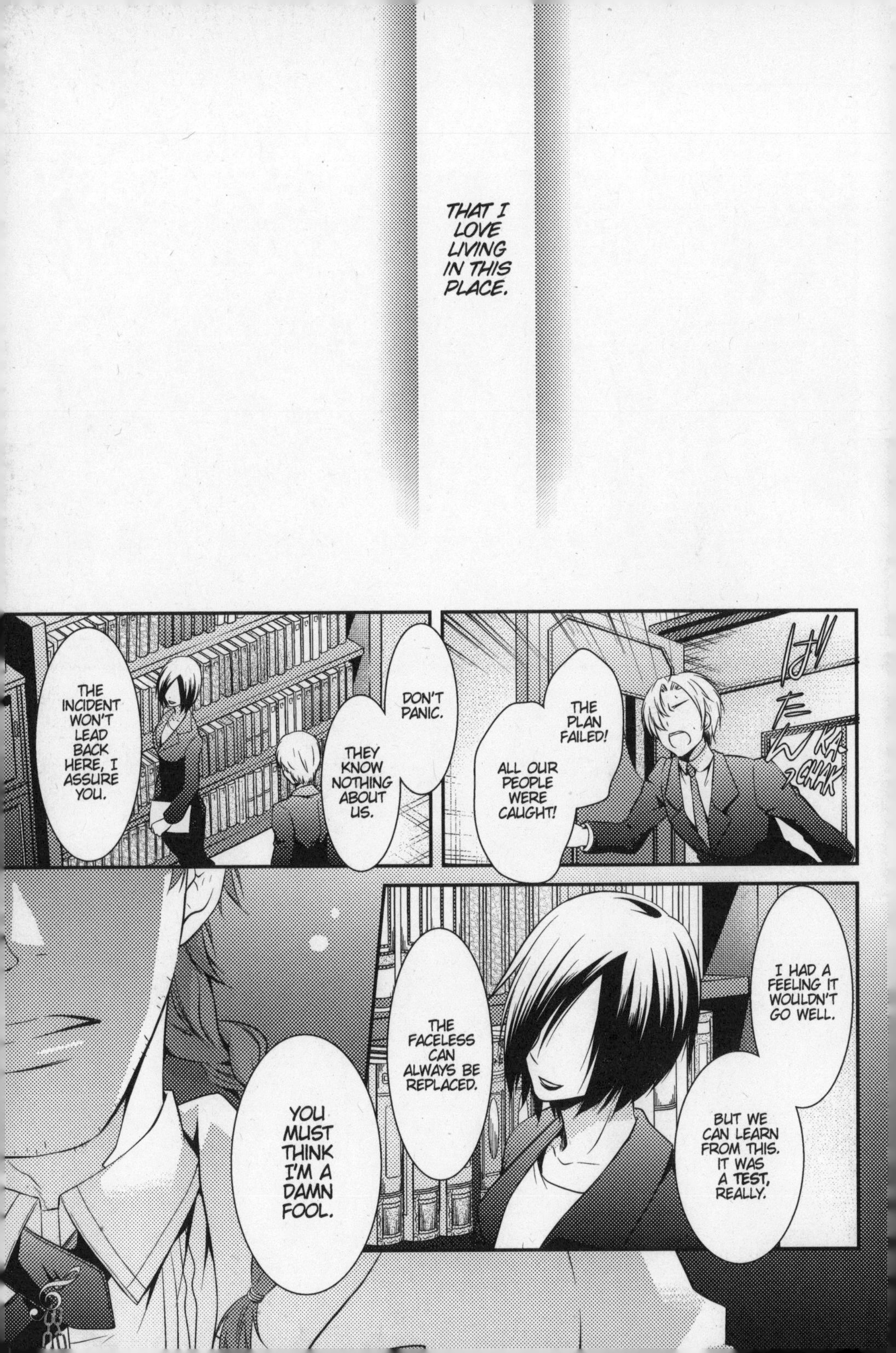
THAT I LOVE LIVING IN THIS PLACE.
ばたんっ
KA-CHAK
THE PLAN FAILED!
ALL OUR PEOPLE WERE CAUGHT!
DON'T PANIC.
THEY KNOW NOTHING ABOUT US.
THE INCIDENT WON'T LEAD BACK HERE, I ASSURE YOU.
I HAD A FEELING IT WOULDN'T GO WELL.
BUT WE CAN LEARN FROM THIS. IT WAS A TEST, REALLY.
THE FACELESS CAN ALWAYS BE REPLACED.
YOU MUST THINK I'M A DAMN FOOL.

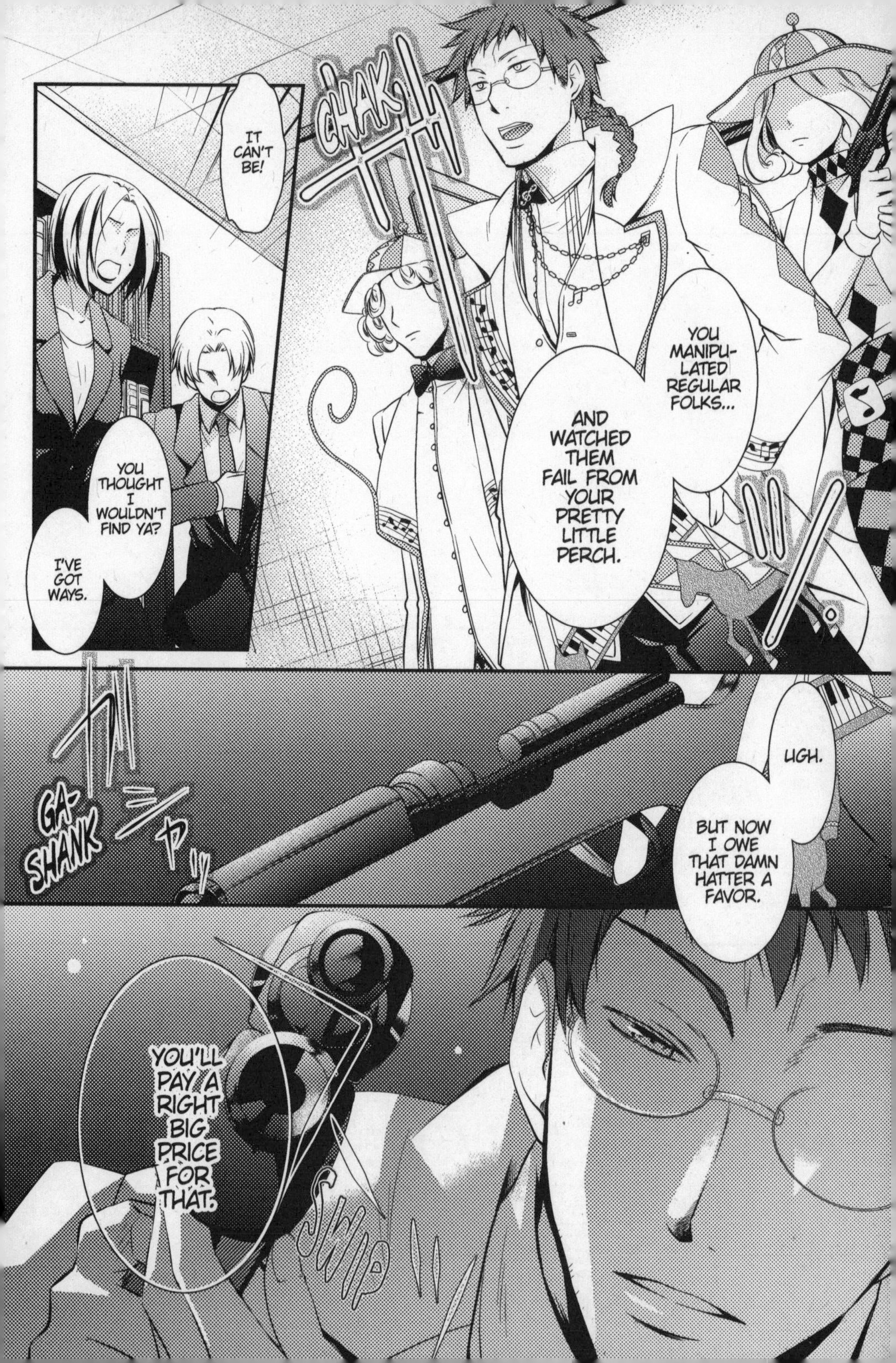
CHAK
YOU MANIPULATED REGULAR FOLKS...
AND WATCHED THEM FAIL FROM YOUR PRETTY LITTLE PERCH.
IT CAN'T BE!
YOU THOUGHT I WOULDN'T FIND YA?
I'VE GOT WAYS.
UGH.
BUT NOW I OWE THAT DAMN HATTER A FAVOR.
GA-SHANK
YOU'LL PAY A RIGHT BIG PRICE FOR THAT.

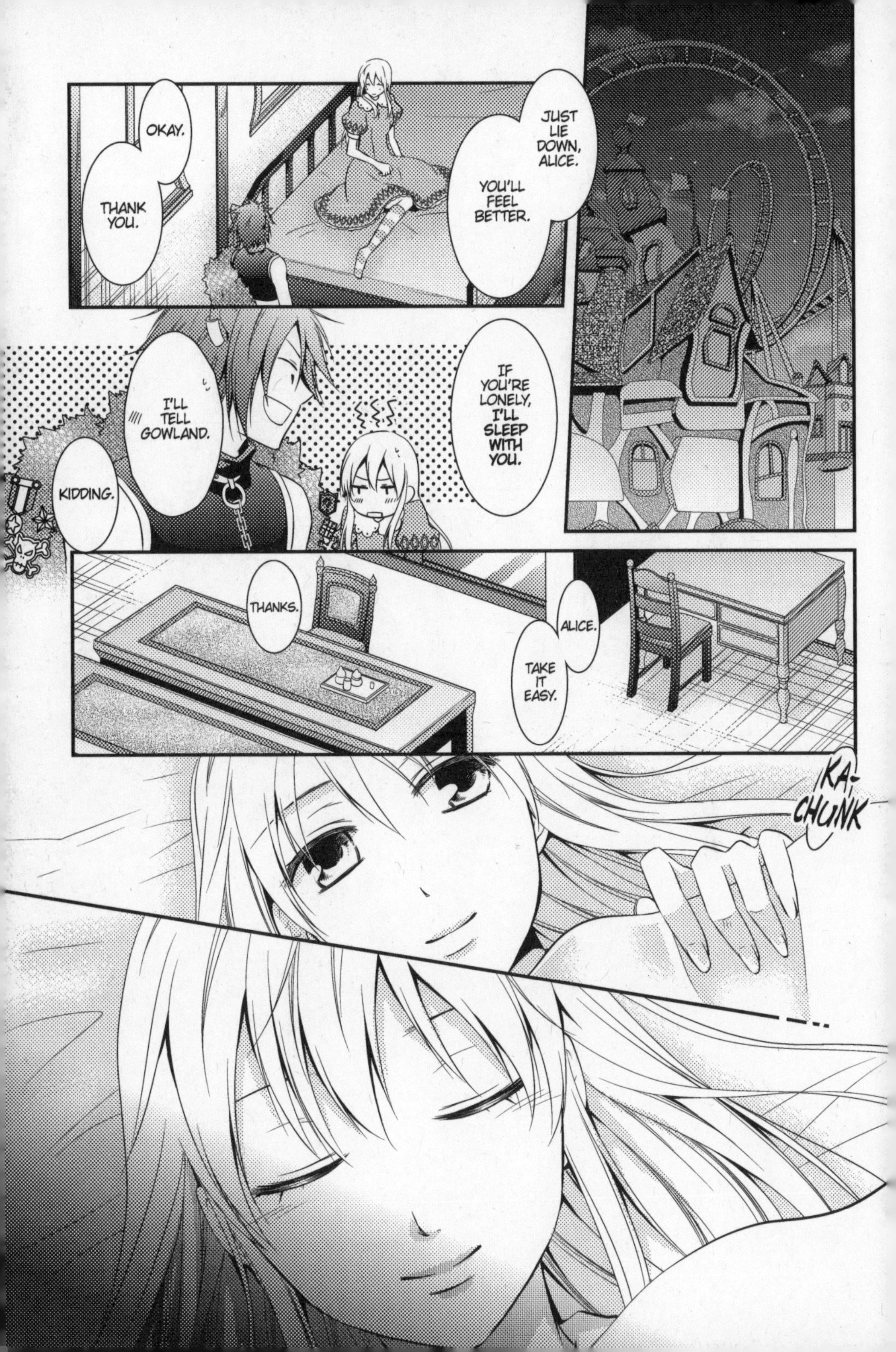
JUST LIE DOWN, ALICE.
YOU'LL FEEL BETTER.
OKAY.
THANK YOU.
IF YOU'RE LONELY, I'LL SLEEP WITH YOU.
I'LL TELL GOWLAND.
KIDDING.
ALICE.
TAKE IT EASY.
THANKS.
KA-CHUNK

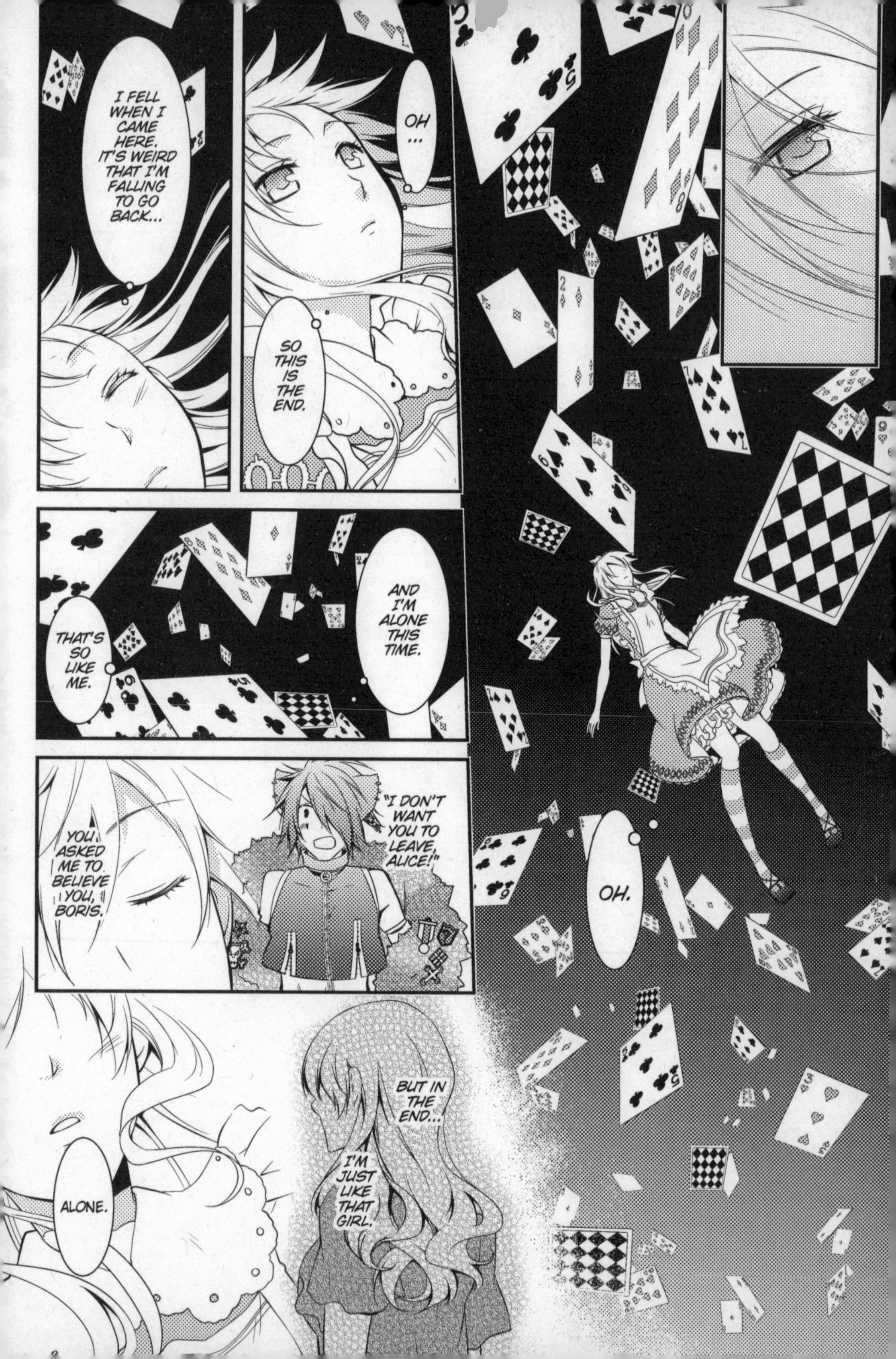
OH.
OH...
SO THIS IS THE END.
I FELL WHEN I CAME HERE. IT'S WEIRD THAT I'M FALLING TO GO BACK...
AND I'M ALONE THIS TIME.
THAT'S SO LIKE ME.
"I DON'T WANT YOU TO LEAVE, ALICE!"
YOU ASKED ME TO BELIEVE YOU, BORIS.
BUT IN THE END...
I'M JUST LIKE THAT GIRL.
ALONE.

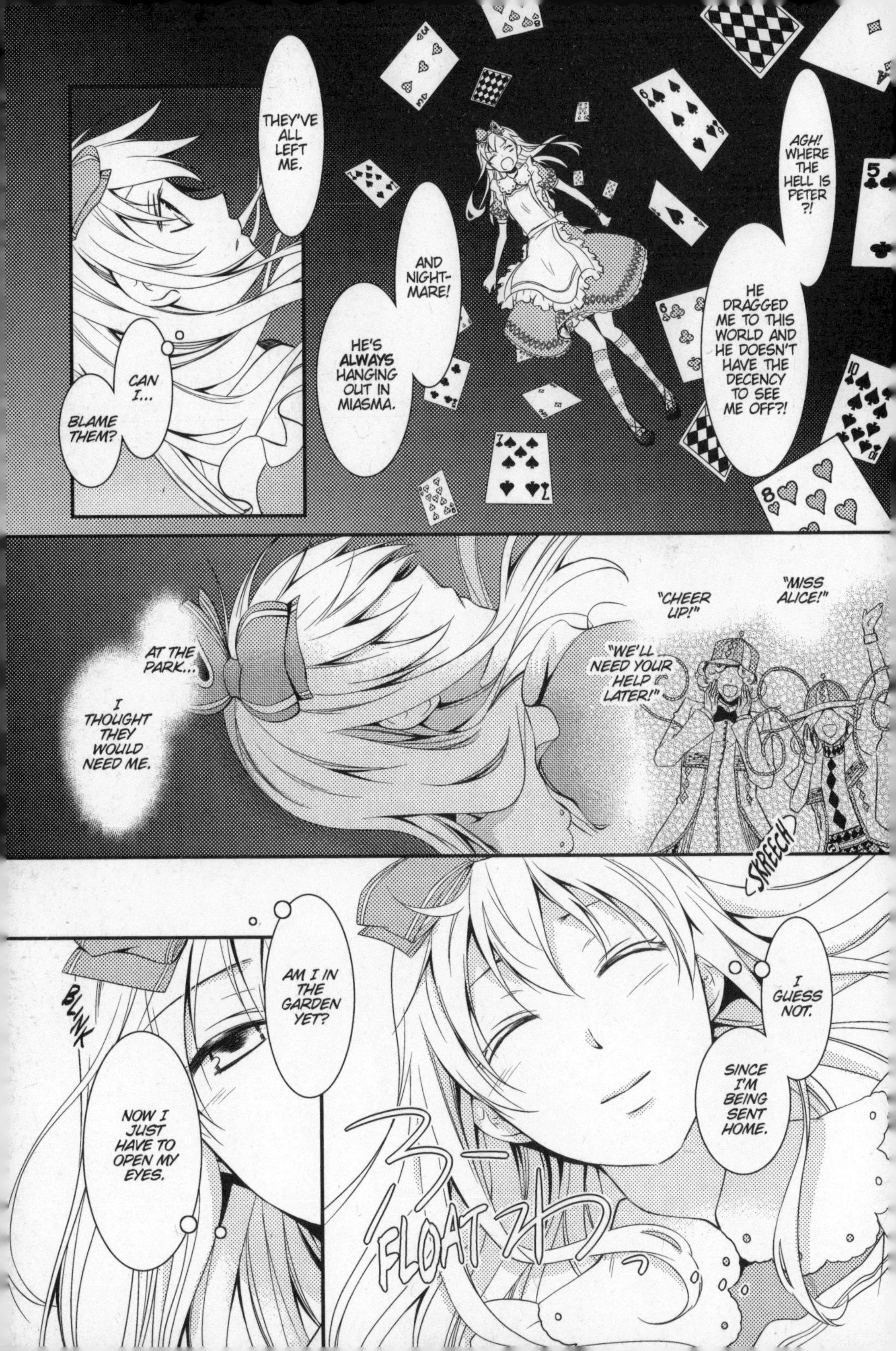
AGH! WHERE THE HELL IS PETER?!
HE DRAGGED ME TO THIS WORLD AND HE DOESN'T HAVE THE DECENCY TO SEE ME OFF?!
AND NIGHT-MARE!
HE'S **ALWAYS** HANGING OUT IN MIASMA.
THEY'VE ALL LEFT ME.
CAN I...
BLAME THEM?
"MISS ALICE!"
"CHEER UP!"
"WE'LL NEED YOUR HELP LATER!"
AT THE PARK...
I THOUGHT THEY WOULD NEED ME.
SKREECH
I GUESS NOT.
SINCE I'M BEING SENT HOME.
FLOAT
AM I IN THE GARDEN YET?
BLINK
NOW I JUST HAVE TO OPEN MY EYES.

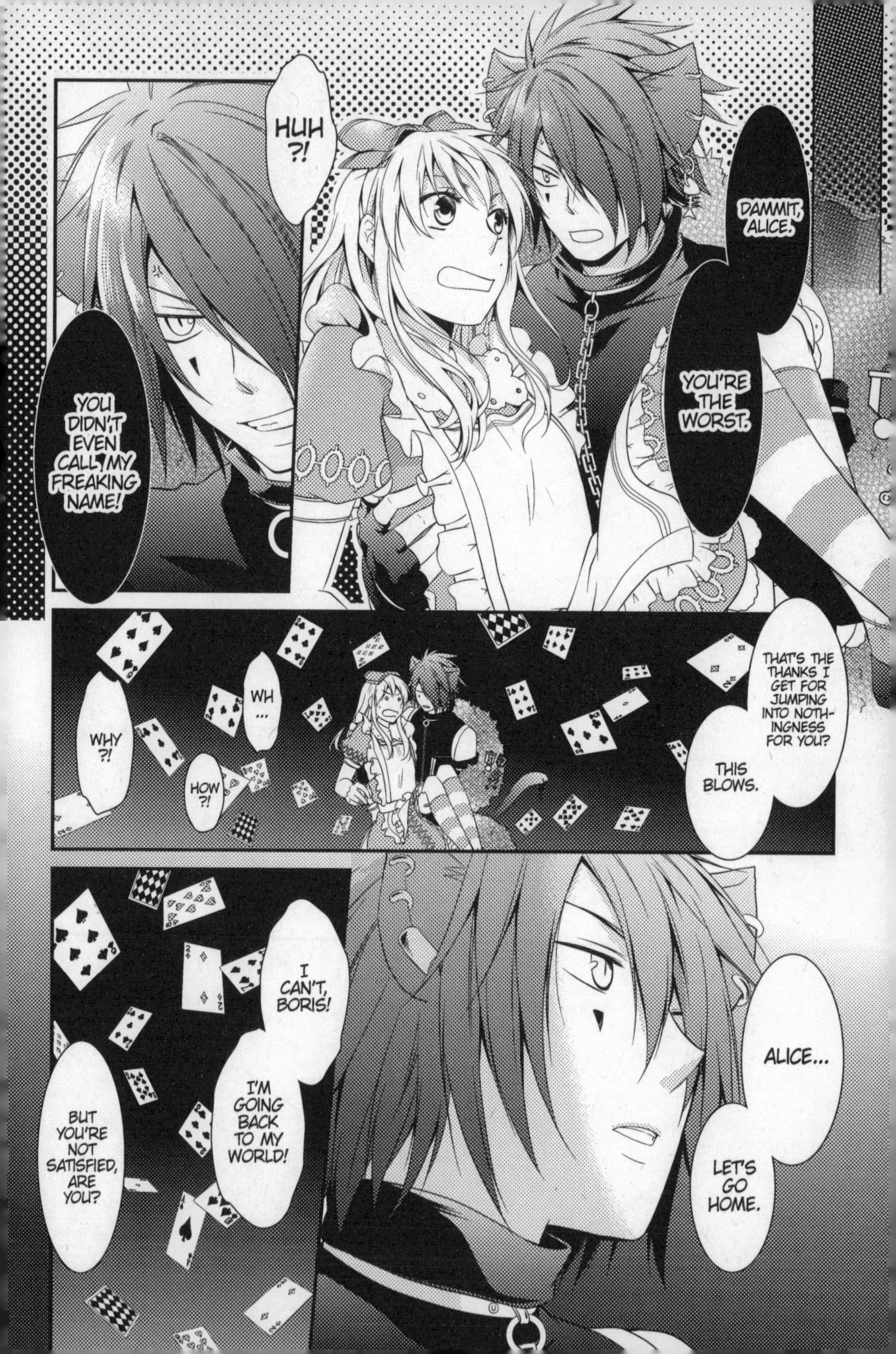
DAMMIT, ALICE.
YOU'RE THE WORST.
HUH ?!
YOU DIDN'T EVEN CALL MY FREAKING NAME!
THAT'S THE THANKS I GET FOR JUMPING INTO NOTH-INGNESS FOR YOU?
THIS BLOWS.
WH ...
HOW ?!
WHY ?!
ALICE...
LET'S GO HOME.
I CAN'T, BORIS!
I'M GOING BACK TO MY WORLD!
BUT YOU'RE NOT SATISFIED, ARE YOU?

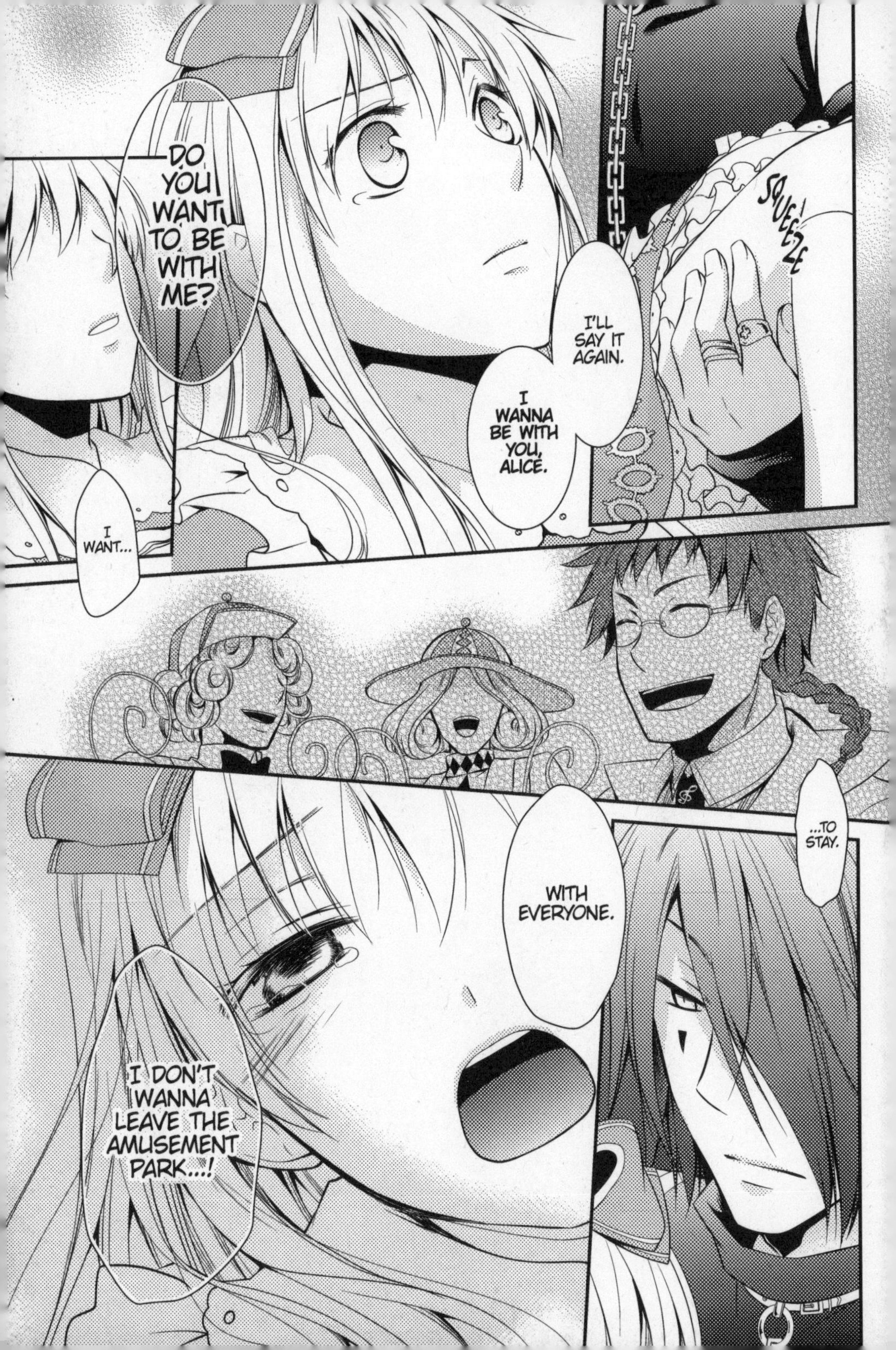
SQUEEZE
I'LL SAY IT AGAIN.
I WANNA BE WITH YOU, ALICE.
DO YOU WANT TO BE WITH ME?
I WANT...
...TO STAY.
WITH EVERYONE.
I DON'T WANNA LEAVE THE AMUSEMENT PARK...!

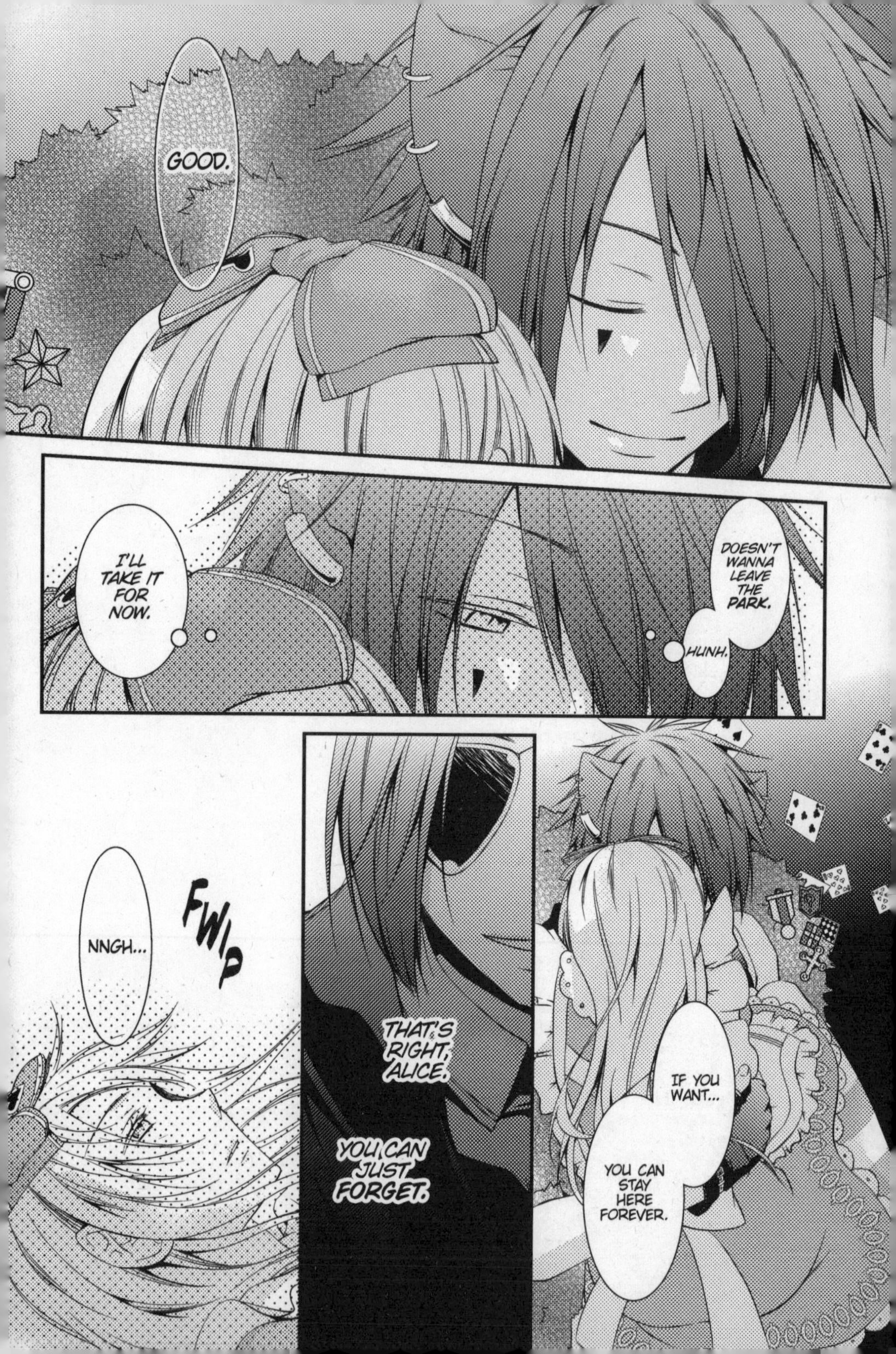
GOOD.
DOESN'T WANNA LEAVE THE PARK.
HUNH.
I'LL TAKE IT FOR NOW.
IF YOU WANT...
YOU CAN STAY HERE FOREVER.
THAT'S RIGHT, ALICE.
YOU CAN JUST FORGET.
NNGH...
FWIP

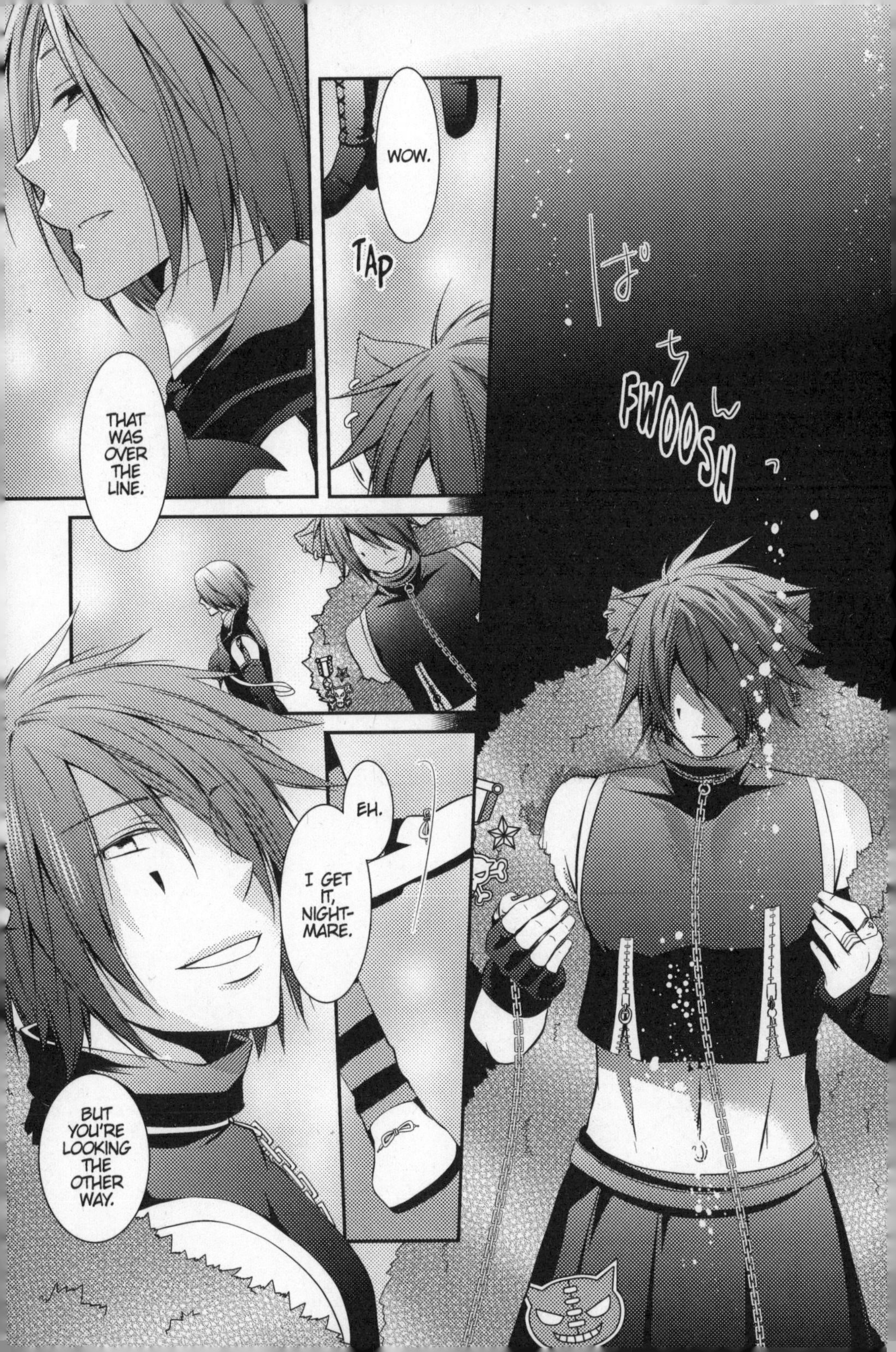
ぱちん
FWOOSH
WOW.
TAP
THAT WAS OVER THE LINE.
EH.
I GET IT, NIGHTMARE.
BUT YOU'RE LOOKING THE OTHER WAY.

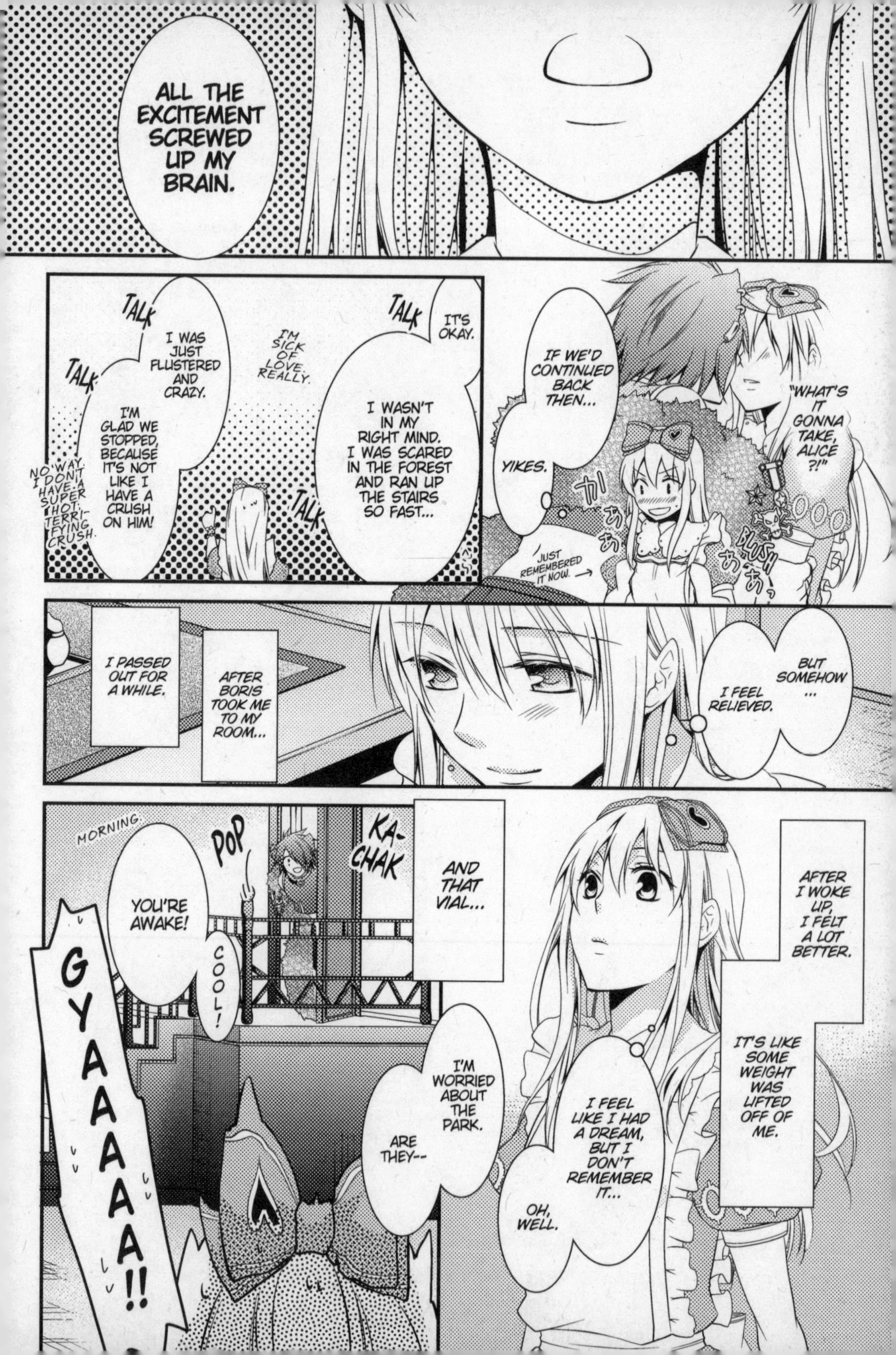
ALL THE EXCITEMENT SCREWED UP MY BRAIN.
"WHAT'S IT GONNA TAKE, ALICE ?!"
IF WE'D CONTINUED BACK THEN...
YIKES.
BLUSH
JUST REMEMBERED IT NOW.
IT'S OKAY.
TALK
I WASN'T IN MY RIGHT MIND. I WAS SCARED IN THE FOREST AND RAN UP THE STAIRS SO FAST...
TALK
I'M SICK OF LOVE. REALLY.
TALK
I WAS JUST FLUSTERED AND CRAZY.
TALK
I'M GLAD WE STOPPED, BECAUSE IT'S NOT LIKE I HAVE A CRUSH ON HIM!
NO WAY. I DON'T HAVE A SUPER HOT, TERRIFYING CRUSH.
BUT SOMEHOW ...
I FEEL RELIEVED.
AFTER BORIS TOOK ME TO MY ROOM...
I PASSED OUT FOR A WHILE.
AFTER I WOKE UP, I FELT A LOT BETTER.
IT'S LIKE SOME WEIGHT WAS LIFTED OFF OF ME.
I FEEL LIKE I HAD A DREAM, BUT I DON'T REMEMBER IT...
OH, WELL.
AND THAT VIAL...
I'M WORRIED ABOUT THE PARK.
ARE THEY--
KA-CHAK
POP
MORNING.
YOU'RE AWAKE!
COOL!
GYAAAAA!!

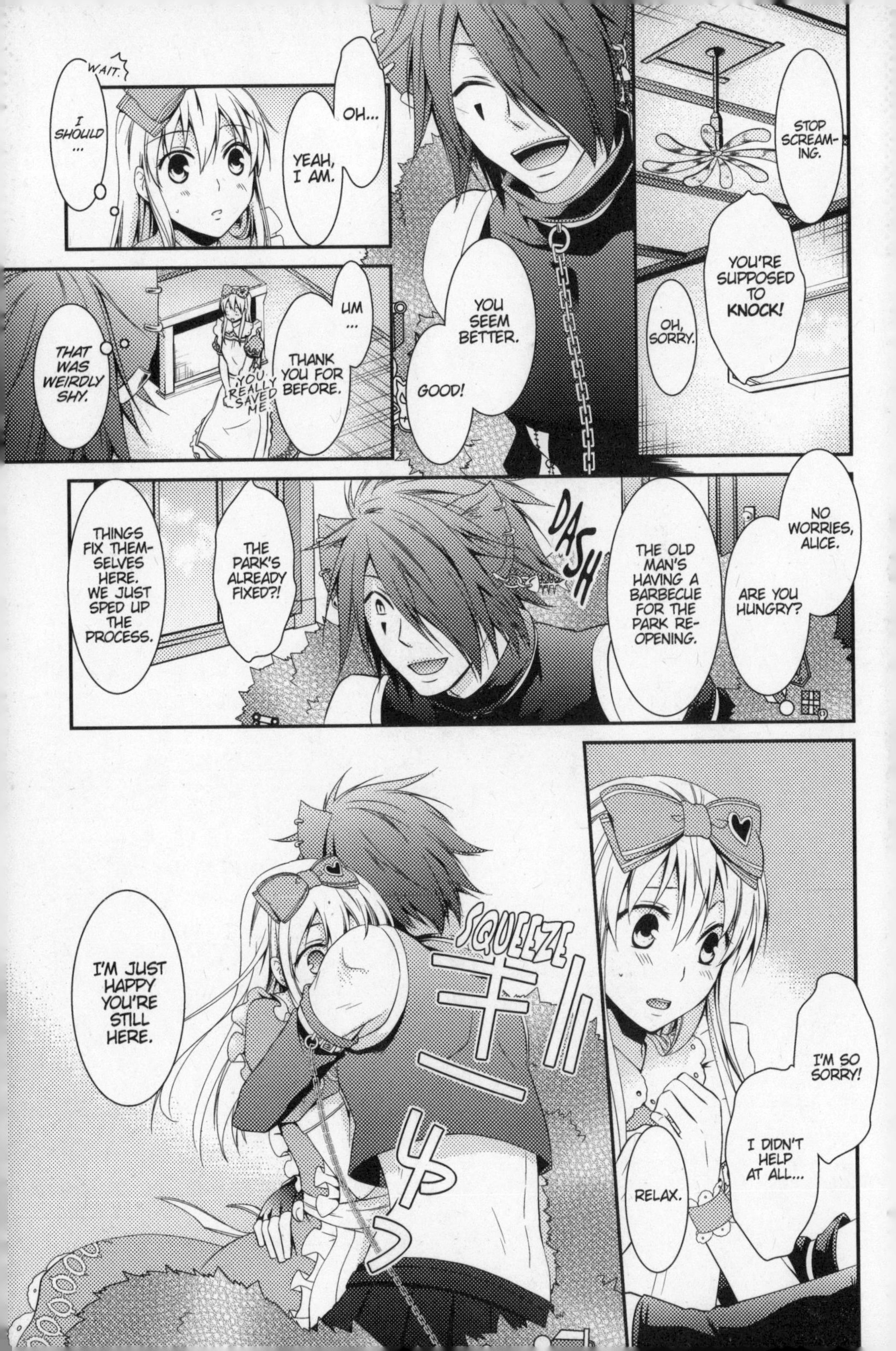

STOP SCREAMING.
YOU'RE SUPPOSED TO KNOCK!
OH, SORRY.
OH... YEAH, I AM.
YOU SEEM BETTER.
GOOD!
WAIT.
I SHOULD...
UM... THANK YOU FOR BEFORE.
YOU REALLY SAVED ME.
THAT WAS WEIRDLY SHY.
NO WORRIES, ALICE.
ARE YOU HUNGRY?
THE OLD MAN'S HAVING A BARBECUE FOR THE PARK RE-OPENING.
DASH
THE PARK'S ALREADY FIXED?!
THINGS FIX THEMSELVES HERE. WE JUST SPED UP THE PROCESS.
I'M SO SORRY!
I DIDN'T HELP AT ALL...
RELAX.
SQUEEZE
I'M JUST HAPPY YOU'RE STILL HERE.

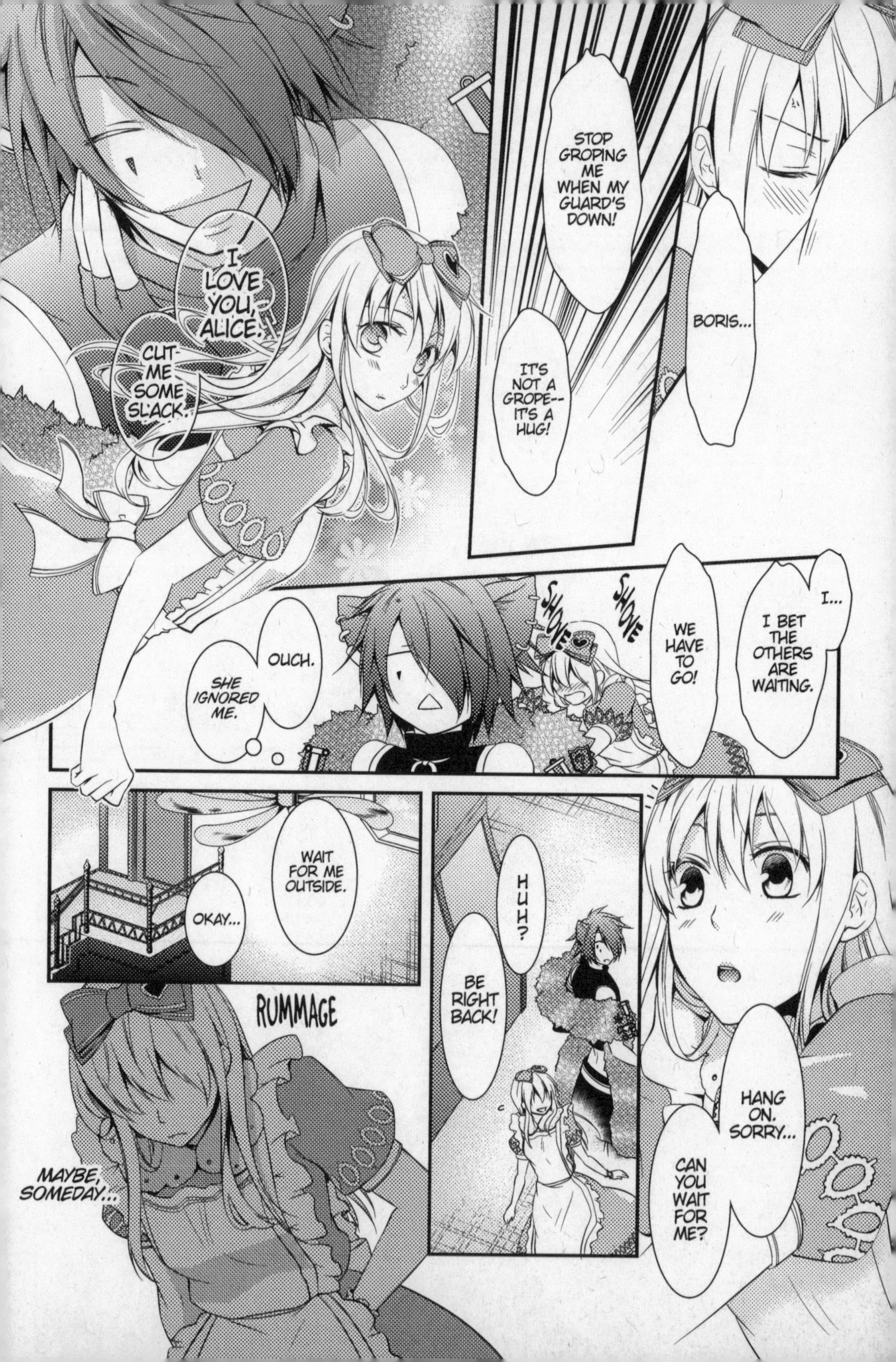
BORIS...
STOP GROPING ME WHEN MY GUARD'S DOWN!
IT'S NOT A GROPE-- IT'S A HUG!
I LOVE YOU, ALICE.
CUT- ME SOME SLACK.
I...
I BET THE OTHERS ARE WAITING.
WE HAVE TO GO!
SHOVE
SHOVE
OUCH.
SHE IGNORED ME.
HANG ON. SORRY...
CAN YOU WAIT FOR ME?
HUH?
BE RIGHT BACK!
WAIT FOR ME OUTSIDE.
OKAY...
RUMMAGE
MAYBE, SOMEDAY...

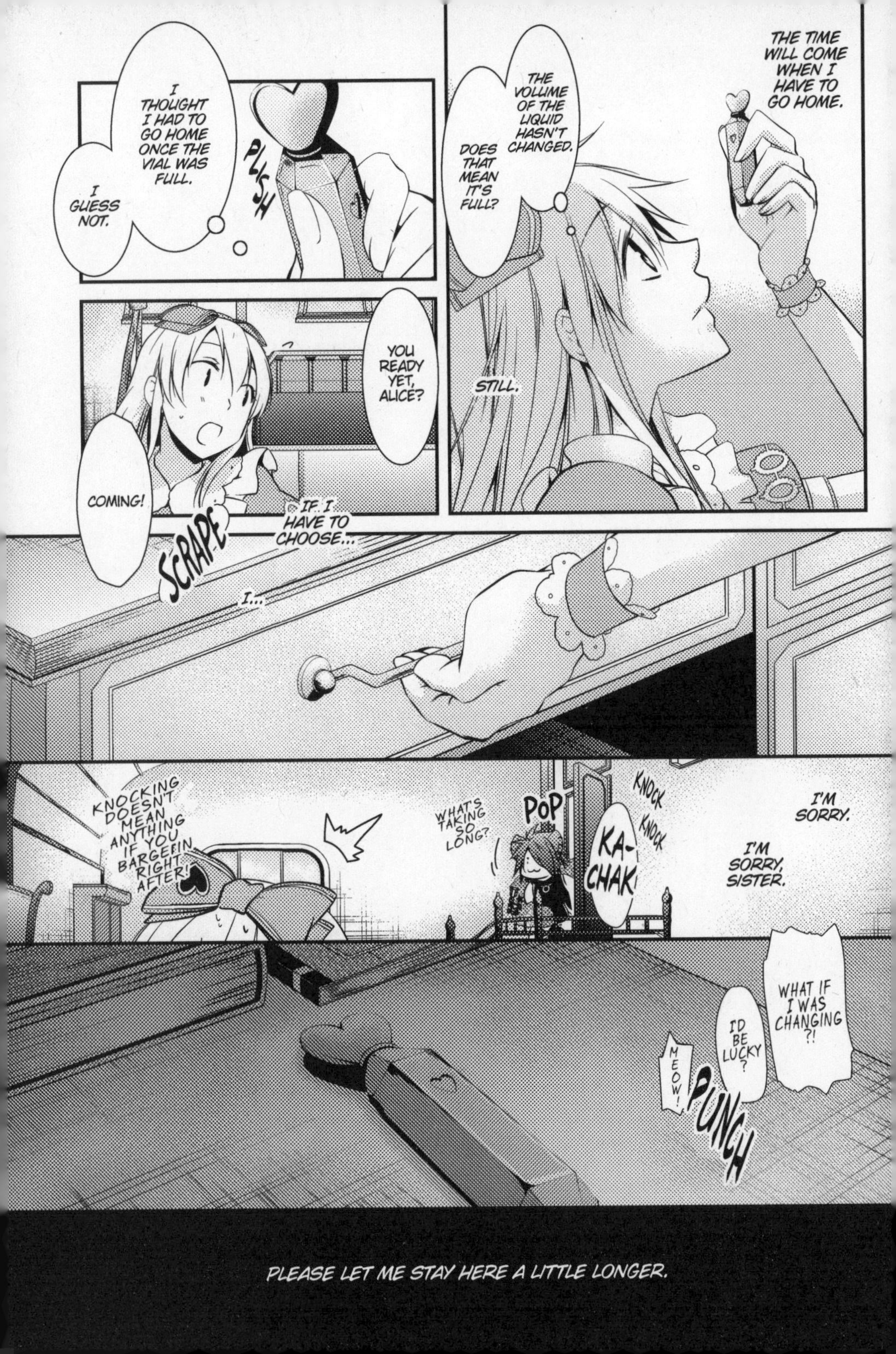
THE TIME WILL COME WHEN I HAVE TO GO HOME.
THE VOLUME OF THE LIQUID HASN'T CHANGED.
DOES THAT MEAN IT'S FULL?
STILL.
I THOUGHT I HAD TO GO HOME ONCE THE VIAL WAS FULL.
I GUESS NOT.
PLISH
YOU READY YET, ALICE?
COMING!
IF I HAVE TO CHOOSE...
I...
SCRAPE
I'M SORRY.
I'M SORRY, SISTER.
KNOCK
KNOCK
KA-CHAK
POP
WHAT'S TAKING SO LONG?
KNOCKING DOESN'T MEAN ANYTHING IF YOU BARGE IN RIGHT AFTER!
WHAT IF I WAS CHANGING?!
ID BE LUCKY?
PUNCH
MEOW!
PLEASE LET ME STAY HERE A LITTLE LONGER.

Side Story 5: "18+"

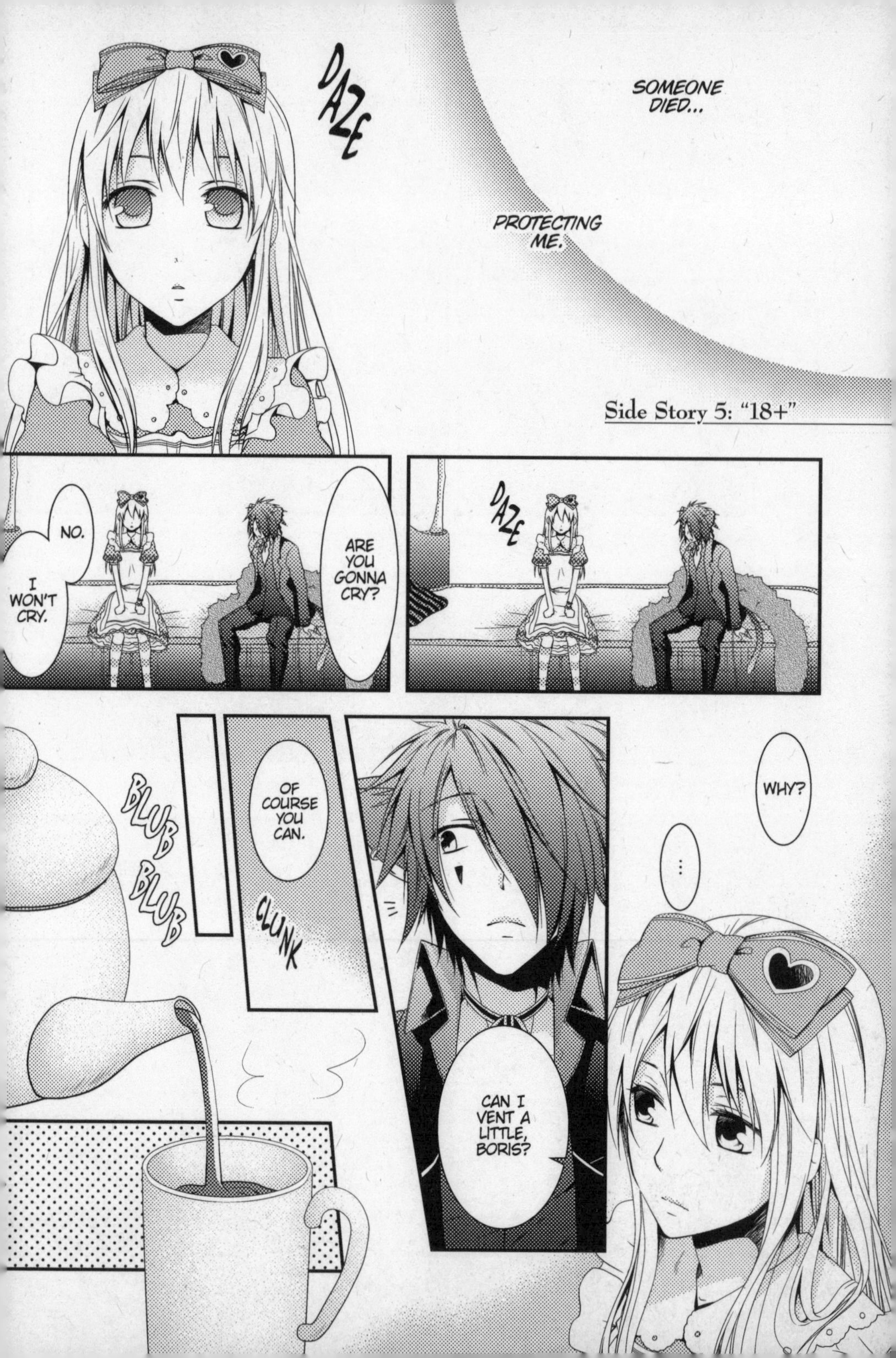

SOMEONE DIED...
DAZE
PROTECTING ME.
DAZE
ARE YOU GONNA CRY?
NO.
I WON'T CRY.
WHY?
...
CAN I VENT A LITTLE, BORIS?
OF COURSE YOU CAN.
CLUNK
BLUB BLUB

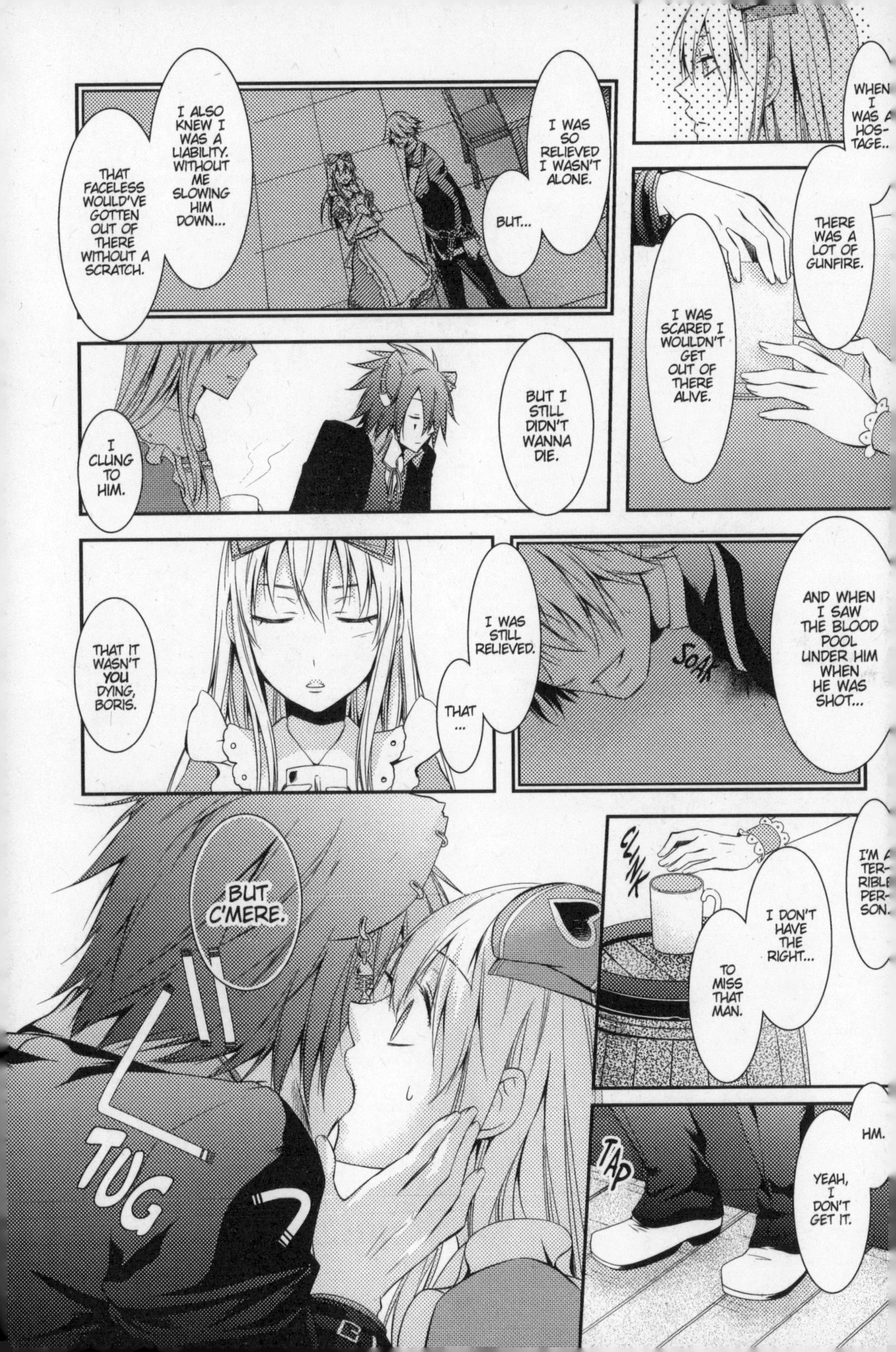
WHEN I WAS A HOSTAGE..
I WAS SO RELIEVED I WASN'T ALONE.
BUT...
I ALSO KNEW I WAS A LIABILITY. WITHOUT ME SLOWING HIM DOWN...
THAT FACELESS WOULD'VE GOTTEN OUT OF THERE WITHOUT A SCRATCH.
THERE WAS A LOT OF GUNFIRE.
I WAS SCARED I WOULDN'T GET OUT OF THERE ALIVE.
BUT I STILL DIDN'T WANNA DIE.
I CLUNG TO HIM.
AND WHEN I SAW THE BLOOD POOL UNDER HIM WHEN HE WAS SHOT...
SOAK
I WAS STILL RELIEVED.
THAT ...
THAT IT WASN'T YOU DYING, BORIS.
I'M A TERRIBLE PERSON.
CLINK
I DON'T HAVE THE RIGHT...
TO MISS THAT MAN.
HM.
YEAH, I DON'T GET IT.
TAP
BUT C'MERE.
TUG

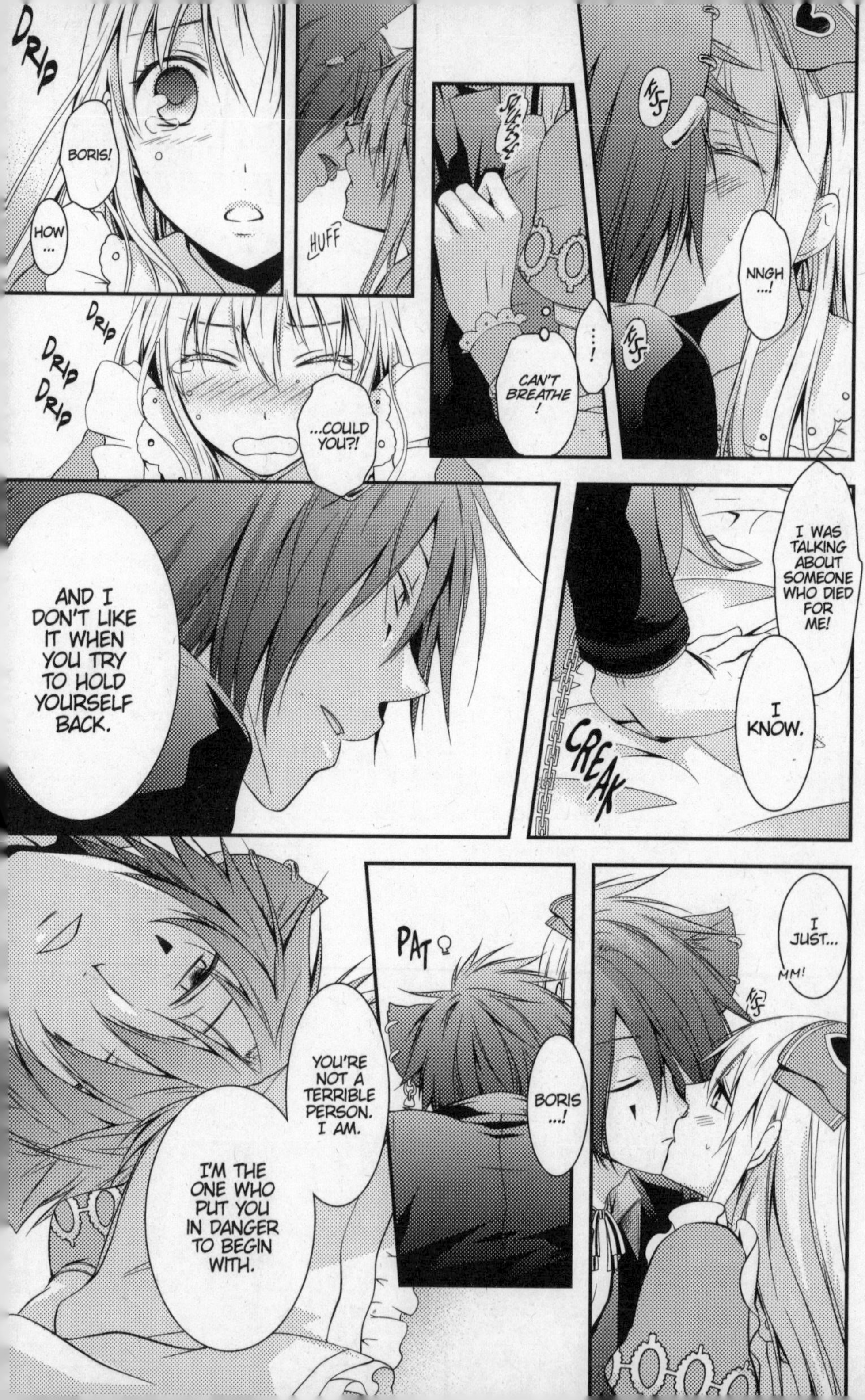
KISS
NNGH ...!
KISS
SQUEEZE
...!
CAN'T BREATHE!
HUFF
DRIP
BORIS!
HOW ...
DRIP
DRIP
DRIP
...COULD YOU?!
I WAS TALKING ABOUT SOMEONE WHO DIED FOR ME!
I KNOW.
CREAK
AND I DON'T LIKE IT WHEN YOU TRY TO HOLD YOURSELF BACK.
I JUST...
MM!
KISS
BORIS ...!
PAT
YOU'RE NOT A TERRIBLE PERSON. I AM.
I'M THE ONE WHO PUT YOU IN DANGER TO BEGIN WITH.

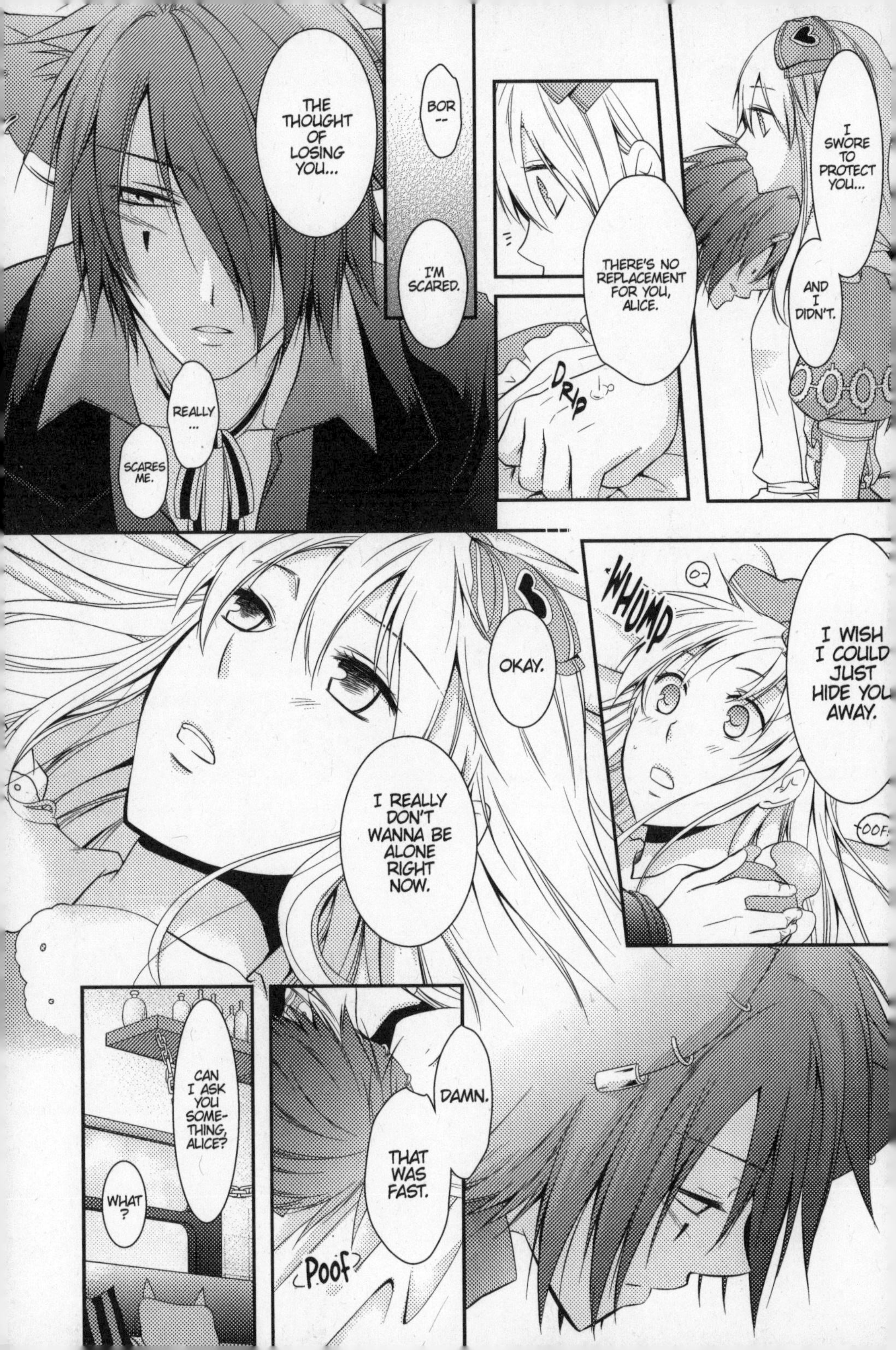
I SWORE TO PROTECT YOU...
AND I DIDN'T.
THERE'S NO REPLACEMENT FOR YOU, ALICE.
DRIP
BOR--
I'M SCARED.
THE THOUGHT OF LOSING YOU...
REALLY...
SCARES ME.
WHUMP
I WISH I COULD JUST HIDE YOU AWAY.
OOF
OKAY.
I REALLY DON'T WANNA BE ALONE RIGHT NOW.
DAMN.
THAT WAS FAST.
POOF
CAN I ASK YOU SOME-THING, ALICE?
WHAT?

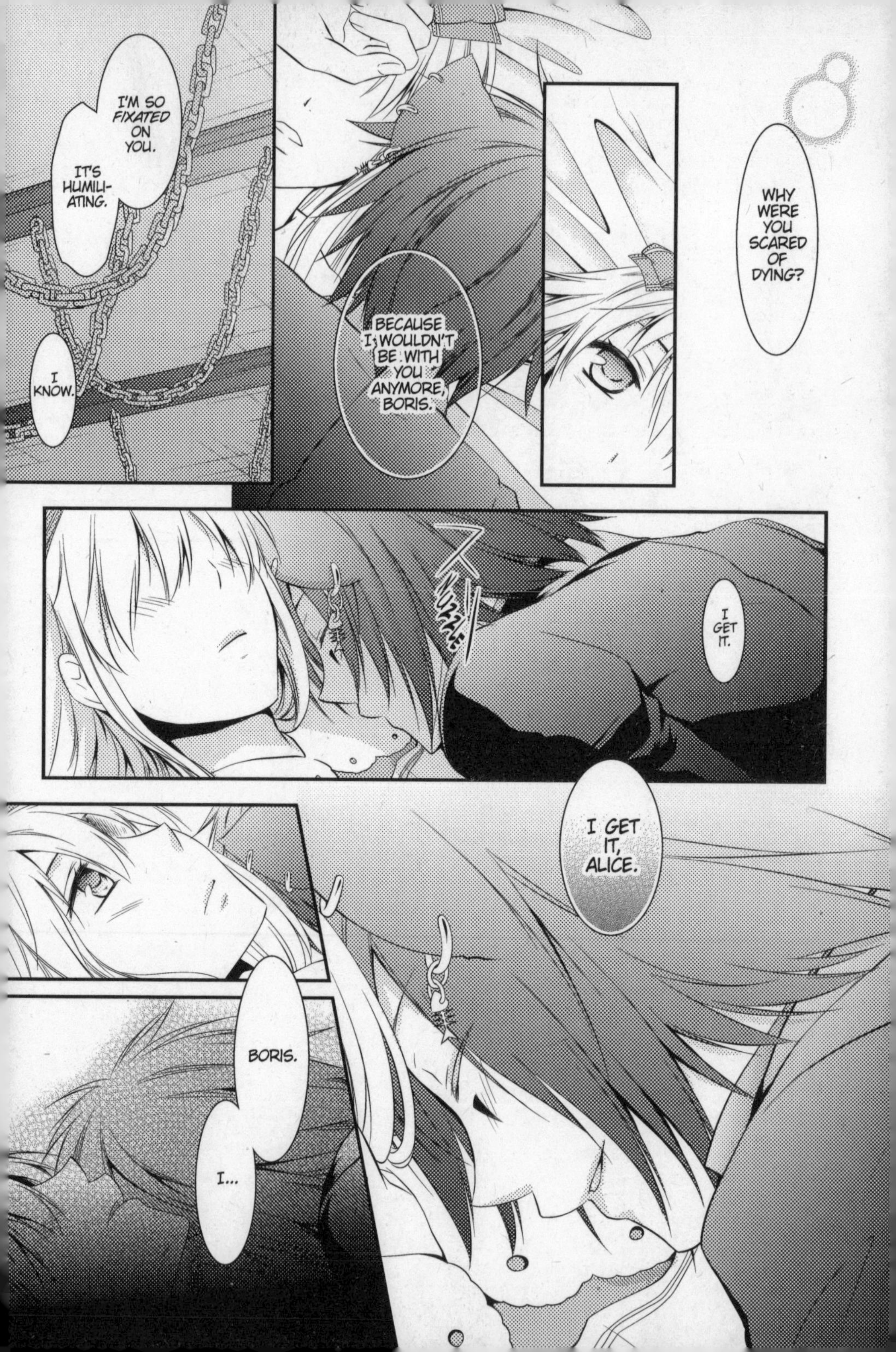
WHY WERE YOU SCARED OF DYING?
BECAUSE I WOULDN'T BE WITH YOU ANYMORE, BORIS.
I'M SO FIXATED ON YOU.
IT'S HUMILIATING.
I KNOW.
I GET IT.
SNUZZLE
I GET IT, ALICE.
BORIS.
I...

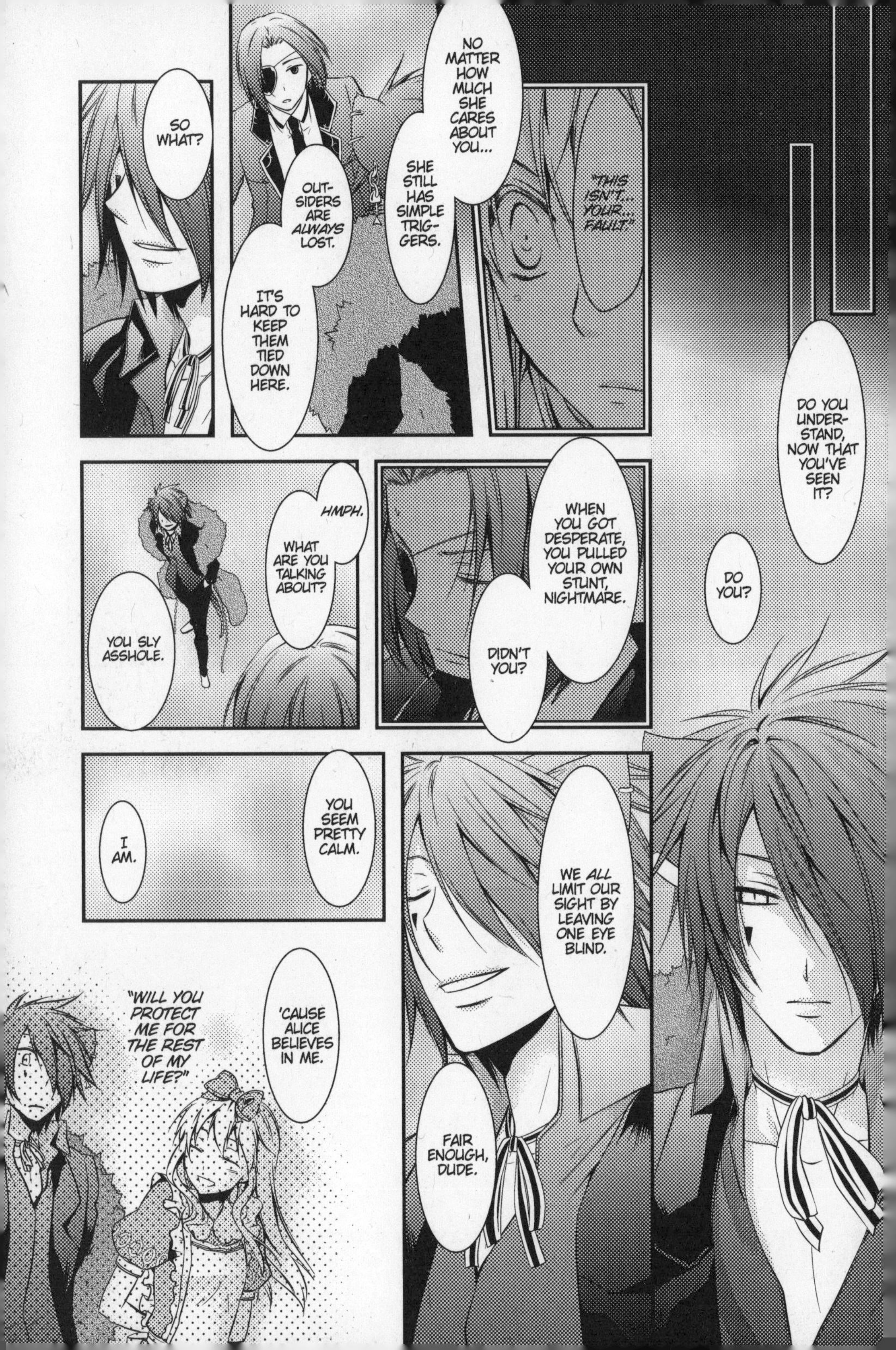
"THIS ISN'T... YOUR... FAULT."
NO MATTER HOW MUCH SHE CARES ABOUT YOU...
SHE STILL HAS SIMPLE TRIGGERS.
SO WHAT?
OUTSIDERS ARE *ALWAYS* LOST.
IT'S HARD TO KEEP THEM TIED DOWN HERE.
DO YOU UNDERSTAND, NOW THAT YOU'VE SEEN IT?
DO YOU?
WHEN YOU GOT DESPERATE, YOU PULLED YOUR OWN STUNT, NIGHTMARE.
DIDN'T YOU?
HMPH.
WHAT ARE YOU TALKING ABOUT?
YOU SLY ASSHOLE.
YOU SEEM PRETTY CALM.
I AM.
WE ALL LIMIT OUR SIGHT BY LEAVING ONE EYE BLIND.
'CAUSE ALICE BELIEVES IN ME.
"WILL YOU PROTECT ME FOR THE REST OF MY LIFE?"
FAIR ENOUGH, DUDE.

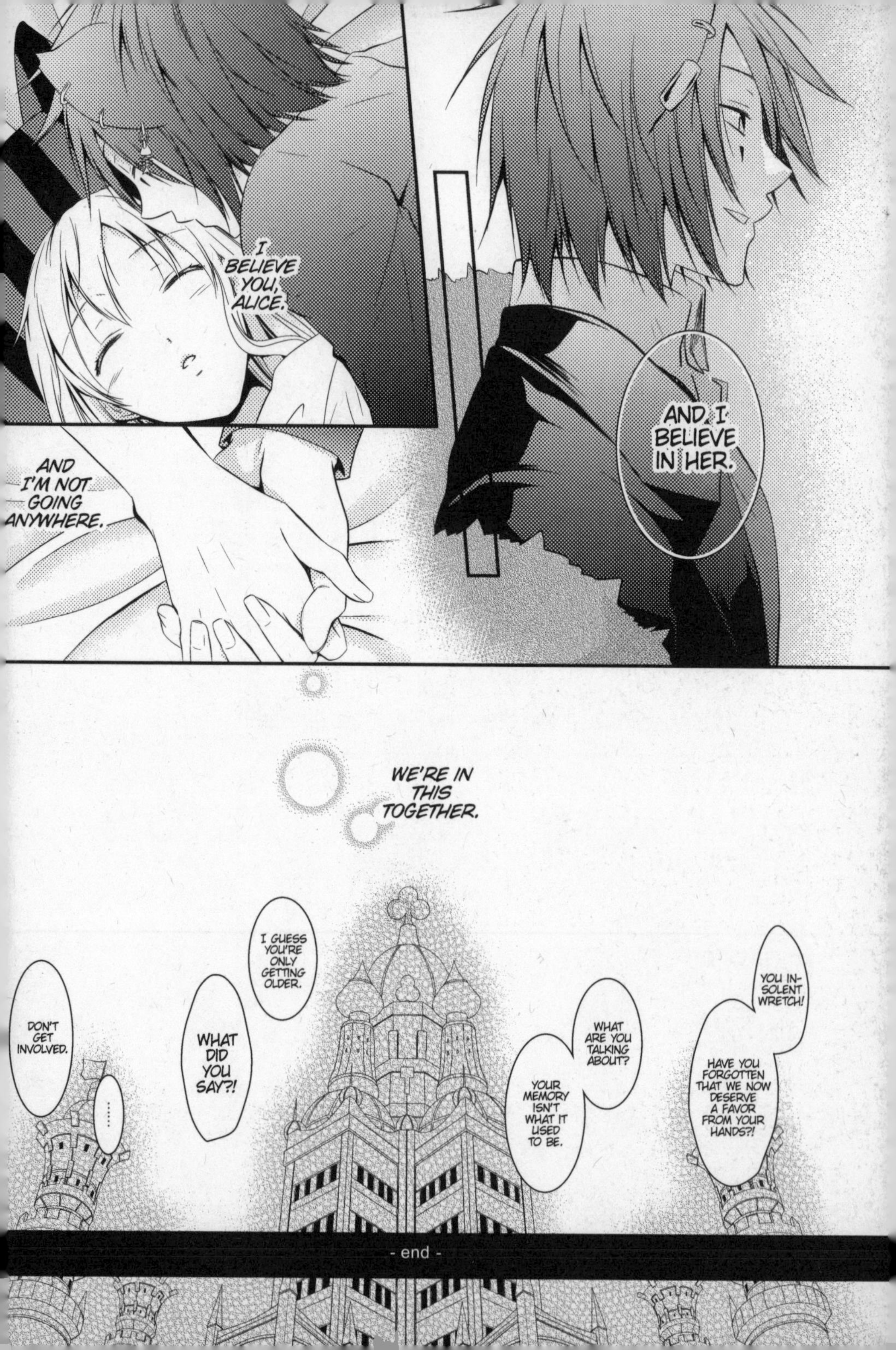
AND I BELIEVE IN HER.
I BELIEVE YOU, ALICE.
AND I'M NOT GOING ANYWHERE.
WE'RE IN THIS TOGETHER.
YOU IN-SOLENT WRETCH!
HAVE YOU FORGOTTEN THAT WE NOW DESERVE A FAVOR FROM YOUR HANDS?!
WHAT ARE YOU TALKING ABOUT?
YOUR MEMORY ISN'T WHAT IT USED TO BE.
I GUESS YOU'RE ONLY GETTING OLDER.
WHAT DID YOU SAY?!
DON'T GET INVOLVED.
......
- end -

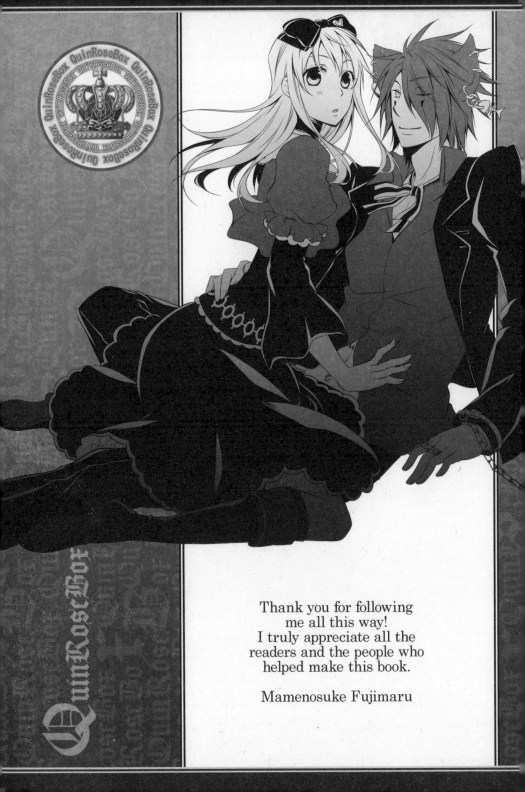

Thank you for following
me all this way!
I truly appreciate all the
readers and the people who
helped make this book.

Mamenosuke Fujimaru

CHESHIRE CAT WALTZ VOL. 7 - POST-MORTEM

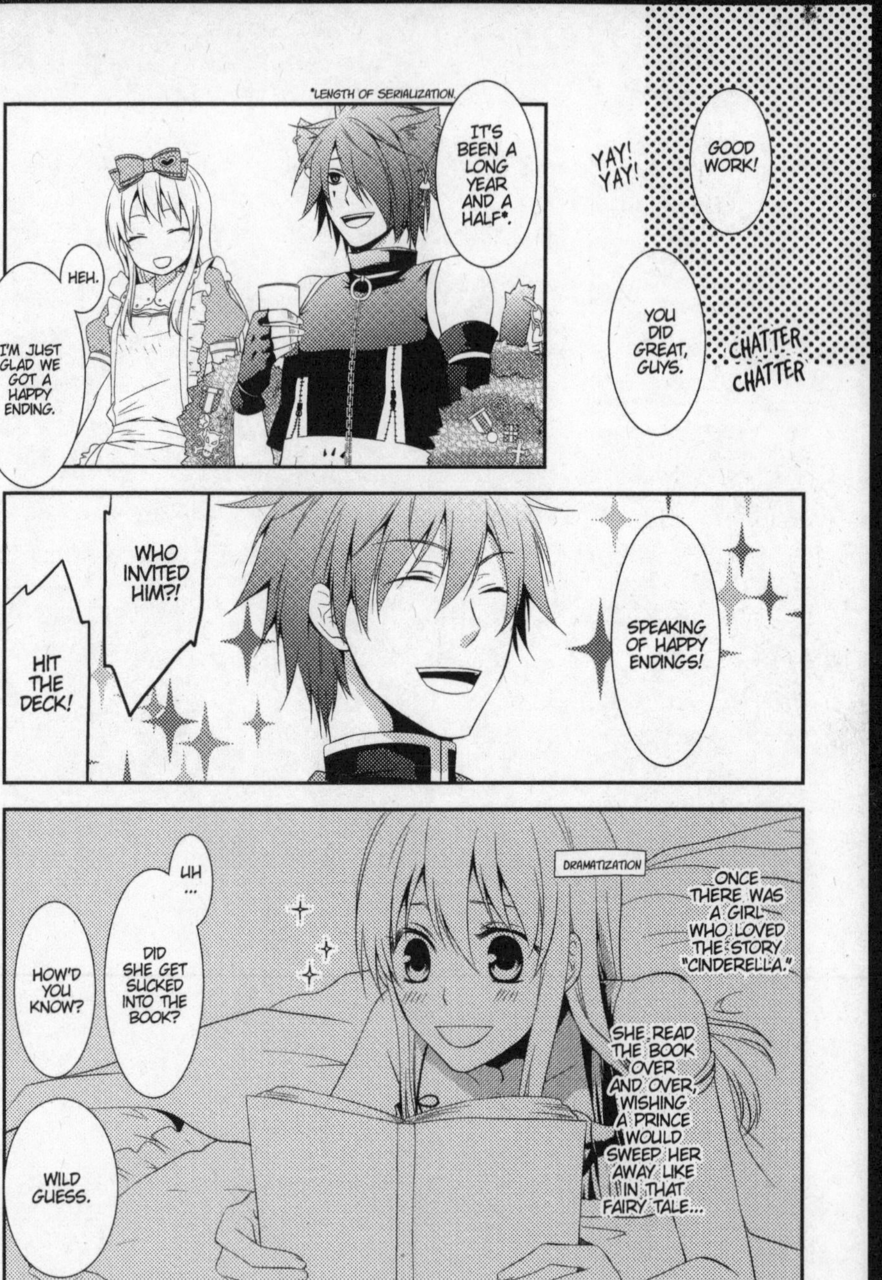
GOOD WORK!
YAY! YAY!
YOU DID GREAT, GUYS.
CHATTER CHATTER
IT'S BEEN A LONG YEAR AND A HALF*.
*LENGTH OF SERIALIZATION.
HEH.
I'M JUST GLAD WE GOT A HAPPY ENDING.
SPEAKING OF HAPPY ENDINGS!
WHO INVITED HIM?!
HIT THE DECK!
DRAMATIZATION
ONCE THERE WAS A GIRL WHO LOVED THE STORY "CINDERELLA."
SHE READ THE BOOK OVER AND OVER, WISHING A PRINCE WOULD SWEEP HER AWAY LIKE IN THAT FAIRY TALE...
UH ...
DID SHE GET SUCKED INTO THE BOOK?
HOW'D YOU KNOW?
WILD GUESS.

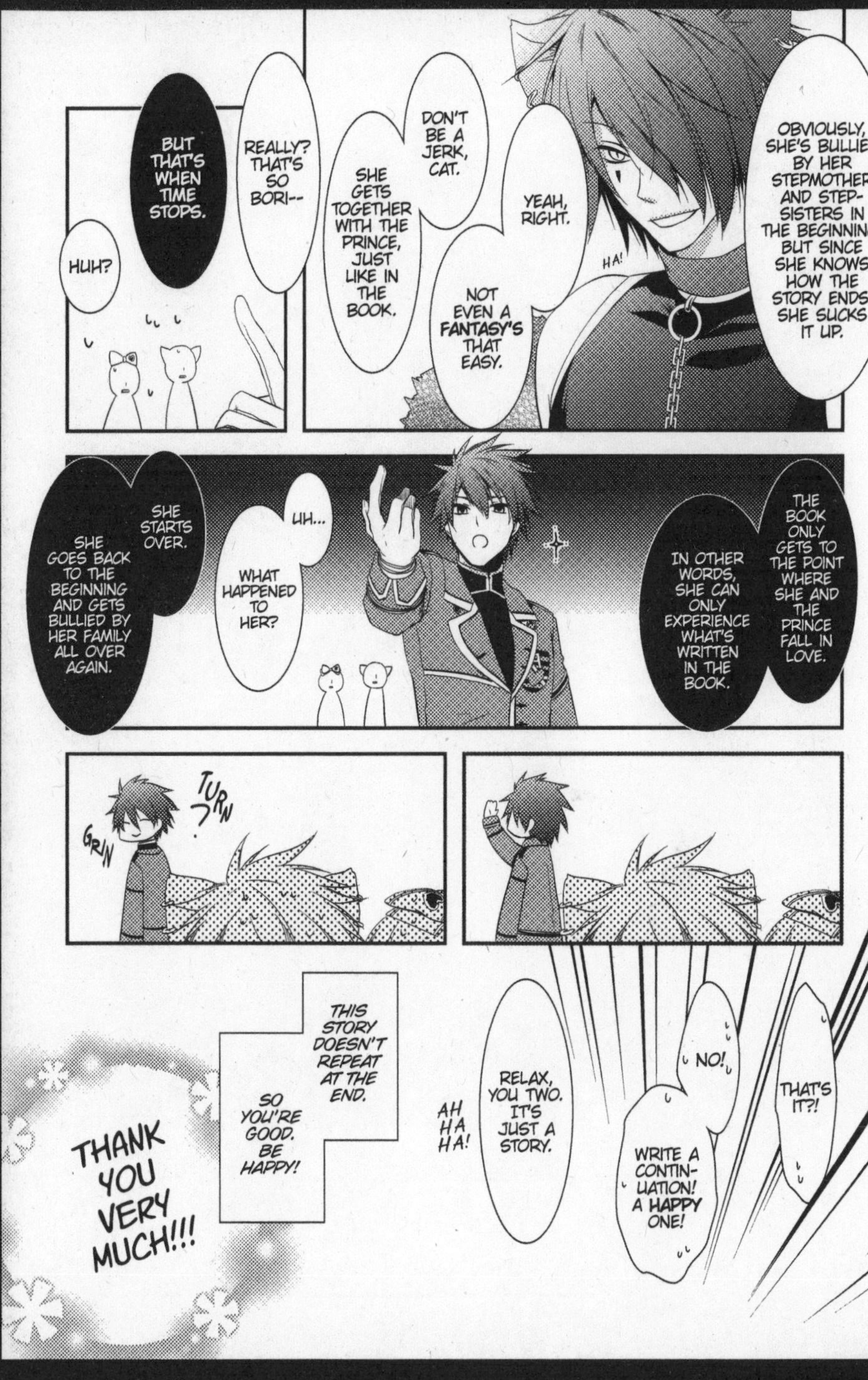

OBVIOUSLY, SHE'S BULLIED BY HER STEPMOTHER AND STEP-SISTERS IN THE BEGINNING. BUT SINCE SHE KNOWS HOW THE STORY ENDS, SHE SUCKS IT UP.
HA!
YEAH, RIGHT.
NOT EVEN A FANTASY'S THAT EASY.
DON'T BE A JERK, CAT.
SHE GETS TOGETHER WITH THE PRINCE, JUST LIKE IN THE BOOK.
REALLY? THAT'S SO BORI--
BUT THAT'S WHEN TIME STOPS.
HUH?
THE BOOK ONLY GETS TO THE POINT WHERE SHE AND THE PRINCE FALL IN LOVE.
IN OTHER WORDS, SHE CAN ONLY EXPERIENCE WHAT'S WRITTEN IN THE BOOK.
UH...
WHAT HAPPENED TO HER?
SHE STARTS OVER.
SHE GOES BACK TO THE BEGINNING AND GETS BULLIED BY HER FAMILY ALL OVER AGAIN.
TURN
?
GRIN
THAT'S IT?!
NO!
WRITE A CONTIN-UATION! A HAPPY ONE!
RELAX, YOU TWO. IT'S JUST A STORY.
AH HA HA!
THIS STORY DOESN'T REPEAT AT THE END.
SO YOU'RE GOOD. BE HAPPY!
THANK YOU VERY MUCH!!!

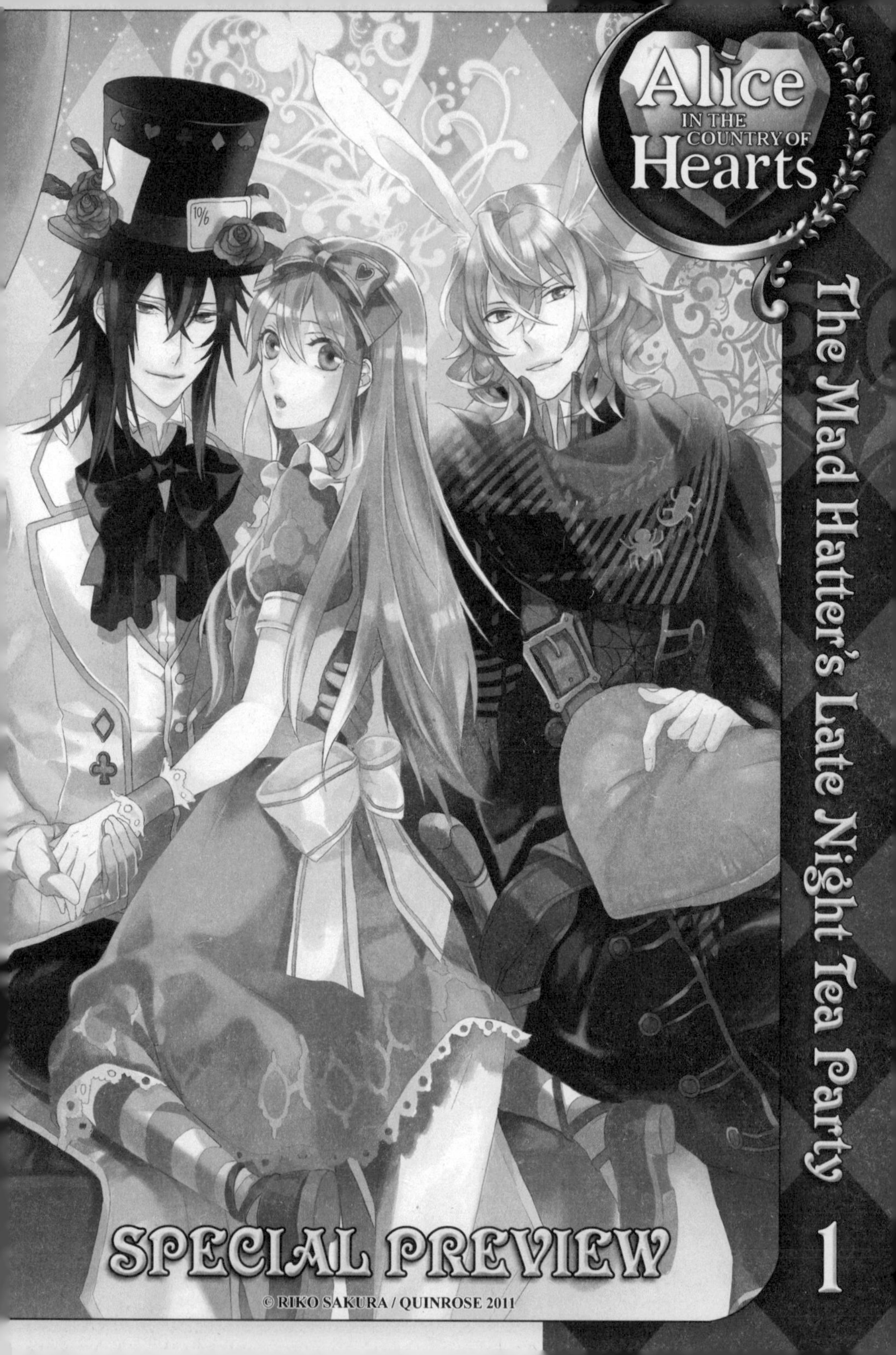
Alice
IN THE
COUNTRY OF
Hearts
The Mad Hatter's Late Night Tea Party
1
SPECIAL PREVIEW
© RIKO SAKURA / QUINROSE 2011

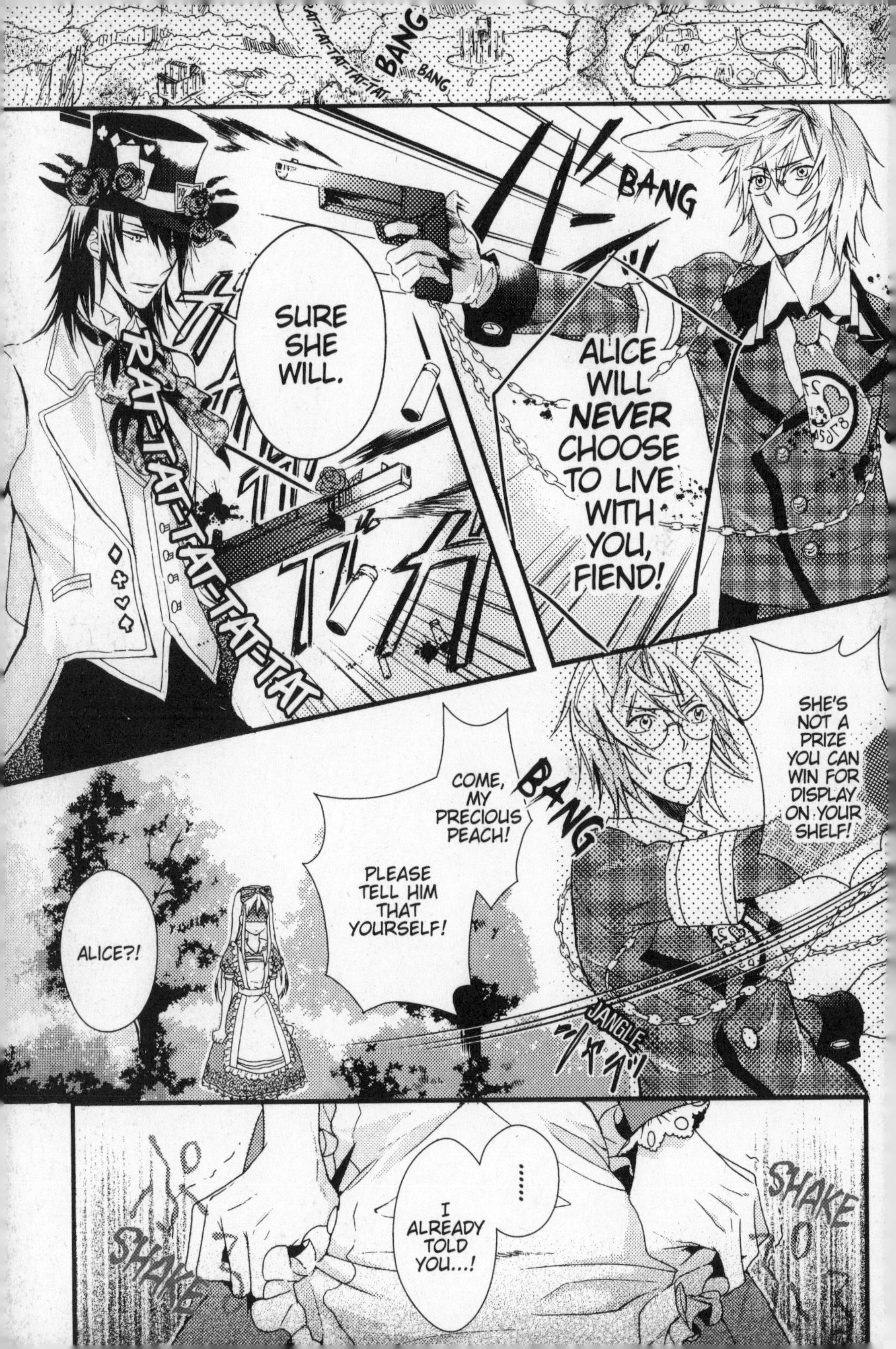
BANG
BANG
TAT-TAT-TAT-TAT
BANG
ALICE WILL NEVER CHOOSE TO LIVE WITH YOU, FIEND!
SURE SHE WILL.
RAT-TAT-TAT-TAT-TAT
SHE'S NOT A PRIZE YOU CAN WIN FOR DISPLAY ON YOUR SHELF!
BANG
JANGLE
COME, MY PRECIOUS PEACH!
PLEASE TELL HIM THAT YOURSELF!
ALICE?!
SHAKE
......
I ALREADY TOLD YOU...!
SHAKE

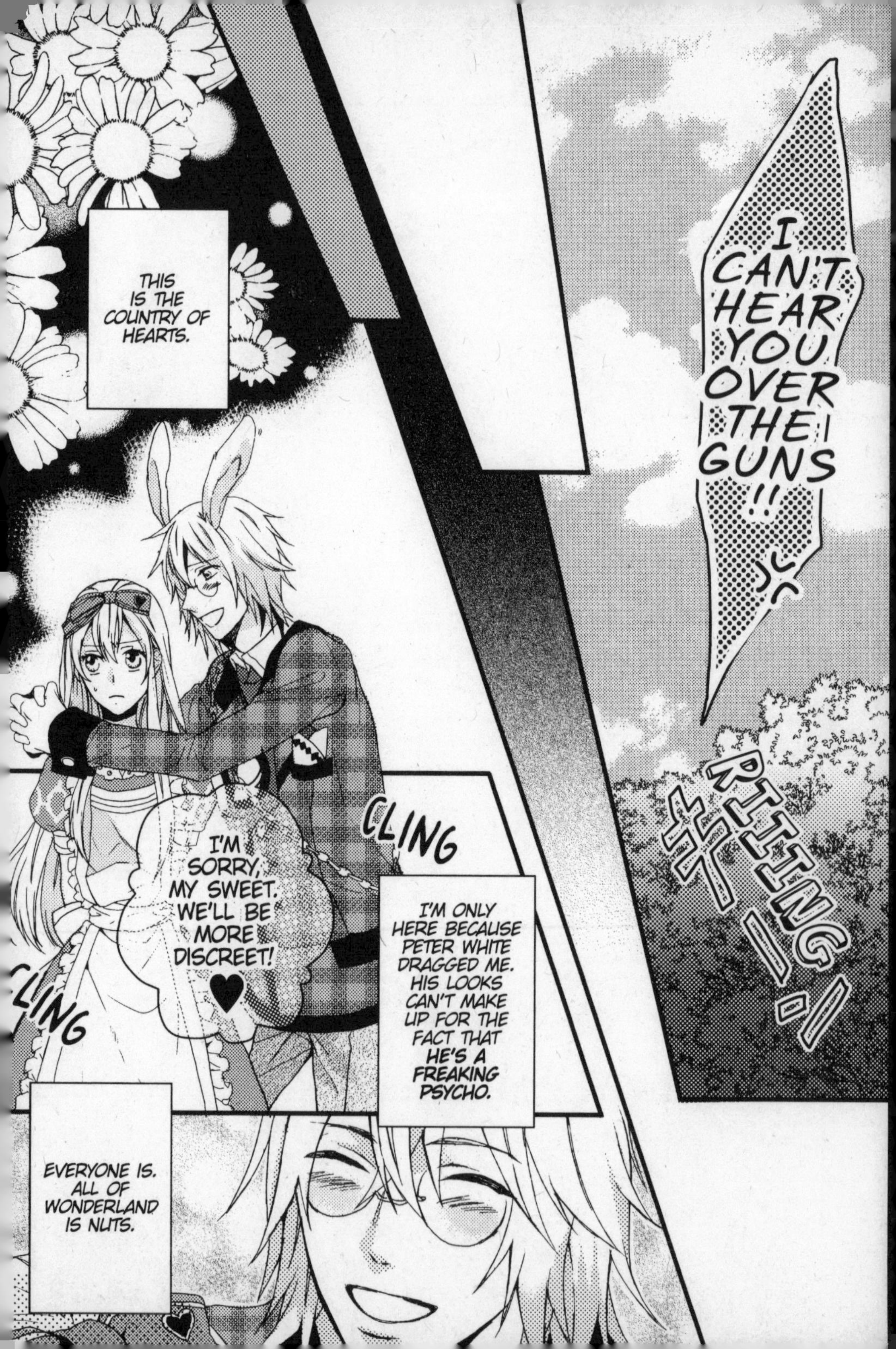
I CAN'T HEAR YOU OVER THE GUNS!!
RIIIING—!
THIS IS THE COUNTRY OF HEARTS.
CLING
I'M SORRY, MY SWEET. WE'LL BE MORE DISCREET! ♥
I'M ONLY HERE BECAUSE PETER WHITE DRAGGED ME. HIS LOOKS CAN'T MAKE UP FOR THE FACT THAT HE'S A FREAKING PSYCHO.
CLING
EVERYONE IS. ALL OF WONDERLAND IS NUTS.

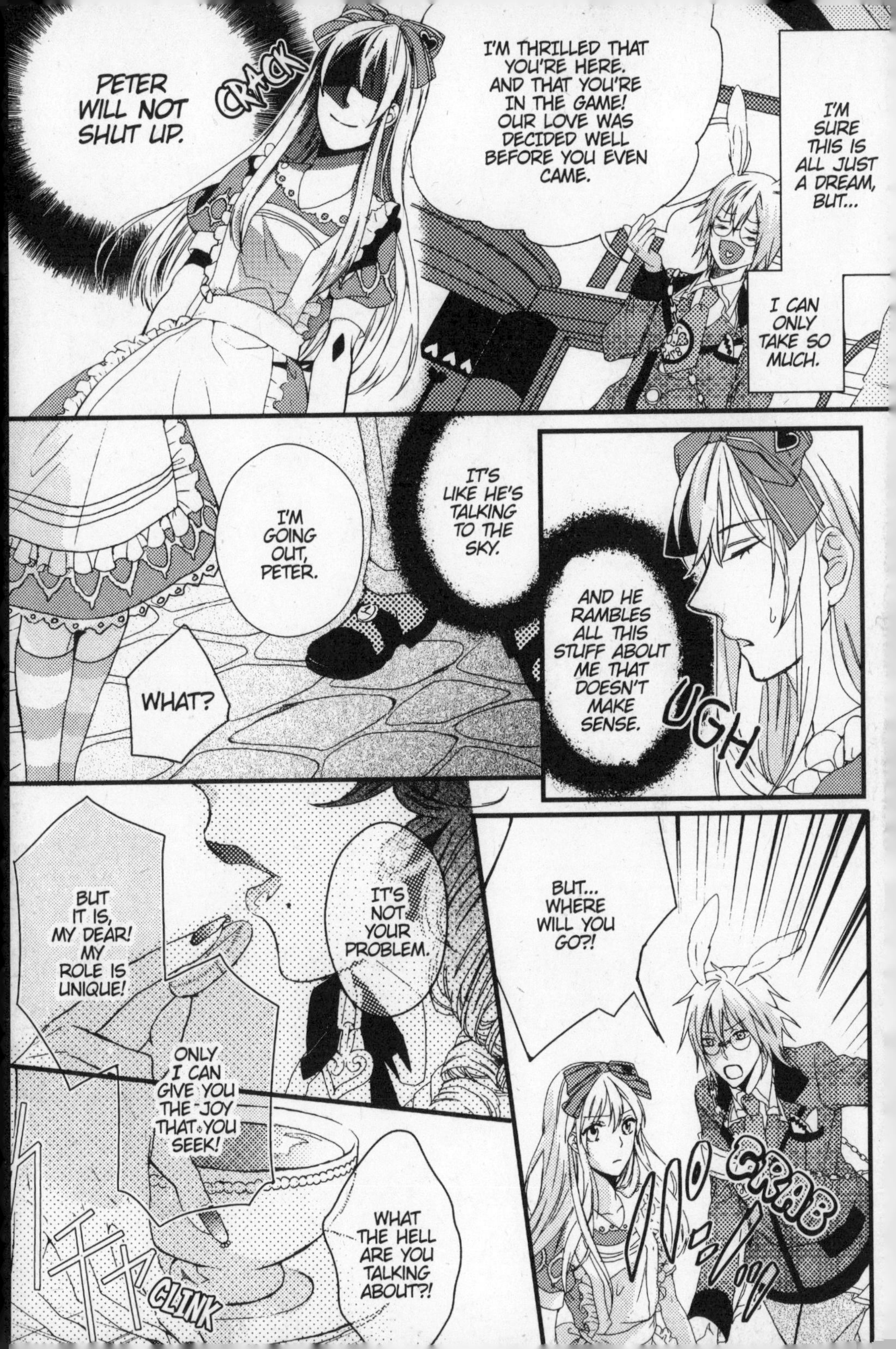
I'M SURE THIS IS ALL JUST A DREAM, BUT...
I CAN ONLY TAKE SO MUCH.
I'M THRILLED THAT YOU'RE HERE. AND THAT YOU'RE IN THE GAME! OUR LOVE WAS DECIDED WELL BEFORE YOU EVEN CAME.
CRACK
PETER WILL NOT SHUT UP.
IT'S LIKE HE'S TALKING TO THE SKY.
AND HE RAMBLES ALL THIS STUFF ABOUT ME THAT DOESN'T MAKE SENSE.
UGH
I'M GOING OUT, PETER.
WHAT?
BUT... WHERE WILL YOU GO?!
GRAB
IT'S NOT YOUR PROBLEM.
BUT IT IS, MY DEAR! MY ROLE IS UNIQUE!
ONLY I CAN GIVE YOU THE JOY THAT YOU SEEK!
WHAT THE HELL ARE YOU TALKING ABOUT?!
CLINK

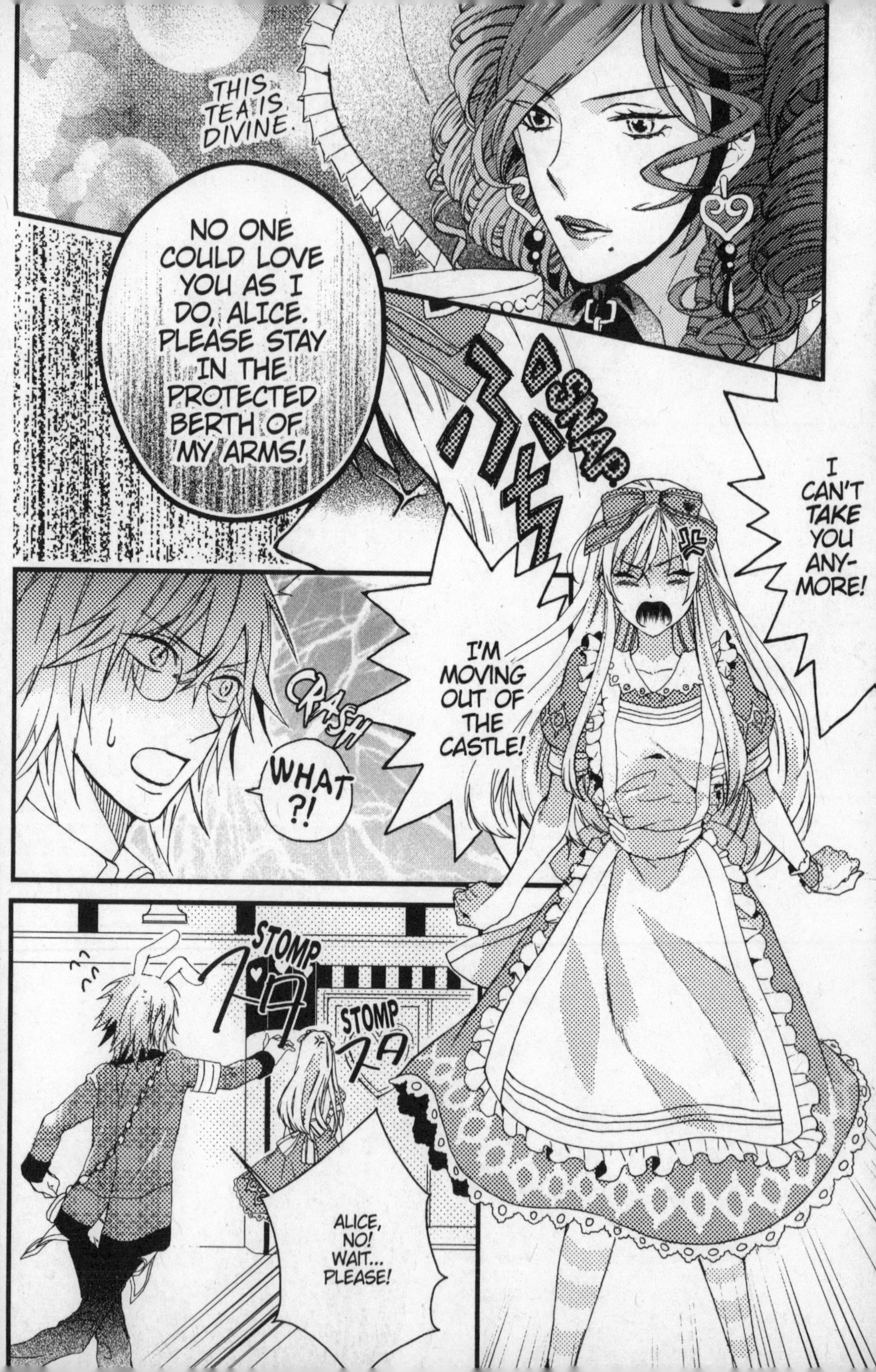
THIS TEA IS DIVINE.
NO ONE COULD LOVE YOU AS I DO, ALICE. PLEASE STAY IN THE PROTECTED BERTH OF MY ARMS!
SNAP
I CAN'T TAKE YOU ANYMORE!
I'M MOVING OUT OF THE CASTLE!
CRASH
WHAT?!
STOMP
STOMP
ALICE, NO! WAIT... PLEASE!

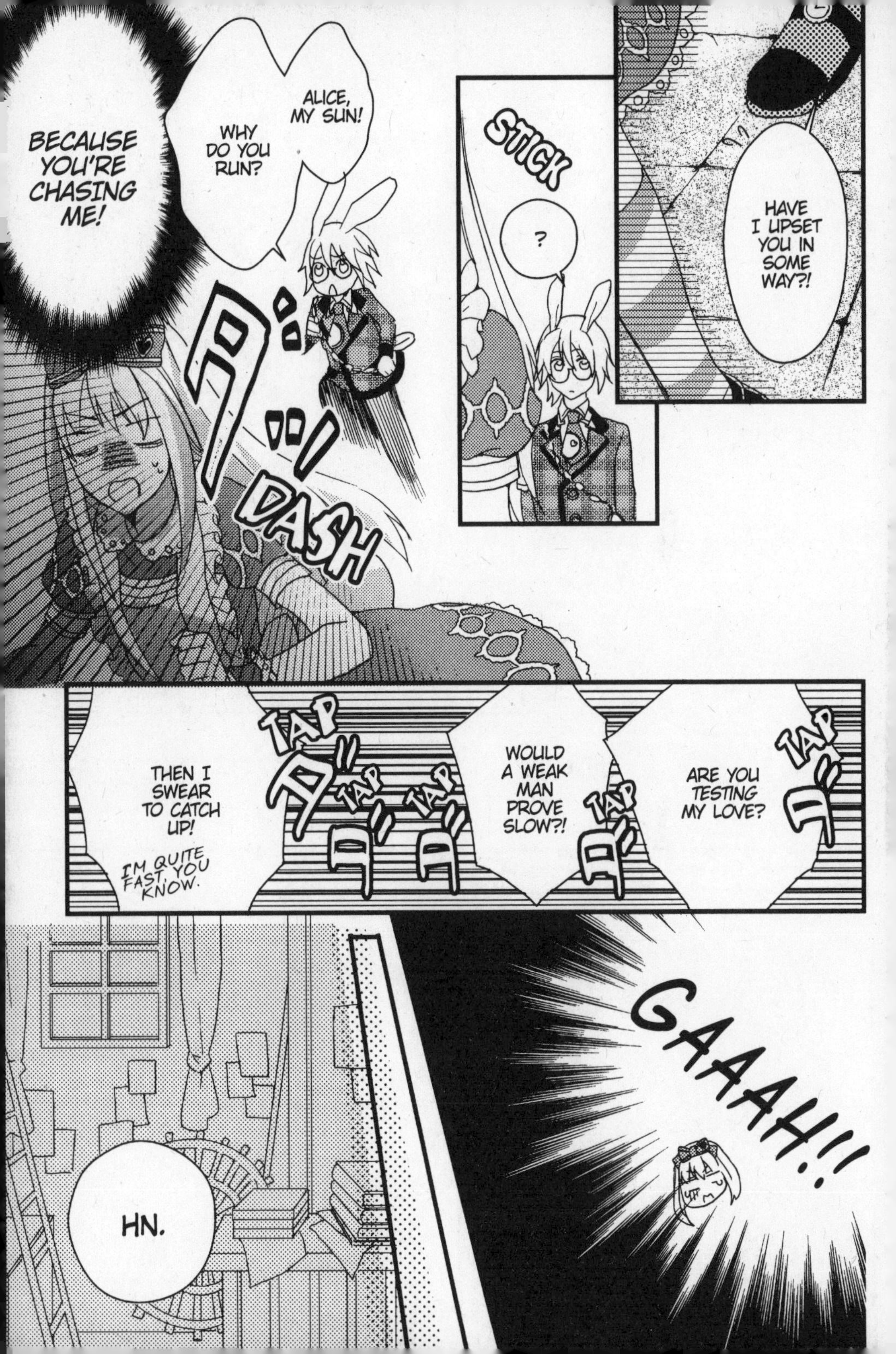
HAVE I UPSET YOU IN SOME WAY?!
STICK
?
ALICE, MY SUN!
WHY DO YOU RUN?
BECAUSE YOU'RE CHASING ME!
DASH
TAP
ARE YOU TESTING MY LOVE?
TAP
WOULD A WEAK MAN PROVE SLOW?!
TAP
TAP
TAP
THEN I SWEAR TO CATCH UP!
I'M QUITE FAST, YOU KNOW.
GAAAH!!!
HN.

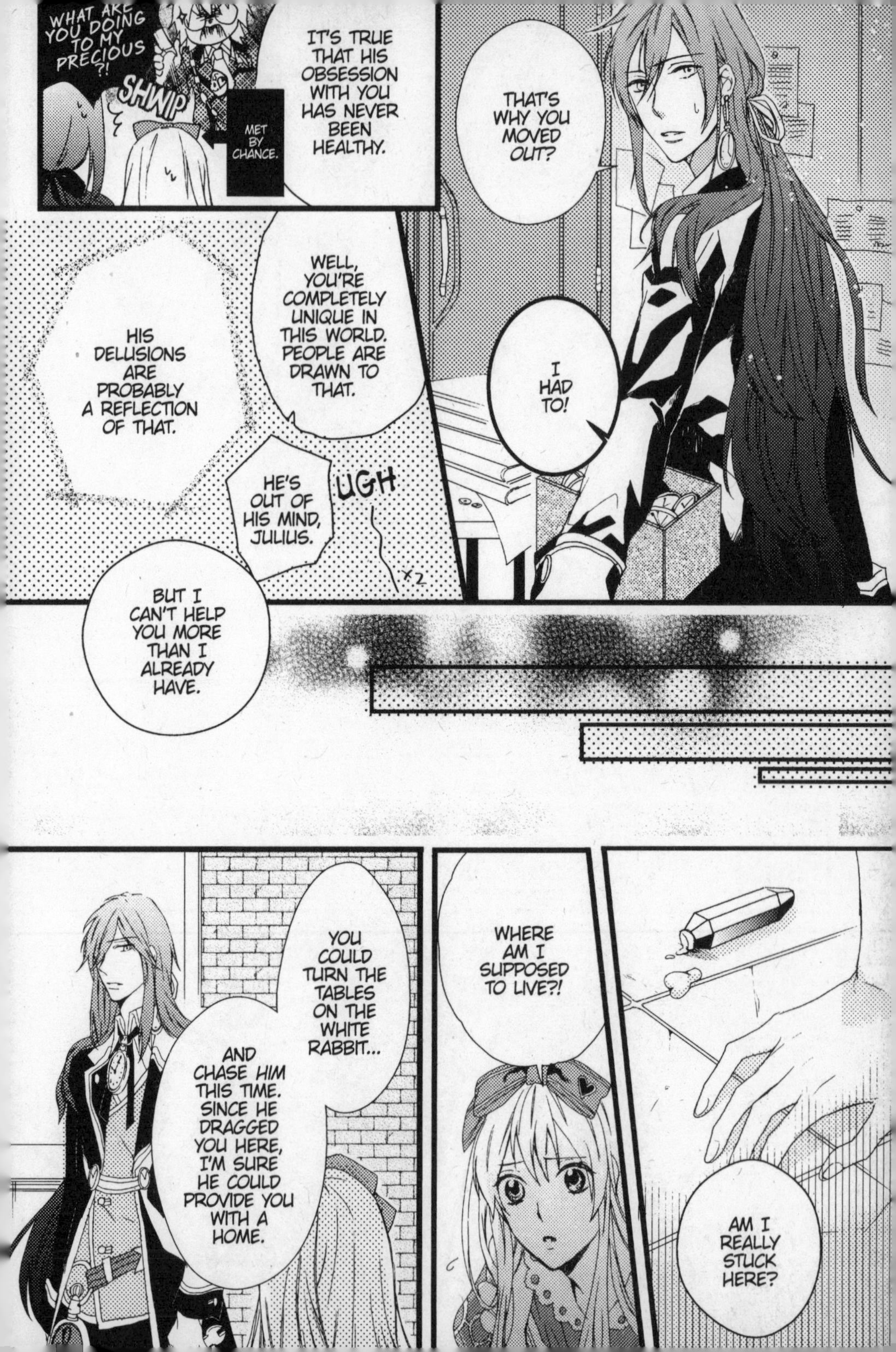
THAT'S WHY YOU MOVED OUT?
I HAD TO!
WHAT ARE YOU DOING TO MY PRECIOUS ?!
SHWIP
MET BY CHANCE.
IT'S TRUE THAT HIS OBSESSION WITH YOU HAS NEVER BEEN HEALTHY.
WELL, YOU'RE COMPLETELY UNIQUE IN THIS WORLD. PEOPLE ARE DRAWN TO THAT.
HIS DELUSIONS ARE PROBABLY A REFLECTION OF THAT.
HE'S OUT OF HIS MIND, JULIUS.
UGH
x2
BUT I CAN'T HELP YOU MORE THAN I ALREADY HAVE.
AM I REALLY STUCK HERE?
WHERE AM I SUPPOSED TO LIVE?!
YOU COULD TURN THE TABLES ON THE WHITE RABBIT...
AND CHASE HIM THIS TIME. SINCE HE DRAGGED YOU HERE, I'M SURE HE COULD PROVIDE YOU WITH A HOME.

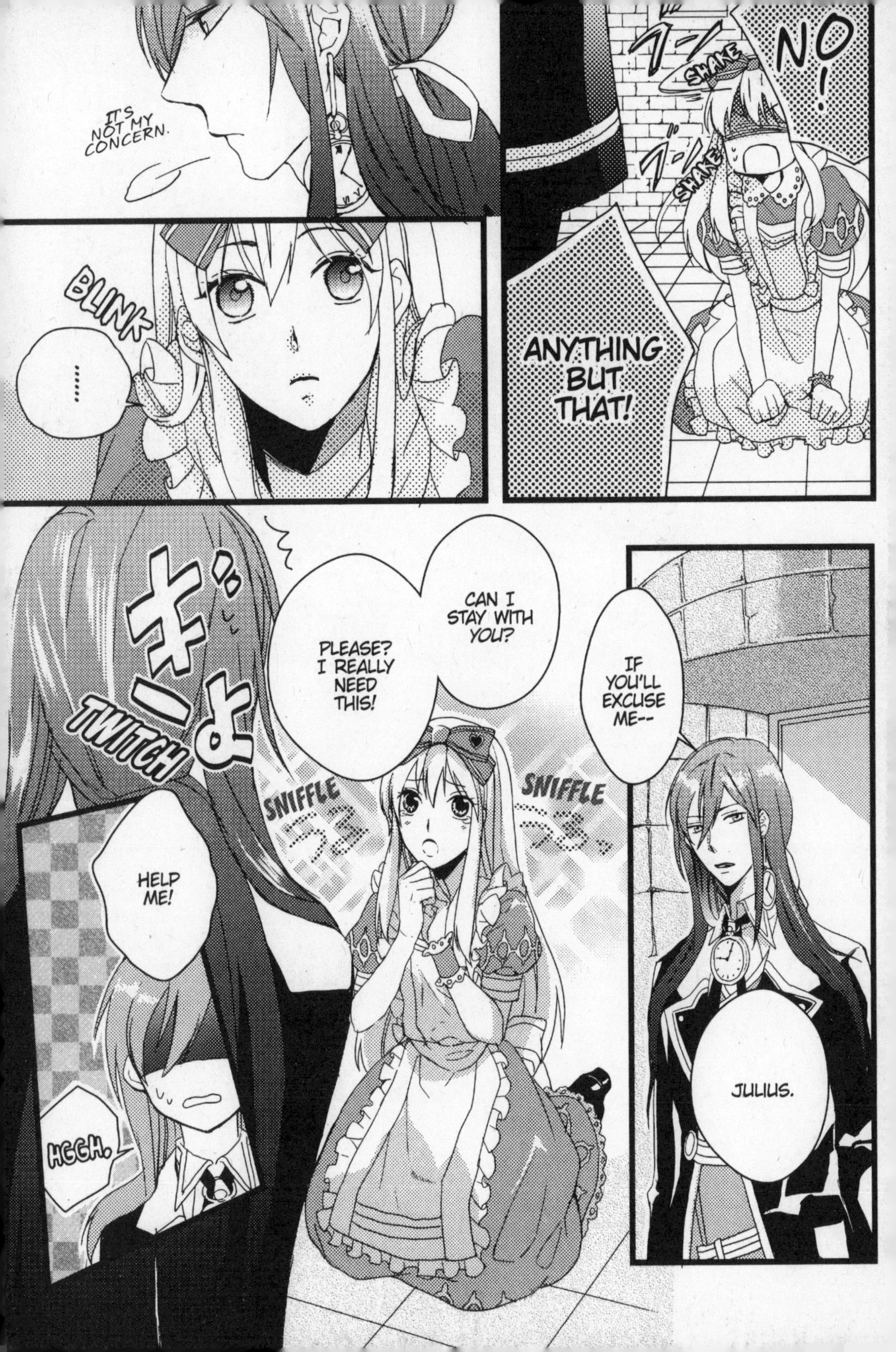
NO!
SHAKE
SHAKE
ANYTHING BUT THAT!
IT'S NOT MY CONCERN.
BLINK
......
IF YOU'LL EXCUSE ME--
JULIUS.
CAN I STAY WITH YOU?
PLEASE? I REALLY NEED THIS!
SNIFFLE
SNIFFLE
TWITCH
HELP ME!
HGGH.

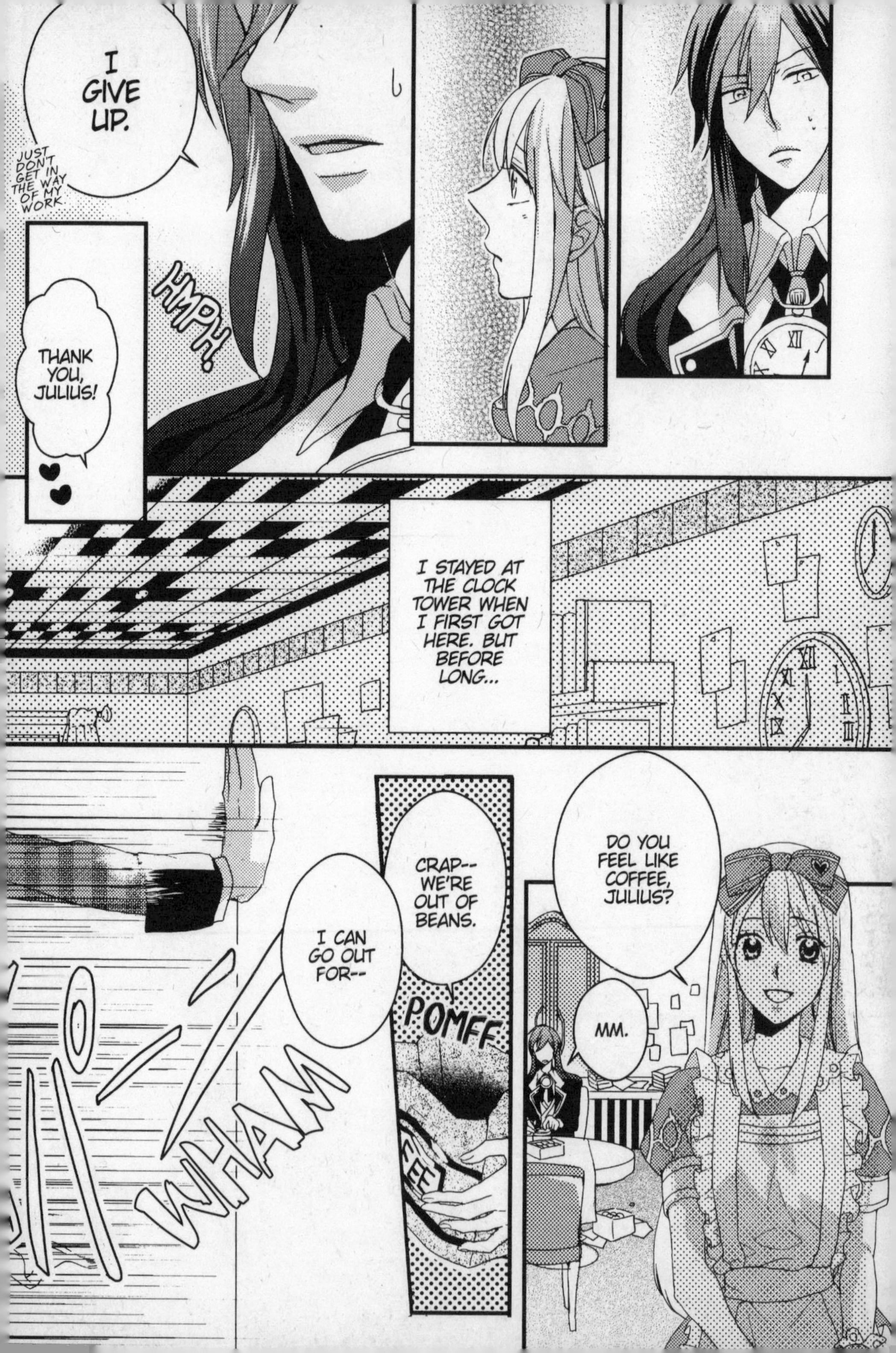
I GIVE UP.
JUST DON'T GET IN THE WAY OF MY WORK.
HMPH.
THANK YOU, JULIUS!
I STAYED AT THE CLOCK TOWER WHEN I FIRST GOT HERE. BUT BEFORE LONG...
DO YOU FEEL LIKE COFFEE, JULIUS?
MM.
CRAP-- WE'RE OUT OF BEANS.
POMFF
I CAN GO OUT FOR--
WHAM

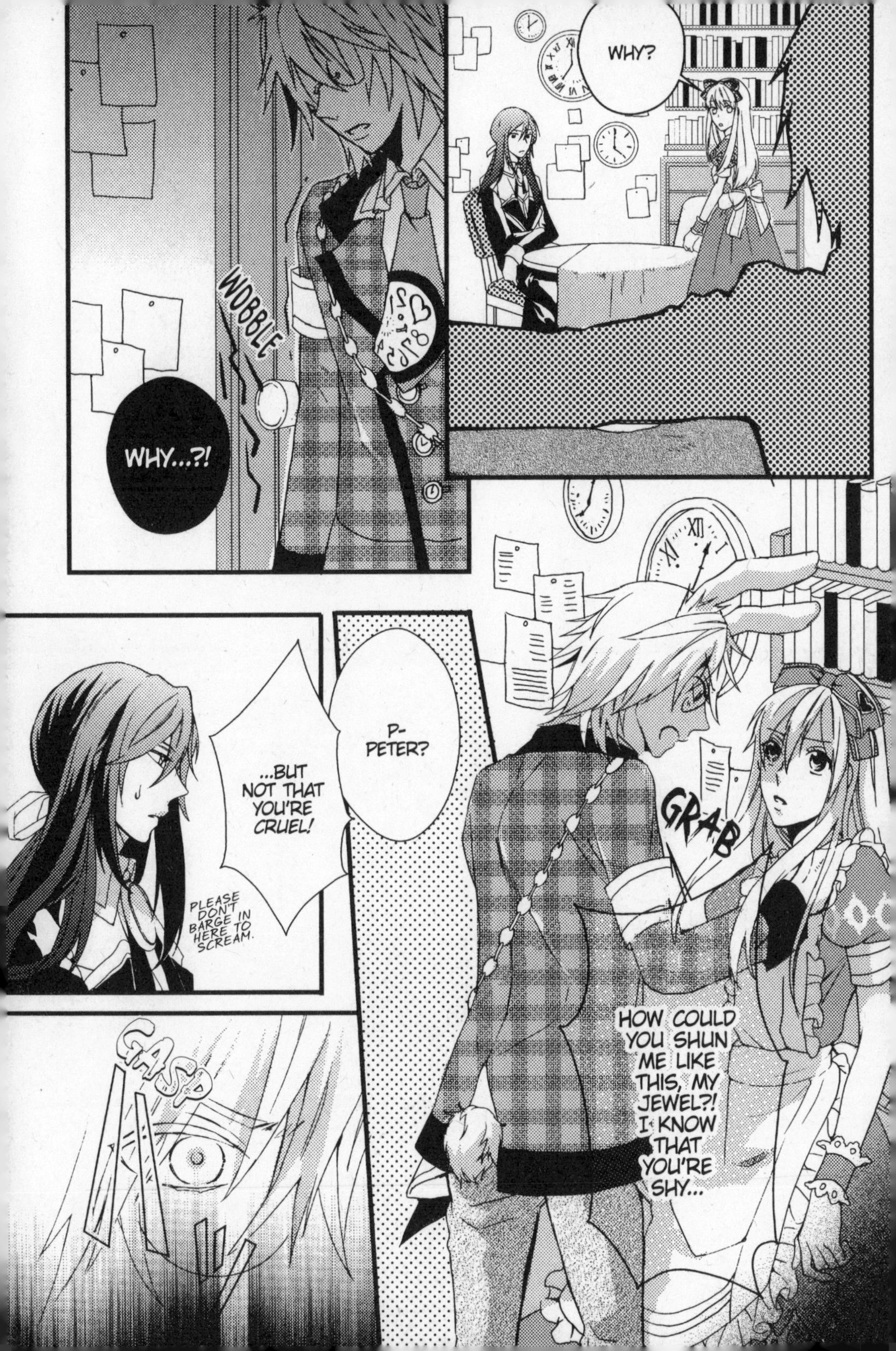
WHY?
WOBBLE
WHY...?!
GRAB
HOW COULD YOU SHUN ME LIKE THIS, MY JEWEL?! I KNOW THAT YOU'RE SHY...
P-PETER?
...BUT NOT THAT YOU'RE CRUEL!
PLEASE DON'T BARGE IN HERE TO SCREAM.
GASP

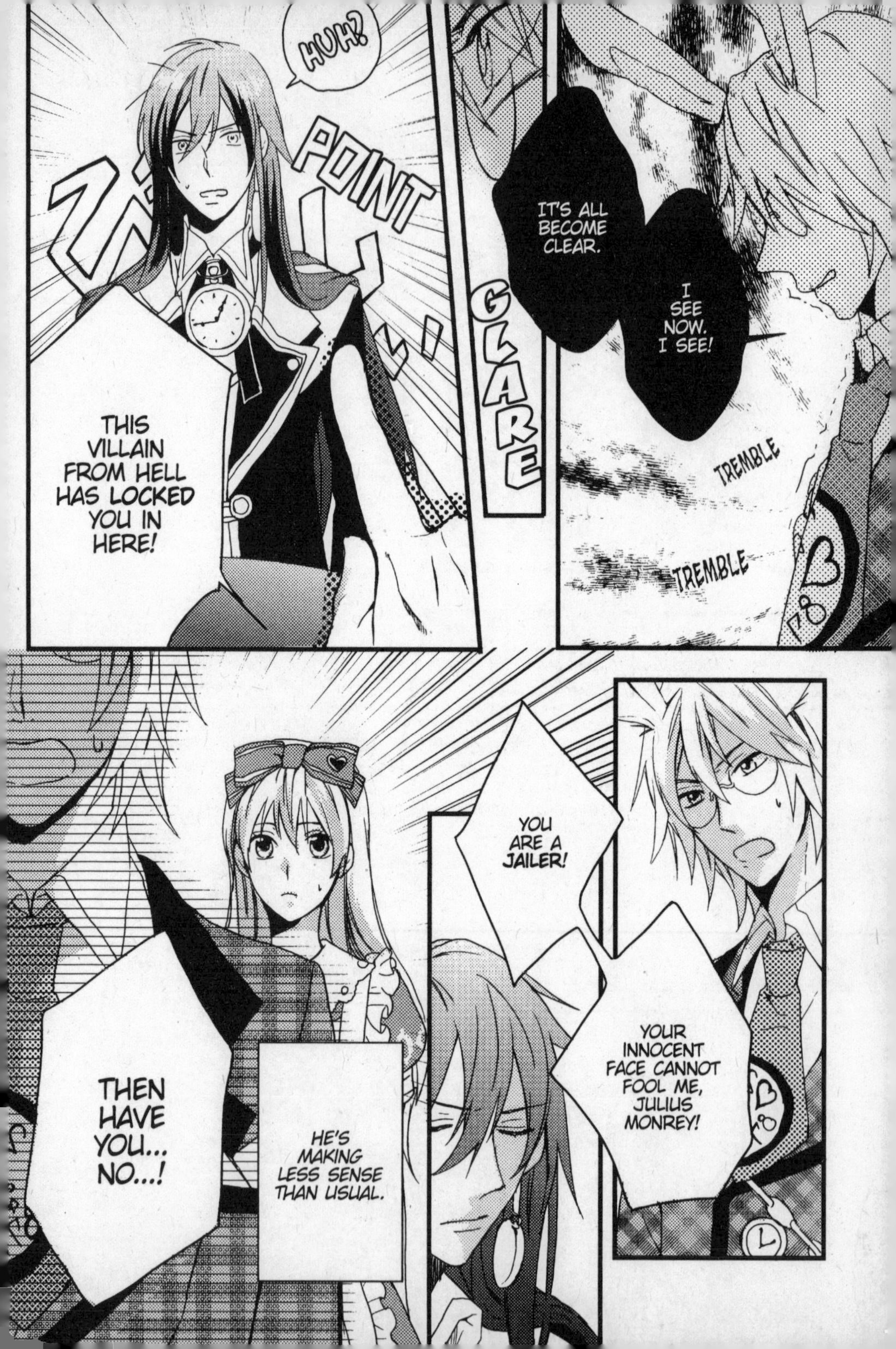
IT'S ALL BECOME CLEAR.
I SEE NOW. I SEE!
TREMBLE
TREMBLE
GLARE
HUH?
POINT
THIS VILLAIN FROM HELL HAS LOCKED YOU IN HERE!
YOU ARE A JAILER!
YOUR INNOCENT FACE CANNOT FOOL ME, JULIUS MONREY!
HE'S MAKING LESS SENSE THAN USUAL.
THEN HAVE YOU... NO...!

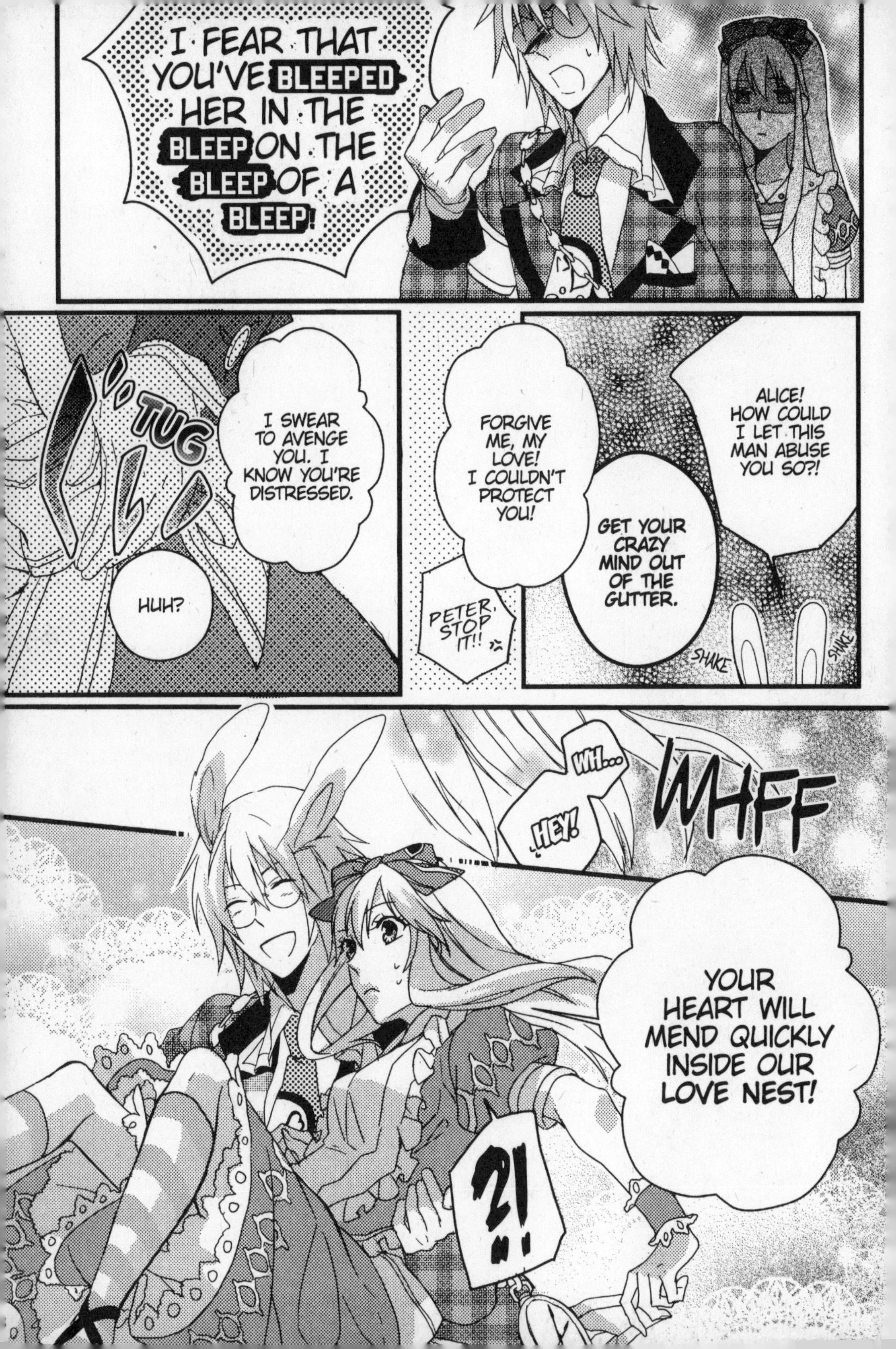
I FEAR THAT YOU'VE BLEEPED HER IN THE BLEEP ON THE BLEEP OF A BLEEP!
ALICE! HOW COULD I LET THIS MAN ABUSE YOU SO?!
GET YOUR CRAZY MIND OUT OF THE GUTTER.
SHAKE
SHAKE
FORGIVE ME, MY LOVE! I COULDN'T PROTECT YOU!
PETER, STOP IT!!
I SWEAR TO AVENGE YOU. I KNOW YOU'RE DISTRESSED.
TUG
HUH?
WHFF
WH...
HEY!
YOUR HEART WILL MEND QUICKLY INSIDE OUR LOVE NEST!
?!

COMING SOON

NOVEMBER 2013

Alice in the Country of Hearts:
The Mad Hatter's Late Night
Tea Party Vol. 1

DECEMBER 2013

Alice Love Fables: Toy Box

Crimson Empire Vol. 3

JANUARY 2014

Alice in the Country of Hearts:
The Mad Hatter's Late Night
Tea Party Vol. 2

FEBRUARY 2014

Alice in the Country of Joker:
Circus and Liars Game Vol. 4